Praise for *Wonde* T0053454

"If *Wonderworks* had been around then, I would have sat my son down and read Angus Fletcher's exploration of the history and the psychology of literature to him, word by word. . . . I hope it will convince others that there are benefits and pleasures that you can get from literature that are unique and valuable."

—Jane Smiley, *The Guardian*

"Fascinating. . . . It blew my mind!"

—Malcolm Gladwell

"Intelligent, engaged and erudite. . . . Speaks to the inner reader in us all, as well as to the inner neurologist."

—Simon Ings, *New Scientist*

"I'm totally obsessed with *Wonderworks*. It swallowed me whole."

—Brené Brown, "Unlocking Us with Brené Brown,"
Parcast Network, and author of *Daring Greatly*

"*Wonderworks* contains many instances of critical insight. . . . What's most interesting about this compendium is its understanding of imaginative representation as a technology."

—*The New York Times*

"I've been living in *Wonderworks* for several weeks now, dazzled by its innovations, wild surmises, gifts of insight, unlikely readings and—perhaps most of all—its inspirational force. Angus Fletcher is that rare critic who actually has something to say, who grabs us by the collar and hopes to shake sense into us. This may be one of the most important and truly useful books about literature written in the past decade. . . . Refreshing and remarkable on so many levels."

—Jay Parini, author of *Borges and Me: An Encounter*

Wonderworks

Literary Invention
and the Science of Stories

ANGUS FLETCHER

Simon & Schuster Paperbacks
New York London Toronto Sydney New Delhi

Simon & Schuster Paperbacks
An Imprint of Simon & Schuster, Inc.
1230 Avenue of the Americas
New York, NY 10020

Illustration credits:
Illustrations on pages 145, 364 and 366 by George 'Agas
Art on page 351 from *Fun Home* © 2006 by Alison Bechdel

Cover artwork: (From L to R, T to B) Kafka by Hulton Archive/Getty Images; Fey by Jaguar PS/ Shutterstock; Alice courtesy of the Library of Congress; Bechdel by Dia Dipasupil/Getty Images for Tribeca Festival Shelley by GL Archive/Alamy Stock Photo; Douglass courtesy of the National Park Service; Beckett by Louis MONIER/Gamma-Rapho via Getty Images Allan Poe courtesy of *American Bookmen*; Woolf by George Charles Beresford; Angelou by by Jack Sotomayor/ New York Times Co./Getty Images; Shakespeare courtesy of The Metropolitan Museum of Art; García Márquez by Ulf Andersen/Getty Images; TS Eliot courtesy Everett Collection/Everett Collection/Adobe Stock; Plato by © Ted Spiegel/CORBIS/Corbis via Getty Images; Aesop by Diego Velázquez; Cao Xueqin by Sovfoto/Universal Images Group via Getty Images; Homer by Rosa Irene Betancourt/Alamy Stock Photo; Spine: George Eliot courtesy Mary Evans Library/Adobe Stock

First Simon & Schuster trade paperback edition March 2022

SIMON & SCHUSTER PAPERBACKS and colophon are registered trademarks of Simon & Schuster, Inc.

For information about special discounts for bulk purchases, please contact Simon & Schuster Special Sales at 1-866-506-1949 or business@simonandschuster.com.

The Simon & Schuster Speakers Bureau can bring authors to your live event. For more information or to book an event, contact the Simon & Schuster Speakers Bureau at 1-866-248-3049 or visit our website at www.simonspeakers.com.

"This Is Just to Say," by William Carlos Williams, from *The Collected Poems of William Carlos Williams, Vol. 1, 1909–1939* (Norfolk, CT: New Directions, 1938). Reprinted by permission of New Directions.

Interior design by Carly Loman

Manufactured in the United States of America

10 9 8 7 6 5 4 3 2

Library of Congress Cataloging-in-Publication Data
Names: Fletcher, Angus, 1976- author.
Title: Wonderworks : the 25 most powerful innovations in the history of literature / Angus Fletcher.
Description: First Simon & Schuster hardcover edition. | New York : Simon & Schuster, 2021. |
    Includes index. | Summary: "A brilliant examination of literary invention through the ages, from
    ancient Mesopotamia to Elena Ferrante, showing how writers created technical breakthroughs
    as sophisticated and significant as any in science, and in the process, engineered enhancements to
    the human heart and mind"—Provided by publisher.
Identifiers: LCCN 2020012458 | ISBN 9781982135973 (hardcover) | ISBN 9781982135980 (trade
    paperback) | ISBN 9781982135997 (ebook)
Subjects: LCSH: Literature—History and criticism.
Classification: LCC PN523 .F54 2020 | DDC 809—dc23
LC record available at https://lccn.loc.gov/2020012458

ISBN 978-1-9821-3597-3
ISBN 978-1-9821-3598-0 (pbk)
ISBN 978-1-9821-3599-7 (ebook)

For Ronan, aged nearly three:

"Are there two Ronans here?"
"No. Just me!"

Contents

Wonderworks

O for a Muse of fire, that would ascend
The brightest heaven of invention

—WILLIAM SHAKESPEARE, *Henry V*

A Heaven of Invention

I t was barely sunrise.

Yet even in the faint, rose-fingered light, there could be no doubt: the invention was a marvel. It could mend cracks in the heart and resurrect hope from the dark. It could summon up raptures and impossible days. It could chase away dullness and unlatch the sky.

The invention was literature. And to catch its marvel for ourselves, let's return to that dawn. Let's learn the story of why literature was invented. And all the things it was invented to do.

The Invention of Literature

Sometime around 2300 BCE, in what is now Iraq, literature's first known inventor was born within a great mudbrick palace near the snowmelt waters of the Tigris River. There, upon a fragrant cedar cot, the newborn babe was lullabied to sleep amid white rock sculptures of armies famed for the most remarkable deeds: turning mountains to ash, pouring blood into cups, and vanquishing beasts in a chasm of thorns. But soon the dreamful infant would become even more famous. Everywhere throughout the city-states of Mesopotamia, all the way from the silver mines of Anatolia to the beaches of the Persian Gulf, her name would be sung. And her name was Enheduanna.

Enheduanna's journey to renown began when, barely older than a girl, she was sent south to an almond-shaped city on the willowed mouth of the Euphrates. The city was Ur, and it was revered as a place of tremendous imagination. Its night-haired, moon-praying people had devised the wheel, the sailboat, and the multiplication table, and to supply their busy workshops with the raw materials to engineer more wonders still, they'd fashioned a massive walled harbor to import lumber from forest slopes in Lebanon, copper from fire-mined quarries in Magan, and jeweled blue stones from ore veins in Afghanistan. So intricate was this network of commerce that by 3000 BCE, it had spurred perhaps the most world-changing creation of all: *namdub*. Or as we know it now: writing. Stamped down as cuneiform characters on quick-drying clay tablets, writing tracked every cargo transaction on Ur's sandy anchorage, allowing receipt ledgers to be kept and taxes calculated to the fraction.

Ur's fertile innovations made it the richest city on earth, its traders adorning their courtyard homes with pearl mosaics and burying themselves in tombs of gold. And so Enheduanna was tasked by her father, King Sargon the Great, with ensuring that the bountiful wealth from Ur continued to flow, borne north by donkey caravans across the steppes to the imperial treasury at Akkad. It would be a giant task, Sargon knew, to tame Ur's proud merchant folk. But he had the greatest confidence in his daughter. It was not simply that she was the most agile minded of his off-spring. Or the most ruthless. It was that she had her mother's tongue. A honey tongue that sweetened salt and charmed all anger from the heart.

Enheduanna began her royal mission by using that honey tongue to forge an invention: her name. For "Enheduanna" wasn't what her father had called her when she lay in swaddle on her infant cot; it was an original title that she tinkered up for herself. And although the title sounded strange when it first echoed through the air, the cleverness of its engineering became clear when Enheduanna arrived at last in Ur. The sun had sunk hours before, leaving the shore air cool and the sky a cloudless black. Above, at heaven's top, hung the holy moon in rounded full, illuminating Enheduanna as she glided down the city's main canal upon a papyrus barge rowed by clerics in feathered camelback robes. Crowding the waterway on all sides were throngs of citizen sailors, scribes, and sweet-beer brewers, armed with sickle swords of bronze. And surging into view ahead, blocking starshine with its shade, loomed the Old Ziggurat of Ur.

The Ziggurat was Ur's stronghold of the gods. Its foundation bricks had been baptized by the rainstorms of the Flood, and within its mammoth tabernacle, high platformed and ziggedly asymmetric, stretched the oblong bedchamber where the moon had lain with the Queen of the Marsh, birthing the sun's hot rays and the ambisexual goddess of love. These heavenly beings were notoriously blood hungry, but they gave Enheduanna no pause. She docked calmly at the Ziggurat's silhouetted jag of angles, perfumed by scents of bloom weed and the river rose. And with her eyes aglow in midnight moonlight, she bade her clerics to chant in fevered tones: "She is the high lord of the moon." Or, as the chant went in its original syllables: "*En-hedu-'anna. En-hedu-'anna. En-hedu-'anna.*"

This was the reason for Enheduanna's self-made name. It claimed for her the mantle of the city's astral overseer, crowning her as archpriest of the fifty thousand lunar worshippers now surrounding her on Ur's canal banks. It was a might invested through a word invented.

And the name was just the beginning of Enheduanna's inventions. Debarking her barge, she climbed a thousand pink-beige stairs until she reached the hidden shrine that capped the Ziggurat. There, upon a dais that seemed to touch the firmament, she bathed herself within a sacred pool, its sides cleverly leak proofed with bitumen caulk. And glistened bright by holy waters, she brought her congregation to its knees by lifting up her voice in incantation:

> O Feeder of life,
> Rising like a bull from snake shallows,
> Born from a great mother,
> Light above all.

As Enheduanna sang, the song answered back, glimmering the horizon with the milk fire of a thousand moons. In the heart of night, a new morn was breaking, unlike any imagined before.

Enheduanna had invented literature.

She wasn't, of course, the first to invent it. Her verses were preceded by other ziggurat canticles, such as *The Kesh Temple Hymn*, dating to a handful of generations earlier. And prior to that, there were many generations more of oral literature, generations that may have stretched back before our species to the *Homo erectus* hunter-gatherers of the

Afro-Asian Stone Ages, where perhaps upon the volcanic lakeshores of Kenya's Great Rift Valley or among the buzzing wetlands of Shaanxi, an archaic hominid bespoke the world's first myth or metaphor, a million years ago or more.

But Enheduanna is the first inventor whose name we know. She's the first author we can credit for an original piece of literature.

Partly, this is because she was lucky enough to be born into an age of literacy; the same cuneiform print that diligently logged Ur's dockyard traffic allowed Enheduanna to breathe her mind into pages of clay, passing her spark on to readers beyond. And partly, this is because her creations were so compelling that Sumerian city clerks copied them afresh for hundreds of years, long after Enheduanna's less adroit brothers had been bludgeoned to death by the stone writing seals of palace assassins—and her father's whole bloodline had been rolled under by mountain raiders from the east.

But mostly, this is because Enheduanna *wanted* to be known as an inventor. She flagrantly identified herself within her verses:

> O goddess, from my altar days,
> I, Enheduanna, sang your name.

And after she'd collected an anthology of her choicest poetry, she ended it by boasting:

> I, Enheduanna, created this booklet—
> a thing which no one else had ever created.

So, in Enheduanna, we have our earliest glimpse of what it was to invent literature. And although it's only a glimpse, it's enough to see why our ancestors did the inventing.

Why Literature Was Invented

Enheduanna coined her ziggurat verses for the same purpose that she coined her moon-catching name: to grab hold of forces above. And her belief in literature's almighty properties would endure long after, leaving its trace in the ancient world's most holy writings. Eight centuries or so after Enheduanna, metaphoric similes danced across the Hindu *Vedas* as they praised the twin horse gods, Nasatya and Dasra. Another eight centuries after that, alliterations chimed through the Hebrew Torah as it told of death's coming to the Garden of Eden. And a half century later still, poetic repetitions latticed the Greek *Theogony* as it revealed how Sky and Soil immortally begat the titan Cyclopes.

So it came to be that in the world's earliest libraries, scripture and literature were joined. And indeed, so tight was the jointure that *literature* and *scripture* would be fashioned with identical root meanings: "that which is writ." They were two ways of saying the very same thing.

What prompted this ancient reverence for literature? What great powers did Enheduanna and our other ancestors detect within its pages? The powers were many, but two in particular stood out.

The first great power was narrative, or, more colloquially, story. Story connected events. And story provided beginnings—and endings. So, story could answer the question "Where did our universe come from?" As in this Mesoamerican parable, recounted by highland Anahuac peoples who predated the Aztecs:

> Amid darkness, the gods gathered together. To make light, they needed fuel, and a proud god, Tecuciztecatl, volunteered to burn himself. But at the heat of the flame, Tecuciztecatl faltered. So, before the flame could perish, Nanauatzin, a sick god and lame, jumped in, becoming the sun. Ashamed, Tecuciztecatl leapt after, becoming the moon.

And story could also answer "Where will we go when we die?" As in this Saqqâra pyramid text, fashioned around 2320 BCE in the Egyptian Old Kingdom: "The good soul will row the eastern sky-boat across the water of the Fields of Reeds."

The second great power of literature was the stirring of emotion: love, wonder, faith. For such was the strength of these feelings that they could fend off life's mightiest demons. Against the demon of loneliness, there was the "Love prayer to Shu-Sin," sung three centuries after Enheduanna upon another moony tabernacle at Ur:

O man,
I ask
you freely,
Master me;
Open up your temple to my touch,
And sweet my dark night with your love.

And against the demon of fear, there was India's Vedic Age *Samhita*, brushed with ash-tar ink upon a birch-bark choral sheet: "Great lightning god, fling wide the doors of strength, making us heroes."

These heart-raising, universe-explaining texts are the heirs of Enheduanna's belief that literature can support and guide us through the darkness: "O Feeder of life . . . Light above all." And literature's two powers of story and emotion aren't all that we can learn from Enheduanna. We can also discover how to pull those powers down from heaven, becoming dawn makers ourselves.

Enheduanna's Other Discovery

Enheduanna did more than treat literature as immortal scripture. She also treated it as an earthly invention. Which is to say: she treated it as a technology.

In our modern epoch, we tend to think of technology as gadgetries of steel and silicon. And even in Enheduanna's age, it was perceived not so differently by most of her father's subjects as contrivances of copper, bronze, and tin. But technology doesn't need to be forged from metal. It can be built of any substance: clay, paper, ink, or even breath. For if we look back to the very earliest beginnings of engineering, we can see that a technology is any human-made thing that helps to solve a problem.

To help solve the problem of cold, there's the technology of fire taming, such as the heating pits that Paleolithic humans dug out of Huang He limestone. To help solve the problem of hunger, there's the technology of meat scavenging, such as the quartzite knives that Pleistocene hominids flaked from Tanzanian creek rock. To help solve the problem of not knowing what lies ahead, there's the technology of signaling, such as the whistles that Paleo-Indians drilled into North American bird bone.

As Enheduanna saw, literature can also help to solve a problem. And indeed, part of what drew her to literature is that it tackles a different class of problem from the archaic technologies above. Those technologies seem wildly diverse, but beneath their branching actions lies a deeper mutual enterprise: domesticating our planet. By transforming cold nights, hungry landscapes, and uncertain futures into warmth, nourishment, and information, fire and knives and whistles bend the physical environment to our will.

This archaic task is such an omnipresent part of human existence that even today it remains the goal of our most futuristic engineerings. Our drones, our phones, our algorithms, our virtual realities, and our smart homes have all been built to shuttle around meals and data and other stuffs, turning space-time into an extension of our needs and wants. Yet if we work backward, we can see that life poses an even more basic challenge than the problem of being human in a nonhuman world. That challenge is: the problem of simply being human.

To be human is to wonder *Why?* As in, *Why are we here? What's the purpose of our hours? Does this life mean anything?* And to be human is to have irrational desires, and uncontrollable passions, and griefs that split us into pieces. Or to put it in the frank language of our scientific present: to be human is to be saddled with the problem of having a human brain. A brain capable of asking vast questions that it cannot answer. A brain fueled by emotions that propel us forward but that also cause us to crave things that harm, and to fear things that don't exist, and to rage against age and death and other parts of our nature that can't be escaped.

As scientists have recently discovered, this problem isn't unique to us humans. Our animal relatives share bits and pieces of our neural circuitry, which is why chimps suffer anxiety, elephants lament their departed, dogs get lonesome, and antelopes spook. Yet even so, the singular sophistication of the hardware in your head and mine means that the problem is particularly profound in us. We can achieve unprecedented success—and still feel that life is pointless. We can have a thousand friends—and be overwhelmed by loneliness. We can walk in daylight's brightest gold—and see all the world as gray.

So deep, so sprawling, and so intangible is this problem that it can seem beyond the grip of any technology. But it's the problem addressed by Enheduanna's ziggurat verses and the world's other original literary scriptures. By drawing on literature's great power of story, these works answered existential doubts with narrative purpose. And by harnessing literature's great power of emotion, these works imbued faltering spirits with togetherness and courage.

Thus it was that literature's technology distinguished itself from Neolithic axes and Bronze Age plows and other creations forged of metal, stone, and bone. While those creations turned outward to grapple with the problem of surviving in our world, literature turned inward to grapple with the problem of surviving as ourselves.

To be sure, this grand intention probably wasn't in the mind of literature's very first author. And, in fact, we know that in many ancient cultures, authors claimed to have no intention at all, preferring to credit their work to muses or other spirits above. But then we arrive at Enheduanna. And in her writings, we get our earliest glimpse of the technology-making discovery that authors could be innovators:

> I, Enheduanna, created this booklet—
> a thing which no one else had ever created.

How brazen was this boast? Was Enheduanna simply announcing herself as a partner in a creative act—"born from a great mother"—one womb passing on the vital energy of another? Or did Enheduanna believe more boldly that she and she alone was the maker of her inventions? Did she dare in moments to think that even the gods she named were fictions built to do her bidding, taming the merchants of Ur and preserving her dynasty? Did she go so far as to dream that heaven was a story that she could fashion herself?

It's impossible to say. But either way, the authors who followed Enheduanna would learn that they could work literature's gears and switches without the magic of supernatural assistance. They could target story to answer specific life questions. They could mold emotion to generate particular mind balms and uplifts. They could engineer new worlds—and new eternities too.

So it came to be that by the time of the first millennium BCE, about two thousand years after Enheduanna's midnight arrival in Ur, literature had gained repute for delivering hope and hospice in shadows where no priest or medic ventured. When the Hellenistic sage Epicurus declared that the gods had bobbed away, his followers revived their greater sense of purpose with the epic poem *On the Nature of It All*. And when Zhou dynasty doctors confessed that they could mend bones but not sorrows, this lyric remedy was painted on bamboo by a resourceful wife upon the Yangtze marshes:

> After you return from the hunt,
> With red-footed geese and wild duck,
> We will feast
> To songs of silk,
> And I will wish for life's long years
> To keep me, gray haired,
> In your arms.

The medicine men may have run out of unguents and potions; the heavens may have vanished or grown cold. But still, literature could fix hearts and lift souls.

That, in brief, is why literature was invented and what it was invented to do. It was a narrative-emotional technology that helped our ancestors cope with the psychological challenges posed by human biology. It was an invention for overcoming the doubt and the pain of just being us.

And the technology didn't suddenly stop working when our ancestors departed this globe. It can still reckon with death and unshatter the psyche. It can still give us the stuff past the stars and the meaning immortal.

Our ancestors' blueprint can show us how.

Our Ancestors' Blueprint for Using Literature

To get the most out of literature, our ancestors treated it as more than a great invention. They treated it as *many* great inventions.

Each of these inventions had a unique purpose, engineered with its own intricate circuitry to click into our psyche in a different way. So, there was one special invention for lightening sorrow, another for banishing loneliness, another for diminishing anxiety, another for treating the symptoms of trauma, another for bringing hope, another for heightening joy, another for stirring love, another for ushering in tranquility, and so on and so on.

Since these inventions were all very different in both how they were built and what they did, our ancestors initially stumbled at random into finding them. But then sometime around 500 BCE, roughly a hundred generations after Enheduanna, a breakthrough occurred: our ancestors discovered an invention-finding method. The method was straightforward enough to be explained in a few moments yet versatile enough to be applied to any piece of global literature, no matter how original its design or far-flung its creation. And with the help of the method, our ancestors began scouring the world's libraries, gathering up a toolbox of literary inventions for improving daily mental health and happiness—when abruptly, a few short centuries after the project began, it was halted. No more inventions were added to the toolbox, while its existing inventions gradually fell into rusted neglect, until, at last, the technology of literature was lost.

If you're curious to learn how this loss occurred—and to explore why our modern schools and universities don't train us to use literature as an innovation for troubleshooting our humanity—you can discover the story in the coda that concludes this book. But our purpose over the following chapters won't be to dwell on the literary toolbox's demise; our purpose will be to undo it. We'll start by re-exhuming the original inventions unearthed by our ancestors, dusting off their dormant flywheels and patching their corroded circuitries so we can put their health-and-happiness boosters back to work. And then we'll go further. We'll expand the toolbox many times over by deploying our ancestors' old invention-finding method in a pair of fresh ways.

First, we'll turn to the vast abundance of literature created in the centuries since our ancestors departed the earth, using the method to excavate the inventions of modernist novels and Renaissance stage plays, nursery rhymes and superhero comics, crime sagas and computer-animated movies, love songs and prime-time soaps, slave narratives and space operas, cartoon memoirs and single-cam sitcoms, pulp fiction adventures and postmodern elegies, horror flicks and detective fictions, surrealist short stories and fairy-tale anthologies, and many, many genres more.

Second, we'll combine our ancestors' method with a more recent revealer of secrets: twenty-first-century neuroscience. Over the past decade or so, neuroscientists have begun using pulse monitors, eye trackers, brain scanners, and other gadgets to look inside our head as we consume novels, poems, films, and comic books. This scientific project is still in its infancy and is thick with unresolved questions and scholarly disagreements. But even so, its early findings have been tremendously revealing. And when they're combined with established areas of psychological and psychiatric research, they produce an intricate picture of how literature's inventions can plug into different regions of our brain—the emotion centers of our amygdala, the imagination hubs of our default mode network, the spiritual nodes of our parietal lobe, the heart softeners of our empathy system, the God's-Eye elevators of our prefrontal neurons, the pleasure injectors of our caudate nucleus, the psychedelic pathways of our visual cortex—to alleviate depression, reduce anxiety, sharpen intelligence, increase mental energy, kindle creativity, inspire confidence, and enrich our days with myriad other psychological benefits.

Remarkably, then, our ancestors were righter than they knew. Enheduanna's moonlit engineering feat was followed by countless more, filling literature with inventions for healing our heart and enhancing our mind, refreshing our lives and making us new.

So, let's go back to the future. Let's discover our ancestors' long-ago method and the modern science behind it.

Let's turn the page and see what followed the dawn.

The Lost Technology

O ut of the evergreen wilds of northern Greece, in the morning years of the fourth century BCE, walked a young man with dark, shaggy hair.

The young man hailed from a family of curious minds. His great-grandfather had plumbed the secrets of disease by dissecting wild dogs—and perhaps even the still-beating heart of a Barbary ape. His older sister had hungrily pestered their mother for tales of enchanted huntresses who rode blonde-antlered deer, and of resurrector goddesses who washed away death's ache with poppy blooms, and of titan queens whose boundless memory stored every song and story ever breathed. And he himself was determined to delve deeper still into the mysteries of medicine and myth, dedicating his days to a far-reaching quest that would lead him at last to a method for finding literature's inventions.

This young man from Macedon was Aristotle. Driven by his teenage ambition to learn, he quit the provincial ravines of his boyhood years, hiking east through forests of lynx, then three hundred miles south down the turquoise-watered Aegean Coast, to make his way to a vast circuit of white-marble walls—built from toppled temple arches and smashed-up statues of forgotten heroes—that guarded the city of Athens. Just outside the walls lay the ancient Mediterranean's most famous school, the Academy of Plato, where, amid a sloping olive grove, all the fabled wisdom of Babylon, Egypt, and Atlantis was studied—and superseded. So, Aristotle enrolled, and, making good on his lofty self-improvement scheme, he became a pupil of extraordinary renown; the only one, it was said in later times, who could comprehend Plato's abstruse theories of immortal beauty and arithmetic afterlives. Until sometime around 347 BCE, the now middle-aged man from Macedon broke away from the academy, heading off to think in his own way.

It's not exactly clear why Aristotle decided to break away. At the time, it was whispered that he was just being a provocateur. That, after all, was the way of ambitious students: they came up with outrageous new ideas to make a name for themselves. And certainly Aristotle was fond of being the center of attention. He enjoyed expensive clothes, covered his fingers with glittering rings, and liked to announce in public places that he had a theory of *everything*.

Or perhaps Aristotle broke away from the academy because he was a born outsider. Unlike Plato, Aristotle wasn't a high-blooded Athenian aristocrat. He was a resident alien; a foreign son. So, he might have thought that it was simply in his pedigree to trouble the status quo.

Or perhaps Aristotle broke away because he was more practically minded than his great teacher. He was a man of the world, and not just because he took pleasure in clothing and rings. He also had an interest in the way things *worked*, and he delved into nature with a scientist's eye, searching for clues to how acorns sprouted and tongues tasted and heavens rotated.

But whatever the reason for Aristotle's departure, he most definitely went rogue. Renouncing the academy's commitment to reason and reason alone, he ambled off to chat with beekeepers, vivisect bird eggs, catalogue mortal emotions, classify wildflowers, and chronicle stage shows, laying the empirical foundations of zoology, physiology, psychology, botany, and dramaturgy. And somewhere in the course of these investigations into the nuts and bolts of life, he discovered the method for finding all of literature's inventions.

Aristotle wasn't the first to discover the method. In fact, he almost certainly learned it from a mysterious group of peripatetic instructors known as the literary Sophists, whose own history is sketched in the coda that concludes this book. But the writings of the literary Sophists and all their students except for Aristotle have since been scattered by the winds of passing years. So, without Aristotle's eager thirst to learn how literature worked, the method would have evaporated forever, like Atlantis and its misty genius, into the stuff of legend.

Aristotle's account of the invention-finding method appears in a cragged paragraph that falls about one-third of the way into a treatise known as the *Poetics*. The *Poetics*, we now think, may not have been physically composed by Aristotle. In fact, there's a strong possibility that it was handwritten by one of his students. The student may have been a trained amanuensis who employed a cryptic intellectual shorthand. Or the student may have struggled to follow every detail of Aristotle's fast-paced lecturings, forcing him to hastily jot down all the words he could in the hope that he'd unpuzzle their full brilliance later. Or the student may have felt fuzzy headed from the hyacinth wine sloshed out at last night's symposium, leading his mind and his note-taking to meander erratically. But however it was that the *Poetics* came to be writ, it doesn't make for an easy read. It gallops through intricacies and delivers revolutionary ideas with stilted matter-of-factness. For long stretches, it feels pedantically boring. And then it shifts into being exasperatingly enigmatic.

Yet as knotty as the prose paragraphs of the *Poetics* can be, they manage to preserve the invention-finding method with enough clarity for us to recover its essential action. That action consists of two linked steps: first, identify *what* literature does, and second, work backward to uncover *how* literature does it. The *what* is the specific psychological effect of a literary work; an effect that's typically linked to emotion. The *how* is the unique literary invention that drives the effect; an invention that's usually engineered from one of the core elements of narrative: plot, character, storyworld, and narrator.

In theory, this two-step process of reverse engineering literature is simple. In practice, it's a bit more difficult. But the more we practice, the easier it gets. So, to slip in a little practice, let's follow along with the *Poetics* as Aristotle unearths one hidden literary invention.

And then another, more hidden still.

The First Invention Unearthed by the *Poetics*

The first invention is what the Greeks saw as a soul lifter.

Prior to Aristotle, his teacher Plato had sagely concluded that there existed only one soul lifter: reason. But when Aristotle visited the theater, he noticed audiences of Greek tragedy experiencing a nonrational—indeed, emotional—up. That up was *thaumazein*, or as we might translate it today, *wonder*. Wonder is life through the eyes of a child. It's the first glimpse of a flower, or the discovery of oceans, or the parting of clouds at the high touch of heaven.

So, what's the literary source of this uplifting feeling? What invention did the Greek playwrights devise to impart wonder's joyous sense of greater possibility? The answer provided by the *Poetics* is: the plot twist. Sounds straightforward. But, of course, there's some twist to it.

The first part of the twist is this: the plot twist isn't a twist. It's the final link of a chain of untwisted events, where each link connects smoothly with the one before, carrying the story forward without bends or breaks. Yet even though the chain of the story is arrow straight, its final link is so stunning that it feels like a swerve. It overthrows all precedent, delivering us to a destination unexpected.

Here is Aristotle's favorite example:

> Once upon a time, a prince of Thebes was born with a hideous prophecy: he was fated to sleep with his mother. Determined to prevent that prophecy from coming true, the prince's mother took immediate action. She ordered a shepherd to get rid of the boy, and the shepherd stole the boy far away, to another land.
>
> In that other land, the prince was raised up by a different mother. Until one day, the prince got curious about his future and visited an oracle. There, the prince heard a hideous prophecy: he was fated to sleep with his mother. Determined to prevent that prophecy from coming true, the prince took immediate action. Fleeing the home of the only mother he'd known, he journeyed far away to another land, until he came to a city known as Thebes, where he met a lovely widowed queen. . . .

That's the story of Oedipus. You can clearly see its unbroken chain. Step by step, a mother and son act entirely logically, hearing a prophecy and doing the sensible thing to thwart it. And then, surprise! Their sensible plots cancel out, and the mother and son end up together.

This twist produces horror in Oedipus and his mother. But in us, the viewing audience, it produces *thaumazein*, lifting our mind with awe at the farseeing powers above.

And this isn't the only wonder that we can take from the plot twist. Because the twist contains a further twist: an invention for making wonder without any plot at all.

The Deeper Invention for Making Wonder

Buried within the plot twist is a more basic literary invention: the *stretch*.

The *stretch* is the taking of a regular pattern of plot or character or storyworld or narrative style or any other core component of story—and extending the pattern further. So, taking a great battle—and making it greater. Taking a bold girl—and making her bolder. Taking a blue lake—and making it bluer. Taking a star—and making it everywhere.

The *stretch* is the invention at the root of all literary wonder: the marvel that comes from stretching regular objects into metaphors, the dazzle that comes from stretching regular rhythms of speech into poetic meters, and the awe that comes from stretching regular humans into heroes.

And the *stretch* is also the invention at the root of the plot twist. The plot twist takes a story chain and *stretches* it one link further, as when *Oedipus Tyrannus* takes the old plot of a person who tries to outwit a prophecy and elaborates it into the mind bender of two people trying to outwit the same prophecy—and so double-negatively fulfilling it.

The *stretch* is a simple device, but its effects on our brain can be profound. It's been linked in modern psychology labs to a shift of neural attention that flings our focus outward, decreasing activity in our parietal lobe—a brain region associated with mental representations of our self. The result is that we quite literally feel the borders of our self dissolving, even to the point of "self-annihilation."

This neural feeling is why we can "lose ourselves" in a book or a film, forgetting our personal limits in horizons beyond. And although such forgetfulness has been dismissed by many an outside observer as idle escapism, it ushers our brain into what twenty-first-century psychologists term a self-transcendent experience, or what the early-twentieth-century founder of modern psychology, William James, described more vividly as a "spiritual" experience. These experiences are the mystic mental states that sages from days immemorial have preached as the highest good of human life. And in the case of literature, at least, the good really exists. The *stretch* has been connected by modern neuroscientists to significant increases in both our generosity and our sense of personal well-being. Which is to say: fictional plot twists, metaphors, and heroic characters dispense a pair of factual benefits. By immersing our neural circuitry in the feeling of things bigger, they elevate our charity and our happiness, spiriting us closer to a scientific Shangri-la.

The literary blueprint for this mind-lifting experience is an extraordinary thing. It might even have made you feel a little burst of wonder yourself. But it's only half of the extraordinary contained in the *Poetics*. Because as Aristotle was staking out the theater, studying audiences, he realized that Greek tragedy contained another great invention. And that invention worked very differently from the *stretch*.

Its function was less spiritual. And more medical.

The Medical Function of Greek Tragedy

When Aristotle went to the theater, he saw that Greek tragedy didn't just make people feel good. It also made them feel less bad. The feeling good came from enriching the brain with positive experiences such as wonder and hope, while the feeling less bad came from the inverse: emptying the brain of negative experiences like grief and anxiety. Or to use modern psychiatric parlance: the feeling good came from boosted mental well-being, that neural condition of happy thriving where our life reaches its fullest potential, while the feeling less bad came from improved mental health, that psychological foundation for mental well-being—and for normal daily functioning.

Literature can improve our mental health in all sorts of ways, but in the particular case of Greek tragedy, Aristotle emphasized a therapeutic process that he called catharsis. Catharsis is an old doctorly term for purging something unhealthy. And as Aristotle recorded in the *Poetics*, one something purged by Greek tragedy is fear.

Fear isn't always bad. In fact, it can be very healthy, steering us away from cliff drops and crocodiles and other perils. But Aristotle noticed that unhealthy fear can build up in our brain when we suffer trauma.

That posttraumatic fear, as it's now termed by modern psychiatrists, is meant to be a form of emotional self-protection; a way of maintaining our distance from the world so that we don't get harmed again. But its frequent effect is to increase our suffering. It can disrupt our lives with pervasive feelings of helplessness, isolation, and hypervigilance. And it's often associated with generalized anxiety, anger, and depression.

Traumatic fear will be experienced by about 90 percent of us over our lives, and its posttraumatic residue will linger in roughly 10 percent of cases. There's no universally effective treatment for the residue; different therapies are more or less effective in different individual situations. But over the past two decades, psychiatric studies involving thousands of patients have yielded a pair of unexpected findings.

The first finding is that it can be therapeutic to revisit our memories of the trauma. This psychiatric process, known as autobiographical review, seems counterintuitive and doesn't always work; some of us find more relief, particularly at first, by instead focusing on forward-looking stress management. But in general, if we imaginatively play back our experience of trauma within a safe and supportive environment, then the "flashbulb" intensity of our remembrance will gradually decrease. This isn't the same thing as erasing our memory: the trauma will always remain part of our lived experience, kept within the long-term storage of our neural cortex. But autobiographical review can make the memory less emotionally raw and intrusive, receding the trauma into the background of our consciousness, and decreasing our symptoms of helplessness, isolation, and hypervigilance.

The second finding is that it helps to sweep our eyes from side to side while we mentally review the trauma. This curious fact was stumbled upon by the California psychologist Francine Shapiro in the late 1980s, and, at the time, it appeared so random, even magical, that it was regarded warily as a drift into pseudoscience. But recent studies on mice have suggested that side-to-side eye movement may stimulate a small region of our brain, the superior colliculus–mediodorsal thalamus circuit, which is involved in fear attenuation. And eye movement has proved effective enough in clinical trials to produce its own trauma therapy—eye movement desensitizing and reprocessing (EMDR) — that has been formally recommended by the American Psychiatric Association, the World Health Organization, and the Department of Veterans Affairs.

As surprising as these findings have been for many modern psychiatrists, versions of both autobiographical review and EMDR were incorporated into ancient Greek tragedy. Greek tragedy encourages us to revisit our past experiences of trauma by staging suicides, murders, and assaults that are interspersed with choral chants such as the ones found in Aeschylus's *Agamemnon*:

> The law of our world is pain,
> the scar that teaches
> the hardness of days
> and leaves its mark
> in every heart.

This chant was first performed in 458 BCE within the Dionysus Eleuthereus, an open-air theater hewn into the south cliff face of Athens's Acropolis. That rock enclosure turned its back on the city's marketplaces and legal forums, casting the eyes instead across the honeyed ridges of the Hymettos Mountains and the dolphin wavelets of the Saronic Gulf. So, as the audience sat upon long, curving pinewood benches, surrounded by thousands of neighbors and extended family members, they were prompted to recall their own past hardships—"The law of our world is pain . . . the hardness of days . . . every heart"—in a venue that removed them from life's daily pressures to enfold them in a greater community of care.

And the audience didn't just hear the chant of *Agamemnon*. They saw it too. The chant's words flowed from the twelve actors of the *koros*, or "chorus," a word that now simply means "song," but which was synonymous in Attic Greek with "dance." As the Greek warrior Ajax snaps in Homer's *Iliad*: "The Trojans are calling us to a fight, not a chorus dance!"

In the case of Greek tragedy, the space for that dance was an ample one. It was situated at the bottom of the Dionysus Eleuthereus in a semicircular area that spanned more than sixty-five feet in diameter. The area was known as the *orkestra*, or "orchestra," which in our own age has come, like *chorus*, to mean a thing of sound. But it translates literally as "dancing place." To the ancient Greeks, the orchestra was seventeen hundred square feet for choreographed movement back and forth.

When *Agamemnon* premiered more than twenty-five centuries ago, it therefore gave its audience a chance to experience ancient literary versions of two modern psychiatric treatments for posttraumatic fear. Like autobiographical review, *Agamemnon* prompted spectators to review their posttraumatic memories in a physically safe and emotionally supportive environment. And like EMDR, the play's chorus delivered that prompt in a dynamic performance that shifted the eyes left and right. And although we cannot travel back in time to gauge the therapeutic effectiveness of these long-ago treatments, we have been able to observe their healing action on twenty-first-century trauma survivors. Over the past decade, performances of the chorus of *Agamemnon* and other Greek tragedies have been staged for combat veterans by initiatives such as Bryan Doerries's Theater of War Productions and Peter Meineck's Aquila Theatre Company (which places particular emphasis on the side-to-side movement incorporated into EMDR). And in response to these performances, veterans have self-reported a decrease in feelings of isolation, hypervigilance, and other symptoms of posttraumatic fear. Just as Aristotle describes in the *Poetics*, they've undergone an experience of catharsis.

This doesn't make Greek tragedy a miracle cure; ancient plays such as *Agamemnon* don't work automatically, in every case, to lessen posttraumatic fear. But perhaps the most remarkable feature of Greek tragedy is that its historical evolution suggests that its authors were aware of its therapeutic limits—and devised an innovation to address them.

The Innovation for Improving Greek Tragedy's Therapeutic Effect

The innovation was revealed to modern eyes by a twenty-first-century psychiatric discovery: therapy for posttraumatic fear is more effective when we possess "self-efficacy."

Self-efficacy is the inner conviction that we can deal successfully with posttraumatic fear, managing and eventually overcoming it. The conviction can be conscious; we might, for example, tell ourselves that unlike trauma, which is an external force that damages, posttraumatic fear is an inner shield flung up by our brain, so that instead of fighting or fleeing its psychic distress, we can calmly acknowledge it as a protective part of our own self. Or the conviction can exist as an unconscious attitude—*I'm stronger than this fear*—embedded deep within our gray matter, that we feel without articulating. But either way, the conviction is powerful medicine. If we possess self-efficacy, then autobiographical review and EMDR are significantly more likely to work for us. And if we don't possess it—if we instead suspect in our bones that the pain of posttraumatic fear can harm us permanently in ways that we cannot stop—then the reverse holds true: our process of mentally revisiting trauma through autobiographical review or EMDR can be alarming and even harmful, exacerbating our symptoms instead of alleviating them.

Twenty-five centuries ago, the Greeks seem to have realized this. Because as Greek tragedy evolved, it developed a mechanism for increasing our self-efficacy—a mechanism that's precisely identified by Aristotle in the *Poetics*.

Aristotle makes the identification in *Poetics* 1452a, where he observes that the healing effects of catharsis can be boosted by a specific kind of tragic plot: one where a character suffers trauma but doesn't acknowledge it until later. Aristotle refers to this belated acknowledgement as anagnorisis. We can call it the "Hurt Delay."

To illustrate the Hurt Delay, Aristotle turns to Sophocles's *Oedipus Tyrannus*. Written three decades after the *Agamemnon* chorus, the play reveals that Oedipus has fathered children with the lovely Theban widow who birthed him long ago. So catastrophic is this tragedy that it's now ravaging the whole city of Thebes with plague. Yet Oedipus is completely unaware. He has no idea that he's wedded his mother, and, in fact, angrily rebuffs a prophet who tries to alert him. It's only in the play's final moments that Oedipus sees at last the horror of what he's already undergone. And with a terrible scream, he acknowledges the devastation that happened years before.

This is a highly intricate structure for a story. It requires the storyteller to construct a way for trauma to strike a character without the character realizing it; hence Sophocles's use of prophets and prophecies that necessitate a future disaster that Oedipus cannot see. These time-bending devices have often been used in modern classrooms to draw students of *Oedipus* into contemplating the infinite philosophical labyrinths of fate and free will, but their storytelling purpose is entirely uncomplicated: to place us, the audience, in the position of knowing the trauma *before* it's felt.

That position of foreknowledge stimulates a powerful sensation of cosmic irony in the "perspective-taking network" of our brain's prefrontal cortex, giving us a godlike experience of looking down on Oedipus's mortal tragedy from above. This God's-Eye vantage reduces activity in our brain's deep emotion zones, acting as a neural shock absorber against the traumatic events before us. And it also does something else: it primes us to increase our self-efficacy.

The increase begins at the climactic moment of the Hurt Delay, when Oedipus endures his terrible epiphany. To escape from seeing the horror of what he's done, Oedipus slams a pair of golden broaches into his eyes, blinding himself. Yet this desperate act doesn't accomplish its purpose. Instead, Oedipus cries out in agony that he's been "pierced by memory." That memory is the deep source of posttraumatic fear, and when its edge cuts Oedipus, it seems to doom him to a life of unending flashbacks. What bodily eyes can perceive no more, the mind's eye will never forget.

But then, unexpectedly, relief arrives in the form of the chorus, which cries out to Oedipus: "We understand your pain; it's catastrophe upon catastrophe." To which Oedipus responds gratefully: "O friend, you are my steadfast care giver still."

The chorus is able to provide Oedipus with this caregiving respite because its members possess a perspective on his tragedy that he does not. That perspective comes from their own posttraumatic memory, which is revealed when the chorus members first arrive in the orchestra, confessing the fear bred of their painful past. The memory then recurs throughout the play, prompting the chorus to shake as they feel flashbacks ensuing. Until at last, in Oedipus's terrible time of need, the memory is converted unexpectedly into a source of healing, empowering the chorus to console Oedipus as a fellow trauma survivor: *You are not alone*.

The Hurt Delay provides us with the same empowerment. By imbuing our brain's perspective-taking network with an ironic up-aboveness, the Hurt Delay makes us feel as if we're floating on a higher plane from which we, like the chorus, can see Oedipus's catastrophe as part of a larger cosmic pattern—and from which we can reach down to Oedipus and lift him up. This neural feeling of being able to support Oedipus is deeply therapeutic: when we experience our ability to assist others through their trauma, we increase our belief in our ability to cope with trauma ourselves. And, in fact, such is the boost to our self-efficacy that, in clinical group-therapy settings, it has been correlated with significantly higher rates of trauma recovery. So, even though we're no more able than Oedipus to stop the inevitable, the Hurt Delay strengthens our capacity to manage when the inevitable arrives. Shifting our tragic feeling of helplessness into a psychological sensation of help*ful*ness, it supplies our brain with a visceral belief in our power to heal.

In the *Poetics*, Aristotle credits this therapeutic innovation for elevating Greek tragedy to a state of perfection. That's an overstatement, at least as far as Greek tragedy's medicinal action is concerned; no work of literature has ever become a universal cure-all. But Aristotle is nevertheless right to claim that the Hurt Delay enhanced Greek tragedy's cathartic effect, and this fact of medical improvement is the most eye-opening of the many eye-opening details inscribed in the *Poetics*. It reveals the Greek stage as an experimental laboratory where new literary inventions could be developed. And it establishes Greek tragedy as a wonderwork that *stretched* to amplify its healing power over time.

Yet despite all this empirical research, ancient and modern, you might still be thinking: *Hold on, hold on. I've flipped through a Greek tragedy or two. But it didn't make me feel any better. And now that I think back, I also didn't find my way to Shangri-la.*

If you're thinking those thoughts, don't put down this book just yet. You can still reap all the psychic benefits of Greek tragedy. The invention-finding method can show you how.

Using the Method to Reap the Benefits of Literature

Not all our brains work the same. In fact, all our brains work a little bit differently. Some of the differences come from our DNA. Some from our culture. Some from our personal history and individual life choices.

All those differences are good for us as a species; they mean that humanity possesses an immense neural diversity that we can exploit to adapt and grow through changing times and shifting environments. But they do present a problem for our everyday consumption of literature: if we're each a little bit different, then how can we all appreciate the same poems, novels, TV shows, and plays?

There are two broad answers to this question. The first is that our brain is flexible. Not infinitely flexible; our brain has its limits. But human gray matter has survived by being adaptable, so it's often able to adapt itself to different kinds of literature.

The second broad answer is that literature, too, is flexible. The same basic literary invention can be deployed in richly varied styles and genres. So, if we're not able to adapt our mind to literature, then literature is often capable of adapting itself to us.

The invention-finding method can help with both kinds of adaptation:

1. *Adapting Our Mind to Literature*. By providing us with the blueprints for how literary inventions are meant to operate, the method saves us from interacting with classic poems and plays in the way that we interact with alien technologies: randomly mashing at buttons to see what happens. Instead, we can work in sync with literature, clicking into its circuitry to become an active partner.

   In the case of the Hurt Delay, the blueprint guides us to (1) embrace the feeling of ironic God's-Eye triggered by our foreknowledge of Oedipus's disaster, (2) reach out with the chorus to affirm Oedipus's pain, and (3) feel Oedipus's reciprocal gratitude. If we take these three steps, we can boost Greek tragedy's cathartic effect.

2. *Adapting Literature to Our Mind*. By handing us the deep blueprints for literary inventions, the invention-finding method enables us to locate versions of those inventions in contemporary literature that more organically suits our taste.

   In the case of the Hurt Delay, there are shelves full of modern novels, from F. Scott Fitzgerald's *The Great Gatsby* (1925), to Kazuo Ishiguro's *Remains of the Day* (1989), to John Green's

The Fault in Our Stars (2012), that contain the time-bending
device of a trauma that happens *before* it's acknowledged, providing our brain with the lightly empowering feel of cosmic
irony. And Greek tragedy's interactive experience of supporting another living soul through trauma can be found in many
moments of modern drama, as when nurse Sue Monahan plays
the part of the chorus at the end of Margaret Edson's *Wit* (1999),
or when Mama Cates makes her lonely phone call in the final
moments of Marsha Norman's *'Night, Mother* (1983), or when
we turn to the person in the seat next to us at the curtain drop
of Eugene O'Neill's *A Long Day's Journey into Night* (1956). In
all these instances, we're able to feel another person's gratitude
for our physical presence in their moment of tragedy, dosing
ourselves with a neural boost of self-efficacy.

That's the adaptive power of the method. It can deepen our appreciation for the world's ancient classics—or direct us toward newer works
that have the same psychological benefit, enriching our lives with a vast
catalogue of time-tested literary inventions.

Inventions like the Hurt Delay that can improve our mental health.
Inventions like the *stretch* that can enhance our greater well-being.

The Plan for the Following Chapters

Aristotle was a pragmatist. He viewed literature as a multipurpose tool
for making life better. So, this book will be equally pragmatic, expanding the *Poetics* with a catalogue of twenty-five literary inventions that
you can put to work right now.

Some of these inventions target what modern psychiatrists have identified as common forms of mental distress: grief, grudges, pessimism,
shame, heartbreak, rumination, reactive thoughts, self-doubt, numbness, loneliness. Some impart what modern psychologists have identified
as well-being boosters: courage, love, curiosity, belief, energy, imagination. And some indirectly support our mental health and well-being by
nurturing practical life skills: freethinking, problem solving, de-biasing,
counterfactual speculating, cognitive flexing, relearning, introspecting.

These benefits are by no means replacements for modern psychiatry. They're supplements, just as a healthy diet and regular exercise are supplements for doctor visits and blood pressure medications. But no less than the daily food we eat, the daily literature we consume can have significant benefits, and to convey a broad selection of those benefits, each of the following chapters delves into a different literary invention, giving you all three things you need to use it: (1) *why* the invention matters, (2) *how* the invention works, and (3) *where* you can find a copy of the invention for yourself.

The *why* comes in the form of the invention's origin story, or in other words, the historical reason that humans developed it. This origin story, like all excursions into history, is a best guess. The invention's earliest maker may have been lost to record, her creative genius forever hidden in the later songs and stories that we now praise for her discovery. And even when we do have a high degree of certainty about who the first inventor was, there's inevitably a shroud of mystery around her process of engineering. Was it driven by conscious intention or subconscious intuition? Individual brilliance or cultural inheritance? Careful experiment or happy accident? Sometimes the inventor might have stumbled into one pharmacology while pursuing another; sometimes she might never have realized her invention's psychological benefits: they may have been uncovered only by later generations. But when the issue lies in doubt, as it almost always does, this book will err on the side of generosity and credit the inventor's volitional intelligence. By doing so, it will celebrate the undeniable fact of human literary inventiveness, which forms the deeper hero of our story.

The *how* is the invention's operational blueprint, including the basic neuroscience behind it. Since neuroscience is a specialized field rife with arcane terminologies and byzantine complexities, the following chapters will not belabor the technical. They will fold in the highlights of what we know, doing so as colloquially as possible, with a view to assisting you in using the invention more effectively.

The *where* are reading recommendations to help you locate the invention in a novel, poem, film, or comic book, so you can experience its effects firsthand.

The chapters are interconnected but independent, like books on a shelf. So, if you're seeking a particular benefit from literature, you can jump to reading that chapter now. If you like to be surprised, you can browse out of order. And if you're a committed bibliophile, you can start at chapter 1 and read right through.

We'll begin by recovering more inventions that were known in Aristotle's day, from courage boosters hammered together on Mediterranean isles, to love increasers constructed in Chinese river valleys, to empathy generators engineered amid biblical kingdoms. And as we proceed, we'll move on through history to uncover later inventions: medieval, Renaissance, and modern.

Learning the literary secrets of our ancestors.

And then a library beyond.

ONE

Rally Your Courage

Homer's Iliad *and the Invention*
of the Almighty Heart

The boy with the quiet brown eyes was about to die.

His sisters and his brothers had already been eaten. And now his father was hunting him, too, flashing long teeth and waving a blood-crusted scythe.

But the boy did not run. He faced his father on the mountaintop, the skies live with fire, the valleys howling with the tongues of giants. And fate was with the boy that day. He tore his father's belly open, ripped out his swallowed siblings, then hurled his father into hell.

The boy was Zeus. From that act of heaven war, he became tyrant lord of Greece. And he would go on to rule for generations, from the late Neolithic era of the fourth millennium BCE to the steel age of the fourth century CE, when the Roman Empire wielded whips and roadside crucifixions to impose a new god, Jesus Christ, upon the Greeks.

During the years of Zeus's reign, the Greeks constantly repeated the story about how he'd disemboweled his father on the mountaintop. And the Greeks repeated many other stories about Zeus too. There was the story about how Zeus flooded the earth, drowning a million infants in their cribs. There was the story about how Zeus assassinated the world's first doctor, Asclepius, with a jealous lightning bolt. There was the story about how Zeus descended in swan feathers to rape the Spartan queen Leda; and in satyr hooves to rape the night-haired Antiope of Thebes;

and in goddess flesh to rape the virginal Callisto of Arcadia; and in bull shape to rape the seafaring Europa of Lebanon; and in tandem with Hades to rape his own daughter, Persephone; and in eagle feathers to rape a little Trojan boy with quiet brown eyes named Ganymede.

Why did the Greeks tell these stories? Why did they imagine their sky master as a child born of violence, a child who grew up to re-inscribe that violence endlessly upon the tender lives within his care? Why did they gather round hearths, and shaded fountains, and red-opium altars to terrify one another with fables of the monster in the atmosphere above?

The Greeks told their fables because they believed them. The Greeks may never have witnessed a god plunge in lusting from a cloud bank, but they'd seen many an infant perish, and many a doctor struck down, and many a young life pointlessly damaged. They'd felt their mortal fragility and the harshness of powers on high. In a word, they'd felt scared. And their tales about Zeus reflected that fear, painting a heaven that matched their existence below.

With their frightful stories, the ancient Greeks took the first step of literature: crafting a representation of life. But as the Greeks would learn around 750 BCE, there was another step that literature could take. Literature could go beyond representing our worldly fears—and it could help to *remedy* those fears.

The year 750 BCE, give or take a decade or two, was when a new story arrived in Greece from the East. The story was borne in the brain of a wandering balladeer who quickly became enveloped in gossip: "His name is Homer. . . ." "He caught a disease of the eye and went blind in his youth. . . ." "He once earned his keep as a schoolteacher, composing children's tales of river frogs and mice. . . ." And since those ancient times, still more rumors have come to swirl: "He was in a collective of folk singers. . . ." "He stole half his verses from his daughter. . . ." "He was not one poet but many."

Perhaps these tales have truth to them. Or perhaps they're just engaging fictions. But what we know for sure is this. The balladeer's own fiction is titled the *Iliad*; it's set during the Greek assault on the Bronze Age trading city of Ilium (or more commonly, Troy); and it captures the massiveness of that assault by unfurling a catalogue of mighty heroes:

Achilles, Hector, Ajax, Aeneas, Odysseus, Agamemnon, Menelaus, Patroclus, Diomedes—the list goes on and on and on.

This epic list has dazzled audiences for almost three thousand years. Yet the *Iliad*'s real triumph isn't its heroes. The *Iliad*'s real triumph is a literary invention that doses our brain with the courage to face down lightning and death and even Zeus, transforming us into heroes ourselves.

The Origins of the Invention

The courage started with the literary technology that we now call the narrator.

The narrator is the mind behind a story. It's the feelings, memories, instincts, attitudes, enthusiasms, desires, and beliefs of the story's teller. That storytelling mind, like all minds, is hidden from view. It reveals itself only through its public acts, and in the case of a story, those acts take the form of the narrator's *voice*.

Back at the very beginning of stories, perhaps on Stone Age Moroccan shrublands or in the red-tinged firelight of Daoxian caves, the voice was a literal voice. All storytelling was oral, uttered by living mouths. Those mouths were richly diverse, and they could inflect stories in many vibrant ways, but the main two were the *tone* and the *taste*:

> The tone was the ring and timbre of the voice. Maybe the voice trembled when it spoke of terrible creatures or chuckled when it spoke of ridiculous coincidences. Maybe the voice was rich with empathy when describing the pains of the poor, or deep with wonder when talking of the gods.

> The taste was the subject matter preferred by the voice. Maybe the voice liked to concentrate on nature and the seasons. Maybe the voice preferred to speak at length about love, or war, or urban architecture, or sea leviathans.

Every storyteller had her own tone and taste, filling the world with different voices. And then astonishingly, the world became even more full. Because there was a storytelling breakthrough.

The breakthrough began in an indistinct era that predated 8000 BCE. During that era, at sites such as India's Bhimbetka sandstone juts and Indonesia's island of Sulawesi, storytellers discovered how to translate their oral voices into the visual media of painting, sculpture, and dance. To translate tone from oral into visual, storytellers devised the endlessly inventive characteristics of individual *style*. And to translate taste, they engineered the remarkable tool now known as narrative *focus*, enabling them to narrow and sharpen their story like a movie-camera lens, zooming tight on some objects and events—while turning others into background scenery.

The next stage of the storytelling breakthrough occurred a little more than five millennia ago, with the advent of writing. Writing, like painting, was a form of visual media, set down as Sumerian cuneiforms upon mud tablets, or Egyptian glyphs upon stone blocks, or Chinese oracle scripts upon cloth strips, or Mesoamerican logographs upon wood planks. And when the ancient authors of this visual media availed themselves of the painters' tools of style and focus, they engineered a brand-new kind of narrator: the literary—that is, literally, the "written"—narrator.

The literary narrator was a seeming impossibility. It existed as inertly monotone script upon a printed page, and yet through the tools of style and focus, it could warmly emote, or solemnly articulate, or fearfully whisper, or dryly remark, or do anything else that a living mouth could do.

We don't know who the very first literary narrators were; the mud, stone, cloth, or wood upon which they were written has long since passed into oblivion. But we can hazard a guess that they were psychological extensions of the human minds who birthed them. If those minds took a wryly detached view of life's impermanence, then their narrators' style might have coupled cosmic *we*-speak with gentle irony, as in this modern rendition of an age-old Akan tale:

We do not really mean, we do not really mean that what we are about to say is true. A story, a story; let it come, let it go.

If those minds believed in Nature's cosmic import, then their narrators' focus might have blurred (or even excluded) supernatural forces while sharply delineating the desires, actions, and memories of natural characters, as in this nineteenth-century transcription of an ancient Cherokee creation story:

> When all was water, the animals were above in Galûñ'lătĭ, beyond the arch; but it was very much crowded, and they were wanting more room. They wondered what was below the water, and at last Dâyuni'sĭ, "Beaver's Grandchild," the little Water-beetle, offered to go and see if it could learn. It darted in every direction over the surface of the water, but could find no firm place to rest. Then it dived to the bottom and came up with some soft mud, which began to grow and spread on every side until it became the island which we call the earth. It was afterward fastened to the sky with four cords, but no one remembers who did this.

From these organic beginnings, our ancestors then used further innovations of style and focus to engineer original literary narrators who sounded nothing like their human authors. Narrators who spoke in the voices of trees or rivers or beasts. And narrators who did something more extraordinary yet.

Narrators who spoke in the voices of gods.

The Narrator God

"Let there be light."

This is the voice of a supreme God. Its style is declarative, simple, absolute. And its focus is galactic: the light-shine of stars.

Gods don't need to speak like this; gods are gods, so they can speak however they wish. But the basic "Let there be light" blueprint is the one adopted by the narrators of the world's most ancient scriptures, from the Old Egyptian *Pyramid Texts* (circa 2400 BCE), to the Sanskrit Rigveda (c. 1500 BCE), to the Hebrew book of Genesis (c. 750 BCE). The style of these scriptures is forceful, austere, and unequivocal. And the focus is giant entities: Life, Truth, Heaven, Beauty, Law. This combined style and focus creates the impression of an almighty being who sees into the deepest nature of things. Which is why we usually refer to the almighty being as the "God's-Eye Narrator," or more concisely, the "God Voice."

The God Voice is an extraordinary literary invention. It allows anyone with a pen to sound like a deity. And by sounding like a deity, that
anyone can touch the minds of audiences with two powerful emotions:

1. *Wonder*. Wonder, as we saw in the introduction, is generated by
   the *stretch*. And *stretch* is what the God Voice does. It *stretches*
   truth into Truth, and law into Law, and light into cosmic
   brightness, making all the stuff of life feel bigger, expanded
   from the familiar to the divine.

2. *Fear*. Fear is a near cousin to wonder; things that inspire awe
   were once said to be "awe-full" or "awful," because the same
   bigness that *stretches* our brain can easily alarm. So, it's only
   to be expected that a narrator who booms like an omnipotent
   deity would make us nervous. Its gigantic size is scare inducing; it skips our pulse and sends a light chill down our spine.

Both these emotions, wonder and fear, were actively cultivated by the
earliest known authors of God Voices. The cultivation of wonder wasn't
especially remarkable; almost all literature, regardless of its historical era or
cultural origin, uses wonder to entice us to listen. But the cultivation of fear
was remarkable. Fear is often unpleasant for audiences: it can be upsetting
and even traumatizing, lodging in our memory to cause recurrent distress.

And indeed, just such distress seems to have been the goal of many
ancient God Voices. *The Epic of Gilgamesh* (c. 2100 BCE) offered this
glimpse of Death: "His brow of darkness, his hands of a lion, his claws
of an eagle, he walks the path to the Temple of Dust." The Egyptian
Book of the Dead (c. 1500 BCE) warned: "The heaven-house of Osiris is
guarded by a mouth of flame, and a spirit of knives, and a destroyer of
hearts, and an eater of blood."

Some ancient authors may have thought that the sweating terror inspired by these God Voices was good for us. But other authors had a
more sinister intent. Fear was (and remains) a common tool of psychological control: in the Egyptian noondays of the twentieth dynasty, amid
the golden valleys of the Theban Necropolis, the gruesome spook of the
Book of the Dead was wielded by the high priest Ramessesnakht to ag-

grandize himself above even the pharaohs, and many another ancient tyrant and ecclesiastic similarly employed a God Voice to dispossess his subject peoples.

But then was built the *Iliad*. And its builder (who, for simplicity's sake, we'll call Homer) revealed that the God Voice could do the opposite of treading us down with fear. It could lift us up with courage.

Courage—and Its Neural Source

Our word *courage* derives from the Old French *cuor*, which itself goes back to the classical Latin *cor*, both of which mean: "heart." So, to Old French and Latin wordsmiths, courage wasn't a stoic virtue or a rational choice. It was a feeling that collided with the terror that rushed through our veins in times of danger, counterbalancing one emotion with another, and rousing us with the psychological desire to hold our ground.

The wordsmiths' old insight into courage has been extended by modern neuroscience. The neural origins of courage start deep in the primordial center of our brain, where there sits, ensconced upon a drop-shaped double throne, the coward despot known as our amygdala. As soon as our amygdala senses danger, it panics. Hastily overruling whatever else we're doing, it triggers our sympathetic nervous system, our periaqueductal gray matter, and the other components of our brain's threat-response network to release a mix of adrenaline and natural opioid painkillers, boosting our heart rate, numbing our hurt, and filling us with energy. This heated feeling of fearful strength isn't courage; in fact, its original biological purpose is to help us flee danger. But it can be converted into bravery through the addition of one more neural ingredient: oxytocin.

Oxytocin is the hormone that bonds mothers to newborns, and as neuroscientists have discovered, it can also be released in response to threats. The release is made by our pituitary gland, a more courageous part of our inner brain that sits just below our amygdala in a bone command bunker, the *sella turcica*. From that bunker, our pituitary carefully gathers intel on our surroundings. And when it learns that there are other endangered humans in our vicinity, it releases oxytocin.

This oxytocin release prompts us to respond to threat differently from most animals. Most animals, be they a lion or rodent, respond to threat by trying to avoid it. First, the lion freezes, hoping to evade detection. If that doesn't work, the lion attempts to flee. Only if flight is impossible does the lion at last turn and fight. But even then, the fight isn't a committed battle. It's a frenetic lash-out; an attempt to startle the threat, creating an opportunity for the lion to ghost away.

That solo fight-or-flight response has enabled lions and rodents to survive down to our present day. But the social tie of oxytocin has guided us humans into an even more effective survival strategy, referred to by scientists as "tend and befriend." In times of chronic danger, such as famine or plague, tend and befriend encourages us to share our food and our medicines with the other threatened people sensed by our pituitary. And in times of acute danger (like an ambush), it prompts us to band together in a combat pack. Within that pack, we're more likely to endure than as a fleeing person. We can stave off—even conquer—threats that would devour us alone.

This survive-together strategy isn't universal to every human situation. There's evidence that testosterone-heavy brains are less inclined to tend and befriend; and when things get truly dire, all of our brains can turn selfish, nudging us to hoard our resources and betray our comrades. Yet even so, the potency of oxytocin is such that our friendliness under fire is remarkably durable. The annals of history are rich with episodes where people have risked their lives to fight alongside a stranger. Together, we feel that we can be bigger than any threat. And together, we feel that even if our individual self should perish on this muddy field, our greater humanness will carry on.

When that feeling of vaster humanity is combined with the neurochemicals stimulated by our primary fear response, the result is a threefold chest heat: the blood-pumping warmth of adrenaline, the pain-dulling warmth of our native opioids, and the social-bonding warmth of oxytocin. This neurochemical elixir makes us feel energized, impervious to harm, and willing to sacrifice ourselves. It's the heart flame that we hail as courage.

Homer and his fellow Greeks knew none of these later discoveries, but like the later Latin and Old French wordsmiths, the Greeks related courage to heart. The *Iliad* has barely begun before Achilles snarls at Agamemnon: "O, you man with the face of a dog and the heart [*kardia*] of a deer, you've never had the courage to fight alongside your people."

And like modern neuroscientists, the ancient Greeks also learned that it was possible to convert the nervous energy of fright into valor's heroic grit by adding oxytocin. Not that the Greeks called it oxytocin, of course. Instead, they hailed it by a literary name: paean.

The Paean and Its Neurochemical Effect

A paean is a song to a god.

In 480 BCE one such song echoed from the lungs of an Athenian in the tense prelude to battle. The battle was Salamis, where a few hundred Greek rowing galleys were daring to lock oars with Persia's imperial armada. And the Athenian was the forty-five-year-old playwright Aeschylus, who, in the world's earliest surviving work of theater, *The Persians*, would later celebrate the song for kindling valor:

> Fear seized the Persians, baffling their minds,
> For the Greeks sang their paean,
> Rushing into war with couraged hearts.

This long-ago depiction of the paean's courage boost has been upheld by two intersecting strands of modern scientific research. The first has revealed that group song in times of duress can amplify our pituitary's sensation of being close to other anxious souls, prompting a rise in our blood level of oxytocin. The second has shown that a similar rise can be stimulated by prayers that prompt us to feel the immanent presence of a god who shares our hardship concern.

Both these oxytocin triggers are incorporated into paeans, which combine a massed vocal chorus with a holy supplication. And thus it was that the paean at Salamis served as a potent martial alchemic, transmuting Greek fear into a forward charge.

This neuro-literary invention was already ancient by the time of Aeschylus. So ancient that it was possible for Homer, who was born at least two centuries prior, to enhance it. Homer invokes the term *paean* about five hundred lines into the *Iliad*: "to Apollo, the Greeks sang their noble paean." But the epic's first paean occurs earlier—and, in fact, starts on the epic's very first word. For all of the *Iliad* is a paean, a mammoth twelve-thousand-line battle hymn designed to stir the latent courage of our heart.

By itself, the sheer size of this hymn is remarkable. Yet the *Iliad* is more than just a long song. It's also a new kind of song, one that would revolutionize global literature by reengineering the paean to release oxytocin without requiring us to sing. This seems a flat-out contradiction: How can there be a song unsung? But the contradiction is resolved by the tools of style and focus. These tools, as authors before Homer had shown, make it possible to convert a power of oral voice into a narrator. So, to replicate the valor boost of a battle hymn, Homer simply needed to create a narrator who did what a sung paean did: give our brain the feeling of joining a holy chorus that sensed danger nearby.

Which Homer achieved by beginning the *Iliad* like so:

"Sing, goddess, of the anger."

To read these five short words is to feel instantly involved in a greater hymn amid the encroachment of a furious violence. With a bare handful of syllables, the *Iliad* has tricked our pituitary into a tend-and-befriend warming of our bloodstream.

And the beginning of the *Iliad* isn't a one-off trick. It's the first stroke of a grand blueprint for courage.

The Blueprint for Courage

We can uncover the blueprint by contrasting the style and focus of the *Iliad*'s opening lines with the style and focus of the "Let there be light" from the book of Genesis.

Genesis

In the beginning God created the heaven and the earth.

And the earth was without form, and void; and darkness was upon the face of the deep. And the Spirit of God moved upon the face of the waters.

And God said, Let there be light: and there was light.

Iliad

> Sing, goddess, of the anger, the anger of Achilles born of Peleus,
> the anger all-a-damaging that brought countless pains to men,
> sending many stout souls to Hades before their time,
> making heroes into food for dogs and vultures.

Both these beginnings boom with God Voice. Yet their booms are different. In the beginning of Genesis, there's "the heaven and the earth." In the beginning of the *Iliad*, there's "the anger, the anger." So, Homer's narrative doesn't spring from Light or Law or some other higher Truth. Instead, its origin and purpose are a mortal emotion. Or to be technical: its focus is the human heart.

The style of the *Iliad* achieves the same human-heartedness through its use of adjectives. Adjectives are absent from the opening lines of Genesis, which unfurls as a succession of galactic nouns: *God, heaven, earth, form, void, darkness, the face, the deep, the waters.* These nouns, like all nouns, are objects, so they feel object-ive.

Such objectiveness isn't unique to nouns; many adjectives (such as those used later in Genesis) can feel objective too: *round* or *living* or *blue* present a thing more or less as it really is. But adjectives can also reflect the subjectiveness of how something seems from our personal perspective: *tall* and *fast* appear that way only because we're shorter and slower.

You can feel that subjectiveness in the *Iliad*'s initial adjectives: *all-a-damaging* and *countless*. These communicate the experience of being too astonished by Achilles's anger to accurately quantify its destructive effect. The narrator can say only that the anger seems to be ruining everything and killing too many people to count. Which is exactly how we, too, would feel if we saw Achilles raging in full massacre. So, just like Athena, Apollo, and the other anthropomorphic deities of the Greek pantheon, the God Voice of the *Iliad* is huge but human. It's not a divinity aloof. It's a vaster version of ourselves, an "Almighty Heart" that echoes our emotional response to the spectacle of war and death.

This human God Voice is Homer's great invention. Prior to Homer, literary narrators had spoken in the voices of humans or gods. But the

Iliad hybridizes the two species of voice, blending mortal sentiment and cosmic scope into an anthropomorphic far-sightedness.

Throughout the *Iliad*, this style-and-focus blueprint for courage is maintained by a litany of smaller literary inventions, including Homer's most legendary stylistic device: the "Epic Simile." The Epic Simile was known to authors before Homer; one appears in the book of Genesis when a dying Jacob prophesizes to his sons:

> "Judah is a lion's whelp; from the prey, my son, thou art gone up: he stooped down, he couched as a lion; and as an old lion, who shall rouse him up?"

But even though Homer didn't invent the Epic Simile, he became its most famous practitioner by doing what he'd done to the God Voice: anthropomorphize it. You can experience the anthropomorphizing in Homer's own man-lion comparisons, such as this one from the *Iliad*'s book 3:

> Like a lion is glad to find the carcass of a wild deer or goat
> When he is hungry, and devours it greedily
> Even as eager hunters and their quick dogs rush upon him,
> So was Menelaus glad to see Alexander.

This simile flips the narrative structure of Jacob's biblical simile. The biblical simile starts on the human and proceeds to the lion, so it begins where we are and then *stretches* toward a mystery beyond, amazing us with a vaster Truth that we can't quite fathom in our here and now. (For more on how this literary technique can generate religious awe, see chapter 6.)

The Homeric simile does the reverse. It starts on the lion and proceeds to the human, comprehending an outside being through one of our mortal sentiments: gladness. So, when we look at the lion—or at any of the trees and birds and boars and fires and bugs and stars and deities contained in Homer's Epic Similes—what we see is not the work of an inscrutable God, but the emotion of a fellow Heart. We and the lion and all of nature are a part of a greater human pulse that animates the world. Sky and leaf and light and life: all of it is us.

This feeling of connection to a cosmic human community triggers our pituitary in the same way as singing in a battle chorus or praying to a sympathetic deity. So, it replicates the physiological effect of a paean, prompting a rise in our blood oxytocin. And as you can discover first-hand, the *Iliad* can go even further than a paean: its printed speech can produce an oxytocin boost even when we're reading silently, alone.

This seems an impossible sleight, but its imaginative effect is no different from the one that inspires a soldier in a lonely foxhole to find bravery in remembering loved ones back home. In the *Iliad*, that imaginative effect begins when the epic's fearsome war depictions trigger our brain's threat-escape dyad of adrenaline plus opioids. And it reaches its fullness when Homer's Almighty Heart adds courage's third neural ingredient, turning fear into its blood opposite and giving us the heated strength to stare down death.

Using the Almighty Heart Yourself

In 1915 a red-bearded British soldier-sailor by the name of Patrick Shaw-Stewart returned to the Aegean shores where the Trojan War had raged.

Those shores had again become a war zone, and perhaps even worse: *We wear our gasmasks because of the smell of the dead* and *shrapnel took his head away* and *flies clog our mouths by millions*. But into that place of horror, Shaw-Stewart brought the *Iliad*, and as he remembered how Homer's verses had once braced his mettle, he picked up a pen to compose his own poem, "Achilles in the Trench."

Was it so hard, Achilles,
So very hard to die?
Thou knowest, and I know not;
So much the happier am I.

I will go back this morning
From Imbros o'er the sea.
Stand in the trench, Achilles,
Flame-capped, and shout for me.

In the first stanza, we feel our distance from Achilles, and when we think of death, we are afraid. But in the second stanza's last lines, we imagine the hero's booming voice with us at its heart, and out of fear, the note of courage comes.

If you're not feeling that paean note in your copy of the *Iliad*, you can find Homer's invention in thousands of later poems, novels, films, and more. Start by searching your bookshelf for a far-seeing narrator with a human heart, such as the sentimental God Voice of Charles Dickens's *A Tale of Two Cities*: "It was the best of times, it was the worst of times." Or the Epic Similes spoken by the narrator of Toni Morrison's 1987 novel, *Beloved*: "like a child's house, the house of a very tall child."

And you can also venture beyond the printed texts of your library into literary works that, like Homer's original recitations of the *Iliad*, take a dramatic form. Many modern films and TV shows, from battle epics such as Ridley Scott's *Gladiator* to primetime soaps such as *Peyton Place*, achieve the neural effect of an anthropomorphic God's-Eye by marrying the objective sight of the camera lens to a human focus and a soundtrack rich with oxytocin-releasing musical effects.

Once you've spotted a few Homeric narrators on the page or on-screen, find one that's woven into a tale that lays bare your deepest dread. If you dread that life is empty of purpose, watch *Game of Thrones*. If you dread that we're all doomed to end as strangers inhabiting the lives of others, watch *Gray's Anatomy*.

Then feel the greater voice connect with you.

And in this world of fear, take heart.

TWO

Rekindle the Romance

Sappho's Lyrics, *the* Odes *of Eastern Zhou,*
and the Invention of the Secret Discloser

A s the twentieth century broke across Europe, ushering in the mad
dash of Western civilization toward the Great War's barbed wire
trenches and howitzer slaughter, two Englishmen set sail for Egypt.

The Englishmen were friends, possibly more. And just west of the
Nile River, on a stretch of the great Mer-wer canal once famed for its
sacred elephant fish, they made an astonishing find.

Not that the find initially appeared so astonishing. It seemed at first
a moldy pile of paper garbage, dumped millennia ago by Ptolemaic accountants who were cleaning out their office filing baskets. But as the
two Englishmen picked gingerly through the ancient bureaucratic
waste, they were stopped short by a discovery: a papyrus poem older
than algebra, or stirrups, or the waterwheel.

The poem was inked in ancient Greek, yet not the ancient Greek
the Englishmen had learned at school. There they'd studied the Attic
lexicon of Homer's combat epic the *Iliad*. But this trash-heap poem had a
different vocabulary, one that was, the Englishmen agreed, quite queer.
And as they read the poem's unusual speech to each other, their wonder
at it deepened. They forgot about the battles brewing back home. And
they lingered in the desert, intoxicated by a sweet-strange feeling.

Love.

Love—and Its Literary Origin

What's the secret to love?

Ah, well, love has many secret sources. The ancient denizens of the Nile knew that love came from crocodile aorta. The Chinese emperor Shennong found it in ginseng. The Aztecs got it out of copious amounts of chocolate, hot. The Bantu peoples of the sub-Sahara extracted it from yohimbe bark. And in nineteenth-century America, the spiritualist Andrew Jackson Davis propounded a source of love that has since become proverbial: "What we must not fail to notice is, that likes repel, and opposites attract."

Unfortunately, modern science has failed to confirm any of these antique theories. In fact, in many cases, scientific experiments have done the reverse. They've shown that crocodile aortas do not cause swoons and that opposite hearts quite often repel.

But all this scientific cold water hasn't doomed us to fumble aimlessly after love. Because at the same time that twenty-first-century neuroscientists have debunked the aphrodisiacs of yore, they've also uncovered one of love's genuine sources: poetry in the voice of *I*.

The Poetic Power of the *I*

As far back into history as we're able to see, literature has included the voice of *I*.

There's the Sumerian *Instructions of Shuruppak*, from 2600 BCE: "My son, let me enlighten you. Do not ignore the words I speak!" And there's the Babylonian hero of *The Epic of Gilgamesh*, from the eighteenth century BCE: "My mother, I dreamed a dream of stars that fell upon me."

Yet even as these *I* voices echoed out from legends and scriptures, they weren't powerful enough to echo out alone. They were, after all, merely individual voices. They didn't boom a cosmic truth; they just relayed a personal opinion. They were limited—and fragile.

So, in both *The Epic of Gilgamesh* and *The Instructions of Shuruppak*, the *I* voice is buttressed by an epic voice of *he-she-they*. That epic voice starts *The Instructions* from on high: "In years long gone, a wise man of silver tongue lived in the land of Sumer, and these were the instructions *he* bestowed to his son."

And in *The Epic of Gilgamesh*, the epic voice begins even more thunderously:

The gods made Gilgamesh, and *they* made him perfect. The sun god gave him glory and the storm god gave him valor.

For century after century, the *I* voice continued to exist like this inside the epic *he-she-they*. Quite likely, there were authors during those ancient times who dared to write stand-alone *I* poems. But none of those poems has survived, seeming to prove that the *I* could not endure on its own.

And then among the mulberry trees and cucumber patches of eastern China, about a thousand years after *The Epic of Gilgamesh*, a woman whispered out:

The great cart hud-huks past,
With its judge robed green like new grass.
It is you I remember;
But I see the law and I tremble.

The great cart hud-huks by,
With its judge robed bright like ruby.
It is you that I want;
But I know the law and I halt.

We must live in separate rooms,
But in death, we will have one tomb.
Do you think that I lie?
I swear it by the sun's unending light.

That this ode has endured, all the way down to our here and now, is extraordinary. The only other *I* poems to survive from so ancient an era are the Hebrew Psalms. And those Psalms, like *The Instructions of Shuruppak* and *The Epic of Gilgamesh*, are infused with epicness. They're part of a divinely inspired scripture, uttered by a biblical king.

The Chinese ode is different. It's authored by a mortal woman who's terrified of being punished for an illegal act of love. Unlike the Psalms, her poem wasn't written to be shared in public; it was slipped to her lover on a folded note. And unlike the Psalms, her feelings aren't condoned by some higher authority; in fact, they're *condemned* by a lofty judge in his great hud-huking cart. The only thing backing up the poet is the strength of her own word: "I swear."

We might believe that oath. Or we might not. But either way, the ode allows us the choice. It doesn't attempt to compel our mind with an epic declaration such as "This woman spoke true." It is entirely and only the voice of an *I*.

How did this individual voice survive? How is it with us still?

As we'll see, there are two reasons that the Chinese ode has managed to bob across time's deep waters. But let's start with the more exciting one: the ode reaches into our cold neural circuits and warms them with the touch of love.

The Neuroscience of Love

You might have heard that, scientifically speaking, love is a matter of chemical attraction: *Invisible pheromones, manufactured by subdermal glandular factories, waft off the skin of our prospective mates to seduce the hedonic centers of our brain. . . .*

It's all very unromantic—and probably untrue. There's no evidence that human pheromones actually exist. If they did, wooing would be a much simpler matter. But even so, there *is* a scientific formula for love. It doesn't involve yohimbe bark, chocolate, or any other physical stuff. It involves speech. Not magic speech. Just regular speech that you already know.

The scientific speech formula has two parts. Its first part is: self-disclosure.

Self-disclosure is revealing things about yourself. Anytime you share the details of your personal life, you're making a self-disclosure. If you tell people where you were born, or how old you are, or what happened to you on Tuesday, that's a self-disclosure.

Any and all self-disclosures can be a source of love. But some self-disclosures have greater potency than others. Those self-disclosures are more hidden, more private. They're not your birthplace or your birthday. They're secrets you don't ordinarily confess. Perhaps they make you feel embarrassed or awkward. Perhaps they're goofy quirks that aren't of public interest. Perhaps they're treasured memories that you like to hold close to your chest. Perhaps they reveal private hopes or desires or fears or mistakes.

Whatever these secrets may be, they're powerful sources of love. And their power increases with their secrecy. If there's a deep secret that you've carried for years, never sharing it with anyone else, that's a tremendously potent ingredient for love.

But don't go out and use that potent ingredient just yet! Because it'll be wasted if you don't combine it with the second part of the scientific speech formula. That second part is: wonder.

Wonder is a feeling of awe, of specialness. It's not always easy to engineer. But as we learned back in the introduction, it does have its own reliable blueprint, known as the *stretch*: the taking of a regular pattern of style, or character, or story, or any other literary element, and extending the pattern a step further.

Without the *stretch* of wonder, self-disclosure can often be less love-exciting than off-putting. If someone inundates us with unwonderful personal details, it makes us feel uncomfortable. We don't want to retire with that someone to a perfumed bower. We want to flee.

But when someone woos us with a self-disclosure that's mixed with *stretch*, the combination has a potent neural effect: it primes dopamine neurons in the reward centers of our brain, sweetening our thoughts with a touch of pleasure. Our brain is happy—and knows that it will become even happier if it can get its primed neurons to fire.

What causes those primed neurons to fire is another self-disclosure, yet not from the wooer this time. To complete the circle of romance, the second self-disclosure must come from us. By wooing back the wooer, we release our brain's cued-up dopamine, delighting ourselves with its chemical sweet. This self-gratifying experience isn't love; it's an infatuation, a flirt, a prelude to more. But to get that more, we don't have to do anything different. We can keep on exchanging wonder-enriched self-disclosures with our wooer, creating a reciprocal cycle of dopamine prime and release that makes us feel increasingly happy together and encourages us to disclose more personal details to each other until we've built an intimate emotional bond.

This happy state of emotional intimacy is love. Admittedly, as just explained by science, it's not much more romantic than glandular pheromones. It's all formula and molecules, and it reveals that a great deal of love's bliss comes from the pleasure of our own self-disclosures, so that our brain is rather egoistically swooning for itself: *I like myself more when I'm with you.*

But as unromantic as this all might be, science has at least revealed that as love deepens, the second part of the blueprint, the *stretch*, becomes less important. We no longer have to seduce our loved one with dazzle; we can simply confess our intimate secrets in all their humdrum ordinariness, and we'll still deepen our emotional bond. That's the real wonder of love: not needing anything more wondrous than ourselves.

Now that you know science's love blueprint—self-disclosure married with wonder—you can go out and woo the world. Just marry some intimate revelations to a bit of *stretch*. And if that sounds uncertain work, or if you'd rather just be wooed yourself, don't fret: you can get all the love you need from poetry.

Because long before science, poets figured out the two-part blueprint. And they folded it into heart catchers like the ode of the ancient Chinese poet.

The Two-Part Blueprint in Poetry

The ancient Chinese poet opens her ode with a self-disclosure: "It is you I remember; but I see the law and I tremble."

And she then enriches this disclosure with poetic *stretches* that extend our mind to the time after death and the space past the night: "In death, we will have one tomb . . . by the sun's unending light."

By revealing a secret that fills us with a quiet awe, the Chinese poet deploys the scientific formula for amorous attraction. She catches our brain's dopamine reward centers. She stirs us to imagine a reciprocal self-disclosure—a silent thank-you for her honesty, a dreamful admission of our own hidden desires, a requited promise to be faithful always—that glads our thoughts with love.

That love is why the poet's ode was retold in its day. It whisperingly seduced its listeners. It made them feel the personal power of the *I*. But as powerful as that love was, it still wasn't enough to save the Chinese ode by itself. The second, and rather less exciting, reason why the ode has survived to our modern age is that it attracted the attention of Zhou dynasty scholars who admired the ode's romance-quashing judge: "It is you that I want; but I know the law and I halt."

Impressed by this love halt, Zhou scholars copied down the ode into a Confucian guidebook, the *Shijing* of the Five Classics, whose precepts on lawful behavior were passed along dutifully to the present day. (For more on these precepts, see chapter 10.) Which meant that, really, the *I* of the Chinese ode didn't endure through its own power. It endured because of an epic *he* who blocked the *I* from acting.

But the *I* wouldn't remain in this disempowered state forever. A century or so after the Chinese ode, another poet would sing from the heart. That poet was Sappho. And her song wasn't preserved as part of a greater epic voice.

It endured entirely through love.

The Power of Sappho

Sappho's life is largely a mystery. We think that she was born on Lesbos, an arch-shaped island in the northeastern Aegean, right across from the sandy plains where Hector and Achilles fought their Trojan War. And we think that she lived her life in the mid-seventh century BCE, which was probably a little more than a hundred years after Homer composed the *Iliad*.

The *Iliad* was well known to Sappho. And she rejected its epic style. Instead, she wrote in the *I* voice. Or as the ancient Greeks called it, the lyric, which literally means "sung with a lyre."

Sappho wasn't the first Greek poet to write in the lyric. A generation or so before, the warrior-poet Archilochus had become famous for lyrics such as:

The fox has many tricks; the hedgehog has one big one.
Don't boast in victory or weep in defeat. Life is always up and
    down.

> I lie here, hurting with lust. The gods have put this pain in my
>   bones.
> The enemy has my shield now; I threw it aside when I ran. Why
>   should I have kept it? This is my only life. I can buy another
>   shield.
> I wish I could touch Neobule by her hand.

The last of these lyrics seems to follow the Chinese ode in sounding a
note of romance: "I wish I could touch Neobule by her hand." Yet the romance is, in fact, a joke. Neobule is a made-up name that means "fickle
female," and Archilochus's extended discussions of her are all domineer-
ing bits of porno-satire that are the antithesis of intimate: "her flesh like
old fruit . . . dipping her lips, she slurped on my straw."

Archilochus's other lyrics are similarly lacking in genuine personal
disclosures. Instead of exposing a vulnerable heart, they follow the
Psalms and *The Instructions of Shuruppak* in hewing to the age-old blueprint of buttressing the *I* with the *he-she-they* voice of ironies or greater
truths: "The fox has many tricks." "Life is always up and down." "The
gods have put this pain in my bones." "I can buy another shield."

So, just imagine how astonished the Greeks were when Sappho
dared to write this:

> He seems to me a god
> that man
> listening to you
> chat sweetly
> and laugh like music,
> scattering my heart.
>
> When I look at you,
> I can't speak.
> My tongue breaks
> and my skin is on fire.

This is a genuine self-disclosure. Sappho is confessing something private: her love for a woman who is in a public relationship. And it's a

confession that might come back to hurt Sappho. Her love, after all, may not be wanted by the woman. The woman already has an epically god-like lover. The woman is already smilingly happy. What does she need from Sappho? Perhaps nothing. Perhaps she'll read Sappho's lyric and snicker.

If all that Sappho did was make a personal self-disclosure, we might snicker too. But Sappho doesn't just expose her private secrets. She mixes in wonder. She *stretches* her inner feelings into simple but awe-summoning metaphors of heart scatter and skin fire.

This mix of awe and self-disclosure is the same blueprint used in the Chinese ode. And like the Chinese ode, Sappho's love poem has survived time's blade because it was copied by a scholar's pen. But unlike the scholar who preserved the Chinese ode, the scholar who recorded Sappho's poem wasn't a government moralist. Instead, he was a literary aficionado: the mysterious, probably pseudonymous, Longinus of the Roman Empire.

Longinus wrote a first-century treatise, *On the Sublime*, which celebrates Sappho's poem for producing the same potent emotion as the epic verses of Homer's *Iliad* and the Hebrew Bible. And as modern science has since revealed, Sappho doesn't simply equal the epic power of Homer and the Bible; she upends it. Where epic gains its emotional force from giganticness, Sappho's lyric gains its emotional force from intimacy.

If this were the only lyric that Sappho had written, it would be an innovation. The innovation is the depth of self-disclosure. That depth had been seen by earlier authors as dangerous; it bared the heart naked, inviting destruction and prompting Sappho's *I*-poem precursors to temper their innermost feelings with irony, judge-abiding common sense, or *he-she-they* heft.

Sappho revealed that authors had nothing to fear by being more intimate. She discovered the counterintuitive truth that science would later uphold: the more private the self-disclosure, the more potent it is. She showed that lyric poetry could be as mighty as epic, not by incorporating gods and other outside voices, but by revealing more of the *I*.

And then Sappho went further. Much, much further. She wrote another poem.

The poem found inside that trash heap.

Sappho's Second Innovation

The two Englishmen who voyaged to Egypt in the winter of 1905 were the papyrological archeologists Bernard Pyne Grenfell and Arthur Surridge Hunt. And the poem they discovered runs like so:

> Some say that horsemen,
> or soldiers, or ships,
> are the most beautiful things on earth—
> but I say it's your love.
>
> Isn't that why
> Helen, the most beautiful
> of women,
> left the best of men
> and sailed to Troy?
>
> Forgetting her child
> and her mother, because
> in a glance she felt
>
> Love.

With elegant brevity, this lyric retells the *Iliad*. The *Iliad* had spun a tale of horsemen, ships, and soldiers that warred at Troy over a stolen woman: Helen, queen of Sparta, wife of Menelaus. But according to Sappho's lyric, Helen wasn't stolen. She sailed freely after desire. So, the real story of Troy isn't war. The real story is love.

If we were dry and dusty philosophers, we could debate Sappho's lyric redo of Homer. We could say, "Yes! A love story! Sappho has given voice to the silenced heart of the Trojan War!" Or we could say, "Harrumph! How daft! War is war; there's nothing romantic about it!" Or we could even say, "It can be both! The truth is always multiple! The greatest wisdom sees both sides!"

But Sappho doesn't want us to be dry and dusty philosophers. She doesn't want us to riff intellectually about the rightness of her lyric. She wants to *feel* the love that launched the Trojan War. Which is why she touches our heart with an intimate disclosure.

That disclosure is about Helen. And it comes as a surprise because, at first, Sappho's poem is anything but disclosing. Instead of giving us Helen's lyric voice, the poem presents her in the *he-she-they* voice of epic. And instead of revealing Helen's inner heart, the poem glides across her exterior: "Helen, the most beautiful of women."

This "most beautiful" woman is the Helen from the *Iliad*, the Helen who was kidnapped because of how she looked. But having provided us with that familiar picture, Sappho's lyric then does the unprecedented: it guides our eye beneath Helen's famous surface. And what we discover there is something so deeply socially unacceptable that any Greek mother would have been mortified to confess it: Helen forgot her own child, the long-haired, horse-cantering Hermione.

This is exactly the opposite of what the *Iliad* tells us. In its third book, it booms that Helen is "torn with longing for her husband and her family." Such familial longing is what the ancient Greeks expected every woman to feel; why else did a woman exist, if not to be a dutiful caregiver to her children and a loyal wife to the man her father selected? So, really, even though the *Iliad* pretends to lay bare Helen's heart, it doesn't make a private disclosure. It does the reverse, establishing Helen as a public stereotype.

Sappho breaks this stereotype to reveal the true secret of Helen's heart: she was so struck by love that she no longer remembered the child she had born. This revelation would undoubtedly have repelled some of Sappho's initial Greek readers. Deep personal secrets are often unsocial; that's why they've been kept secret. But in the same way that our friends and lovers come to care for us *because* of the things that we don't like to admit about ourselves, so would some of Sappho's readers have been moved by Helen's feeling of being more than a mother. In that feeling, they'd have discovered what was special about Helen's heart. They'd have touched the hidden rhythm of her love.

This feeling of closeness to Helen was a revolution in poetry, and not just because it challenged the old feeling of the *Iliad*. It also dramatically expanded the prior blueprint of the lyric. In the past, that blueprint had been used by poets to make intimate disclosures about themselves. But now Sappho was using it to make an intimate disclosure about someone else. Innovating the *he-she-they* voice of epic to reveal a hidden *I* of history, she conjured up feeling for a character who never spoke herself.

With this, Sappho did far more than rewrite the *Iliad*. She threw open a vast new horizon for literature. For if literature could make self-disclosures on behalf of Helen, then it could make self-disclosures on behalf of every epic *she* or *he* or *they*.

It could take any story and make it a love story.

Using the Secret Discloser Yourself

Love isn't the only way that we can care about others. We can also feel empathy, or sympathetic identification, or friendship (the literary recipes for which are laid out in chapters 3, 19, and 25, respectively).

But love is an enormously rich emotion. It can come in many different shades and varieties, from the erotic love of Sappho, to the ethereal love of the Chinese poet, to the familial love of Dylan Thomas's "Do Not Go Gentle into That Good Night," to the social love of Emily Dickinson's "I Should Not Dare to Leave My Friend" and Walt Whitman's "Crossing Brooklyn Ferry."

And love is also one of the most powerfully rewarding emotions that our brain can experience. It's been shown scientifically to improve our mood, increase our energy, and make us enjoy everything more. (Although you probably didn't need science to tell you that.)

And if you ever want more love in your life, you can find its blueprint of intimate disclosure mixed with wonder in poetry that spans the ages, from the early-ninth-century outlaw verses of the Abbasid princess Ulayya bint al-Mahdi . . .

I have tucked our love inside this lyric
Like silver in a pocket

. . . to the epic inverse of e. e. cummings:

here is the deepest secret nobody knows
i carry your heart (i carry it in my heart)

You can also find love's blueprint in the first-person narration and dialogue of novels, from the elegantly swift disclosure of Charlotte Brontë's *Jane Eyre* ("Reader, I married him. A quiet wedding we had"), to the painfully tender disclosure of nurse Catherine Barkley in Ernest Hemingway's *A Farewell to Arms* ("I'm not brave any more, darling. I'm all broken. They've broken me. I know it now"), to the wistfully romantic disclosure of teenage Jim Burden in Willa Cather's *My Ántonia*:

> One dream I dreamed a great many times, and it was always the same. I was in a harvest-field full of shocks, and I was lying against one of them. Lena Lingard came across the stubble barefoot, in a short skirt, with a curved reaping-hook in her hand, and she was flushed like the dawn, with a kind of luminous rosiness all about her. She sat down beside me, turned to me with a soft sigh and said, "Now they are all gone, and I can kiss you as much as I like."
>
> I used to wish I could have this flattering dream about Ántonia, but I never did.

And finally, you can journey with Sappho into love beyond the lyric. Her epic-changing invention of disclosure on behalf of someone else endures in modern musico-poems such as Percy Sledge's 1966 rhythm and blues ballad "When a Man Loves a Woman": "When a man loves a woman / Can't keep his mind on nothing else."

And it endures, too, in every awe-rich moment where a novel uses its narrative focus, or a film deploys its camera closeup, to reveal a character's untold secrets. Including perhaps the most devastatingly potent love scene in literature, the at-last togetherness of Elizabeth Bennet and Mr. Darcy in Jane Austen's *Pride and Prejudice*:

> Elizabeth, feeling all the more than common awkwardness and anxiety of his situation, now forced herself to speak; and immediately, though not very fluently, gave him to understand that her sentiments had undergone so material a change, since the period to which he alluded, as to make her receive with gratitude and pleasure his present assurances. The happiness which this reply

produced, was such as he had probably never felt before; and he expressed himself on the occasion as sensibly and as warmly as a man violently in love can be supposed to do. Had Elizabeth been able to encounter his eye, she might have seen how well the expression of heartfelt delight, diffused over his face, became him; but, though she could not look, she could listen, and he told her of feelings, which, in proving of what importance she was to him, made his affection every moment more valuable.

Like Helen of Troy, Elizabeth and Mr. Darcy feel too awkward to share exactly how they feel. But then the narrator discloses for them, summoning love.

Literature brims with more of these moments than your lifetime can exhaust. Any lyric voice that lays bare a private feeling can make you feel a close affection. Any *he-she-they* story that makes a personal disclosure about its characters can spark an emotional connection. And that connection can come in endless fresh varieties, each as queer and unique as the secrets kept inside an individual heart.

So, every day, you can be like those two Englishmen in Egypt.

And discover wonder intimate.

THREE

Exit Anger

The Book of Job, Sophocles's Oedipus Tyrannus,
and the Invention of the Empathy Generator

I n the land of Uz, there lived a man who honored God and turned
away from evil. Yet still God was not convinced the man was holy. So,
God resolved to test the man from Uz.

For that test, God stripped the man of everything: his home, his
health, his children. God took so much that the man's wife lost her faith.
She cursed God and looked to death. But the man from Uz, he did not
waver. He called his wife a fool. And kneeling down upon the ashes of
his life, he kept God in his heart.

Then God saw that the man was truly righteous, so God returned
him everything—and more. The man from Uz became lord of fourteen
thousand sheep and six thousand camels. He had seven sons and three
daughters and saw his grandchildren in his twilight age.

The man from Uz was Job. And the story of his godly test was
authored many thousands of years ago by a Gentile people who lived
among the peach tree gorges and plateau vineyards that ringed the Dead
Sea basin. Those people may have been Edomites, or Moabites, or Am-
monites, or Arabians. They may have lived in the Iron Age, or before, in
the Bronze. So old is the story of Job that we cannot glimpse its origins.
They're lost for good behind the dust of time.

Yet although we can no longer see the origins of Job's story, we can
reconstruct its original purpose: to strengthen our neural commitment to

justice. That commitment is challenged by what seems to be the story's opening *in*justice: God inflicting harm upon a man who's done nothing wrong. But when the story concludes by undoing the harm and compensating the man double for his perseverance, our brain is reassured: *Eventually the righteous soul will be uplifted.* So, just like Job, we're carried by the story through a two-step process. Our faith in life's fairness is tested, and our faith is then rewarded.

That faith was important to the people of the Dead Sea gorges. They recited the story of Job over and over, spreading it down through generations and nations. So, people believed that life was just, and they did their best to live in justness.

Until one day, a poet did the unthinkable: he took Job's story—and rewrote it.

The Poet and His Changes

We don't know who the revisionist poet was. But we think that he was a Hebrew who lived in the sixth century BCE, when the Babylonians conquered the kingdom of Judah, destroying the First Temple in Jerusalem and deporting its people. For fifty years, those deported Jerusalemites endured in exile until Babylon was conquered by King Cyrus the Great of Persia and his hoop-earringed Immortals. Then the Jerusalemites were at last permitted to return home, where, in 537 BCE, they began constructing the Second Temple.

The original story of Job must have resonated deeply with the temple builders of this era. Like Job, they'd watched their homes dashed to rubble, their children killed, their health snatched away. And like Job, they'd then seen their fortunes repaired: they'd remade their holy sites, cradled their grandchildren, and filled their halls again with gold. Their belief in justice had been tested, and their belief had been restored.

Yet despite all this, the Hebrew poet changed the story. Why? Why did he meddle with Job's tale of fairness? Why did he tinker with the justice blueprint?

It started with a realization: the life that had existed before the Babylonian invasion couldn't be restored by justice alone. Justice alone called upon the righteous Jerusalemites to avenge every dead Hebrew infant with a slain Babylonian child, nursing an uncompromising fury that escalated the conflict with eye-for-an-eye reprisals.

To get back the life of nonviolence that the invasion had disrupted, justice therefore had to be tempered with something else: forgiveness. Forgiveness released the injured heart from anger, halting the back-and-forth killings and returning the lost days of harmony.

So it was that the Hebrew poet decided to invent a new forgiveness technology and install it in the old Gentile story about Job, enriching righteousness with peace.

The Poet's New Lines

To preserve justice, the Hebrew poet left the original prose story of Job intact. But to imbue forgiveness, he inserted a thousand new lines of poetry. Those new lines expand the story to twenty times its original length, transforming a prose parable into a verse epic.

In the expanded story, Job is not so stoically patient in the face of God's test. Instead, he demands, "Wherefore is life given to him that is in misery, and life bitter unto the soul?" And when no answer is forthcoming, Job becomes frustrated, complaining, "I cry unto thee, O God, and thou dost not hear me: I stand up, and thou regardest me not."

With this challenge to God, Job strays from the strict path of righteousness. So, our brain begins to feel that Job has failed his test. And our feeling is confirmed when God responds to Job in sudden anger:

"Hast thou an arm like God? Or canst thou thunder with a voice like him? Canst thou draw out leviathan with an hook?"

This rebuke tells our brain: *You were right to think that Job did wrong. So, now Job must be punished; justice demands it.* But then, just when our heart is fixed against Job, the poet adds his new technology: "I abhor myself, and repent in dust and ashes."

These words are uttered by Job. They don't seem like much, nor do they seem especially original. Job isn't expressing a novel theology or conjuring up a fresh philosophical argument. He's just repeating what our brain has already concluded: Job is a sinner who deserves to end in dust and ashes.

Yet even though Job's words seem utterly familiar, they do something that no known work of literature had done before: they temper our brain's desire for justice with the forgiveness bringer that modern neuroscientists call empathy.

Empathy is the feeling of understanding another person's actions. That feeling doesn't make us *condone* those actions. It doesn't make us *identify* with the person, or share the person's values or beliefs. Instead, it allows us to disagree with the person while simultaneously accepting that the other person's actions weren't wrong.

How is it possible for us to feel this way? And how do Job's words trigger this experience in our brain? To see, let's take a quick tour of the neuroscience of forgiveness, starting with where forgiveness itself begins: our brain's desire for justice.

Justice and Its Neural Origins

Our brain has a natural desire for justice.

The desire runs so deep inside our nature that it predates our species. Chimps, gorillas, and macaque monkeys all possess an innate hunger for fairness, hailing from some archaic simian who swung the jungles ten million years before the first human judges created justice instruments such as the widow-protecting Laws of Urukagina (Sumer, c. 2400 BCE) and the eye-for-an-eye Code of Hammurabi (Babylon, c. 1750 BCE).

And our brain's desire for fairness isn't just ancient. It's also very, very strong. So strong that, as modern psychologists have discovered, we're willing to trade our wealth and our health to enforce fairness, even when the wrongdoing isn't against us. If someone cheats our neighbor, then we feel the wrongness in our own heart, and, indeed, can feel it with such emotional intensity that we risk our own safety to bring the perpetrator to justice.

To understand why our brain has evolved to crave fairness this powerfully, imagine a village where you and I forsake justice to act instead in our own immediate self-interest, ignoring any cheating that doesn't affect us directly. If I get defrauded, I go after the perpetrator; but if you get bilked, I stay home and let you handle it. In that kind of village, the only ones who can protect themselves are the mighty. The weak have to seek shelter from the nearest strongman, paying him for protection and joining his gang. So, gradually, our village disintegrates into rival factions that punish and counterpunish each other, turning our streets into a war zone.

Now let's imagine that same village *with* justice. Let's imagine that when one of us cheats another, we all join together to punish the cheater. That act of punishment brings our village together. We do it communally, so it strengthens the ties among us, building trust and civic cohesion. And since the source of our strength is the community, we don't need to value weapon-wielding strongmen as the ultimate social good. Instead, we can live in a culture that recognizes lots of goods: the ability to bake bread, and raise crops, and make pottery, and heal sickness, and tell stories.

That's the biological answer to why our brain desires justice. Justice is better for the long-term health and diversity of our communities. But to attain that long-term good, our brain has to desire justice very, very powerfully. After all, in the short term, justice isn't always in our interest. It doesn't benefit us to get hurt or killed enforcing fair play for our neighbors. So, to override our short-term impulse toward self-preservation, our brain has to really *crave* justice. It has to have a deep emotional drive for fairness.

That deep emotional drive has been good for us as a species. It's encouraged us to develop fairer societies—and to reinforce those societies with justice parables such as the original story of Job. But the golden rule of biology is that nothing is always good in every situation. Different things are good in different contexts. So, scientifically speaking, there can be too much of a good thing. Including justice.

Too Much Justice

Our biological craving for justice can cause two major problems.

The first problem is social. When our brain becomes inflamed with the conviction that someone has done wrong, our neural desire to rebuke that wrong can grow so powerful that we stray into mob violence and cruel and unusual punishments, breeding communal fear and misery instead of trust and peace.

The second problem is individual. The more that our brain obsesses over the unfairness of life, the more that we become consumed with unhealthy emotions such as anger and bitterness. So, instead of leading us into lives of deeper trust and social exchange, our emotional investment in justice can breed isolation and hate.

These two negative consequences of justice are why our brain developed the counterbalance of empathy. Empathy is powered by some of our newest neural circuitry: the perspective-taking network of our cortex. That network can imagine the wrong from the wrongdoer's perspective, searching for mitigating factors. And almost always, such factors exist. Perhaps the perpetrator acted out of ignorance or desperation; perhaps he made an honest mistake; perhaps he's willing to change his ways and be rehabilitated. If so, then we can forgive him, avoiding the harsh social consequences of total justice and freeing our brain from the negative effects of persistent anger and distrust.

This neural leap inside a perpetrator's head is an astounding feat. It allows our brain to be us while also being someone else. Yet just like justice, empathy alone is far from perfect. Since our perspective-taking neurons aren't connected directly to other people's gray matter, there's no way for us to know for certain what those other people are thinking. The best we can do is guess—and our guesses are inevitably skewed by our natural self-centeredness. We start off on the wrong foot by deducing, *If I did that, I'd have done it for this reason,* when, in fact, other brains have their own personal motivations. And we often compound our error with an equally self-centered tendency to assume that other people do what they do because of us. So, we might think, *She did that just to hurt me!* When, in fact, she wasn't thinking about us at all and harmed us only accidentally.

This unreliability of empathy puts us in a bind. On the one hand, empathy is a boon for our social and mental health. But on the other, it's fickle enough to make us feel softhearted toward psychopaths and hardhearted toward innocents.

And so it was that our ancestors invented an ancient tool for improving our powers of empathy. That ancient tool was: the apology.

The Science of the Apology

An apology is an acknowledgement of blame and an expression of regret. "I'm sorry I did that; I won't do it again."

This simple word formula triggers an intricate subregion of our brain's perspective-taking network, making us feel like we can see the wrong from the wrongdoer's point of view. And what we see is that the wrongdoer didn't mean to cause the pain that he did. He made a mistake that he now forswears, allowing us to forgive.

That's the basic neuro-mechanism behind an apology, anyway. But apologies aren't always effective. Wrongdoers can, after all, lie. And our brain is wise to that. It knows that someone who cheated us maliciously will be happy to repeat the trick by spewing fake tears. So, our brain accepts apologies only after it has first consulted our empathy circuits. If our empathy circuits are strongly convinced that the wrong was intentional, then our brain disregards the wrongdoer's stated remorse. But if our empathy circuits can't decide—if they think that the wrongdoer *could* have made a mistake that he now regrets—then our brain credits the apology, tipping our internal scale of justice toward clemency.

This isn't a perfect system. But it has proved historically robust. It allows us to act with justice when a wrongdoer is clearly guilty, and it inclines us toward forgiveness in cases of doubt. So, the apology nurtures a society with the maximum amount of *certain* justice and the maximum amount of *possible* forgiveness, making us as fair as our brain can be— and as generous as life allows.

And apologies don't just do good things for our broader society. They also do good things for us individually. When our brain accepts an apology, negative emotions such as anger and victimhood decrease, while positive emotions such as trust and love increase. We feel relieved, even happy, to let go of the urge for punishment. Our overall mental health improves.

Which is what happens when we hear Job's words to God.

The Apology in the Book of Job

Job's words are an apology: "I abhor myself, and repent in dust and ashes."

This is an acknowledgment of blame and an expression of regret. Job admits that he did something wrong and commits to not doing it again, so his words reach out toward our empathy circuits, encouraging us to soften righteous anger with forgiveness.

As we'll explore in a moment, Job's words aren't guaranteed to have this effect on our brain. Individual brains are different, and some of us might feel that Job's apology is lacking. But in the context of the ancient Hebrew story, the apology is clearly meant to be effective. That's why God forgives Job and restores his lost prosperity. So, in the end, Job is uplifted not simply because God is just but because God is also empathetic.

God's empathy encouraged the ancient Hebrews to accept Job's apology, too, and when they began compiling the third section of the Hebrew Bible, the Ketuvim, in the sixth century BCE, they included Job's revised story—now officially titled the Book of Job—alongside the Psalms and the book of Proverbs. As those scriptures were transmitted across the world, the literary blueprint for forgiveness went along. And as it went, its range and its power were boosted by a series of clever innovations.

The first of those innovations took place about a century after the Hebrew poet and about eight hundred miles west. There, in a little white-hilled suburb of the city of Athens, lived a silver-tongued civic exchequer.

His name was Sophocles. And he wrote Greek tragedies.

The Apology Blueprint in Greek Tragedy

Greek tragedy was invented sometime in the later sixth century BCE, shortly after Job's story was revised to include the apology. There's no evidence that the original architects of Greek tragedy knew of Job's apology. In ancient Greek, the word *apologia* meant an unapologetic defense of one's behavior, not an expression of regret. And in the oldest known Greek tragic trilogy, Aeschylus's *Oresteia*, forgiveness is conspicuously generated without any Job-like voicing of remorse. Instead, the goddess Athena uses brute force to browbeat a horde of righteous beings, the Furies, into softening their commitment to absolute justice.

But in the middle of the fifth century, about fifteen years after the *Oresteia*, the apology blueprint was introduced into Greek tragedy by Sophocles. Sophocles might have gotten the blueprint directly from the

Bible: his white-hilled suburb lay about six miles northeast of Piraeus, a port that traded with Judah and Israel via Phoenician cargo galleys. Or Sophocles might have gotten the blueprint from a nonliterary source: oral apologies had been circulating the Mediterranean for years, inspiring the Greeks to coin the term *suggnômê*, which literally means "like-thinking," and which was used in Sophocles's time to connote "empathy for the person I hurt."

Either way, Sophocles began using the apology blueprint early in his playwriting career. In his tragedy *Antigone*, he portrays a king who imposes justice with such strictness that he's accused of impious cruelty. The king initially ignores the accusation, but when his pursuit of justice sets in motion an eye-for-an-eye cycle that costs him his own family, he at last lets loose a wail of regret:

> "Oh, the crime is mine and mine alone! There can be no exoneration! I am a fool, a fool. My wife! My child! I have slain you. "

With this apology, Sophocles triggered empathy for a man who'd crossed the gods, going as far as the Hebrew poet a century before. And then Sophocles took a step further. He innovated the apology blueprint to make it more effective.

So effective that it couldn't fail.

Sophocles's Innovation

There's only one kind of apology that cannot fail to generate empathy: an apology that instantly convinces us of its sincerity.

In real life, no apology can do that. There will always be skeptics, and appropriately so. The truth of an apology doesn't lie in its words. It lies in the mind behind those words, and that mind can never be perceived with total certainty.

But in literature, there *are* apologies that can instantly convince us of their sincerity. That's because literature allows us to peer into characters' heads, inspecting their minds for an apology's neural proof: remorse. If we see that remorse, then we know that the apology is genuine. And, indeed, if we see that remorse, then we don't even need a formal apology.

The character can simply wail, collapse, or gibber incoherently, and we'll feel: *That's because he regrets what he did. That's because he accepts blame and repents his mistake.*

This is precisely how we come to feel about the title character of Sophocles's tragedy *Oedipus Tyrannus*. Like Job, Oedipus has done wrong: he's murdered his father and begot with his mother. So, when Oedipus steps onstage, our brain's justice circuitry burns hotter and hotter—until finally, Oedipus screams: "*Eeeoouuu! Eeeoouuu!* It's true! I am an unholy son!"

This isn't an apology. Oedipus doesn't say, "I'm sorry, and I won't do it again." Nor does Oedipus direct his words toward a judge or a deity or anyone else with the power to forgive. Instead, Oedipus just cries out wildly.

But this half-inchoate cry is no less effective than a formal apology. In fact, it's *more* effective, at least as far as our neural circuitry is concerned. The spontaneous informality of Oedipus's howl reveals that he's having an epiphany in real time: *I abhor myself, and repent in dust and ashes.* What Job speaks aloud, Oedipus believes inside. And because an inner belief cannot be faked, Oedipus's cry automatically triggers our empathy.

This mind-reading glimpse of a character's remorse is Sophocles's great invention: the "Empathy Generator." Drawing on literature's special power to carry us inside the minds of others, it reveals the unquestionable truth of a person's regret, opening our heart with compassion toward them.

Once this literary breakthrough had been made by Sophocles, later authors expanded it. Two millennia after Oedipus, Shakespeare introduced audiences to an even more criminal tyrant: England's King Richard III. Richard not only kills—he kills children. He not only woos incestuously—he does so intentionally. So, Richard sends our justice neurons into overdrive, filling us with a violent ache to see his crimes punished. Until at last, Richard has this private realization:

> I shall despair. There is no creature loves me;
> And if I die, no soul shall pity me:
> Nay, wherefore should they, since that I myself
> Find in myself no pity to myself?

Richard is mistaken here. We do pity him. For his spontaneous regret has prompted empathy in our brain. And so it is that literature's technology saves us from reiterating Richard's vicious heartlessness, keeping us from turning tyrant ourselves.

Two hundred years after Shakespeare, Sophocles's invention was enhanced again, this time by refining its mechanism. The original mechanism of the Empathy Generator had been engineered by playwrights like Sophocles and Shakespeare upon the theater stage, where the only way for characters to express remorse was to utter it aloud. But nineteenth-century authors such as Jane Austen, George Eliot, and Charles Dickens had at their disposal a newer literary technology, the novel, that could communicate the *unspoken* regrets of Emma Woodhouse, Maggie Tulliver, and David Copperfield:

> Her mind had to pass again and again through every bitter reproach and sorrowful regret.
>
> —*Emma*, Jane Austen

> The song suggested distinct memories and thoughts, and brought quiet regret in the place of excitement.
>
> —*The Mill on the Floss*, George Eliot

> I could not be here once more, and so near Agnes, without the revival of those regrets with which I had so long been occupied.
>
> —*David Copperfield*, Charles Dickens

Flashing these inner sentiments into our head, the novel's technology directly connects another person's mind to ours, convincing us that the remorse could not be faked.

Thus it was that Sophocles's invention allowed writers to generate empathy like never before. They could summon empathy not just for the righteous man of Uz but also for archfiends like Richard III. And they could make empathy almost irresistible, activating our neural networks more reliably than the best-crafted apology.

But still, Sophocles wasn't satisfied. Still, he wanted more empathy in the world. So, he kept inventing.

Sophocles Innovates Again

Sophocles's second innovation may not have been intentional. But it was credited to him by a very erudite scholar. So, we'll follow the scholar and credit Sophocles as well.

The very erudite scholar was Aristotle, who claimed that Sophocles engineered his plays in such a way that their remorseful characters were never actually guilty of moral crimes; they were guilty only of what Aristotle termed a *hamartia*. This word has a long history of being mistranslated as "tragic flaw," leading generations of teachers to instruct their students to rather uncharitably sift through literature in search of the psychological traits that have rightfully doomed the defeated. But *hamartia* means something more ethically neutral: it's a mistake of perception, like a misheard word or a moment of blurred vision.

Take Oedipus. Oedipus didn't *mean* to sleep with his mother. He simply mistook her for a different woman. Nor did Oedipus *mean* to kill his father. Oedipus's eyes betrayed him, telling him that his father was someone else.

Aristotle's case here is debatable. He's right to point out that Oedipus's crimes are not intentional, but even so, this fact seems irrelevant to Sophocles's play. Oedipus himself doesn't claim ignorance as a mitigating factor. Instead, he takes an old-school view of public decency that makes the *why* of his crime far less consequential than the *what*.

Yet although it's possible for us to quibble with Aristotle, his larger point is undoubtedly correct: literature can inspire empathy for individuals who've done very little, or even nothing, wrong. Literary empathy doesn't need to be restricted to characters who violate our justice circuitry by challenging God or committing other tragic sins. Literary empathy can be extended to characters who simply goof.

In the years since Aristotle, this extension is exactly what authors have done. They've used Sophocles's invention to soften our heart for literary characters who regret the most minor mistakes, like in Theodore Dreiser's *Sister Carrie*, when the saloon manager George Hurstwood repents his drunken decision to embezzle; or in Louisa May Alcott's *Little Women*, when Jo March rues accidentally burning her sister Meg's hair; or in Lucy Maud Montgomery's *Anne of Green Gables*, when the titular hero has a pang of remorse after coldly declaring: "No, I shall never be friends with you, Gilbert Blythe; and I don't want to be!"

And then, authors have gone further still: they've stirred our empathy for characters who've done nothing at all wrong but who simply regret the way that they are. Maybe the characters regret their too-big ears, or their hand-me-down clothes, or their clumsy feet. Maybe they regret their anxieties, or their enthusiasms, or their love for someone who doesn't love them back.

Whatever the regret is, it functions just like an apology. Clicking into our brain, it prompts us to feel empathy for anyone who isn't perfect . . . and forgive them for the crime of simply being human.

Using the Empathy Generator Yourself

Almost every work of literature produced in the past two hundred years contains a character who touches our heart with empathy. Which means that almost every modern novel, memoir, comic book, children's story, film, and sitcom contains a mind-reading glimpse of a character's remorse.

The vast reach of this invention hasn't turned us all into paragons of compassion. There's only so much empathy that our head can hold, and the amount varies brain by brain. Some of our brains are naturally more flinty; some naturally more forgiving.

Nor is more empathy always a good thing. Just as there can be too much justice, there can be too much empathy. We can feel pity for people who don't deserve it—or want it. And we can also crash from compassionate caring into hurtful false empathy, thinking that we understand others better than we actually do: "I know just how you feel," saith the freeman to the slave.

But in general, the world could benefit from a little more empathy. Since our brain's perspective-taking circuits are less powerful than our primate urge for justice, empathy tends to be less prevalent than optimal. And by using literature to practice forgiveness, we can condition our neurons to respond with empathy more powerfully and more frequently, reducing our anger and personal stress, while making our societies more inclusive, more richly abundant, and more peacefully happy.

If you're not getting those empathy benefits from Job and Oedipus, perhaps it's because the poetic or theatrical qualities of the book of Job and *Oedipus Tyrannus* make their apologies feel contrived or melodramatic. In which case, look for a literary work with more subtle moments of admission, like that of Newland Archer at the end of Edith Wharton's *The Age of Innocence* or that of Gabriel Grimes in James Baldwin's *Go Tell It on the Mountain*:

> He lifted up his head, and she saw tears mingled with his sweat.
> "The Lord," he said, "He sees the heart—He sees the Heart."

Or perhaps you have a natural skepticism about the genuineness of people's regrets. In which case, find yourself a story where a character proves his remorse by punishing himself. Like in Thomas Hardy's *Jude the Obscure*, in which a child overhears his parents miserably admit that they don't have enough money to feed their growing family. Prompting the child to feel so deeply guilty for contributing to his parents' misery that he hangs his siblings then himself, leaving behind the hand-scrawled note: "Done because we are too menny."

No matter how stern your heart, there are characters in literature whose remorse will ring true. So you don't just feel the primal zeal of righteousness.

You feel the human touch of kindness too.

FOUR

Float Above Hurt

Aesop's Fables, *Plato's* Meno, *and the*
Invention of the Serenity Elevator

The poison was known to be excruciating.

It stank of rotten parsnip and slipped with acrid vileness down the throat into the chest, where it went to work upon the lungs, slowly paralyzing them. The gulps of air came hard, then harder, until at last, they stopped completely, and the eyes gaped in helplessness, alive for a few last dreadful moments after the flesh below had choked to death.

And now the poison had been handed to old Socrates. And he'd been brusquely told to drink.

It was 399 BCE in the democratic city of Athens. A few weeks earlier, Socrates had been indicted by the prosecutor Anytus of Euonymeia, a witty legalist whose family had grown prosperous as leather merchants in the southern suburbs. According to Anytus, Socrates was guilty of a terrible impiety: he'd renounced Zeus and seduced a school of impressionable youths into worshiping a fantastical metaphysics instead.

The allegation baffled Socrates. He'd never questioned the existence of Zeus, he averred. He'd merely questioned a few priests. Those priests had been the ones unable to provide any straight answers. Those priests were the ones who really seemed ignorant of the gods.

The trial that ensued was a spectacle: the jury alone numbered five hundred citizens. And in the end, a great many of them sided with Socrates. Yet it was not enough. The elderly defendant was convicted by a narrow margin. And the triumphant Anytus ordered a mugful of poison prepared.

But Anytus would have to wait. There could be no public executions until Athens had been purified, and Athens could not be purified until a ship with a celery wreath had sailed around the isle of Delos. The city priests had been trying to complete that tour for quite some time, yet mysteriously, the wind always blew them back to harbor. It was almost as if the gods didn't want Socrates put to death.

That's what Socrates's friends suggested, anyway. And they whispered to Socrates that they had a plan. They'd smuggle him out of prison and whisk him off to Sparta, Delphi, or anywhere else he chose.

Socrates smiled. He was grateful for his friends' love. But he saw no need to run. His physical location was unimportant. All that mattered was the situation of his mind. And his mind was already far, far above. It couldn't be harmed by fear, pain, or poison. It was as untouchable as the high-flying gods.

So, Socrates accepted the fatal brew from Anytus and quaffed it cheerfully. He didn't flinch at the foul taste or the strange tightening of his breath. His thoughts were elsewhere, in the clouds. And as his body perished gruesomely, his psyche floated up to find a painless calm.

Socrates's Secret

Socrates knew that the world would want to know his secret for dying free from care or hurt. So, he left behind a simple answer: "True philosophers train for death with their philosophy."

Yet like all of Socrates's simple answers, this answer has turned out not to be so simple. Socrates himself never explained exactly what his philosophy was. The most he would say was: "I know that I know nothing." Which was a logical contradiction. Or at least a riddle. And so, to this day, Socrates's philosophy remains a brain teaser. Some bright mind will explain it to you, and then another bright mind will explain the opposite, just as convincingly.

Eventually, no doubt, those bright minds will puzzle it out. But in the meantime, the rest of us can take advantage of a less enigmatic path to Socrates's higher peace. That other path was preserved by the ransomed slave Phaedo of Elis, who witnessed Socrates's death and later revealed what he'd seen to Plato, a student who'd missed the execution due to a stomachache.

What Phaedo of Elis revealed to Plato was that Socrates had spent his final hours "imitating Aesop." Imitating Aesop? That was strange, thought Plato. Aesop wasn't one of the "true philosophers" who trained for death. He was instead a storyteller who'd become mildly notorious for his fables about foolish animals. There was the fable about the fox who couldn't reach a sweet bunch of grapes—and huffily declared them sour. There was the fable about the mule who wished for a new master—and got a worse one. There was the fable about the lovestruck lion who agreed to be declawed—and then found himself attacked.

Why, Plato wondered, was Socrates frittering away his final moments on these childish beast tales? Phaedo of Elis couldn't say, but he did recall Socrates remarking that Aesop's fables weren't the animal fictions they seemed; they were really clandestine commentaries on humanity. Aesop had only populated them with foxes, mules, and lions because he knew that people would get angry if he pointed out their faults directly.

Then at last, Plato began to understand: Socrates wasn't just talking about Aesop; Socrates was also talking about himself. Like Aesop, Socrates had spent his life wryly pointing out people's follies. And like Aesop, Socrates had tried to avoid people's wrath by pretending to be a harmless gadfly. So, like Aesop, Socrates had been a covert satirist.

As Plato was struck by this epiphany, he began to wonder if perhaps the secret to Socrates's superhuman death lay in those final hours spent "imitating" Aesop. Perhaps the mystery of eternal serenity could be unveiled, at least in part, by studying the ancient satirists who'd inspired Aesop and Socrates. And such was the intense curiosity sparked in Plato by this possibility that he decided to leave philosophy's temple of reason and descend into the disreputable literary grotto where the satirists' writings were shelved.

The descent proved startlingly illuminating. For as Plato fumbled through literature's murky cave, hunting for Socrates's painkilling secret, he discovered that satire contained more than one secret. It contained three, each in the form of a different invention.

Satire's First Invention: Parody

The most basic, and probably the most ancient, of satire's inventions is parody.

Parody is an exaggerated imitation. So, if you exaggeratedly imitate your friend's talk or his walk, that's parody.

Literary parody is so old that the Greeks thought that it dated back to Homer, who, it was said, had just finished the *Iliad* when he was inspired to write a parodic epic, *Batrachomyomachia*, or the *Frog-Mouse-Feud*, which told the story of how the frogs mortally offended the mice, leading the two species to launch their own Trojan War.

And as post-Homeric authors discovered, parody could caricature more than epic seriousness. It could caricature religion too. According to the Greeks' most solemn priests, the gods were remarkably human: Zeus, Athena, and all the rest possessed not only human hearts but also human limbs—and even human clothes.

Could this human-looking heaven be a symptom of our own deluded self-importance? Could we have arrogantly imagined the divine in our own image? Yes, the poet Xenophanes decided, that's exactly what had happened. And a few centuries after Homer, he wrote a parody where horses and cows drew pictures of the gods, who—surprise, surprise!—happened to look just like horses and cows.

The *Frog-Mouse-Feud* and the poems of Xenophanes prompted a great deal of sniggers at military fictions and manmade scriptures. But still, humans continued to act nonsensically. Parody hadn't cured their follies.

So, the satirists continued to invent.

Satire's Second Invention: Insinuation

A century after Homer, the Greek lyricist and reputed verbal assassin Archilochus forged satire's second invention: insinuation.

Insinuation implies an insult by engineering what logicians refer to as an incomplete syllogism, or in other words, two dots for our brain to connect. Here's an example from Archilochus:

I'm not one for tall, swaggering generals who comb their hair
and shave. I'm for short, bow-legged generals, who don't turn
and run.

First dot: the poet likes generals who don't turn and run. *Second dot*: the
poet doesn't like tall, swaggering generals. *Connect the dots*: tall, swaggering generals must turn and run.

If those dots don't connect for you, here's a more recent insinuation,
courtesy of the nineteenth-century American wit Mark Twain:

Reader, suppose you were an idiot. And suppose you were a member of Congress. But I repeat myself.

First dot: you're an idiot. *Second dot*: you're a congressman. *Connect the
dots*: congressmen are idiots.

Insinuation has a double action: it tears down fools while making
the satirist seem clever. Cleverness is, after all, required for insinuation.
Unlike parody, which is also called aping because any primate can do it,
insinuation requires a higher intellect. That's why we don't just snicker
at congressmen when we read Twain's insult; we also admire Twain
for being brainy. So, insinuation goes beyond abusing the dunces of the
world. It tries to reform them by illustrating a smarter way.

Yet still the dunces continued to multiply. And so the satirists crafted
one last great invention.

Satire's Third Invention: Irony

The third and most powerful of satire's inventions is irony.

Irony's literary blueprint is the revealing of a truth that someone else
doesn't see. That revelation triggers our brain's perspective-taking circuitry (as described in the introduction), making us feel like we have a
God's-Eye view of the situation. So, it gives us the neural experience of
literally being hoisted up to a loftier plane.

Here's an ancient example of an irony hoist that Plato might have
found in his studies, courtesy of Hipponax, a grump from the sixth cen-

tury BCE who lived amid the silver mints and fermented fish condiments of the Eastern Mediterranean seaport of Klazomenai:

> There's two times a woman most delights a man:
> On his wedding night and at her funeral.

The ironic reveal arrives on the final two words. Up to this point, Hipponax seems to be earnestly celebrating the joys of marriage. But when he utters, "her funeral," he lifts us up to a higher vantage, enlightening us with the wry truth unknown to all the foolish grooms below. (If you don't appreciate Hipponax's gross misogyny here, there's a deeper feminist irony lurking. We'll get there in just a moment.)

When Plato unearthed irony, insinuation, and parody from the writings of the ancient satirists, he thought, *This is it! This is how Socrates lifted himself up! Satire elevates you above worldly folly, making you superior!*

But then Plato paused. No, he realized. Socrates hadn't just used satire; Socrates had innovated it.

Socrates's Innovation

Socrates's innovation is laid out by Plato in the Socratic dialogues, which are staged conversations between Socrates and various folk about Athens. More than two dozen of these conversations have survived down to our present day, but the most introductory is *Meno*.

Meno begins when Socrates remarks to the youthful student Meno that even the world's wisest men don't know what virtue is. This leads Meno to respond that he's quite sure that the rhetorician Gorgias *does*, in fact, know what virtue is. To which Socrates replies:

> "Unfortunately, I've forgotten what Gorgias thinks. So, could you remind me? Or why don't you just tell me, Meno, what *you* think of virtue. I bet that you and Gorgias think just about the same."

Did you spot the satire here? It's an insinuation. In fact, it's *two* insinuations. Delicately embedded in Socrates's response to Meno are a pair of connect-the-dots:

First dot: the wise can't define virtue. *Second dot:* Gorgias can define virtue. *Connect the dots*: Gorgias is not wise.

First dot: Gorgias is not wise. *Second dot:* Meno thinks like Gorgias. *Connect the dots*: Meno is not wise either.

Meno doesn't catch these insinuations. And there you have the second element of satire's technology: parody. Plato's literary imitation exaggerates the simplemindedness of Meno, caricaturing a naïve young man into a clueless dilly-doo.

Then finally, Plato adds the third and final satiric invention: irony. After Meno agrees that he does, indeed, have some thoughts on virtue, Socrates says: "Be kind, then, dear Meno, and tell me what you know. For I swear to god, I'd love you to educate me." The irony being that Socrates is about to do just the opposite and educate Meno. So, the hidden truth is that the one asking questions is really the teacher.

By this point in the dialogue, Plato has proved himself a master of satire. He's joined the three inventions of the ancient satirists into a single dialogue for mocking the unfortunate Meno. But still, there seems to be no big innovation here; no grand literary breakthrough, no Socratic secret.

Except there is. Plato is doing more than just combining the prior blueprints of Xenophanes, Archilochus, and Hipponax. He's adding a twist. He's using the ancient technology of satire in a radically new way.

Have you spotted that innovation? Have you identified the Socratic twist? If not, keep reading, and you'll see.

The Socratic Twist on Satire

The twist is that you're Meno. That's why you didn't catch the twist; Meno is a mental peanut, so he never catches anything. But don't feel bad about being Meno. We're all vegetable intelligences. Every one of us (even Socrates).

I know, I know, I'm going too fast for you, Meno. Here, I'll slow it down so that you understand.

In *Meno*, Plato turns around the inventions of satire. Instead of using them to satirize our enemies, he uses them to satirize ourselves:

1. *Parody.* First, Plato parodies our behavior in Meno. We, after all, like to think that we've learned a thing or two. No matter how humble we might be, none of us believes that we're complete fools. So, when someone asks us for our opinion on a topic such as virtue, we're happy to share. And the more we share, the more we stray into contradictions, confusions, and unsubstantiated nonsense, revealing that, in fact, we knew less than we thought.

2. *Insinuation.* Second, Plato insinuates that we're Meno by giving us two dots to connect. *Dot one:* Meno is a student looking for enlightenment. *Dot two:* we're reading *Meno* because we're a student looking for enlightenment. *Connect the dots . . .*

3. *Irony.* Third, Plato snares us in the coils of irony. We think we're smarter than Meno, just as Meno thinks that he's smarter than Socrates. So, the hidden truth is that Plato has tricked us in the same way that Socrates has tricked Meno.

And there you have it. We're Meno.

We didn't see it at first, just as we didn't see that the animals in Aesop's fables were also us. But now that our slow-moving brain gears have finally caught up, we've got two choices. Choice one is to do what the Athenians did to Socrates: get angry and sentence the author to death. (This, by the way, is also what Aesop's audience did to him; as the legend goes, the citizens of Delphi took umbrage at his zoological barbs and pitched him off a cliff.) Choice two is to go along with the satire, satirizing ourselves.

Since we're Meno, choice one probably sounds pretty good right now. But as neuroscientists have recently discovered, choice two is the key to enriching our brain with Socrates's pain-quenching secret.

The Pain-Quenching Secret

Satire was invented to make us laugh at others. But as scientific studies have revealed, laughing at others isn't always good for our health. It feels good, certainly. It gives us the pleasure of feeling superior. But this pleasure is only momentary. And it can have negative long-term effects: condescension and negative judgments of others (as we'll explore more in chapter 21) have been correlated with increased anxiety and elevated blood pressure, boosting our risk of heart attacks and strokes.

Yet that doesn't mean satire is necessarily bad for us, for science has also shown that when we turn satire around, it can be healthy in both the short term and the long. In the short term, laughing at ourselves releases feel-good neuro-opioids and drops our blood level of cortisol, diminishing stress. And in the long-term, laughing at ourselves reduces anxiety, nurtures emotional resilience, and helps us bond with other people.

This doesn't get us all the way to being Socrates. But it's a start. Socrates was calm, resilient, and surrounded in his final moments by friends. And Socrates was also resistant to pain, which, as it turns out, is another benefit of laughing at ourselves. Psychologists have found that when we laugh with others (as opposed to laughing *at* them), our brain releases endorphins that can significantly increase our tolerance for pain. And this analgesic effect, as psychologists have also discovered, can be boosted further by self-irony. Self-irony flips around the perspective-taking network of our frontal brain, making us feel like we're looking at our self from outside. That detached vantage reduces the felt intensity of our emotional hurts, which is why wry humor is common among soldiers, paramedics, and other professionals who deal daily with death. Their irony is quite literally numbing; it's a mental novocaine for coping with the horrors of war zones and emergency rooms.

So, by satirizing ourselves, we dose our brain with Socratic up-aboveness and pain-quenching neuro-pharmacologies, while by satirizing others, we drag ourselves down with anxiety and cardiac arrest.

And now you can see that the joke was on Hipponax for sneering at women. He thought that he'd made himself grandly superior. Yet the irony is that he only made himself sick.

Using the "Serenity Elevator" Yourself

Socrates was very good at self-satire. So good that he floated higher than the priests and maybe even the gods. And to get yourself a bit of that transcendent serenity, all you have to do is accept that you really are Meno. Bespeak thus: "I am Meno and Meno is me." Then get yourself a copy of *Meno* and delete the last two letters of Meno's name, so that Socrates is now having a conversation with *Me*. If that doesn't help, go through the dialogue again and replace Meno's name with your first name, last name, and middle initial.

Or if Plato's not really your style, dip into literature's grotto for some more recent works that combine parody, insinuation, and irony. Most of these works were originally intended as satire, not as a means of Socratic elevation, but they can still be repurposed to lift you into a peace above. Just find a satire that pokes fun at one of your own tendencies and read away. If you think that school is useful, try Aristophanes's ancient Greek comedy *The Clouds*. If you think that you'd learn more by escaping your teachers to voyage the world, try Jonathan Swift's eighteenth-century prank travelogue *Gulliver's Travels*. If you think that state-run socialism is the best option in our imperfect world, try *We*, penned in 1921 by Russian sci-fi novelist Yevgeny Zamyatin. If you think that capitalism would serve us better, try Sinclair Lewis's 1922 novel *Babbitt*. If you seek the enlightenment of ancient sages, try G. V. Desani's *All About Hatterr* (1948). If you believe that a mix of self-medication and pop entertainment will fix your brain, try David Foster Wallace's *Infinite Jest* (1996). If you're sure that things would be better if you were in charge, try George Orwell's *Animal Farm* (1945).

Or, for a fast flight up to the atmosphere, no repurposing required, try Douglas Adams's *The Hitchhiker's Guide to the Galaxy* (1979), where the earthling, Arthur Dent, learns from the alien researcher, Ford Prefect, that the digital encyclopedia of the cosmos has this to say about our spectacular planet:

> "'Harmless'!? Is that all it's got to say? Harmless! One word!"
> Ford shrugged. "Well, there are a hundred billion stars in the Galaxy, and only a limited amount of space in the book's micro-

processors," he said, "and no one knew much about the Earth, of course."

"Well, for God's sake, I hope you managed to rectify that."

"Oh yes, well, I managed to transmit a new entry off to the editor. He had to trim it a bit, but it's still an improvement."

"And what does it say now?" asked Arthur.

"Mostly harmless."

So, go feel the mostly harmlessness of this world. Lift yourself out of your mortal troubles and your woes. All it takes is a book that turns the satire around.

All it takes is understanding that the greatest cosmic joke is us.

FIVE

Excite Your Curiosity

The Epic of Sundiata, *the Modern Thriller, and
the Invention of the Tale Told from Our Future*

I t all started when the goat went mad.

The goat had been grazing on the Bronze Age slopes of Mount Parnassus, above the charcoal beaches of the Gulf of Corinth. But then the goat had wandered west, sniffing over autumn clover until it chanced upon a jagged crack that split the mountainside apart.

The crack ran deep into the rock—down, it seemed, into the very center of the earth. And wafting from its nightish depths was a peculiar vapor that caused the goat to froth its eyes, buck its spine, and bleat a gruesome cry that sounded like the death shriek of a human child.

Alarmed, a goatherder dashed to the rescue. But then the herder became afflicted too. Smelling the vapor, he collapsed in a scream. And in the scream, he witnessed what the goat had seen: a future red and black and fire. A future blue and white and ice.

When the herder recovered his senses at last, he grabbed the goat and hastened down a narrow footpath to the nearby settlement of Delphi. The villagers there had no idea what to make of the herder's ranting tale of fire and ice, but they decided it must be a revelation from beyond. So, around the crack, the villagers threw up a makeshift oracle. And at the center of the oracle, they perched an old woman on a tripod chair.

The old woman spent her days breathing in the mountain vapor. And the vapor provided hints of a truth remarkable and strange. Because like the herder's vision, that truth came as riddles: "A mule will be king." "Stone statues will stand." "The winds will save this land."

What did the riddles mean? None of the villagers could say. But they could promise one thing with certainty absolute: the oracle's riddles always, always came true.

So it was that Delphi became the classical world's most famous oracle. For almost two thousand years, from the mythic era of Helen of Troy to the days of the last Roman emperor, its hallowed steps were trod by Spartan kings and Phoenician philosophers, Celtic queens and Athenian democrats, Egyptian slaves and Hindustani rajahs, all of them come to glimpse the days ahead.

And if you'd like, you can join those eager seekers. This chapter will teach you all the oracle's secrets—and some further secrets too. So you can excite your curiosity with the racing heartbeat of anticipation as you chase the time beyond tomorrow's lid.

Into the Future

From the beginning, there were warnings that it was unwise to peer into the future.

The grimmest warning came from Croesus, a fabulously rich king of ancient Lydia who, in roughly 550 BCE, approached Delphi to ask: "Should I invade the Persian Empire?" The old woman lifted her head from the vapor and replied: "If you do, a great empire will fall."

Oh good, Croesus smiled. *That means I'll topple Persia.* So, he yoked his gem-studded chariots and attacked. The result was a catastrophe for Croesus. His mammoth army was scattered, and his golden kingdom fell. The oracle had riddled true, but Croesus had solved the riddle backward. *His* was the great empire that collapsed.

Croesus's disaster became as legendary as his wealth, yet it did nothing to deter the flood of visitors to Delphi. Even today people still trek the old footpath to the future. Maybe it's dangerous to know. But as the hikers draw near upon the mountain crack, their pulses quicken in suspense. *What will be my destiny? Will I find wealth or love or joy or infamy?*

The oracle's psychological secret to catching all these curious hearts is an emotion known as wonder. We learned wonder's literary blueprint back in the introduction, but even so, we didn't learn the oracle's secret. That's because wonder comes in two distinct neural varieties:

> The first variety is *passive* wonder. This is the wonder we explored in the introduction. It's the feeling of being overwhelmed with awe. It's pausing in astonishment as a miracle washes over you.
>
> The second variety is *active* wonder. This is the wonder sparked by the Delphic oracle. It's *wonder* as a verb: *to* wonder. It's a curious searching, a seeking, a yearning. It's rushing forward to chase where the miracle leads.

Since the second variety of wonder is different, it has a different literary blueprint. And we can glimpse that blueprint in the oracle's favored manner of speech: riddles.

Riddles work by presenting one thing as two conflicting opposites: "When is a door not a door?" "What gets wetter the more that it dries?" "Why do I have a mouth I never feed—and a bed I never use to sleep?" (So, one thing is a door—and also not a door. One thing dries—and is wetter. One thing looks like a feeder and a sleeper—but acts like neither.)

The riddle formula for active wonder is so old that it goes back even before the Delphic oracle; a scrap of Sumerian cuneiform from 1750 BCE asks: "Where can the blind go to see?" And from those long-ago beginnings, the riddle formula then spread far and wide through history, making its way into Pacific Island burial rites and ancient Chinese festivals, Namibian weddings and the Hindu Rigveda. Old English verses declared: "I came like a fish from the water, but fire's made me like snow." Antique Arabic texts mused: "Without food or drink I grow."

And as globally popular as the riddle formula became, it was only the beginning of the wonder. Because the oracle took the formula—and added a twist.

The Oracle's Twist

The oracle's twist was to send the riddle from the future.

Riddles from the future have answers from the future. So, the only way to get the answers to how "a mule will be king" or how "statues will stand" is to wait for the future to arrive. And as we wait . . . and wait . . . and wait . . . the curious wonder inside our brain gets stretched into the emotion known as suspense.

Suspense is the impatience of knowing that an answer is coming— just not yet. And the longer that we sit in suspense, the further we shift to the edge of our seats, trying to lean ourselves nearer to the time ahead. Which is to say: suspense makes us wonder more actively. It fills us with a desire to jump through the hours, so we can get the riddle answers faster.

You might be feeling a little of that more active wonder now. After all, this chapter has given you a string of riddles—"Where can the blind go to see?"—and then rather rudely withheld the solutions. But don't worry, those solutions will be coming soon.

How soon? Well, it depends on how swiftly you read. So, go ahead and read faster, converting this boring old chapter into a blistering page-turner.

The Oracle Transplanted into Literature

After the Delphic oracle put its twist on riddles, the twist began to find its way into literature. Sophocles's *Oedipus Tyrannus* (429 BCE) is packed with future riddles uttered by the blind prophet Tiresias of Thebes:

> "My knowledge will be ignorance to you."
> "Thou hast eyes, but cannot see."
> "This shall be thy day of birth—and death!"

These future riddles fill Oedipus with such unbearable suspense that he desperately attempts to speed the answers up. First, he tries to bully Tiresias into explaining the mystery. And when that fails, Oedipus pulls a Croesus: he leaps to a false conclusion, solving the riddles wrong.

The very same plot unfolded two thousand years later in Shakespeare's *Macbeth*, where a trio of Weird Sisters gleefully shrieked:

> "Fair is foul and foul is fair."
> "When the battle's lost and won."

"Macbeth shall never vanquished be, until
Great Birnam Wood to high Dunsinane Hill
Shall come against him."

The Weird Sisters' tomorrow puzzles make Macbeth so enormously impatient that he becomes an even bigger bully than Oedipus. To get the answers that he craves, the once-noble Scotsman murders a king, then murders his friend, and then tries to murder a child. But like Oedipus and Croesus before him, Macbeth mis-solves the riddles from the future, charging into doom.

To save you from a similar tragic fate, the answers to this chapter's previous literary riddles are: A door isn't a door when it's ajar; that is, "a jar." A towel gets wetter the more that it dries. A river has a mouth and a bed but doesn't feed or sleep. The "blind" can go to school to see. When (sea) water is treated with fire, evaporation leaves behind the "snow" of salt. A fingernail grows without food or drink.

Now that you've got all the answers, you might be feeling less interested in page-turning any further. But don't stop reading yet, because there's still one riddle left for us to solve: *Oedipus* and *Macbeth* perfectly copied the words of ancient oracles—but they didn't give theatergoers the experience of a visit to Delphi. Instead, they did the opposite.

Why?

The Riddle of Literature's First Future Riddles

One riddle can have two contrary effects. That's because the riddle can be the same, but the audience can be different.

So it was with *Oedipus* and *Macbeth*. The spectators who witnessed those plays were different from the seekers at Delphi. Because unlike the seekers, the spectators knew the riddle's answer.

The spectators of *Oedipus* knew the answer because Oedipus's legend was famous long before Sophocles wrote his play. So, while Oedipus was gripped with suspense about his future, his audience sat already in that future, captured by a very different feeling: irony. (See chapter 4 for the blueprint.)

Shakespeare's audience got the same ironic feeling when they watched Macbeth botch the prophecy of Great Birnam Wood. That prophecy had long been recorded in popular history books such as *Holinshed's Chronicles* (1577), and for audience members who hadn't done the reading, Shakespeare tipped them off with a scene that revealed "Birnam Wood" to be a human army disguised with branches. So, while Macbeth was torn apart with baffled suspense, trying to fathom the riddle of a walking forest, his audience experienced a cosmic knowingness.

That audience experience of ironic foresight was the deep gift of dramatic tragedy. It bestowed medicinal benefits (for these, see the introduction) by lifting up the mind to fate's more sacred plane. But it was the very opposite of a trip to Delphi. It was a resigned feeling of knowledge—instead of an active feeling of wonder. It was being the god in the vapor—instead of being Croesus.

So, if the writers of the world wanted to fill audiences with Croesus's impatient curiosity, they would have to venture a step beyond Sophocles and Shakespeare. Rather than simply recycling the famous oracles of yore, they'd have to become oracles themselves.

The Invention of the "Tale Told from Our Future"

For storytellers to fashion themselves into oracles, they needed to invent their own future riddles; ones that the audience couldn't answer—yet.

The most elementary way to do this was for storytellers to make up a fictional oracle, which is what the Assyrian rhetorician Lucian did in *A True Story* (c. 160 CE). *A True Story* was not at all true. It was an elaborate yarn about a sailing trip to the moon, and among its many fabrications was a soothsayer's prediction that the hero would make his way home, provided that he never stoked fire with steel. What did that riddling prediction mean? The tale's original readers couldn't tell you. So, like the tale's hero, their sole option was to forge ahead in growing suspense, turning pages quicker and quicker until the answer came.

Building suspense like this was a clever literary trick, but it had an obvious limitation: it required the use of fictional prophets. And what if you didn't want to incorporate those soothsaying characters into your story? What if you wanted a more flexible way to stimulate active wonder?

The answer was discovered independently by oral storytellers in multiple cultures across the globe. Since those oral storytellers never wrote down their finding, leaving it to be preserved (or lost) by later generations, there's no way for us mortal historians to determine who made the discovery first. Only an oracle could know.

So, let's visit an oracle, perhaps the oldest in the world. An oracle in the sub-Saharan lands where humans first emerged. There, in the east-west realm of Igboland, sit age-old augury houses that remain in use today. And just north of the houses, on copper-dust savannahs that embank the River Niger, echoes a song known as the *Epic of Sundiata*.

The *Epic of Sundiata* was originally composed in the thirteenth-century kingdom of Mali by a griot: a West African oral historian and bard. The epic tells the tale of a child who is mocked for his physical frailties but grows up to be a warrior king. And although it makes use of the time-tested device of a fictional prophet, it also contains the ground-breaking answer of how to stimulate active wonder without one. The answer is: talk in a voice that interjects the audience's *future* into the narrative's *present*. As the griot does it:

> Listen to my words, you who want to know; by my mouth you will learn the history of Mali. By my mouth you will get to know the story.

We "will" get to know—which makes us suddenly aware: *We don't know yet*.

What gave the Mali griot the idea to speak like this? Did he invent the *Epic of Sundiata*'s future-hinting voice himself? Or did he learn it from oral storytellers more ancient? We cannot say. We know nothing about the griot; not his influences, not his life history, not even his name. All we know is the science of why his invention works on our brain.

The Science of the Mali Griot's Invention

There are three things necessary for life: food, reproduction, and information.

Information might look a little out of place on that list. After all, the world is full of bacteria that get by without knowing anything; they drift along without schools or books, existing in a blissful state of microscopic ignorance. Yet if we peer close, we can see that even those no-knowing creatures require information. They may lack brains, but at the center of their bodies, bobbing through their inner plasma, is a data storage device: the nucleic acid of DNA or RNA. And without the data on that device, bacteria couldn't metabolize food or reproduce; they'd be as lifeless as stones.

The importance of data to life is why information collecting is the first thing that primitive brain cells evolved to do—and why it remains a primary function of our own cutting-edge gray matter. Most of the neurons in our skull exist to amass intel (from our eyes, our pain receptors, and our other sensory organs) and to then store it in various memory banks (short-term, episodic, semantic, procedural).

To help with this life-sustaining endeavor, millions of years of natural selection have exquisitely calibrated our brain's information-gathering circuitry. That circuitry doesn't want to squander valuable time searching for answers that cannot be known. Nor does it want to waste valuable time searching for answers that don't matter. So, to avoid both dead ends, our brain's information-gathering circuitry has evolved to work its hardest when we feel like we have *some* idea about an answer—but also feel *unconfident* about what that answer is. After all, if we have some idea, then the answer is likely not too far away. And if we're unconfident, then the answer is likely different from what we know already, making it that rare (and valuable) sort of information that transforms our view of the world.

When these two conditions are achieved, the reward centers of our brain do a sneaky thing: they give us a little dose of dopamine. The dose is like a nibble of cake: it tastes sweet but doesn't satisfy our appetite. In fact, it makes us *more* hungry than if we hadn't got a taste at all, wracking our brain with a ravenous curiosity.

That ravenous curiosity is the feeling triggered by riddles. Riddles achieve the "some-idea" condition of the dopamine cake nibble by giving us all the pieces of an answer, telling us straight out that a mule will be king or that a lost battle will be won. And they achieve the "unconfident" condition by providing those answer pieces as a contradiction that baffles reason: *How can mules rule human kingdoms? How can defeats be victories?* The resulting combo makes us feel like we've caught a hint of a truth that will rewrite logic as we know it, filling our brain with the irresistible belief: *This is close-at-hand data that will change everything!*

The same neural cocktail is generated by the griot's future-hinting voice: "You will get to know the story." This literary invention turns the entire *Epic of Sundiata* into a riddle, presenting one story as two. The two are: (1) the ongoing version of the story, which gives us some idea of how things will end, and (2) the full version of the story, which has an ending that (as the future-hinting voice has made us suddenly conscious) we're unsure about. And because the solution to this riddle is the story ending that the griot knows, it invests the griot with the aura of an oracle.

That aura is, of course, a literary cheat. The griot isn't seeing our future in the manner of a genuine prophet; instead he's *making* our future by introducing a story that will occupy our hours ahead. But still, the griot's promise strikes our brain the same way as a riddle from Delphi. It makes us conscious of a coming time that the griot sees—and we don't. Filling us with suspense to hear.

Once the griot has begun the *Epic of Sundiata* by hooking us with this blueprint for suspense, he then proceeds to intensify the blueprint's neural action by embroidering his present-future story with further riddle things. There are riddle objects, such as a supple bow of hardest silver. There are riddle animals, such as a starving buffalo fat from feasting. And there are even riddle characters, such as a lame child who sprints like a lion. Each of these two opposite things in one prompts another cake nibble of active wonder that tugs our brain forward, making us even more desperate to know how the story will end.

So, how *will* it end? What will the answer to the future be?

Let's turn ahead through time and see.

The Revolution in Storytelling

Like the blueprint for the riddle, the griot's literary invention spread across the globe through a mix of cultural exchange and independent rediscovery. In English literature, it can be found as early as the fourteenth-century Arthurian ballad *Sir Gawain and the Green Knight*:

But of all the British kings, I've heard tell that Arthur was the most noble. And so I will show you something that's astonished the eyes of many, an outrageous adventure of knightly wonder, and if you will listen to my song for oh just a little, I will tell it as I heard it in town.

There, in the very last phrase, you can see the Tale Told from Our Future: "if you will listen to my song for oh just a little, I will tell it as I heard it in town."

And because the Tale Told from Our Future is a rhetorical sleight of hand that doesn't require literal fortune-telling, its riddle voice has also appeared in detective fictions, realist novels, historical memoirs, and other modern literature without Green Knights or Arthurian wizards or any magic at all. It has even inspired its own original genre, the thriller.

The thriller was invented at the end of the nineteenth century with novels such as H. Rider Haggard's *King Solomon's Mines* (1885):

I am going to tell the strangest story that I remember. It may seem a queer thing to say, especially considering that there is no woman in it—except Foulata. Stop, though! there is Gagaoola, if she was a woman, and not a fiend. But she was a hundred at least, and therefore not marriageable, so I don't count her.

The riddles come so quickly here that they tumble atop of one another. We'll find our future in the narrator's past, where we'll meet no women except one—and a female who's also a fiend.

The same riddle-thick tomorrow voice is used to snare our interest at the start of Scottish author John Buchan's wildly influential thriller *The Thirty-Nine Steps* (1915):

I was just fitting my key into the door when I noticed a man at my elbow.

"Pardon," he said, "I'm a bit rattled tonight. You see, I happen at this moment to be dead."

How is a living man now dead? Ah, well, the answer to that riddle lies in the future. And to whet our wonder for it, the storyteller flies ahead of us into that future, learning the man's tale and then talking back to us from the beyond:

> "Get on with your yarn," I said. . . .
>
> He seemed to brace himself for a great effort, and then started on the queerest rigmarole. I didn't get hold of it at first, and I had to stop and ask him questions. But here is the gist of it. . . .

This story hook was adapted by Alfred Hitchcock into his 1935 movie thriller of the same title, and its suspense-building technique now overflows our modern bookstores and cinema screens: the opening chapter of almost every crime or adventure novel, and the opening teaser of almost every television mystery or action movie, is a flash-forward glimpse of the story ahead. As Stephenie Meyer begins her *Twilight* series:

> I'd never given much thought to how I would die—though I'd had reason enough in the last few months—but even if I had, I would not have imagined it like this.

But as curiosity grabbing as thrillers are, they're still not the most miraculous modern form of the Mali griot's invention. That most miraculous form is: page-turning nonfiction.

Page-turning nonfiction is another riddle. By itself, nonfiction is the antithesis of thrilling. It's the domain of textbooks, instructional manuals, and other books that you go to with hungry questions, only to be greeted with a stultifying tedium. But when nonfiction is combined with the Tale Told from Our Future, even the most deathly dull material can elevate your pulse.

Here's how Charles Darwin raises suspense at the beginning of his classic science book, *On the Origin of Species* (1859):

> When on board H.M.S. "Beagle," as naturalist, I was much struck with certain facts [that] seemed to me to throw some light on the

origin of species—that mystery of mysteries, as it has been called by one of our greatest philosophers.

The answer to this "mystery of mysteries" is shrouded by Darwin in futurespeak: "We shall thus see that . . ." And just like the Mali griot, Darwin then goes on to intensify the suspense by piling on more riddles:

> How strange it is that a bird, under the form of woodpecker, should have been created to prey on insects on the ground; that upland geese, which never or rarely swim, should have been created with webbed feet.

What woodpecker never pecks wood? What creature has webbed feet but doesn't swim? Or, in perhaps Darwin's most intriguing riddle:

> It may be difficult, but we ought to admire the savage instinctive hatred of the queen-bee, which urges her instantly to destroy the young queens her daughters as soon as born, or to perish herself in the combat.

We've all heard of maternal love. All of us, that is, except for the queen-bee, who instinctively launches into mortal combat with her newborn daughters. So, the queen-bee's heart contains a riddle: maternal hate.

How to solve these scientific riddles? Well, the future-you knows. She's read to the end of Darwin's book. And she's waiting for you there.

Using the Tale Told from Our Future Yourself

Curiosity is crucial for our survival. But it's also crucial for our happiness. It boosts what psychologists term our positive affect, making us more cheerful, enthusiastic, energetic, and generally glad to be alive. Launching us out of bed with eager purpose, it banishes our world-weary doldrums with the lure of fresh discovery.

And if you're not getting that positive affect from the *Epic of Sundiata,* or *The Thirty-Nine Steps,* or *On the Origin of Species,* there are countless other works that use the griot's invention to spark curiosity and raise suspense.

If you like crime stories, why not try the best-selling author of all time, Agatha Christie? Her 1939 novel *And Then There Were None* is a classic Tale Told from Our Future that begins with a tomorrow-hinting nursery rhyme and then, like the *Epic of Sundiata*, further cranks the suspense with a constant stream of world and character riddles: an island with conflicting histories; a cold-blooded schoolmistress warmed by a passionate heart; a cautious captain who's up for anything.

If Christie is a little traditional for your taste, try a modern thriller like Gillian Flynn's *Gone Girl*. Or if you'd prefer to get your thrills from non-fiction, try the opening prophecy of Truman Capote's 1966 *In Cold Blood*:

> At the time not a soul in sleeping Holcomb heard them—four shotgun blasts that, all told, ended six human lives. But afterward the townspeople, theretofore sufficiently unfearful of each other to seldom trouble to lock their doors, found fantasy recreating them over and again—those somber explosions that stimulated fires of mistrust in the glare of which many old neighbors viewed each other strangely, and as strangers.

Or turn on the group divination of the 1983 docudrama *The Right Stuff*, based on Tom Wolfe's best-selling book about the 1950s US military test pilots competing to be Mercury astronauts:

> There was a demon that lived in the air. They said whoever challenged him would die.

Or dip into the romantically intimate voice from the future of Frances Burney's 1768 *The Early Diary*:

> O my dear—such a charming day! And then last night—well, you shall have it all in order—as well as I can recollect.

Or for a double-oracular experience, try Lytton Strachey's 1918 biographical innovation *Eminent Victorians*, which blends tomorrow voice and riddle characters ("alike in their emphasis and their lack of emphasis, in their eccentricity and their conventionality, in their matter-of-factness and their romance") with the tragic irony-gaze of Tiresias and the Weird Sisters: "His fate was mingled with the frenzies of Empire and the doom of peoples. And it was not in peace and rest, but in ruin and horror, that he reached his end."

Whatever genre piques your interest, you can quickly identify a thriller by its beginning. Does the storyteller talk from the future? Does she offer glimpses of the hours ahead?

If so, she's drunk the vapor from the mountain.

And she has seen your secret time to come.

SIX

Free Your Mind

Dante's Inferno, *Machiavelli's* Innovatori,
and the Invention of the Vigilance Trigger

In July 1513, on a drafty old farm amidst Tuscan sunflower fields, a new computing engine was machined into being. At the time, the engine was too unprecedented a thing to be named. But eventually language would catch up, and the futuristic contraption would be christened with a fluid phrase: *la mente moderna*—"the modern mind."

Its machinist was Niccolò Machiavelli. He'd been born in 1469 inside an overstuffed timber dwelling two blocks southwest of the graceful stone arches of Florence's Ponte Vecchio. And he'd devoted his life to those arches and the rest of his city, serving as a Florentine scribe, diplomat, and militia commander until, as a forty-four-year-old man, he'd been hauled from his quarters, rope tortured, and sentenced to exile by Italy's most powerful clan: the House of Medici. According to the Medici, Machiavelli's crime had been "a conspiracy" to promote revolution. And as much as Machiavelli protested his innocence, his activities in exile suggested that his accusers had smelled out the truth. For although there was no one left amid the sunflowers for Machiavelli to conspire with, he dipped his solitary quill into a pot of iron ink and unleashed revolution with a word: *innovatori*.

Innovatori meant "innovators." The term was, by itself, nothing new. It had existed for centuries in Italian, and for many centuries before that in Latin. But when its ten letters fell from Machiavelli's pen, they became radically unprecedented. In the past, they'd been an accusation. To be an innovator was to be a usurper, a blasphemer, a soul against God. Lucifer had innovated when he'd challenged the hierarchy of heaven; Eve had innovated when she'd eaten the apple in Eden. These novel acts had perverted the perfect work of the Almighty. Their fresh perspectives had quite literally engineered hell.

Machiavelli took a less moral, more pragmatic view of original thinking. His time in Florentine politics and war had taught him that the world was ever shifting. No empire stayed constant; all life pitched in flux. So, to keep above the rolling tides, we had to adapt, to experiment, to improvise, creating new laws, new technologies, new ways of surviving. It was innovate—or perish.

Machiavelli's embrace of innovation no longer seems rebellious today. In fact, it feels banal. We've long ago been convinced by the modern minds of scientists, historians, and business gurus that our lot is turnover incessant. Nothing now is as it was; nothing here will in the future be. But back in the sixteenth century, Machiavelli's celebration of the *innovatori* was so unconventional that he was deemed to be "an enemy of the human race," an atheist, a Satanist, and even the Antichrist. His writings were condemned as heretical by Pope Paul IV in 1559 and were formally blacklisted by the Catholic Church's *Tridentine Index* in 1564.

What prompted Machiavelli to break so radically with the faith of his contemporaries? What encouraged him to flip received wisdom on its head? What drove him to join the ranks of the *innovatori* himself?

Machiavelli's original thinking had many sources. But none was fonder in his heart than the poetry of another exiled Florentine: Dante Alighieri. Two centuries before Machiavelli, Dante had also been forced out of the four-rivered city by a powerful clan, the Black Guelphs. And in his subsequent wanderings, he'd pulled off a remarkable feat of guerilla engineering: he'd camouflaged a mind-liberating invention within an epic poem of such seeming orthodoxy that it was welcomed into the most hidebound libraries.

Inspiring many a Machiavelli to follow Eve . . . and bite the apple to think free.

The Orthodox Literature of Eden

For Dante's guerilla feat to succeed, it had to be disguised in a literary style that aroused no suspicion from Europe's highest authority, the Catholic Church. So, for that literary style, Dante selected allegory.

Allegory is an old Greek synonym for "speaking other," and it operates as a kind of literary code where one thing covertly represents another. Here's a sample of the code, plucked by Dante himself from the ancient Latin epic, Ovid's *Metamorphoses*: "Orpheus used his lyre to tame wild beasts and to move plants and stones."

And here's how Dante cracked the code:

> Orpheus represents the wise man, and his lyre represents the wise man's voice, which he employs to soften the hearts of people who are cruel like "beasts" and to charm people whose "plant" minds are too vegetable to have learned anything—even those with the brains of "stones" he moves.

Allegories like this were embraced by the medieval Church because they produced wonder. Wonder comes from the literary invention known as the *stretch*. (See the introduction.) And you can feel that invention in Dante's decoding, which *stretches* a simple tale about the poet Orpheus into a grand parable about Wisdom Almighty.

This *stretch*-induced feeling of awe activates our brain's spiritual zones, enriching our consciousness with the sensation of meanings beyond. So, to keep those meanings brimming through our consciousness, the medieval Church embroidered allegory into everything it did. Every ritual of Sunday mass, every tassel of the priestly robes, every architectural detail of the altar chancel—all of it represented something *more*.

And allegory didn't just help the Church empower itself. It also helped the Church de-power its rivals, one of which was pagan literature. Pagan literature had long challenged the Church's moral commandments with its alternate lifestyle of martial courage, amorous love, and Socratic elevation. (For their blueprints, see chapters 1, 2, and 4, respectively.) To tamp down on the most dangerous of these heathen feelings, the Church resorted here and there to censorship edicts such as the *Tridentine Index*. But in most cases, the Church found that allegory could do better than silence pagan authors: it could steal their voices.

To effect the theft, monkish scholiasts took pagan stories about Apollo, Oedipus, or the Trojan War and attached allegorical glosses like: *The moral is, hubris is a deadly sin!* These glosses were a literal "speaking other" that retrofitted unchristian mouths with churchly tongues. And to make the retrofitting even more effective, scholiasts occasionally went the additional step of surgically inserting allegorical glosses into the very body of the story itself, leaving suture work that we can still detect in Anglo-Saxon England's most famous poem: the epic *Beowulf*.

Beowulf is set in sixth-century Scandinavia, where its titular hero aids a Danish king by killing monsters. To inspire us to similar heroics, *Beowulf*'s narrative is engineered, like the *Iliad* and its other epic forerunners, to warm our brain with courage. (See chapter 1 for the blueprint.) But sometime after the Christianization of England in the seventh century, *Beowulf* was amended to include a Catholic sermon that warns of the danger of *oferhygd*. The word *oferhygd* means "hubris" or "pridefulness," and although it sounds authentically Anglo-Saxon, it was really hammered together by churchly linguists. Prior to those linguists, pride had been viewed by the Anglo-Saxons as a healthy component of a warrior's identity (for reasons we'll explore in chapter 10). Not so in the spliced-in sermon, which runs:

O much-loved Beowulf, do not give into hubristic *oferhygd*! Do not surrender to pride! Now you are strong—but soon, you will grow feeble and die. So, turn your eyes to the Almighty!

With this inserted gloss, a proud monster killer was turned into a humble Christ worshipper, transubstantiating the old poetic blueprint for pagan valor into a font of Christian reverence.

The Church's allegorical method of modifying pagan fables was well known to Dante. Prior to his days of banishment, he'd used it himself to *stretch* the military conquests, necromantic witchcrafts, and beast mythologies of Virgil's *The Aeneid*, Lucan's *Pharsalia*, and Statius's *Thebaid* into pious Christian homilies. And through such reengineerings, Dante learned the technology of allegory thoroughly. So thoroughly that he saw how to reverse its circuitry.

Dante's Reverse of Allegory

Sometime around 1308, while hiding in exile amid the shadows of northern Italy, Dante wrote *The Inferno*. Like *Beowulf*, Dante's *Inferno* is an epic poem. But its structure is inverted. Where *Beowulf* intersperses Christian allegory into pagan myth, *The Inferno* intersperses pagan myth into Christian allegory.

The Inferno's Christian allegory begins when the poem ushers us to a gate that declares, "Justice built me." Through the gate, we then discover the nine circles of hell, each of which takes the justice blueprint of the biblical book of Exodus—"If there is harm, you are to take a life for a life, an eye for an eye"—and *stretches* it into original eye-for-an-eye punishments. So, in the first circle of Dante's hell, souls who shuttered God's light on earth are now condemned to a shuttered eternity of shadow. Then in the second circle, souls who tossed the world with violent lust are now tossed themselves by perpetual buffets. And so on through hell's other circles, each new punishment elaborating justice with fresh twists that fill our brain with religious wonder ever deeper—until abruptly, the allegory cracks apart. And through the crack, we see a burning wall where three monsters open bloody jaws to shriek: "Turn this intruder into stone, O Medusa!"

Medusa is not a creation of the biblical deity who built hell's fiery circles; her name exists nowhere in the book of Exodus or the Church's other holy scriptures. Instead, as Dante had discovered through his youthful perusals of Ovid's *Metamorphoses*, she was a heathen priestess subjected to a gross miscarriage of justice: after she'd been sexually assaulted by the sea god, Poseidon, she was victim-blamed by Athena and turned into a serpent-haired gorgon.

So, what is this unchristian fiction doing inside the Christian afterlife? How has an embodiment of pagan unfairness intruded into God's grand eschatology of justice? *The Inferno* doesn't say. Instead, it dishes out more glimpses of heathen creatures: a Minotaur who chews his flesh amid the ruined wall of hell's seventh circle, a gang of centaurs who patrol the infernal blood river of Phlegethon, and a mob of shit-feathered harpies who feed on thorns inside the Wood of Suicides—interrupting our religious wonder with a very odd feeling.

That Odd Feeling and Its Neuroscience

To our brain, an object can stick out in two different ways. First, the object can be a familiar thing that sticks out in a strange environment. Second, the object can be the opposite: a strange thing that sticks out in a familiar environment.

The first kind of sticking-out object is a reminder of the things of home. So, it makes our brain feel like home has *stretched* to reach us in a foreign terrain, stimulating a neural burst of wonder.

This is the feeling generated by the Christian revision of *Beowulf*. In the revision, we're wandering through the faraway realms of sixth-century Scandinavia, when we catch an allegorical hint of the religion of our native soil, imbuing our brain with the awe-inspiring revelation *Your faith extends everywhere*. (Or, at least, this is what our brain would experience if we hailed from medieval Christendom. If you'd like an updated version of the same *stretch* effect, try Madeleine L'Engle's 1962 young adult novel *A Wrinkle in Time*.)

The second kind of sticking-out thing—a *strange* object in familiar surroundings—generates a very different emotion: paranoia.

Paranoia originates in one of our brain's most ancient components: the threat-detection network. This network evolved hundreds of millions of years ago, back before we were human, mammalian, or even reptilian. It came to be when we were jawless fishes swimming in primordial seas. Those seas were full of dangers, so whenever something moved in our immediate vicinity, our threat-detection network shouted out a warning: *Beware! Beware! Beware!*

When we left the primordial seas, we carried along our threat-detection network. But the network's original circuitry wasn't enough to safeguard us in our new environment, which presented a more sophisticated kind of threat: one that could sit still. That threat waited quietly until we turned our back. Then it slipped up ever so slowly, opening its jaws . . .

To protect us from such ambushes, our threat-detection network gradually evolved more sophisticated mental machinery that begins working when the dynamic "habitat map" inside our brain's parietal lobe becomes aware of a strange sticking-out object. Maybe the object is a shadow where we'd expect light. Maybe it's a light where we'd expect shadow. Whatever the object is, it doesn't fit the usual pattern of our surroundings, so it suggests that something around us might have moved. And if something has moved, well, then something could move again, leaping upon us the moment we relax.

To guard against that possibility, our mental habitat map rouses our vigilance by flooding our consciousness with a feeling of paranoia. Paranoia is the suspicion that something is lurking where our eyes can't quite see. And the more that our brain becomes convinced of the lurking, the more that our paranoia deepens: *Beware! Beware! Beware!*

As our brain has evolved, that *Beware!* has evolved too. Now it can be triggered by the subtlest environmental irregularities: a smile that isn't quite right, a sales pitch too perfect—or a Medusa in hell.

The Paranoid Feeling of *The Inferno*

Dante had never heard of the brain's threat-detection network. But he knew exactly what he was doing when he inserted Medusa into hell. Just before Dante composed *The Inferno*, he remarked in his educational encyclopedia *Convivio*: "The churchmen use allegory differently than the poets—and it's my intention to follow the poets."

According to Dante, this difference between churchmen and poets isn't a minor one. In fact, the difference is that churchmen and poets use allegory in precisely the opposite way. Churchmen use allegory to *reveal* a hidden truth; poets use allegory to *conceal* a hidden truth. So, where the allegories of the Church create the wonder of revelation, the allegories of poetry generate the sensation of something lurking beneath the surface. Which is to say: they stir up paranoia.

This paranoia is what we experience when we see Medusa in Dante's *Inferno*. Medusa is a thing out of place; an alien creature in a familiar Christian cosmos. So, she triggers our threat-detection network, making us wonder: *Why is there a pagan myth in hell? Is Dante trying to slip us a hidden message? Or is Medusa a trap? Has she been sent, like Satan, to tempt us away from the truth, distracting our eyes with heathen distortions?*

And Medusa and her fellow Greek and Roman legends aren't the only entities in *The Inferno* that activate our threat-detection network. Throughout Dante's poem, we're followed everywhere by an even more discomfiting lurker: Virgil.

Virgil is our infernal tour guide. But he's a strange sort of guide. He's not an angel or a pious Catholic. He's the author of a pagan poem, *The Aeneid*, that's earned him a place in Dante's netherworld. So, are we meant to trust Virgil? Or not? If we listen to his guidance, will we navigate our way from hell? Or will we end up with Virgil, outcast from God for all eternity?

It's enough to make us paranoid about the whole excursion. And Virgil does nothing to alleviate our concerns. He explains that he's been picked as our escort because of his *parola ornata*, or "stylish speech," triggering our threat-detection system to remind us that stylish speakers aren't the same as *truthful* speakers. They can seduce our wits with elegant fictions, like the doublespeak that Virgil uses right in front of us to dupe hell's denizens.

So, is Virgil duping us as well? Is he using his mastery of language to steer us wayward? Are we meant to believe him when he warns us not to pity the tormented souls in hell? Or is his *parola ornata* chasing us away from Christian mercy?

The Inferno supplies no answers. Instead, it heightens our paranoia with a voice from nowhere:

> O you of sound minds,
> seek the doctrine that is hidden
> beneath the veil of verses strange.

Why is *The Inferno* doing this to us? Why is it creeping our brain with flickers of the "strange"? Why is it confessing that there's a "hidden" secret but not disclosing what the secret is?

Let me offer an explanation in my own stylish speech: *The Inferno* hints at a secret it never divulges because Dante believed that the secret was less important than the *looking* for the secret. As he'd later write to Cangrande della Scala, the infamous "dog-lord" of Verona: "My poem is an allegory about how we, through our own free choice, are punished or rewarded by Justice."

This sounds like a gloss that a medieval monk might append to a pagan myth: "The following fiction is a representation of justice." But now that our mind has been woken by Dante's poem, we can see that the crucial word in his gloss isn't *justice*. It's *free*. Our free choice is what determines whether we are "punished" or "rewarded," earning us the high light of heaven—or the dark fires below.

Which is why *The Inferno* has set our mind free. By giving us a Medusa in hell, a slick-speaking tour guide, and an eerie warning of secrets, the poem has triggered our paranoid vigilance, shaking us out of our old mental torpor and liberating us to think for ourselves.

Maybe that freethinking will confirm the orthodox pathways of the Church. Or maybe it will nudge us down some heretical road. Either way, it's our only hope for salvation.

It's our only chance out of hell.

Using the "Vigilance Trigger" Yourself

In 1513, the same year that Machiavelli celebrated the *innovatori* in the scandalous sixth chapter of his political treatise *The Prince* . . .

> Among the world's foremost innovators are Moses, the founding prince of Israel; and Cyrus the Great, the founding prince of Persia; and Romulus, the founding prince of Rome; and Theseus, the founding prince of Athens.

. . . he also penned a quiet letter to a friend:

> I'm living on my farm, hunting sparrows with bird-lime. Each morning, I go for an hour or two to a lumber grove. Then I visit

a brook for bit, before heading off to hang up my bird nets. In my pocket, I carry Dante's *Comedy*.

Dante's *Comedy* was *The Inferno* and its two sequels, *Purgatorio* and *Paradiso*.

By the time that Machiavelli wrote his letter, Dante's *Comedy* was already considered a classic in his hometown of Florence. And over the following centuries, its fame was spread ever further by the Catholic authorities. Those authorities accepted the fundamental orthodoxy of Dante's *Comedy*, going so far as to bless it with a new title: *The Divine Comedy*. And the Church then carried the poem across countries and continents, eventually transporting Dante's paranoia-inducing invention into the hands of Geoffrey Chaucer, Marko Marulić, Martin Luther, Galileo Galilei, Xu Guangqi, Francis Bacon, John Milton, Giambattista Vico, Elizabeth Inchbald, William Blake, Honoré de Balzac, Karl Marx, George Santayana, Jules Verne, F. Scott Fitzgerald, E. M. Forster, Jorge Luis Borges, Cahit Sıtkı Tarancı, Samuel Beckett, Primo Levi, John Kennedy Toole, Giannina Braschi, and countless authors more.

So, if you're not getting enough freethinking from Dante's verses, there are plenty of later works of world literature that have been influenced by his invention. You can find allegories with unfamiliar stick-outs in nineteenth-century fictions such as Nathanial Hawthorne's *The Scarlet Letter* and Charlotte Perkins Gilman's *The Yellow Wallpaper*: "There is a recurrent spot where the pattern lolls like a broken neck and two bulbous eyes stare at you upside down."

And you can find the same basic blueprint in twentieth-century literary unsettlers such as Franz Kafka's *The Trial*, Ken Kesey's *One Flew over the Cuckoo's Nest*, William S. Burroughs's *Naked Lunch*, Philip K. Dick's *Ubik*, Octavia Butler's "Bloodchild," and Amitav Ghosh's *The Calcutta Chromosome*.

Thousands of these mental liberators are waiting in your library right now. And the one you're wanting won't be hard to spot. It'll be the book that juts out from the shelf.

It'll be the myth that doesn't fit.

SEVEN

Jettison Your Pessimism

Giovanni Straparola, the Original Cinderella,
and the Invention of the Fairy-tale Twist

Charles Perrault had been promised a cure for his terrible pessimism. The promise had been made by his niece after she'd swept into his shuttered lodgings and ordered him to don his finest breeches and most immoderate wig, the one he'd worn eons ago to impress King Louis XIV at the Palace of Versailles. The wig had gone brittle with age, and the breeches now sagged across Perrault's underfed waist. But with a sigh, he obeyed his niece's instructions. It was useless to quarrel with her youthful fancies, and perhaps, Perrault reflected as he peered at himself in his rusted mirror, those fancies contained a sliver of wisdom. The outfit, threadbare as it was, had stirred up some of his old optimism: he'd once shone for the Sun King; perhaps he could bedazzle again.

And as it turned out, this change of couture was merely the start of his niece's grand cure. She bundled Perrault into a four-wheeled fiacre pulled by white horses, and off they trotted across seventeenth-century Paris, past cabaret gardens and midsummer fireworks, all the way to the city's enchanted heart. There, in the Rue de Richelieu, Perrault was whirled through a regal gate into a hidden room of gold-leaf clocks and Turkish carpets . . . where, with a pop of light, a mouse-eyed woman floated down, introducing herself as "an escaped princess."

Perrault was now beginning to think that he'd entered a dream. But it was all very real. The escaped princess was Angelique-Nicole Tiquet, renowned about Paris for rebuffing her husband when he'd come to jail her in a closet. And the hidden room was the Tuesday salon of forty-six-year-old Madame de Lambert, a vivaciously open-minded marquise who'd read the great literary classics—and pronounced them tedious. In December 1692 the marquise had established the salon to encourage more exciting new stories. And just now, gliding through the curtained door, was one of the marquise's avant-garde authors. She had a cheerfully plump face and flamingo-pink slippers, and, seating herself on a platinum armchair, she pulled out a manuscript draft of her newest creation: *The Tale of Graciosa and Percinet.*

This, Perrault realized, was the cure his niece had promised. And at the realization, his heart began to sink. Perrault had been imagining a more plausible remedy for pessimism, such as a long-lost Persian elixir, or an immortal Paduan doctor, or a strange-smelling herb from goodness knows where. And Perrault's heart descended further when the pink-slippered author began to read aloud. Her tale involved a princess, a wicked stepmother, and a bewildering number of coincidences. It was, in short, a ramble of nonsense, and Perrault was by now ruing his decision to dust off his wig. He'd allowed himself to get his hopes up, and that was always a mistake. Hoping inevitably led to disappointment; dawn was the most dangerous time of the day.

But then the pink-slippered author reached her final phrase: *"un parfait bonheur"*—"happily-ever-after." And as that phrase sparkled through the air, Perrault experienced an unexpected heart lift. For the first time since he'd lost his place at court to a younger man, for the first time since his beloved wife had died over fifteen years ago, he felt that tomorrow would be better than today.

It was an extraordinary feeling—but could it be trusted? No, Perrault decided. Whatever the pink-slippered author had done, it was certain to be a fleeting trick. So, Perrault curled up on a sofa, clutching a velvet cushion and bracing for the gloom bug to return. Yet wondrously, the bug kept its distance, and the extraordinary feeling persisted. The cure had worked, just as Perrault's niece had promised.

Daring at last to believe, Perrault bounced up from the sofa, joining the queue to thank the author. Who was she? And what was her miracle cure? The author laughed. She was the retired spy, Baroness

Marie-Catherine d'Aulnoy. And her miracle cure was . . . well, there were many names for it, but the one that she preferred was: *conte de fée*—"fairy tale."

Perrault swiftly hailed a white-horse carriage to carry him home. Now that his pessimism was gone, dreams were abloom in his head. He would spread the cure to other suffering souls. He would become famous. He would become rich. So, he grabbed a quill and crafted his own triad of fairy tales. And as he crafted them, he made a careful change to Baroness d'Aulnoy's original formula, one that he felt sure would increase its pharmacological kick.

Perrault's own fairy tale seemed to work out just as he'd dreamed. His writings became instantly renowned, and a few years later, in 1697, he secured his lasting reputation by penning *Sleeping Beauty*, *Puss in Boots*, and *Cinderella*. Over the following centuries, those tales were translated into more than a hundred languages, until, in Perrault's triumphal achievement, *Cinderella* was made into a 1950 Disney animated classic. It rescued Walt Disney Productions from bankruptcy and became the logo for the Magic Kingdom, blessing billions of hearts with the uplift that Perrault had felt in the Tuesday salon.

And yet, something wasn't quite right about it all. Gradually, people started to discover: there was a thorn concealed in Perrault's rosy cure.

The Thorn in the Cure

The thorn in *Cinderella* is this: the film inspires optimistic hopes, but in many of us, the hopes are short lived. And when those hopes fade, we're left feeling more dejected than before.

Ever since *Cinderella*'s Hollywood premiere, its thorn has been blamed on the film's patent lack of realism. Hollywood reviewers criticized Disney's "doll-faced" princess, the Soviet Union issued a proclamation condemning the production as a capitalist fantasy, and *The Atlanta Constitution* pointed out that stepsisters were not, in fact, universally big-footed and cruel. So, as a remedy, post-1950 storytellers have rewritten Perrault's tale with more real-to-life characters, darker storylines, and greater moral ambiguity, spinning modern *Cinderellas* such as *Into the Woods*, *Cinder*, and *Confessions of an Ugly Stepsister*.

These disenchanted fairy tales have accomplished their aim of making us hate ourselves less for not being Disney princesses. Yet unfortunately, their method for countering the down of a *Cinderella* hangover hasn't restored the up of the Tuesday salon. Instead, it has carried us even further away from Baroness d'Aulnoy's cure. That cure didn't come from realism, after all. It came from optimism, which is to say, from focusing less on grim truths and more on sunny possibilities. So, to get back the baroness's cure, let's reverse course from Disney's modern critics. Let's go back to Perrault and see what he changed.

And then let's undo his change, recovering the original fairy-tale lift.

Perrault's Change—and What Came Before

Perrault made no effort to cover his tracks. In the title of his fairy-tale collection *Tales of Times Past, with Morals*, he cheerfully announced that he'd altered *Cinderella* by tacking on this wholesome new moral:

A woman's beauty is a rare treasure, but even richer in value is courtesy. "Courtesy" comes from "court"—it's a royal word, and it made Cinderella a queen. So, take heed! If you wish to win a prince's heart, courtesy is more vital than elegant hair. It's the true gift of the Fairies. With it, you can accomplish anything.

The specific moral here is: Queenly behavior begets queens—so act courteously and you'll find yourself at court. And the broader moral is: In life, we get our just deserts. Which is to say: poetic justice.

Perrault dispensed this fairy-tale lesson with the best intentions. He was a child of the Enlightenment, which traditionally dated its own birth to mid-seventeenth-century philosophes such as René Descartes. Those philosophes had deduced the importance of reason, and reason had then itself gone on to deduce many more truths, including a proof of the benefits of poetic justice: "Like begets like, so bad begets bad and good begets good." Or in other words: "Good things happen to good people, and stories about those good things will create good readers."

But as rational as all this seemed, modern neuroscience has discovered that there's an occasion when poetic justice is *not* so good for us: any time that we're feeling down. On such an occasion, the logic of "good begets good and bad begets bad" leads our brain to think:

> *Since my efforts have come to no good, then I must be no good. I'm the failure who begot my own failure. And if I'm a failure, then I'll keep failing forever.*

This is "catastrophizing." It follows the same like-begets-like logic as Enlightenment reason, so it's a common neural side effect of fairy tales like Perrault's *Cinderella*. We turn to these fairy tales because our lives aren't perfect, and we want an emotional lift. But when the fairy tales whisper, "People get what they deserve," our brain starts to worry: *Maybe I'm unhappy because I deserve to be unhappy. Maybe I'm the opposite of Cinderella.*

Such catastrophizing self-judgment has been linked with pessimism, anxiety, and depression. And it's only the start of the problem with Perrault's morals. That's because Perrault's morals don't just add something harmful to the old fairy tales. They also remove something healthy: Baroness d'Aulnoy's special ingredient for giving us hope.

What is that special ingredient? And how does it work differently from poetic justice? We can't get the story from Baroness d'Aulnoy; like a true spy, she never betrayed her secrets. But we can start to unravel the mystery by consulting another of the Tuesday salon's members: the Countess Henriette-Julie de Murat.

The countess was a free-loving cross-dresser who debuted her own fairy-tale collection in 1699. And in the collection's *Advertisement*, she defended herself against the accusation that she'd plagiarized from Baroness d'Aulnoy by revealing that they'd both plagiarized from somebody else:

> I must warn the reader that I took the ideas for some of these tales from an old book, *The Playful Nights* of Seigneur Straparola, printed for the sixteenth time in 1615. But Baroness d'Aulnoy also borrowed from that old book. So, even though she and I tell a few of the same tales, I never stole from her. We both stole from Seigneur Straparola. And why shouldn't we steal? To have been

printed so many times, *The Playful Nights* must have been very popular.

Who was this Seigneur Straparola? And what exactly did Baroness d'Aulnoy and the other Tuesday salonists steal from his book *The Playful Nights?* To see, let's turn back another chapter into history.

The Mysterious Seigneur Straparola

In 1553 Giovanni Francesco Straparola was nearing the end of his life. And truth be told, it hadn't been the most successful life. As a bright-eyed young man, Straparola had published a poetry folio that had been forgotten immediately. And for the remaining fifty years of his existence, he'd toiled away in utter obscurity. Perhaps he'd been a courtier, a concierge, or a clerk. Whatever he spent his life doing, those labors proved so unmemorable that all their traces have since been swallowed up.

And at the same time that Straparola was being engulfed by nothingness, so too was the historical era around him. That era was the Italian Renaissance, or, as it was then known, the Rinascita. In the fourteenth and fifteenth centuries, the Rinascita had burst forth with buoyant light, dispelling the "dark" ages with the love songs of Petrarch, the metalworks of Donatello, and the vanishing-point portraits of Masaccio. And for the next century or so, the possibilities for Italy's future seemed limitless: Leonardo da Vinci painted the Mona Lisa's infectious smile; Michelangelo frescoed the Sistine Chapel with a sky of bluest blue.

But during Straparola's final years, that blue-sky hope evaporated. French cannonballs battered the five castles of Naples. Swiss mercenaries overran the walled groves of Milan. Spanish cavalry trampled the prized vineyards of Venice. Gallic archers used da Vinci's masterpieces for target practice. Rome was sacked. Turin was captured. Florence was besieged. By the winter of 1553, Italy was bleak with despair. The Rinascita was over. Snow and dusk were everywhere.

And then, just when it seemed like Italy's past hopes were doomed to vanish in a fugue of gloom, Straparola emerged from his oblivion with a remedy. That remedy began, like so many Renaissance creations, with an ancient literary model. But the model wasn't any of the high classics that the Tuesday salons would later deem to be dullness. No, the model was the riotous stage entertainment known as comedy.

Comedy had been invented in fifth-century-BCE Athens and innovated over the next three hundred years by a succession of Greek and Roman authors—Menander, Plautus, Terence—who'd lifted audiences' spirits with slapsticks, puns, burlesques, witticisms, dreams, schemes, reconciliations, jokes, and many other ingenious literary inventions. But among this vast catalogue of merriment boosters, one in particular excited Straparola's interest: the happy ending. The happy ending was a cheerful affair that gave audiences hope, so to learn how to maximize that hope, Straparola perused piles of worm-eaten old comedy scripts. Until, at last, he had a great epiphany: the secret to the happiest of happy endings was the "Lucky Twist."

The Lucky Twist was an arbitrary breaking of the laws of reason, a random swerve into good fortune that shattered all logic, bringing to pass the most unlikely joy. In fact, so wildly improbable was the Lucky Twist that even its own birth had been an upside-down affair. By all rules of common sense, the Lucky Twist would have been invented by the authors of comedy. Yet it wasn't. It was invented by the authors of tragedy.

Tragedy seemed destined, by definition, to end tragically. But some ancient Greek tragedies, such as Aeschylus's *Eumenides* and Euripides's *Orestes*, concluded instead with a plot swerve where a god intervened to make things happy. This divine intervention was later dubbed the deus ex machina, or "god from the machine," in honor of the mechanical pully that swung down an actor in a god mask to arbitrarily upend the story. And sometime in the fourth century BCE, the authors of comedy reengineered the god to provide even more arbitrariness. Where the god in tragedy had been a serious Olympian who enforced cosmic rules of harmony, the god in comedy became a deity of luck who randomly overturned reason with joy. At the end of Menander's *Aspis*, the goddess Chance appears and—*poof!*—a funeral is flipped whimsically into a wedding. At the end of Plautus's *Aulularia*, a puckish spirit waves his wand and—*presto!*—a tight-fisted scrooge blesses a marriage with a potful of gold.

These Lucky Twists are the opposite of poetic justice. They don't logically beget good from good; they arbitrarily beget good from bad. And although the begetting was lambasted by many an ancient theater critic as vapid escapism, modern neuroscientists have discovered that it can do something genuinely healthy for us: it can energize our inner optimist.

The Science of Our Inner Optimist

We all have an inner optimist.

Even if we can't remember our last hopeful thought, that optimist is sitting in our head right now. And it's no lightweight, either. It's a great, big chunk of gray matter. It is: the entire left side of our brain.

Yes, weirdly and wonderfully, our brain's left hemisphere is more optimistic than the right. The first hints of this strange fact were unearthed in the nineteenth century when the European physicians Pierre Paul Broca and Carl Wernicke discovered that our brain's two hemispheres divvy up different tasks between them. This phenomenon became known as lateralization, and in the late twentieth century, it gave rise to the fantastical myth that our left brain was more logical and our right brain more creative. Accountants declared themselves "left brained," while in Southern California, an art teacher by the name of Betty Edwards penned a 1979 best seller that claimed we could boost our creativity by "drawing on the right side of our brain."

This myth has long since been debunked. But twenty-first-century neuroscience has shown that there are nevertheless important differences between our right brain and our left. The differences keep our brain halves from duplicating functions or warring with each other. And one of the more remarkable differences is that the two sides of our brain evaluate risk oppositely. This divergence in risk assessment has been measured by a bevy of peculiar experiments: neuroscientists have muffled our right ear and piped threats to our left; they've interviewed hypochondriacs to see which side of the body contains the most imaginary pains; they've applied magnetic jolts to the heads of pessimists. And from these experiments, neuroscientists have learned that our right brain is more tightly connected to our sympathetic nervous system (which triggers our fearful fight-or-flight response) and that our left brain is more tightly connected to our parasympathetic nervous system (which calms us down). Or in other words: our right brain tends to concentrate more on what could go wrong, while our left tends to concentrate more on what could go right.

This division of labor allows our brain to focus concurrently on perils and possibilities, so that instead of giving the edge to the dark side of life or the bright, we can balance the two, being simultaneously cautious and forward seeking. And it means that no matter how pessimistic we might feel right now, our brain is actually half empty of pessimism—and half full of optimism. To access that optimism, all we need to do is shift our brain's perspective, tilting our head a few degrees so that our left hemisphere comes out on top.

There are several laboratory-approved ways to get that tilt, including magnetic jolts to the right side of our skull. But if you'd prefer a less violent, more enduring, and equally scientific boost, then you can get it by reminding yourself about luck. As modern psychologists such as Martin Seligman have discovered, luck is one of our left brain's preferred explanations for failure: *I got unlucky that time; it just wasn't my day. But maybe tomorrow my fortunes will turn.*

This left-brain emphasis on chance makes us more resilient: by encouraging us to view our struggles as temporary setbacks, it empowers us to forge on till our luck improves. And it also makes us happier: by attuning us to the randomness of life, it stops us from feeling entitled to the positive things we've already got. Instead, it encourages us to feel fortunate to have those positive things, boosting our gratitude (a life-improving feeling we'll explore more in chapter 15). So, even if our hopes don't all pan out, a little reminder of luck can still increase our life satisfaction. It's wishful thinking that doubles as a self-fulfilling prophecy.

All these psychic benefits are conveyed by the Lucky Twist. The Twist short-circuits the rational thinking that leads our brain to catastrophize, nudging us to think instead: *Sure, it's logical for bad times to come from bad. But life isn't always logical. Good fortune could fall right now from the sky.*

And although this literary source of optimism was condemned in the Middle Ages by Christian and Islamic philosophers who saw luck as a blasphemous challenge to God's omnipotence, it was revived again during the Italian Rinascita. In 1509 Ludovico Ariosto cheered the downcast of Ferrara with a comic caper, *I Suppositi*, where fortune randomly veered disaster into festivity. In 1543 Giambattista Gelli uplifted Florence with an adaptation of Plautus's classic luck extravaganza *Aulularia*. In 1548 the Paduan grammarian Francesco Robortello, legendary across Italy as the "syntactical dog," barked that it was the very nature of comedy to "bring unexpected joys from twists of fortune."

This resurrection of the Lucky Twist hoisted Straparola's spirits. And in the glum winter of 1553, it made him think: *What if I could amplify the Twist? What if I could make it bigger and more uplifting, heightening the dose of hope?*

It was an optimistic thought. So, of course, Straparola's left brain told him to give it a go.

The More Uplifting Twist

Straparola saw two ways to increase the emotional uplift of the Twist.

First, he could enlarge the good luck bestowed by the Twist. In traditional comedies, that good luck took the form of a wedding and a splash of gold. So, Straparola could expand the good luck into a *royal* wedding with *endless* gold, amplifying a happy ending into a happily-ever-after.

Second, he could make his royal bride imperfect and even incompetent. That way, her fairy-tale success would suggest to our brain: *It was happenstance, not virtue, that made her a princess. It was a blind chance that could befall anyone.*

With these two innovations in mind, Straparola sat down at his desk and composed a fairy tale titled *Adamantina and the Doll*. The fairy tale begins with two hungry girls: Adamantina and her older sister. Desperate for food, the older sister dispatches Adamantina to the market. But Adamantina doesn't heed her sister's shopping list: bread, eggs, milk. Instead, she becomes enamored by a frivolous doll. And foolishly, she buys it.

When Adamantina returns home with the doll, her sister is dismayed. Now the two of them will starve. But in a stunning Twist, the doll randomly turns out to be a *magic* doll that spits out geysers of coins, making Adamantina and her sister instantly rich. This is a remarkable bit of blind luck, and, even more remarkably, Adamantina's blind luck continues. Her magic doll is stolen, tossed into a cart, and dumped in a refuse field. And who should chance to stroll through that refuse field? Why, an unmarried king, of course! Immediately, the doll attaches its incisors to the king's rear, and when the alarmed monarch finds himself unable to unclamp the doll, he appeals in desperation to the public: "Who will rid me of this troublesome doll?" The call is promptly answered by Adamantina, who coaxes the doll to release the king and go back to belching up gold. Ecstatic, the king marries Adamantina, certain that she'll enrich his kingdom with torrents of loot—and forever protect his backside from magical teeth.

This is the Lucky Twist amplified into the "Fairy-tale Twist." Adamantina is an anti-Cinderella who enjoys a happily-ever-after due not to merit but to chance. So, her tale dispenses a neural hope refresher that's free of *Cinderella* aftertaste, fortifying the hopeful spirit of our left brain without launching the boomerang self-judgment of our right.

Straparola published *Adamantina and the Doll* in his 1553 anthology collection, *The Playful Nights*. And a century and a half later, his invention was rediscovered by Baroness d'Aulnoy. The baroness was guilty as charged of pirating Straparola's plots. And more importantly, she was guilty of pirating Straparola's broader plot technique of engineering fairy-tale endings out of arbitrary happenings. The baroness's arbitrary happenings aren't quite as arbitrary as the ones in *The Playful Nights*; she regarded herself and her friends as royalty, so she bestowed her happily-ever-afters only on princesses, not on regular folk. But still, those happily-ever-afters involve astonishingly random Twists.

In the case of *Graciosa and Percinet*, a princess has just been seized by a terrible stepmother—when, in a wild narrative veer, she's rescued by a previously unannounced fairy prince: "My princess! I am yours and will be yours always!" The princess is baffled, and so are we. Who is this random fairy? Where has he come from? Why has he sworn devotion to this particular princess? The fairy tale never explains. It simply muses: "Alas, O princess, what would have been thy fate if the fairy's everlasting love had not rescued thee?" As far as the fairy tale is concerned, the princess is just lucky that a fairy has fallen in forever love with her. She's the beneficiary of an enchanted Twist, a rupture of the laws of reason, a fairy ex machina.

This fairy from the machine is the secret to Baroness d'Aulnoy's cure for pessimism. And although it seems a most illogical thing, its potent therapeutic action can be felt in two modern Twists that have, between them, uplifted millions of dejected hearts.

The Two Modern Twists

The first Twist was launched in the early 1900s by a magical new technology, the motion picture, which used its flickering silver screen to charm audiences with silent fairy-tale shorts such as *The Cowboy Millionaire* and Selig Polyscope's *The Wonderful Wizard of Oz* (which ends with a scarecrow being crowned king by a fresh kind of deus ex machina: a balloon-riding wizard). In 1922 the first animated adaptations of *Sleeping Beauty* and *Cinderella* were then engineered by the self-taught German special-effects whiz Lotte Reiniger. Until finally in 1925, the world was gifted a feature-length Fairy-tale Twist: Charlie Chaplin's *The Gold Rush*.

The Gold Rush starred Chaplin's most famous comic creation, the Tramp, who, as Chaplin explained, was himself the product of a Lucky Twist:

> I was hurriedly told to put on a funny make-up. This time I went to the wardrobe and got a pair of baggy pants, a tight coat, a small derby hat and a large pair of shoes. . . . My appearance got an enthusiastic response from everyone [and] the clothes seemed to imbue me with the spirit of the character. He actually became a man with a soul—a point of view.

Out of an act of wardrobe happenstance, a new "soul" was born.

This same random serendipity permeates *The Gold Rush*, which portrays the Tramp as an impoverished doof who bumbles through a Klondike snowstorm into a stroke of fortune: a warm cabin where the Tramp meets a prospector who's made a lucky strike. From here, more fortunate Twists ensue, making the Tramp filthy rich. Until at last, *The Gold Rush* ends with the Tramp accidentally bumping into his long-lost true love, who, by mere chance, has boarded the same steamship as him.

And—*ta-da!*—like Adamantina, the Tramp has chanced into wealth and then wedding bells.

The Gold Rush was a blockbuster. It became the fifth-highest-grossing silent film ever, proving so enduring that it was rereleased by Chaplin in 1942. And among its many admirers was an eleven-year-old boy who'd go on to launch the second great modern Twist.

The boy was Jerry Siegel. He grew up in Cleveland, Ohio, as the sixth child of Lithuanian immigrants who ran a modest clothing store. In Siegel's final years of high school, his father died of a heart attack after confronting a shoplifter, ruining the family's finances and destroying Siegel's hopes of college. Yet Siegel didn't abandon hope. Partnering with his friend Joe Shuster, he set out to earn a living as a comic-book creator. One of the duo's early efforts was the failed strip *Snoopy and Smiley*, which Siegel would later describe as an unfortunate attempt to imitate Chaplin's Tramp. But soon Siegel and Shuster would engineer a more successful sequel: Superman.

Superman was introduced to the world in 1938's *Action Comics #1* and June 1939's *Superman 1*. The introduction took the form of a classic Fairy-tale Twist of tragedy into triumph: on a doomed planet, an infant is loaded into an "experimental" spaceship by a mother who wants him to get his "chance at life." And get his chance he does. After he crash-lands on our globe, he's spotted by a pair of passing motorists, who, fortunately, happen to be Ma and Pa Kent, a pair of fairy-tale godparents who raise the interstellar orphan into the Man of Steel. And—*voila!*—a babe who was an ordinary person on his home world has swerved into becoming the most extraordinary person on earth.

Such was the hope-lifting effect of this narrative career that Superman became the most popular comic-book character of the Great Depression. And just like Charlie Chaplin's Tramp, Superman's Twist formula for optimism proved wildly influential. It inspired Stan Lee and other comic-book creators to engineer the Flash, the Fly, the Fantastic Four, the Incredible Hulk, Spider-Man, and dozens of other superheroes who gained magical powers (titanic strength, invisibility, the power to fly) through random strokes of luck (accidental laboratory explosions, cosmic rays, arbitrary bites from radioactive spiders). And in millions of four-color comic books that poured off newsprint presses in the 1950s and 1960s, these fortunate superheroes then paid forward their Twists, becoming global fairy godparents who appeared like masked gods from machines to sweep ordinary folk from certain disaster into unexpected happily-ever-afters: *Poof! Presto! Ta-da! Voila!*

The unexpected happily-ever-afters of Chaplin's Hollywood Twist and Siegel and Shuster's Superhero Twist have lifted multitudes of downcast spirits, just like the random serendipity of Baroness d'Aulnoy's fairy tales lifted Charles Perrault's spirits on that gloomy Tuesday afternoon. So, naturally, the question becomes: Why did Charles Perrault change the optimism formula? Why did he spike the magical cure?

The answer is that Charles Perrault heard a skeptical voice. It's a voice that we all have in our head. In fact, it's probably talking to you now.

Our Skepticism About the Fairy-tale Twist

When Charles Perrault left the Tuesday salon, he had two big concerns about the Fairy-tale Twist.

His first concern was that the Fairy-tale Twist was bad storytelling. For who other than the most incompetent writer would randomly introduce a magical character that waved a wand and turned catastrophe into a happy ending? And his second concern was that the Fairy-tale Twist nurtured feckless behavior. By feeding our belief in dumb luck, it encouraged us to follow Adamantina's thoughtless example of opting for whimsical purchases over sensible shopping lists, abandoning common sense for foolishness.

Perrault's two concerns are probably resonating with you at least a little. That's because his concerns originate in the right side of our brain, and the right side of our brain is very convincing. So, convincing, in fact, that it did more than prod Perrault to dismantle Baroness d'Aulnoy's seventeenth-century fairy tales. It also led to the dismantling of both the Hollywood and the Superhero Twist.

The dismantling began with the Motion Picture Production Code of 1930 and the Comics Code of 1954. The codes squeezed out luck by dispensing a stiff dose of poetic justice: "In every instance, good shall triumph over evil." And even after the codes were abandoned many years later, the right brains of the world continued to insist that luck was bad storytelling and bad life advice. Which is why, in our here and now, the happy endings of motion picture supermen and Disney princesses are overwhelmingly wrought by intelligence, hard work, perseverance, love, or some other virtue rewarded. Perrault's poetic justice has emerged triumphant over Straparola's Fairy-tale Twist.

This victory is as indisputably rational as the Enlightenment. But that doesn't mean it's correct. After all, the right side of our brain is correct only *half* of the time. That's why millions of years of biological evolution have given us another brain hemisphere with a different point of view. So, before we abandon the Fairy-tale Twist, let's take a moment to consider that alternative. Let's hear what our left brain thinks about Perrault's two concerns.

First, our left brain isn't too bothered about illogical storytelling. Our left brain doesn't think that stories have to be strictly logical. In fact, it doesn't think that stories *have* to be anything at all. To our left brain, stories aren't sites of absolute rules. They're zones of open possibility that can expand life's horizons, just as *Adamantina* and *The Gold Rush* and *Superman* do.

Second, our left brain doesn't think that a belief in luck is dangerous. Sure, it would be dangerous to believe that we're guaranteed to be lucky. That's the gambler's fallacy. But the Fairy-tale Twist doesn't encourage us to pawn the last of our silverware to go casinoing. It simply reminds us that we *can be* lucky—and that we *have been* lucky. These reminders are healthy, not hazardous; they strengthen our resilience and help us appreciate the good things that we already have. And indeed, as our left brain sees it, the real danger to our health isn't optimism. The real danger is pessimism, which has been correlated with increased rates of heart disease, stroke, and suicide that can double our odds of death. And such potentially harmful negative thinking, our left brain warns, is what lies beneath our right brain's rejection of luck.

Our right brain will counter, of course, by insisting that it's dishing out *realism*, not pessimism. This distinction between realism and pessimism, like all our right brain's arguments, is very convincing. But here's the flaw with it: no part of our brain can see things realistically. Our brain is too small, and the world too vast. The closest we can get to truth is a balance between the caution of our right hemisphere and the optimism of our left. So, when our mind gets out of balance, tipping us into a despairing funk, our wisest option is to lift ourselves back to center.

Which we can do with a little fairy-tale luck.

Using the Fairy-tale Twist Yourself

Once upon a time, amid the thistle fields and spired kirks of the Scottish Borders, a bonny, dark-eyed lad was born.

The lad was raised by a goodly, wise matron, Mother Enlightenment, who taught him that all of Nature was created by Reason. "From Good comes Good," she instructed sweetly. "And from Bad comes Bad."

The bonny, dark-eyed lad was Andrew Lang, and for the first fifteen years of his existence, he lived happily without a care. But in 1859, calamity struck: Mother Enlightenment was overthrown by a terrible stepmother who sprang from the pages of a most disillusioning book, *On the Origin of Species* by the English naturalist Charles Darwin. Darwin disputed Mother Enlightenment's claim that Nature was created by Reason; instead, he told a tale of how life had been birthed by billions of random mutations and blind natural selections. Every bird, every cherry bloom, every human heart had come to be through luck.

This arrival of Stepmother Luck felt deeply tragic to Andrew Lang and many of his Victorian contemporaries. What "hope" could there be in "a world of chance?" So, when Lang grew up, he tried to undo the tragedy by prescribing Perrault's old rationalist remedy of fairy tales where virtue always won. In 1888, twenty nine years after Darwin's hope-killing book appeared, Lang declared: "Charles Perrault was a good man, a good father, a good Christian, and a good fellow." And the following year, Lang revived Perrault's fairy tales of poetic justice with his own book, *The Blue Fairy Book*, which introduced a new generation of readers to *Little Red Riding Hood, The Sleeping Beauty in the Wood, Aladdin and the Wonderful Lamp, Rumpelstiltskin, Beauty and the Beast,* and *Cinderella, or the Little Glass Slipper.*

Over the next two decades, *The Blue Fairy Book* was followed by twenty-four more Andrew Lang Fairy Books, and together, these books cast a vast spell over the modern world. They were read by J. R. R. Tolkien, Walt Disney, and many other fairy-tale tellers whom they enchanted to drive out Stepmother Luck with tales of virtue rewarded and pure hearts triumphant.

Thus it was that Perrault's thorn slipped into our modern fairy tales. But if you'd like to pluck it out, there's a simple way to restore Straparola's original remedy. That remedy starts with a stiff dose of happenstance, so just as it embraced Baroness d'Aulnoy's illogical fairies, it can embrace Darwin's Stepmother Luck. And indeed, it can do more than embrace Stepmother Luck; it can spin her into the start of a most extraordinary scientific fairy tale in which you and I have come to enjoy life's remarkable treasures against all odds, through countless strokes of chance so blind that they defy any rational logic. Every joy in our days, every smile, every kiss, is a Darwinian Twist so unlikely that even Baroness d'Aulnoy would be left speechless.

Whenever you'd like more of this scientific hope, just walk to your bookshelf and upend your negative thoughts with a few Fairy-tale Twists. To gain the most from those Twists, it might help to start with a fairy tale that's specially engineered to bring along your inner skeptic. So, satisfy your right brain's negative skew by mixing the Twist with a little dark humor, like the golden-ticket deliverance of Roald Dahl's *Charlie and the Chocolate Factory*. Or give your right brain some tales designed to rebut its rational objections, like the exquisitely plotted arbitrariness of Danny Boyle's 2008 film *Slumdog Millionaire*. Or take a page from ancient comedy and warm up your right brain with a bit of song and dance, like when the orphans in *Annie: The Musical* chance into new homes.

And if your right brain is continuing to glower, dose it with the motion picture fairy-tale that's lifted a hundred million downcast psyches: Pixar's *Up*. *Up* begins by acknowledging that life can be rocked by bad luck. But it then carries us on a gleeful story of randomness with a grumpy hero whose main virtue is that he doesn't "talk much." Which is to say: the hero's main virtue isn't really anything at all. He's an ordinary soul who lucks into being chosen by a free-dreaming young woman, just as all us regular folk can be gifted happiness by some unexpected goddess of chance.

All these Fairy-tale Twists come without the *Cinderella* hangover. And should you find any of the hangover lingering from before, you can banish it completely with one last tale: the tale of the original Cinderella.

The original Cinderella lived thousands of years before Charles Perrault. Her name was Rhodopis, or "she of rose-powdered cheeks," and she was courtly in a rather different way than Perrault's Cinderella. She was a professional *court*esan: a self-employed sex worker who earned her living by charming drunken men at banquets. It wasn't an easy career. And it got only harder. Each passing day, the courtesan was informed by her clients that her beauty was fading, and with it, her chance to make money. So, every dawn, Rhodopis arose to find her lot the worse.

Until most unexpectedly, her trajectory reversed. While Rhodopis was outside bathing, a bird swept down upon her pile of clothes and plucked away a shoe. That shoe wasn't a glass slipper, just a leather sandal. But through an extraordinary twist of good fortune, it fell from the bird's grip onto the lap of an Egyptian king. The king was so amazed by the sandal's apparent heaven-sentness that he ordered his men to search far and wide for its owner. And when those men found Rhodopis, the king instantly married her, turning a courtesan into a Cleopatra.

This might sound like a Straparola happily-ever-after before Straparola. But it's not a literary fairy tale. It's a piece of history recorded in the *Geography* of the ancient Greek chronicler Strabo. Which means that the original Cinderella wasn't a magical myth. She was a flesh-and-blood woman. And while modern scholars have doubted whether the tale of Rhodopis is entirely true, there's no question that Strabo got his main fact right: luck really can arrive like a pair of wings from the sky.

That's why luck has worked countless real miracles. And that's why luck has created countless real Cinderellas too. So, if your days are hard and getting worse, don't catastrophize or get down on yourself. Instead, look to the history of life on this planet and remember: good fortune can descend like a flash from the blue . . .

. . . and tomorrow's Cinderella could be you.

EIGHT

Heal from Grief

Shakespeare's Hamlet *and the Invention of the Sorrow Resolver*

On a hot day in August, a child passed away.

The year was 1596; the place, a wattle-and-daub English cottage beside the River Avon's mercury blue. And the child was eleven-year-old Hamnet, the son of Anne Hathaway and the playwright William Shakespeare.

Shakespeare wrote no public words to commemorate his son. And far from doing anything obvious to mourn, he spread mirth. He crafted the madcap antics of Sir John Falstaff in *The Merry Wives of Windsor*. He penned the hopeful wooing of Beatrice and Benedick in *Much Ado About Nothing*.

Until at last, sometime after the summer of 1599, three years past Hamnet's death, Shakespeare put down his comic pen to write a grief-soaked tragedy: *Hamlet*.

Hamlet. Hamnet. *Hamlet*. Hamnet. The connection has seemed so obvious—and so mysterious. If Shakespeare wanted to mourn his son, why not pen a poem with his son's actual name? Why write a play about a historical prince whose name was almost the same? And why write all those comedic jests in the meantime? Why wait three long years to weep?

As mysterious as it all appears, the answer lies in the three-year gap. The gap reveals that *Hamlet* isn't a raw expression of grief dashed out in the terrible aftermath of a child's death. *Hamlet* is a coming to terms with grief—and a healing beyond. That healing beyond is what Shakespeare learned to do in the hard months after Hamnet's passing.

And it's what *Hamlet* is engineered to help us do too.

Hamlet's Engineering Breakthrough

Hamlet was hardly the first work of theater to wrestle with the problem of grief. Indeed, so old was the problem that it formed the axis of history's earliest known plays: Greek tragedies.

Greek tragedies revolved around characters who'd lost parents, siblings, children. And although those bereaved characters responded to loss in different ways, a common pattern quickly emerged: mourning took the form of a plot. Plot had long been literature's standard response to disaster: when something went wrong, heroes sprang into action, waging wars, killing monsters, or embarking on other doings to set things aright. So, what sort of doings could set grief aright? The answer encouraged by Greek tragedy's fiscal patron, democratic Athens, was a narrative of funeral rites: lamentations, cremations, libations. But Greek tragedy itself offered a rather less civilized solution: the revenge plot.

The revenge plot can be found as far back as the oldest surviving Greek tragic trilogy, Aeschylus's *Oresteia*, written in 458 BCE. The *Oresteia* opens with an aggrieved mother, Clytemnestra, who avenges her daughter's murder with an intricate scheme: she lures the killer into a bathtub, entangles him with a net, and then drops an axe upon his head. From here, the revenge plottings portrayed upon the tragic stage grew steadily more elaborate. A quarter century after the *Oresteia*, Athenian audiences were introduced to Euripides's Medea, a barbarian princess who delivered comeuppance to her unfaithful Greek lover by stabbing his two sons, assassinating his new wife with a poisoned wedding gift, and finally, escaping in a dragon chariot hijacked from the gods.

Medea's outlandish revenge seemed to be the plot to end plots, yet it only inspired even more prodigious ones, including a plot that would become particularly influential in Shakespeare's day. That plot was the plot of *Thyestes*, a revenge caper penned by the Roman playwright, Seneca. Seneca was an advisor to Emperor Nero, a man who'd proved himself to be an extraordinary real-life plotter. He'd contrived to murder his mother by means of a mechanical bedroom, and when that cunning tool of matricide failed, Nero finished the job with an even more complex contraption: a collapsible yacht. But even these fantastical plots were outdone by Seneca, who went back to Medea and gruesomely expanded her retribution blueprint. His revenger in *Thyestes* didn't murder two boys; he murdered three. And he didn't simply murder them. He fed them in a casserole to their unsuspecting father.

When *Thyestes* was rediscovered a millennia and a half later in Elizabethan England, audiences were appalled—and delighted. What a bizarre and unexpected plot! So, the playwrights of London set about crafting ingenious revenge plots of their own. There were plots where revengers tricked their victims into kissing venomed skeletons. There were plots where revengers surprised their victims with lethal stage props. There were plots with hobnail hammers, scalding cauldrons, and falling trapdoors. There were plots and plots and plots and plots.

Shakespeare knew all about these revenge plots. In his early twenties, he'd bought penny tickets to watch them unfold in tragedies such as *Hieronimo Is Mad Again* and *The Tragedy of Hamlet* (the first by the secretarial scrivener Thomas Kyd; the second possibly by Kyd as well). And after Shakespeare had marveled at these plots, he'd gone on to craft his own. Most notoriously, sometime in the wake of his twenty-fifth birthday, he'd expanded *Thyestes*'s reprisal narrative into the demented violence of *Titus Andronicus*, which contained, among other gruesome innovations, a human pillow. So, of course, when Shakespeare revealed that he was working on his own version of *Hamlet*, London audiences began to expect a truly, wonderfully, horrifically, outrageous plot.

But to their shock, that wasn't what they got. Instead, they got a plot that stalled . . . and strayed . . . and stuck. A plot that seemed to be no plot all.

The Strange Plotlessness of *Hamlet*

Hamlet was one of the first plays to be performed at the Globe, the sky-open theater constructed in 1599 from salvaged timbers by Shakespeare's company, the Lord Chamberlain's Men, upon the bog-reed wilds of London's southern entertainment district. And when *Hamlet* premiered, for an eager audience that may have been three thousand strong, it appeared to have a clear, clear plot.

That plot began in the play's opening act, where the ghost of a Danish king visited his son Hamlet to inform him:

> Thus was I, sleeping, by a brother's hand,
> Of life, of crown, and queen at once dispatch'd.

Hearing this, the audience concluded instantly that Hamlet would plot a revenge against his murderous uncle. The only question was: *What* plot would Hamlet plot? Would he pull a Medea? Would he nick a page from *Thyestes*? Would he use poison, bathtub nets, or a weapon unprecedented? Would he concoct some terrible death engine that would have impressed even Nero?

The audience craned forward expectantly. But instead of launching forth upon spectacular avengings, Hamlet instead announced his decision to adopt an "antic disposition." What, the audience wondered in puzzlement, was an antic disposition? Well, it was Hamlet acting oddly jaunty. He wandered around the Danish castle with a book, and upon being asked what he was reading, he replied: "Words! Woooords. Words?"

From here, the plot disintegrated further. For long periods, Hamlet did nothing but speak. He raved about his inner doubts. He vented his disgust at life. And most curiously of all, he harangued a troupe of professional actors on the correct way to act: "Hold a mirror up to nature . . . and let your clowns say no more than is set down!"

Was this more of Hamlet's antic disposition? Did he think it was funny to tell actors how to do their jobs? Or had Hamlet genuinely lost his mind? No one could say. But eventually the ghost himself decided that he'd had enough, and he intervened to get the plot on track: "This visitation is but to whet thy almost blunted purpose!"

Yet once again, Hamlet fumbled the narrative. Instead of getting revenge, he disposed of an innocent man in a stairwell, tricked two casual acquaintances into getting royally butchered, and then jumped inside a grave: "Alas, poor Yorick! I knew him, a fellow of infinite jest."

It was madness. It was all out of joint. Other playwrights snickered.

Hamlet wasn't a tragedy; it was a farce. Shakespeare himself had lost the plot.

But then to the astonishment of Shakespeare's rivals, the play proved a popular triumph, earning a vaster tide of printed encores than *Henry V* and *Much Ado About Nothing* and even *Romeo and Juliet*. It affected audiences far more powerfully than a traditional revenge play. In fact, it affected them more powerfully than any tragedy they'd ever seen. It inspired them to deeply weep. And it left them looking restored—even serene.

How was this possible? What power had this plotless plot?

The Power of Stopping the Plot

On Shakespeare's desk sat a book that counseled him on how to handle losing his son. The book was *Cardano's Comfort*, a sixteenth-century best seller legendary for the advice it distilled from the sagacious philosophers of yore. And that advice was: "Call to memory how many worthy men have undeservingly & cruelly by fortune been cast down, and patiently suffered."

In other words: Do not remember your own dead child. Instead, remember other men who have lost children, and remember how they did so with patient dispassion. Or briskly summed: Respond to tragedy with a manly stoicism.

Shakespeare meditated on this ancient wisdom—then flung it away with a heartsick cry that he would dramatize a few years later in *Macbeth*. Toward the play's end, the stalwart warrior Lord Macduff is warned by the thane of Ross that his ears are about to hear "the heaviest sound." Macduff has an inkling of what that sound will be: "Hum. I guess at it." But even so, he is not prepared. Ross reveals, "Your castle is surprised; your wife and babes savagely slaughtered." Prompting Macduff to crack in dismay: "All my pretty ones? Did you say all?"

At this point, the future king, Prince Malcolm, intercedes to counsel Macduff: "Dispute it like a man." To which Macduff rejoins:

I shall do so;
But I must also feel it as a man:
I cannot but remember such things were,
That were most precious to me.

In all of Shakespeare, there is no moment more astonishing. Macduff backtalks his liege and casts off all the virile stoics of antiquity to assert, "I must feel it as a man." And although this rebel assertion would have struck many a Renaissance doctor as a summons to further heartache, modern psychologists have discovered that it's instead a prologue to therapy. A therapy in two parts.

The first part is simply to acknowledge the hurt of bereavement. That acknowledgement releases deep parts of our brain, like the emotion centers of our amygdala and the memory networks of our thalamus, to begin processing our grief. The processing takes time, and we will never forget the loss. But gradually, our extreme symptoms of grief will ease, returning us to our regular emotional balance. And to ease us through this mourning transition, the acknowledgment of hurt also helps us in another way: it reassures our brain, *There's nothing wrong or weak about feeling overwhelmed with sorrow.* That reassurance boosts our neural self-worth, reducing our risk of developing depression and preventing our grief from being compounded by shame.

The second part of the therapy is to dwell on happy memories of the people who were, to borrow Macduff's phrase, "most precious" to us. Happy memories of all kinds prompt our brain to release a little boost of neural self-pleasure in the form of dopamine. The purpose of that dopamine is to train our brain to seek out more of the good that once made us glad, so even though memory pleasure seems backward looking, it's really a future driver. And in the case of our pleasant nostalgia for the departed, the dopamine gradually pulls us into doing things that remind us positively of our loved ones lost. Drawing us out of mourning isolation and back into the flow of life beyond, it eases sorrow with an active gratitude for what the dead have given us.

Long before Shakespeare, this two-part therapy was incorporated into funerals, which encourage both public grief and celebrations of the dead. And the same therapy lies at the root of Greek tragedy, which is, at its core, a pausing of life's hurly-burly to occupy our mind with scenes of death. In that pause, we can acknowledge our unresolved feelings of bereavement—and reminisce about the virtues of the lives no longer here.

Hamlet's contribution to this ancient therapy is to deepen its healing action. The deepening comes from Shakespeare's removal of the feature of Greek tragedy that most interfered with the memorial pause: the plot. The plot was the opposite of a pause. It carried our brain in rapid new directions that diverted us from mourning contemplation. And as tragedy evolved more and more intricate plots, from *Medea*, to *Thyestes*, to *Hieronimo Is Mad Again*, the diversion intensified, sweeping us into a tide of action that served less to help us process our grief than to manically deflect it.

Hamlet dismantles this distractive plot technology. It maroons us for hours in a place where almost nothing happens. And when things *do* happen, they're not the result of Hamlet's conscious planning. In act 2, the plot is diverted by a gang of professional actors who crash the proceedings after a member of the Danish court cotes (that is, overtakes) them "on the [high]way," prompting a surprised Hamlet to react: "What players are they? How chances it they travel?" In act 3, the plot veers again when Hamlet accidentally kills Polonius behind a tapestry, and again in act 4, when Ophelia distractedly drowns. The bulk of Shakespeare's play is thus devoted to two main kinds of viewing experience. First, there are mishaps and other haphazard events that exchange narrative suspense for narrative surreal. Second, there are Hamlet's long breaks from action to engage in slow meditations on mortality and the dead, meditations that elicit our own memories of the ones we've lost: *so excellent . . . so loving . . . most dear life . . .*

This dwelling time made *Hamlet* a revolution in therapy, and its emotional impact was immediate and lasting. In 1604 the doggerel lyricist Anthony Scoloker recorded that of all "Friendly Shakespeares Tragedies," *Hamlet* was the most beloved by the "vulgar" folk, who, unlike the dispassionate sages of *Cardano's Comfort*, felt anguish and shock. And six decades later, when every one of Shakespeare's other tragedies had been bowdlerized or forgotten, *Hamlet* would be revived, first on a rickety stage in London's downtown cattle meadow, then under quiet summer nights at Oxford, and finally, at the Thames's lapping riverfront, to such popular acclaim that the theater frequenter John Downes could cheerily-crassly declare: "No succeeding Tragedy for several Years got more Reputation, or Money."

And as potently effective as Shakespeare's plotless plot would prove, it's not the only mourning innovation of *Hamlet*. The wonder of the play is that it's simultaneously engineered to address the other major problem posed by grief: not being able to shut off our tears once they start.

The Other Problem of Grief

If it can be hard to pause in grief, it can be even harder to move on.

This problem was well known to the ancient tragedians. The author of *Thyestes* mused: "In animals, grief is sharp but quick—in people, it can linger for years." And this problem becomes well known to Hamlet too. Hamlet does just what Macbeth and modern psychologists advise: he acknowledges his grief. Yet he never seems to heal. All about him, others weep and recover. But Hamlet founders in misery.

How can this be? If our brain naturally exorcises our sorrow by pausing to recall the dead, then what's going on with Hamlet? Has his amygdala or his thalamus gone haywire?

No, there's nothing awry with Hamlet's neural circuitry. His unending mourning is a symptom of something very different from unprocessed sorrow. That something is what modern psychologists term complicated grief.

Complicated grief is grief that doesn't resolve itself naturally over time. Instead, it persists and even deepens, triggering psychic disturbances such as depression, detachment, and rage. These disturbances are what entangle Hamlet, inciting him to brood, to drift, and to lash out. And in Shakespeare's play, as is typically the case in real life, the source of complicated grief is guilt.

Guilt catches Hamlet's conscience from the very beginning. In the play's opening act, he insists repeatedly that it's *wrong* to stop grieving his father. He rages against his mother for moving on with her life: "O, God! A beast . . . would have mourn'd longer." And he swears to the ghost that he will himself always remember:

> Remember thee?
> Yea, from the table of my memory
> I'll wipe away all trivial fond records,
> All saws of books, all forms, all pressures past
> That youth and observation copied there,
> And thy commandment all alone shall live
> Within the book and volume of my brain,
> Unmix'd with baser matter. Yes, by heaven!

With this extraordinary promise, Hamlet vows to empty his mind of everything other than his thoughts of his father. And to this promise, Hamlet holds true. He devotes himself obsessively to tearful remembrance, convincing and reconvincing himself that it would be a crime to be happy in a world without his father.

Hamlet's guilt-response bemuses the play's other characters. It's judged by Hamlet's mother to be not "common," by Hamlet's uncle to be "peevish," and by everyone else to be "mad . . . mad . . . mad." But there's nothing weird, perverse, or aberrant about Hamlet's guilt. Almost all of us feel that it's wrong to stop mourning the dead and move on with our lives. And this feeling can easily spiral us, like Hamlet, into melancholy, anger, remoteness, and the other symptoms of complicated grief.

Unless we find guilt's remedy.

Guilt's Remedy

Guilt is a complicated emotion.

It originates in a neural network whose vast intricacy—spanning from the front of our brain, round the outer sides, and then reaching upward to the backslope of our crown—reflects its complex social function. That function is to carefully monitor our relationships and alert us when rifts develop. The alert registers in our consciousness as a guilty feeling of wrongdoing, even if our only "wrong" has been to live our own life while the other person has drifted on her separate way. And the guilty feeling then prods us to reach out to the other person with an apology, a gift, or some other gesture for repairing the distance.

Because guilt is such a motivating emotion, it has helped us maintain our families, our friendships, and our communities for millions of years. But the death of a loved one causes our guilt system to quirk. The quirk begins when the system detects our loved one's physical absence and warns: *You've got to heal the rift!* At which point, we find ourselves caught in a quandary: How can we maintain our bond with the deceased, reassuring them that we care for them as deeply as we ever did, when they're no longer materially here to receive an apology or a gift?

It's to solve this quandary that our ancestors devised posthumous offerings such as burial libations, incense burnings, and most grandly of all, the public memorial. The public memorial can take endless forms: eulogies, poems, funeral arrangements, tombs, statues, named endowments. But all its forms are gifts that bequeath the dead a place in life, transmuting our guilty feeling of social distance into the pleasure of imaginative togetherness and allowing us to gradually exit mourning to resume our daily business.

Thus did our long-ago ancestors discover a scientific solution to the guilt that follows bereavement. But as Hamlet finds, the science isn't always easy to execute. Our love for the deceased makes most memorials feel inadequate, and, unlike a living recipient, the deceased cannot calm our doubts by accepting our offering with a grateful smile. So, the memorial gift with which we intend to pay our obligation to the dead can instead saturate our guilt with a heavy anxiety: Was it a good gift? Was the funeral we arranged or the eulogy we wrote personal and thoughtful enough? Have we really done enough to mourn the loved one that we've lost?

Hamlet's own worries on this score are starkly evident. He scoffs at the clichéd black attire of traditional mourners: "These are but the trappings and the suits of woe." And he resolves to clear his conscience by creating a memorial as special as his father. This resolution is heartfelt. But as Hamlet quickly learns, it's beyond him to fulfill.

Hamlet first encounters trouble when he tries to give the memorial gift that his ghostly father requests: revenge. Revenge can be a fitting memorial only if it's as creatively unique as the life it avenges. As explained by Seneca's *Thyestes*:

O my Imagination! Hatch a deed so far beyond the norm that posterity will never forget.

This is a high plot standard indeed. It requires the revenger to craft a blood show of such shocking originality that it writes itself permanently into history, like a tombstone that burns its epitaph into the mind of every passerby. Yet as daunting as this ambition is, it does at first appear to be in reach of Hamlet's "antic disposition." For here is a crazily anarchic method of revenge never seen onstage before; a method that hints at a reckoning as lawless as Medea and as lunatic as *Thyestes* . . .

But this hope is ultimately disappointed. Hamlet's antic disposition rejects past precedent with such completeness that there's no buying of poisons, sharpening of knives, or building of killing yachts. Instead, Hamlet goes "so far beyond the norm" of traditional revenge plots that he spends his hours howling strange poetry and wounding everybody but his instructed target, delivering his father no vengeance at all.

The collapse of Hamlet's revenge plot strands him in a deepening tide of guilt. He reproaches himself for his unfilial behavior; he wallows in his unfulfilled obligation to his father; he feels his conscience haunting him. Until, at the rough midpoint of the proceedings, he stumbles upon another way to keep his father's memory alive: staging a play.

This literary form of memorial is initially conceived by Hamlet as a forensic device for plumbing his uncle's conscience, but its potential value as a guilt salve emerges when it gets infused, like all of Hamlet's doings, with his grief. As Hamlet labors on his play with his father in his mind, he becomes aware—perhaps as Shakespeare himself became aware while writing *Hamlet* with Hamnet in his mind—that one way to memorialize the deceased is by weaving their biography into a public performance. And auspiciously for Hamlet, such weaving doesn't require the artistic element that doomed his revenge plot: originality. Indeed, it adopts precisely the opposite artistic standard: realism. So long as Hamlet's play reproduces some individual detail of his father's life, it will stand as a fitting testament, enshrining the uniqueness of the dead man by documenting his existence like a faithful eulogy.

Yet as promising as this new mode of remembrance appears initially, it too turns out to be doomed. As Hamlet discovers, no performance can ever be perfectly true to life; no play can ever provide a literal mirror of nature. It's the action of theater, like all art, to shape, to focus, to clarify, to reveal—to give us *more* than nature by narrowing our attention on less. Hamlet tries to evade this unwelcome fact by browbeating the actors of his play into acting *exactly as he says*. But despite Hamlet's micromanaging, the performance goes sideways. Hamlet's uncle interprets it as a threat against his life, while Hamlet himself jokes that his script has earned him a place in the theater troupe. So, rather than functioning as a memorial that captures the deceased's unique essence, Hamlet's play does what art typically does: it puts the focus on the artist's shaping hand.

When Hamlet fails at both his revenge plot and his remembrance play, his hopes for a public memorial seem finished. He's attempted one style of elegiac art (the imaginatively original) and then the contrary (the strictly realistic). Now that both have miscarried, there appear to be no more options for the grieving artist.

Yet in the final act of Shakespeare's play, Hamlet finds a third way, the origins of which lie in the fact that Hamlet's revenge plot and his remembrance play both suffer from the same flaw: the belief that it's up to Hamlet to ensure his father's memory. This belief is intuitive but errant. For public memorials don't succeed because of the artist; public memorials succeed because of the *public*. It's the public that holds on to the memory of the deceased, keeping it "green" long past the days when the gravestones are cracked and the funeral wreaths faded. It's the public that gathers the broken sculpture of past ages to remember: *This was Caesar . . . and this, Cleopatra.*

So, what Hamlet really needs to achieve his memorial isn't greater originality or creative control. What he needs is an audience that he can trust to remember. And Hamlet discovers that audience when he encounters the Danish knight Laertes at Ophelia's fifth-act funeral. By the time of the encounter, Laertes has lost as much as Hamlet, perhaps more: his father and his sister, Ophelia, have both been snatched away. And although Hamlet initially accuses Laertes of feigned grief, he soon comes to grasp that the young knight's suffering is genuine: "By the image of my cause, I see the portraiture of his."

This is the play's great turning point. For the first time since his father's death, Hamlet acknowledges that someone can feel like him. And this acknowledgment prompts an equally major transition in Hamlet's behavior. His lonely guilt vanishes, and he confesses to his friend Horatio that he feels a greater peace: "Since no man has aught of what he leaves, what is't to leave betimes?"

Hamlet's liberation from guilt is so rapid that it can feel as contrived as the hackneyed funeral platitudes that he despises. But it's what happens in our brain when we see our grief mirrored back by other people. The mirroring reveals that we're not alone in our sorrow; there's a wider public that understands what it is to lose someone who can never be replaced. And with their understanding, that public helps not only to support us through our bereavement, but also to relieve our anxiety that we haven't done enough to commemorate our dead.

The relief begins when the members of the public make up for the inadequacy of our elegiac offering with their own sympathetic comprehension, fathoming what it was that we *meant* to say. And the relief deepens when the public then carries our intended meaning beyond us into future days and places. As that shared remembrance spreads forth, the deep centers of our guilt network gently relax. We come to see that we don't need to devote our every waking hour to mourning remembrance. We can return to the rhythms of our daily lives, secure in the emotional discovery that a memorial exists in a human community far vaster than ourselves.

Hamlet is enormously fortunate to find this guilt lift. After all, his collision with a bereaved Laertes doesn't result from any conscious plot. It's an accident, a serendipity, an epiphany stumbled into. And yet as chancingly improbable as Hamlet's crash into healing is, the miracle of Shakespeare's play is that it guides us into the very same good fortune, blindly colliding us with our own guilt lift.

For that blind collision to happen, we need to repeat Hamlet's accidental epiphany. We need to charge forward, craving a plot, when we instead encounter something totally unexpected: A person who feels just like us. A person who shares our disgust at clichéd remembrances and formulaic memorials. A person who shares our deep sense of grief and deeper sense of guilty obligation. A person who feels that it's better to rave and act uncivilly than to betray our debt of love to the dead.

That stumbled-into someone, of course, is Hamlet. Hamlet is our Laertes. He reveals that there are people "in this distracted globe" who understand what we do: each life is special, so each death is a tragedy unprecedented. And because of those understanding people, we're not doomed to be saddled forever with the guilty feeling that we can never do enough to remember the departed. For to help us with the task are all the like-hearted Hamlets around.

Those Hamlets can be the other bearers of the casket. They can be the memorial power of ages.

They can be the life beyond.

Using the Sorrow Resolver Yourself

Hamlet ends with its mortally wounded prince making a plea: "Tell my story." Once again, a life has reached its vanishment. Once again, a public memorial is required.

The memorial is promised by Horatio: "Let me speak to the yet un-knowing world how these things came about: so shall you hear . . ." But then Horatio disappears offstage before he can finish. And so the task must fall to us. Can we remember Hamlet? Can we encapsulate his life's uniqueness?

We cannot, of course. Generations of memorialists have tried and failed, as this chapter has tried and failed, to capture the singularity of Shakespeare's great creation. Yet even so, our efforts have not been in vain, for Hamlet's specialness has not evaporated. Through century after century, his individual character has endured, kept alive by a collective remembrance that grasps what we, poor speakers, cannot articulate.

And by preserving Hamlet, that collective remembrance has pre-served something else: Shakespeare's invention for coping with our own bereavements. The invention, as we've seen, is really two combined. First, there's the "Grief Releaser" of a plot that abandons the usual for-ward momentum of plots in favor of a drifting, eddying, dilating story that provides us with time to acknowledge our heartache and dwell upon memories of our loved one lost. And second, there's the "Guilt Lifter" of a character who shares our disdain, our dismay, and even our anger, at clichéd funerals and formulaic condolences—and who is determined to battle through the apathy and hollow action of this world to honor the uniqueness of the life departed.

Together these inventions are the "Sorrow Resolver." And in the centuries since Shakespeare first engineered it, the Sorrow Resolver's basic blueprint of a stalled plot and a uniquely grieving character has been elaborated by Johann Wolfgang von Goethe's *The Sorrows of Young Werther*, Ernest Hemingway's *The Sun Also Rises*, Robert Redford's *Or-dinary People*, Joan Didion's *The Year of Magical Thinking*, Mariama Bâ's *So Long a Letter*, and many works more. If you suffer from the closed heart of the manly sages, these works can thus unfasten it to grieve.

And if you suffer from Hamlet's heart locked open, these works can lift the burden of your lonely conscience, gifting you the greater memory that heals.

NINE

Banish Despair

*John Donne's "Songs" and the Invention
of the Mind-Eye Opener*

In the early seventeenth century, amid the porched piazzas of the University of Padua, a middle-aged professor decided to learn about heaven.

At the time, most people who decided to learn about heaven did so by perusing the words of the prophets. But this middle-aged professor was a little bit different. His name was Galileo Galilei, and he had a knack for constructing pendulums, thermoscopes, directional dials, and other technological gadgets. So, instead of poring over holy scriptures, he built a star-seeing machine.

The machine had two special lenses, the smaller concave, the bigger convex, installed within a three-foot wooden tube. And after this "telescope" was constructed in 1609, Galileo eagerly pointed it at heaven's center—the sun—expecting to behold a miracle.

The particular miracle that Galileo expected was the "quintessence," or "fifth element." The quintessence had been acclaimed by Greek astronomers, hymned by North African monks, and venerated by Persian alchemists, for unlike the four earthly elements, the fifth never changed. It was the pure fire of heaven, the stuff of the astral, the perfect eternal of God.

But when Galileo used his wooden tube to peer at the sun, he didn't behold the quintessential miracle. Instead, he saw a smudge. More than one smudge, actually. Many, many smudges.

Perplexed, Galileo cleaned the glass lenses of his machine. But no matter how thoroughly he wiped, the smudges remained. And slowly, Galileo realized: the smudges weren't on his telescope. *They were on the sun.* The sun's shining surface was blotched.

This was a strange and terrible discovery. It meant that the fifth element was no more flawless than the four grubby elements below. It meant that the stars were afflicted with the same physical decay that led earthly fruit to rot and mortal hearts to stop. Or to put it frankly: it meant that the heavens weren't heavenly at all.

Galileo called the disenchanting smudges *macchie solari,* or sunspots. And when he announced their existence to the world, the world did what Galileo himself had done: it blinked. Prior to Galileo, the world had been able to brush off the bizarre claims made by middle-aged astronomers. Only a few months before Galileo built his star seer, Johannes Kepler had finished writing *New Astronomy*, an enormous book that attempted to prove that the earth was orbiting at great speed round the sun. Kepler was very earnest about this proof and could show you intricate mathematics to back it. But, of course, that only proved how useless mathematics was. A simple glance out the window revealed that the earth was clearly *not* rushing through space at the hectic rate of twenty miles a second. If it were, life would be a hurricane. The clotheslines, the market signs, the pasture sheep—all of it would be in flight.

Or so the world thought, at least. But the world could not ignore Galileo as easily as it had ignored Kepler. Because unlike Kepler, Galileo was not asking people to trust mathematics. He was asking them to trust their eyes, the very same instruments of common sense that they'd used to convince themselves that the earth was standing still: *Just look at the heavens and you'll see; they're not as perfect as you've been led to believe.*

People did look. Even without a telescope, they could see that there were blemishes on the moon and irregular patterns to the starry constellations. In the past, these inconvenient facts had been creatively rationalized away, but how to explain smudges on heaven's golden heart itself?

The world paused uncertainly, and in that pause, its fears were captured by a poet's couplet:

New Philosophy calls all in doubt,
The Element of fire is quite put out.

The poet behind this couplet was John Donne, born years before in the London ward of Bread Street. Donne was now, like Galileo, in his middle age, and his journey there had not been smooth. He'd begun brightly enough as a courtier with an astonishing way with words; he could charm any prince and seduce any lady-in-waiting. But then he'd fallen in love with Anne More, the niece of the king's trusted advisor, and married her without permission. The crime landed Donne in prison, and although he was eventually released, his career at court was ended. He drifted toward poverty, living in cramped urban apartments with Anne and their ever-growing brood of children: Constance, John, George, Francis, Lucy, Bridget, Mary, Nicholas, Margaret, and Elizabeth. Despairing of his ability to provide for all this family, Donne wrote a defense of suicide: *Biathanatos*. And when one of his children caught a fatal illness, he comforted himself grimly with the thought that he could now afford to feed the others—until he realized that the little coffin's cost would bankrupt him.

Yet as dire as things became, Donne was always able to slip outside and stare up at the sky. *Someday*, he thought, *we'll tumble off this mortal coil into that better place above. Someday, our woes will all be burnt away with holy light*. . . .

And then came Galileo's telescope. For Donne, this was the last and most painful disappointment. His earthly dreams had crumbled, and now heaven had disintegrated too. There would be no afterlife among the stars. There would be no saving miracle.

But happily for Donne, his despair was quickly lifted. For the very same year that Donne published his anguished couplet about the new astronomy, the miracle did what miracles do: it broke all the laws of logic and returned. That return came in the form of an invention as elegantly built as any of Galileo's machines. Yet the invention wasn't a glass-and-wood gizmo like the telescope; it was a literary gizmo, engineered by Donne himself. To common sense, the gizmo seemed as impossible as Kepler's mathematics. But to the eye, it proved as compelling as Galileo's double-lensed tube. One look, and the star fire was rekindled.

One look, and you believed in the fifth element again.

The Origins of Donne's Invention

Many years before Galileo constructed his stargazing instrument, Donne had himself discovered a method for snuffing out the quintessence, a method he coyly disclosed in his erotic lyric, "The Sun Rising."

The lyric began with the poet dozing in his lover's arms—when suddenly bliss was interrupted. The sun rose outside, poking nosy beams into the bedroom and startling the couple awake. Annoyed, the poet chastised the glaring interloper:

> Busy old fool, unruly sun,
> Why dost thou thus,
> Through windows, and through curtains call on us?

This rebuke was ignored by the sun, which continued to prod its unwelcome rays into the lovers' retinas. Until at last, the poet felt compelled to take action. Raising himself up, he threated to "eclipse" the sun, darkening its rays to nothing.

Unfazed by the threat, the sun stayed ablaze. So, the poet was forced to follow through. Dropping back onto his pillow, he eclipsed the sun, casting its fifth element into gloom.

How did the poet achieve this startling feat? How did he quench the sky's eternal king? Well, as he slyly explained, he did it "with a wink." Shutting his eyes, he put out the sun.

An instant later, the poet's eyes were open again. He could not bear, he declared, to be without the sight of his lover, and so off his verses galloped in a different direction. But years afterward, when Donne plucked this faded old lyric from a drawer, it occurred to him that his eclipse boast had contained a miraculous power. The power was that of the literary paradox, a cheeky prose genre (dating back to ancient rhetorical jests such as Cicero's Stoic *Paradoxes* and revived in the Renaissance by entertainments like Ortensio Lando's 1544 *Paradossi, or Claims Unorthodox*) that upturned logic by using witty arguments to "prove" that ice was hotter than fire, that feathers fell faster than rocks, and that night outshone the day.

These literary refutations of reason had so delighted Donne during his university days that he'd attempted a few of his own, leaving them behind on yellowing manuscripts that fell after his death into the hands of the printer Elizabeth Purslowe. And when Purslowe published those manuscripts as the posthumous *John Donne's Juvenilia*, the reading public was astonished to discover that the old were far more imaginative than the young. For wasn't it true that old men constantly fell in love with women half their age? And what could take a greater feat of imagination than supposing that such withered affection would be kissingly reciprocated?

Donne's fascination with literary paradoxes perplexed most of his friends. What was the purpose in rejecting truth for a lie? But Donne discerned something more ingenious at work in the literary paradox. The paradox, he realized, was never compelling enough to get our brain to recant our original truth. No matter how clever the paradox's conceits and rhetorical maneuvers, it couldn't convince us that ice wasn't cold or that night wasn't dark. Instead, the paradox was just compelling enough to crack open our mind to a simultaneous opposite truth. Even as we continued to believe that *ice is cold*, we came to entertain the belief *and ice also is hot*.

So, instead of overturning the truth, what literary paradoxes did was double it. They made us think: *Night is dark—and also is light. Left is left—and also is right.*

And as Donne reread his old eclipse boast, he realized that it had accomplished the same. The boast had never made us believe that the sun had been blotted out. We'd always known that the sun was still up there, casting its beams across the sky. Yet even as we'd held on to this original truth, the boast *had* made us believe that we were eclipsers. We shut our eyes and got the proof: the sun and its beams were no more.

In that winking moment, we'd discovered the remarkable sensation of seeing the sun in opposite ways at once. It was as if we had two sets of eyes: the eyes of our body and the eyes of our mind. The eyes of our body saw that the sun was eclipsed—while the eyes of our mind saw that the sun still shone bright.

So, what if we could experience the same paradoxical marvel when we used Galileo's telescope? What if we could behold the truth of the new science—but also the truth of the ancient belief? What if we could see that the quintessence was flecked with decay—but also unspottedly perfect?

That would be an even greater miracle than the one that Galileo had dispelled. The old miracle, after all, had simply been that heaven was heaven. That wasn't so very wondrous. In fact, in retrospect, it wasn't wondrous at all. It was no different from saying water was water or earth was earth. It was just a boring, straight fact.

The new miracle wouldn't be like that at all. The new miracle would be a genuine wonder, a fifth-element heaven that was also the four elements of the earth. Uniting two opposite truths, it would be the illogical made manifest, a paradox that activated our double eyes, uplifting us with awe.

But could Donne write a poem that made us feel that way? Could he write a poem that showed us the cosmos as it appeared through Galileo's glass lenses—and also as it appeared to angel minds?

Yes, Donne decided, he could. The poem would be impossible. And he would do it anyway.

Donne's Impossible Poem

Donne's impossible poem is "A Valediction: Forbidding Mourning." He wrote it in either 1611 or 1612, less than a year after the publication of his couplet about the dousing of heaven's fire. And it begins with this scene:

> As virtuous men pass mildly away,
> And whisper to their soul, to go,
> Whilst some of their sad friends do say,
> "The breath goes now," and some say, "No."

This scene isn't particularly remarkable. Every day, all around us, people pass away. And yet this scene *is* remarkable. Because those dead people are also alive. "A Valediction" guides us into this paradox by asking us to imagine a friend's body at the very last instant of life—and also at the very first instant of death. Then the poem asks: What's different about our friend in those two moments?

The answer is: nothing. And the answer is also: everything.

The first answer comes from the eye of our body, the eye that can wink out the sun. As far as that eye can see, our friend looks exactly the same at the first moment of death. So much the same, in fact, that our friend seems about to draw another breath: "Some . . . do say, 'The breath goes now,' and some say, 'No.'"

The second answer comes from a different eye, the eye inside our mind. That eye sees that everything has changed. The object now before us is a corpse's empty shell. Our friend exists inside no more.

This feeling of double sight is the same feeling that we get from winking out the sun. It's the feeling of two opposite truths in one. And as much as this double sight might feel like a poetic trick, it reveals something genuine about our brain: our brain really does possess two sets of eyes. And those two sets of eyes can see impossible things.

The Science of Seeing Impossible Things

The impossible things seen by our brain are known to neuroscientists as impossible objects. Impossible objects are objects that can be drawn on two-dimensional paper but cannot exist in our three-dimensional universe:

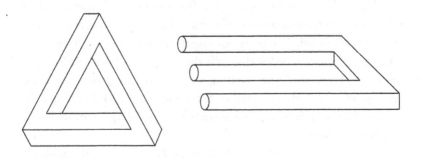

These objects look very different, but they're impossible in exactly the same way: they're two possible objects combined impossibly into one. The left object is a possible triangle that juts left and a possible triangle that juts right; the right object is a possible fork with three prongs and a possible fork with two prongs. Each half of the impossible object is thus conceivably real; it's the intersection that breaks physics.

By breaking physics in this precise way, impossible objects trigger a very specific short circuit in our brain's seeing system. That system consists of two primary components: our visual cortex and our eyes. Our eyes work like cameras that take snapshots of every object around. And just like the snapshots of cameras, the images captured by our eyes are flat; they exist, as if on a digital screen or upon a roll of film, in two dimensions. So, to give us a full picture of the nonflat object that we're seeing, the two-dimensional snapshots from our eyes are shuttled by our brain to the enormously powerful circuitry of our visual cortex, which merges the snapshots into a three-dimensional mental image.

This process of converting the three-dimensional world into two dimensions and then back to three is a miracle of biological evolution, and because everything in nature is a possible object, the miracle proceeded smoothly for millions of years—until human artists invented impossible objects. And then it was that the miracle became even more miraculous. Since impossible objects can exist in two-dimensional space, our eyes are able to photograph them. But since impossible objects cannot exist in three dimensions, our visual cortex cannot assemble the photographs into a completed picture. Instead, it stalls in an infinite loop, going round and round from half of one possible object to half of another.

This endless cycle has a knock-on effect on our visual memory, which is tasked with recording every new object that we see. To make sure that the object is recorded properly, our visual memory releases a little neurochemical burst of wonder that tells the rest of our brain: *We're seeing something novel here!* The resulting sensation of awe pauses our brain, giving our eyes and our visual cortex a few extra moments to double-check their snapshottings and imaginative modelings, improving the memory's quality.

That's how it works normally, anyway. But when an impossible object throws our visual cortex into a loop, our visual memory jams open. It can't finish recording the object because it has no idea what the object is, so instead of releasing a single burst of wonder, our visual cortex keeps releasing more bursts and more, telling our eyes: *Keep pausing! Keep looking! We need a little more time to record this correctly!*

This stretched-out experience of visual wonder creates a special feeling in our brain, so special that it has been honored with its own unique name.

Psychedelic.

The Psychedelic and Its Science

The term *psychedelic* was coined in 1956 by the British psychiatrist Humphry Fortescue Osmond.

Osmond served as a naval psychiatrist during World War II, and after the conflict's end, he became interested in the intense hallucinogenic visions sparked by the drug LSD. These visions, he concluded somewhat overhastily, mimicked the delirium tremens of schizophrenia. And when this conclusion was greeted with bafflement by the London medical establishment, Osmond decided to immigrate to a railroad town in the frosted grain prairies of Saskatchewan, Canada, where he found employment in a vast and foreboding brick asylum: the Weyburn Mental Hospital.

The Weyburn housed hundreds of chronic alcoholics, deemed unfit for public release, who spent their days playing cards, taking cold baths, and receiving electroconvulsive head shocks. None of these therapies had cured the alcoholics, so Osmond saw an opportunity to test his theory about LSD. He reasoned that the schizophrenic terrors induced by the drug might spook the alcoholics into going sober, and to test this rather callous hypothesis, Osmond helped administer LSD to some two thousand Saskatchewan alcoholics in the years between 1954 and 1960. To Osmond's delight, the therapy worked: more than 40 percent of his patients quit drinking. But to Osmond's surprise, his patients didn't quit because the LSD was terrifying. They quit because the LSD triggered intense feelings of spiritual wonder that helped alleviate two of the underlying psychological causes of their alcoholism: depression and anxiety.

After hearing patient after patient euphorically describe this neural transformation, Osmond decided that the best moniker for LSD's heavenly visions was "soul sight." And since soul sight didn't have the ring of medical officialese, Osmond merrily reverse translated it into ancient Greek: *psyche* (soul) + *delos* (visible) = *psychedelic*.

Despite this official-sounding name, psychedelics remained on the medical fringe during Osmond's lifetime, and LSD itself was declared illegal in the United States in 1968. But in our own era, LSD's reputation has been improved by a number of intriguing scientific discoveries, including that psychedelics operate in the same basic way as impossible objects: they flood our visual cortex with images that it can't reconcile with physical reality, locking our brain in a state of open wonder.

This wonder is so incredibly strong that it has been shown in patient trials to reduce anxiety and depression for days and even weeks. But unfortunately, it's not without drawbacks: LSD is unpredictable in its effects, which can include psychosis, panic, vertiginous loneliness, and terrifying flashbacks. So, to minimize those drawbacks, psychologists have begun exploring the effects of "microdoses" of LSD. And if you'd like to try a microdose without any drawback at all, you can get it from John Donne's "A Valediction."

"A Valediction" gets psychedelic with its image of the dead-living body. That body is two possible objects—a deceased friend and an ongoing breath—impossibly joined into one. So, when our brain perceives this impossible object, it triggers the same neural pathways that go active in soul sight, stimulating a wonder loop that goes on for as long as we look.

And the dead-living body isn't the only source of soul sight in "A Valediction." The poem ends with an even more potent psychedelic object: an earth and a heaven made impossibly one.

The Poetic Psychedelic

To guide us into a psychedelic experience of earth-heaven, Donne begins by getting our visual cortex to imagine a simple tool: a geometer's compass. The compass has two pointed legs fastened into an upside-down V, so if we stick one leg down and spin the other around, we trace a perfect circle.

This circle-drawing instrument is introduced into the closing stanzas of "A Valediction," where a poet departing on a long journey urges his wife to visualize their souls as two legs of a single compass:

If [our souls] be two, they are two so
As stiff twin compasses are two,
Thy soul the fixed foot, makes no show
To move, but doth, if th'other do.
And though it in the center sit,
Yet when the other far doth roam,
It leans, and hearkens after it,
And grows erect, as that comes home.
Such wilt thou be to me, who must
Like th'other foot, obliquely run;
Thy firmness draws my circle just,
And makes me end, where I begun.

When we get to that final line—"And makes me end, where I begun"—what do we see? What's the "end" where the poet began? What final shape does the compass draw?

The answer is: Our brain sees two things. It sees two endings. It sees two compass shapes. One half of our brain sees with the eye of the body. That eye sees the second leg of the compass completing its loop and making a perfect circle: a "circle just." The other half of our brain sees with the eye of the mind. That eye reads the phrase "end where I begun" and imagines the poet returning to where he started his farewell: in the arms of his wife, bending the compass closed into a single point.

So, we see a circle—and also its center. We see the curve traced by the sun in the sky—and also the world at its hub. We see, in other words, an impossible union of two possible shapes—showing us a heaven and an earth as one.

Using the "Mind-Eye Opener" Yourself

Your head is itself an impossible object. It combines a brain of neurons with a mind of experiences, each of which is possible. But how are those two things combined into one? How is insentient gray matter merged with sentient consciousness?

This brain-mind impossibility began to excite interest among philosophers in the seventeenth century and among psychologists in the nineteenth century—and then in the early 1950s, at the same time that Humphry Osmond was launching his psychedelic investigations, it fell under the purview of an entirely new species of investigator: the neuro-anatomist. There was the serendipitously named British neuroanatomist Dr. Russell Brain, president of the Royal College of Physicians, who reckoned that even when the "cold eye" of science had exposed every secret of the brain, the mind would remain explicable only by poetry. There was the neuroanatomist Dr. Hartwig Kuhlenbeck, an emigre from Nazi Germany, whose pioneering study of "brain death" led him to reach the extraordinary conclusion that the mind existed in a parallel dimension. And most influentially of all, there was the American neuroanatomist Dr. Roger Wolcott Sperry, a 1981 Nobel laureate in medicine or physiology.

Sperry began his career by mad-scientisting a possible salamander into an impossible one: with deft surgical technique, he removed a salamander's eyes, rotated them 180 degrees, and then reinstalled them. The result was a salamander that existed in the perpetually psychedelic state of having a mind's eye that saw the world as right-side up, while its bodily eyes saw the world as upside down. In 1952 these visionary investigations inspired Sperry to author an article on the "Mind-Brain Problem" in *American Scientist* magazine, where he rejected the then-prevailing belief that the mind was a mirrored representation of the brain. Instead, Sperry proposed that our mind saw objects while our brain saw actions, such that when our mind beheld *water*, our brain beheld *drinking*, endowing our head with endless double sight.

From here, Sperry's research got even more trippy. He took a cat and severed its corpus callosum, splitting the left half of its brain from the right, and making the astounding discovery that both halves were conscious—*but that neither was conscious of the other*. So, which consciousness was the cat? Somehow, both were. The cat was of two different minds in one.

Then Sperry took one last psychedelic step: he transferred his attention to humans and found that we're like that cat. We possess two distinct zones of consciousness, right and left, that we perceive as one: "Both the left and the right hemisphere may be conscious simultaneously in different, even in mutually conflicting, mental experiences that run along in parallel."

Our head is thus even more impossible than the philosophers and psychologists knew. Each waking instant is really instants twinned, making every second of our mental life a paradox.

If your mind doesn't know this yet about itself, you can help open its eye with Donne's invention. The blueprint fell into disuse for much of the eighteenth and nineteenth centuries, but it was reborn in certain modern strains of visual poetry, such as the Imagist "This Is Just to Say" by William Carlos Williams:

> I have eaten
> the plums
> that were in
> the icebox
>
> and which
> you were probably
> saving
> for breakfast
>
> Forgive me
> they were delicious
> so sweet
> and so cold

Can the eye of your body taste the cold and the sweet while the eye of your mind simultaneously knows: the plums are no more?

You can also discover Donne's double sight in paradoxical visual narratives such as M. C. Escher's *Relativity* and *Waterfall*, or in filmic psychedelia such as Terrence Malick's *The Thin Red Line*, which uses polyphonic voiceover to mingle the thoughts of the dead with the sights of the living, doubling our consciousness and looping our awe. And the more that you open your mind's eye to these mystical art experiences, the closer you'll come to the deepest physics buster of all, a miracle beyond suns of pure gold and quintessence smudge free.

The miracle of the impossible you.

The one that glimpses two.

TEN

Achieve Self-Acceptance

Cao Xueqin's Dream of the Red Chamber,
*Zhuangzi's "Tale of Wonton," and the
Invention of the Butterfly Immerser*

At a wobbly elm desk in the shadow of the Xishan Hills, a student hung his head in shame.

The student was young Cao Xueqin, later to be reputed as China's greatest novelist. But as Cao hung his head on that early-eighteenth-century afternoon, all he knew of his future was the looming verdict of the imperial exams.

"Excel at the exams," his father had lectured only that morning, "and you will find your way inside the Forbidden City, swathed in silk as you attend the emperor himself."

"Do adequately at the exams," his uncle had encouraged more gently, "and you could enjoy a comfortable life as a regional salt commissioner."

But what if Cao didn't excel—or even do adequately? Well, then he would be forever stuck where he was now: the hard-soiled badlands west of Beijing. Which was to say: forever stuck in nowhere.

His stomach tightening at the thought, Cao tried to focus on his schoolbooks: *Great Learning* and *Doctrine of the Mean* and *Analects*. They contained the ancient teachings of Kǒng Fūzǐ (anglicized as Confucius but literally meaning "Master Kǒng"), a royal advisor who'd retreated from public life during the last years of the Spring and Autumn Period in the six and fifth centuries BCE to mentor six dozen disciples in virtues such as *zhi* (wisdom), *zhong* (loyalty), and *chi* (shame).

For many centuries now, those virtues had been a mandatory part of the imperial exams. Millions of students had faithfully memorized *zhi*, *zhong*, and *chi*, before then going on to careers as government ministers, tax collectors, and regional salt commissioners. Yet poor Cao knew that he'd never join such esteemed company. He could barely recall a fraction of what Master Kǒng had said. His exam scores were disastrous.

Cao's ineptitude at the exams came as an unpleasant surprise to his family. Not that Cao's family thought that the exams were easy. They knew that exam takers were locked for days in guarded cells with only a water jug, a chamber pot, and a bed of straw. They knew that most exam takers flunked, and that more than a few actually died, at which point, their corpses were unceremoniously wrapped in floor mats and tossed over the exam center's fortified rampart. But despite all those notorious horrors, Cao's father and uncles had been very good at the exams. They'd diligently memorized Kǒng's words and risen to eminent positions amid the wing-roof pavilions of the imperial court.

In the end, Cao's father and uncles had lost those positions, tumbling into their current slough of country poverty. Yet still, they were sure that, soon, they'd return to the heights. It was in their family's nature, after all, to succeed at tests. So, they'd raised Cao from his earliest days to study Kǒng. Cao had a quick and inquisitive mind, and they felt sure that he was destined to restore them to the emperor's grace.

But it was not to be. No matter how many hours Cao spent cramming, all he ever managed to pick up from his labors was *chi*, the virtue of shame. "Shame is the root of Duty," Master Kǒng had preached among the ancient bamboo groves of Lu. Nodding his head in sage agreement was Kǒng's great apostle Mèng Kē: "Shame is one of Nature's four sprouts, without which we cannot be human." And the lesson remained the same two thousand years later in the days of Cao, when the Chinese emperor dispatched imperial officials twice a month to warn every villager: *Never forget to look to your superiors and be ashamed of your faults; they walk the upright way and you do not.*

The emperor needn't have worried that Cao would forget. When it came to this one teaching, Cao was a true follower of Kǒng. He felt *chi* when he bungled his studies; he felt *chi* when he saw his mother's disappointed face; he felt *chi* when he witnessed his cousins wallowing in penury. Yet unfortunately, Cao's shame didn't do what Kǒng's acolytes had taught: rather than prompting him to sprout more human, it simply made him feel that he was worthless. Until at last, the feeling grew so great that poor Cao gave up on himself. Closing the covers of Kǒng's books and leaving the elm desk to wobble gently on its own, he exiled himself to his school's darkest corner, hoping to find a hole of oblivion that would swallow him up.

But in that corner, Cao instead stumbled onto something else: a faded old codex of boiled-bark paper. It had lain there, forgotten, for more than fifty years, ever since the Kangxi emperor had sternly instructed the Chinese people in his 1670 Sheng Yu, or Sacred Edict, to "exalt the true doctrine" of Master Kǒng and "cast away" the codex for its "strange teachings." And when Cao ignored the edict and peered disobediently at the codex's banished pages, what he saw was . . .

The Revelation of the Bark-Paper Codex

In the middle of the world lived Wonton.

Wonton had two neighbors: the emperor of the North and the emperor of the South. And he was always very kind to them. So, one day, the emperors decided to repay Wonton. They said: "We have seven holes in our heads. Two for hearing, two for seeing, two for smelling, and one for tasting. But poor Wonton has no holes like us. We should give some holes to him."

Pleased by their plan, the two emperors got a drill. Each day, they drilled a new hole in Wonton's head.

And on the seventh day, Wonton died.

When Cao finished these forbidden words, he knew just how he'd feel: full of *chi*. He'd once again defied his superiors, reading things he wasn't meant to.

But then Cao noticed to his astonishment that he didn't feel ashamed at all. In fact, he felt quite the opposite. His pangs of *chi* had lightened, and for the first time since he didn't know when, he felt comfortable being the less than perfect pupil he was.

Had the tale of Wonton done this? Had it somehow eased the head drill of Cao's shame? Curious to find out, Cao toted the codex back to his wobbly desk. And there he studied like he'd never studied before, poring over the outcast story until he glimpsed a hidden blueprint.

Wonton's Blueprint

Wonton was invented by the mysterious sage Zhuangzi, who is traditionally believed to have lived a century or so after Master Kŏng in the Warring States Period, when seven major states (and dozens of minor warlords) feuded over what is now central and eastern China. The feud was staggeringly violent. Its combatants wielded bronze-tipped artillery and iron dagger-clubs to slaughter one another in numbers unprecedented; one general alone, the unmerciful Bai Qi, was purported to have caused a million deaths. The mass killing didn't end until Bai Qi's masters, the Qin dynasty, conquered all the other states, prompting the Qin king to proclaim himself *Huáng dì*, or celestial emperor.

The violence of this period was condemned by the followers of Master Kŏng. Unlike the celestial emperor, who believed that the Chinese people were so fundamentally bad that they needed virtue imposed with law and blade, Kŏng taught that the Chinese were so fundamentally *good* that they'd spontaneously become dutiful if their rulers acted nobly. Indeed, such was the friction between Kŏng's disciples and the warlords that when the *Huáng dì* triumphed at last, he was subsequently accused of burying hundreds of the disciples alive.

Yet in spite of all this, Kŏng's disciples did share one common doctrine with the warlords: they too believed that China should be unified beneath one rule. Kŏng had called that rule the Tao, or "Way of the cosmos." Live with the Way, and we flowed with the eternal law of justice, honesty, and kindness; live against it, and we felt the shame of *chi* prodding us back to the path of our moral superiors.

Zhuangzi knew all about Kŏng's doctrine of the one true Way. And he knew, too, that Kŏng had conceived of shame as a goad to keep us off the dangerous path of cosmic nonconformity. But Zhuangzi couldn't bring himself to agree with Kŏng; like the iron discipline of the celestial emperor, the psychic rod of *chi* felt unnatural to him. So, Zhuangzi left Kŏng's classrooms and the celestial emperor's battlefields to wander through the lotus peaks and plum rains of eastern China, moving peacefully without pondering much where he was going. Until one warm afternoon, as Zhuangzi was gazing idly at koi fish in a pond and sparrows in the sky, he had an epiphany: koi and sparrows were not the same! Koi and sparrows each had their own Way, and the Way of one was not good for the other. If koi tried to live the Way of sparrows, they wouldn't make it very high in the sky. And if sparrows tried to live the Way of koi, they'd drown.

So, there isn't, after all, one Way of life, Zhuangzi thought. *There are many Ways. And each living thing has its own.*

Inspired by this discovery, Zhuangzi decided to share it with the world: *I shall write a great tome of wisdom, like the* Analects *of Master Kŏng. And I shall train a legion of six dozen disciples to spread my insight far and wide, teaching schools of students to be as wise as me, Zhuangzi . . .*

When suddenly Zhuangzi realized: he couldn't do any of that. If he taught others to think in his Way, he'd be contradicting his own epiphany and repeating the imperial mistake of Master Kŏng's schools and the Warring States.

Chastened, Zhuangzi sat down beside the koi pond and thought. How could he guide people into finding their own Way? How could he empower them to instruct themselves? Somehow he had to teach but *not* teach. It was a paradox . . .

Then, in a burst of inspiration, Zhuangzi saw a solution: he wouldn't teach; he would *unteach*, dismantling the one Way instituted by Kŏng and freeing people's minds to recover their own personal flows.

To pull off this educational reverse, Zhuangzi turned back before the Celestial Empire, back before Master Kŏng, back all the way to the Yellow River Valley of the second millennium BCE, where the pyromancers of the Shang dynasty had etched turtle bones with a pair of interlinking words: *yin* and *yang*. *Yin* meant "night." *Yang* meant "sunlight." And together they suggested a larger duality in nature. Just as night was paired with sunlit day, so too was every natural thing connected with an opposite: summer had winter, smooth had rough, waking had dream.

Kǒng's followers had explained away these couplings by claiming that each contained one higher partner: summer was superior to winter, smooth superior to rough. But Zhuangzi would change that. He'd demonstrate that yin and yang were two equal goods: summer was good for the lady beetle, and winter for the snow lynx; smooth was good for the bark of the wutong tree, and rough for the bark of the elm. Once people learned about this duality, the One imposed by Kǒng would crack apart, releasing a million individual Ways . . .

And then Zhuangzi halted again, realizing that he'd re-entangled himself in the old imperial error of trying to instruct people in the right way to think. If he genuinely wanted to un-One the world, he couldn't go around teaching the yin and the yang. The only way to do it was to *un*teach the *un*-yin and *un*-yang.

Thinking about this backward curriculum gave Zhuangzi a minor headache. And it made him decide that he was himself philosophizing entirely too much. He needed to stop with all the mental gymnastics and get back into his own spontaneous Way. So, Zhuangzi shut off his conscious mind. And relaxing into his flow, he picked up an ink brush to write.

What Zhuangzi Wrote

What Zhuangzi wrote was the "Tale of Wonton." This tale doesn't teach the rule of yin and yang. It doesn't teach the rule of anything. But it does fill our brain with startled dismay at Wonton's brutal end. It does make us feel: *Wonton didn't deserve to die for being different from the emperors.*

So, just as Zhuangzi had unplanned, the tale unteaches the un-yin and un-yang. It dismantles our belief in an absolute, imperial One.

Yet Zhuangzi didn't set down his ink brush when he'd finished the "Tale of Wonton." He kept on writing and writing. Why? Zhuangzi himself didn't know. He was in the flow of his Way, not thinking. But if we permit ourselves a few moments of conscious reflection, we can see that the neural power of the "Tale of Wonton" comes at a potential cost: it prompts such dismay at the two emperors that it threatens to tip us into condemning them. Instead of just making us feel that *Wonton was all right his own Way*, it can also make us think that *Those emperors were bad people.* When we think that, we're back in the mind-set of the One. We're back to believing that some Ways are bad and others are good.

So it was that Zhuangzi balanced the "Tale of Wonton" with stories like this:

> I, Zhuangzi, once dreamed that I was a butterfly, flitting about and enjoying myself. I didn't know that I was Zhuangzi. Suddenly I awoke, and I was myself again, the genuine Zhuangzi. So, had Zhuangzi dreamed that he was a butterfly? Or was a butterfly now dreaming that he was Zhuangzi? I didn't know. But there's clearly a difference between Zhuangzi and a butterfly. And such is the transformation of things.

This is "Dream of the Butterfly." Unlike the "Tale of Wonton," it doesn't contain any characters who can be seen as villains. Instead, it draws us into experiencing two different but equally positive experiences of life. First, we're Zhuangzi dreaming of the butterfly, and then we're the butterfly dreaming of Zhuangzi. In both cases, we're happy, enjoying ourselves. So, even though we change from one thing to another, the transformation isn't an improvement or a decline. Like moving from a summer beetle to a winter lynx, we appreciate two sides of life.

Now, if you're still consciously reflecting on Zhuangzi's storytelling, you might have started to wonder: *If "Dream of the Butterfly" communicates the experience of two more completely than the "Tale of Wonton," then why didn't Zhuangzi go back and blot out the "Tale of Wonton"?* Good question, my summer beetle. And the answer is this: "Dream of the Butterfly" may communicate yin and yang more completely than the "Tale of Wonton," but that doesn't make it better than the "Tale of Wonton." Each story has its own Way:

> The "Tale of Wonton" is more powerful and more narrow in its neural action. It vigorously demolishes our mind's belief in the One.

> "Dream of the Butterfly" is gentler and more broadening in its neural action. It teases our mind open to Two.

If Zhuangzi had written only "Dream of the Butterfly," it might not have been strong enough to break the grip of the One. If Zhuangzi had written only the "Tale of Wonton," it might not have been broad enough to unfurl Two. So, Zhuangzi wrote both stories, giving our brain smooth and rough, summer and winter.

And with this storytelling yin and yang, Zhuangzi also gave our brain something else: the neural experience of self-acceptance that young Cao found in the bark-paper codex.

Self-Acceptance and Its Neuroscience

Self-acceptance, as young Cao Xueqin discovered, is disrupted by feelings of shame.

Shame is one of our "moral" emotions, the other major ones being guilt and pride. These emotions aren't really moral. They spring not from a universal right and wrong but just from our brain, and they can vary as widely and as wildly as human life. But modern psychologists nevertheless refer to shame, guilt, and pride as moral because these emotions reinforce the ethical codes of our local community. Shame and guilt discourage us from doing things that our community sees as bad, while pride encourages us to do things that our community sees as good.

Pride has often been denounced by philosophers and theologians, and group pride has a long history of encouraging destructive behaviors such as sexism, hooliganism, and nationalism. But modern psychology studies have shown that pride in our individual characteristics—be they unique ideas or idiosyncratic interests or quirky skills—can improve our mood, strengthen our resilience, and even make us a more supportive friend. By imbuing us with a calm confidence in our own Way of being, it can make us less inclined to view alternate Ways as a threat, encouraging us to value other people for what makes them different.

Shame, meanwhile, is almost always unhealthy. It can contribute to lowered self-esteem, substance abuse, depression, anxiety, and poor relationships, all of which stem from shame's vicious neural mechanism, which cuts far deeper into our brain than guilt. Where guilt makes us self-conscious about our outer actions, shame makes us self-conscious about our inner *nature*. So, instead of prompting us to feel a salubrious remorse for correctable behaviors such as lying and cheating, shame prods us to experience a damaging disgust at what we permanently are: *I'm ugly. I'm stupid. I'm worthless.*

If we're going to feel bad about ourselves, it's therefore healthier to feel guilty than to feel ashamed. And our own biology seems to have recognized this. Guilt appears to have evolved in our brain more recently, reducing shame to something of a vestigial organ, like tonsils and wisdom teeth. And although shame can't be surgically removed in the manner of these other vestigia, its self-destructive effects can be minimized by targeting its neural origin: our inner list of cultural norms.

That list inheres in record-keeping brain regions such as our medial frontal gyrus, and, in fact, inheres so strongly that it can't be wiped clean; our brain feels a need to possess at least *some* cultural norms. But even though our norms can't be deleted, our shame can be minimized another way: our inner list can be *enlarged,* expanding our brain's sense of what constitutes socially acceptable behavior. And one simple, prosocial method for accomplishing this expansion is to befriend people who act differently from us; the more varied the norms of our companions, the more comfortable that our brain feels just being itself.

The same shame-reducing therapy is stimulated by "Dream of the Butterfly." By transitioning us from the life of Zhuangzi to the life of the butterfly, the story allows us to experience the acceptability of one Way and then another, increasing our inner list of norms and lightening our self-judgment. Which is why the story eased the *chi* that pained young Cao Xueqin.

As welcome a remedy as this was to young Cao, however, its effect is limited by the workings of our brain. Our brain can't free itself from unhealthy shame by reading a single short story about a butterfly; our medial frontal gyrus absorbs norms over hours of organic immersion, so to achieve full self-acceptance, we would need to butterfly through literature for quite a while. And although Zhuangzi sought to facilitate this extended literary experience by authoring dozens more stories upon a long scroll that would later become known as the *Zhuangzi*, those stories were composed many centuries before the development of an even more potent butterfly-immersion technology that would be discovered by Cao in another ill-lit corner of his school.

At the time that Cao made his discovery, the technology was such an odd and idiosyncratic thing that no one knew quite what to call it. It wasn't poetry, musical theater, or any of the other ancient literary arts celebrated by the scholars of the Qing imperial court. So, eventually, in years after Cao, the technology became known by a kind of no-name that simply marked its novelty.

That no-name was "the novel."

The Technology of the Chinese Novel

The Chinese novel was invented in the 1300s, many centuries before its European counterpart.

Its reputed inventor was the playwright Luo Guanzhong, a semi-legendary character who styled himself "the playboy of the seas." In the last days of Kublai Khan's golden empire, or possibly in the first days of the million-man-army Ming dynasty, Luo paused his playboy ways to author *Romance of the Three Kingdoms*, a mythic-historical novel about the rise of the dynasties of Shu Han, Cao Wei, and Eastern Wu. And at roughly the same time that Luo was composing *Romance*, another author (possibly Luo's teacher or maybe even Luo himself) was crafting the second classic Chinese novel, *Outlaws of the Marsh*, which recounts how a gang of outlaws repent their crimes to join forces with the rightful emperor.

Both *Romance* and *Outlaws* were read by young Cao Xueqin. And as Cao buried himself in their pages, he realized that they were even more psychologically transporting than "Dream of the Butterfly." That increased transport was generated primarily by two literary inventions. The first was the "Secret Discloser," which generates love and forms a basis for literary romance. (See chapter 2 for the blueprint.) The second was the Empathy Generator, which stirs compassion and forms a basis for literary tragedy. (See chapter 3.) Together these inventions encouraged Cao's brain to care for the characters of *Romance* and *Outlaws*, a caring that was lent an erotic dimension in *Outlaws* by the inclusion of lightly pornographic material.

Cao was struck by the emotional power of this loving-empathetic-erotic caring. But he noticed that it was mobilized by the two classic Chinese novels to induce another less positive feeling: shame. Both *Ro-*

mance and *Outlaws* hinged on a conflict between order and chaos, and both used their literary technologies to encourage us to care more for the Way of order than for the Way of chaos, elevating a yang over a yin, and inculcating our brain in the One.

So, Cao decided to repurpose the literary technologies of *Romance* and *Outlaws*. He wrote his own Chinese novel, *Dream of the Red Chamber*, set in a yin-yang world populated with dozens of complex characters who aren't heroes or villains, but who all follow their own different Ways. And to tease open our brain to these many Ways, Cao's narrative is enriched with hundreds of Secret Disclosers and Empathy Generators, filling us with attraction and care for the characters' sundry styles of life.

The neural result of this literary innovation is to give our brain the experience of joining a vast cosmopolitan community. Each new character in *Dream of the Red Chamber* gently expands our inner list of norms, drawing us into a widening panoply of human diversity that, like a richly varied set of friends, makes us more comfortable being ourselves.

And after Cao had finished repurposing the literary technologies of Zhuangzi and the classic Chinese novelists, he carried his engineerings a step further, inventing two original shame reducers of his own—the first of which was the "Dream of the World."

The Dream of the World

You might have noticed that the title of Cao's novel, *Dream of the Red Chamber*, sounds similar to "Dream of the Butterfly." That's because Cao constructs his novel like Zhuangzi's little parable, only with one gigantic twist: instead of having one character dream of another, Cao has one *world* dream of another.

The first world is the realm of the Qing dynasty. The second world is the Land of Illusion. So, which world is the dream, and which world is the dreamer? Well, of course, the answer is: both. In the opening chapter of Cao's novel, a Qing man dreams of the Land of Illusion, where a thing of illusion then reciprocates by journeying into a dream life in Qing. And so it goes in later chapters, with characters waking from one world into the other.

Each world feels real in its own distinct Way. The Land of Illusion contains all the secrets of Qing's mortal inhabitants, so it must be the *real* real. And yet the Qing dynasty is the place where illusions go to shed tears and feel love, so it must also be the *real* real.

Together, these two worlds immerse us in the experience of waking up as something else. Back and forth we move, from the dreamer of one world to the dreamer of the other. Each different and equally true. Each unteaching the un-yin and un-yang.

And to keep this process going, the novel then introduces its second invention: the "Equilateral Love Triangle."

The Way of Two Hearts

The Equilateral Love Triangle is a special kind of love triangle.

In a regular love triangle, a boy falls in love with two opposite girls, but only one of those girls is really right for him. The other girl *seems* right, but that's just because our boy needs to wise up.

In the Equilateral Love Triangle, a boy falls in love with two opposite girls—and *both* of those girls are really right for him. One is his yin and the other, his yang.

(Equilateral Love Triangles don't have to involve one boy and two girls. They can involve any combination of boys and girls—or even characters who don't identify as boys and girls at all. But Cao's Equilateral Love Triangle involves one boy and two girls, so for clarity's sake, we're using that model here.)

In *Dream of the Red Chamber*, the boy is Baoyu. Baoyu is supposed to be studying Master Kǒng's teachings to prepare himself for a career at the imperial court. But instead, he prefers reading the "Tale of Wonton" on the sly. Perhaps because of that reading, Baoyu has a spontaneously double nature: he's a boyish boy who loves women's clothing.

The two girls of the Equilateral Love Triangle are Baoyu's cousins, Baochai and Daiyu. Baochai is wise and reserved, generous to others, and unshowy in her dress, while Daiyu is witty and musical and has a strongly possessive heart. The two girls could not be more different yet Baoyu loves them both. (His name, in fact, is a combination of one syllable from each of theirs.)

And the novel encourages us to feel that same love. Because of our own natural Way, many of us may be initially drawn more to either Baochai or Daiyu. But to open our mind to an equilateral caring, *Dream of the Red Chamber* uses Secret Disclosers and Empathy Generators to convey the intimate confessions and unspoken sorrows of both girls, touching us with affection and compassion for two opposite souls.

So, we don't just observe the Triangle. We join it, embracing its yin-yang romance ourselves.

Using the "Butterfly Immerser" Yourself

To find your Way, you have to go with your spontaneous flow. You can't read *Dream of the Red Chamber* like we've done in this chapter. You can't mull over its Equilateral Love Triangle or Dream of the World. You have to enjoy it thoughtlessly, immersing yourself in pages of love and empathy and the occasional erotic twist.

And when you're done with those pages, there's plenty more literature that can boost your self-acceptance by reducing your shame. Equilateral Love Triangles can be found in the 1942 film *Casablanca*, Milan Kundera's *The Unbearable Lightness of Being* (1984), and Chimamanda Ngozi Adichie's *Americanah* (2013). Dreams of the World can be found in Ralph Ellison's *Invisible Man* (1952), the Philip K. Dick–inspired *Total Recall* (1990), David Mitchell's *Cloud Atlas* (2004), and Jaco Van Dormeal's *Mr. Nobody* (2009). And you can always jerry-rig a yin for your yang by reading any novel that dips you into a tragic romance set in a society with norms opposite from your own.

So, go read like Wonton; go read like a butterfly. And leave behind this night-day world to wake up in another dream.

ELEVEN

Ward Off Heartbreak

Jane Austen, Henry Fielding, and the
Invention of the Valentine Armor

B eneath the medieval beech roof of the Steventon market arcade, her turquoise ribbon aflicker in candlelight, twenty-one-year-old Jane touched a gloved hand to the arm of Tom Lefroy, a recent graduate of Dublin's Trinity College. And as a cotillion change played out from a country violin, Jane and Tom began to dance.

Jane liked many things about Tom, but most of all his taste in books. The comic novel *Tom Jones* was a mutual favorite. Tom liked it so much that he decided to dress up like its hero. Jane liked it so much that she decided to become a novelist.

And then, just a few weeks after Tom and Jane met, the dancing was no more. Jane wrote to her older sister, Cassandra, "The Day is come on which I am to flirt my last with Tom Lefroy. . . . My tears flow as I write at the melancholy idea."

Were Jane's tears really flowing? Or had she already smiled them all away? It was hard for Cassandra to know. Jane had a way of being lightly ironic about love. It was an antidote to heartbreak that she'd picked up someplace; Cassandra wasn't sure where.

But Jane herself knew exactly where: her copy of *Tom Jones*. And before the antidote had found its way into that much-thumbed book, it had been invented across the waters to the south, amid the Mediterranean heat of the Castilian city of Valladolid, where, in a long brick house that was rumored to double as a hall of *prostitución*, the Spanish marine corps veteran and disgraced tax collector Miguel de Cervantes had dipped a worn accounting nib in ink . . . and penned the opening of *Don Quixote*.

Don Quixote Sallies Forth

Cervantes drafted *Don Quixote* in 1604 with a clear purpose in mind: to rid the world of the pain caused by literary romance.

Literary romance traced its origin back twenty-four centuries to Homer's *Odyssey*, a twelve-thousand-line song about a mortal man who outwits the gods, talks with the dead, feasts on endless ox flesh and Dionysian drink, enjoys the most gorgeous music in history, spends seven years in the embrace of a nymph and another year in the bed of a beautiful witch, and finally returns home to find his ageless wife waiting faithfully.

This chronicle of wish fulfillment does more than show Odysseus getting what he hungers for; it seduces our own brain into believing that our desires will be similarly fulfilled. That seduction is accomplished by the technology of the Almighty Heart (see chapter 1), which conjures up the anthropocentric feeling that the cosmos cares for the same things that we do. What we love, the sky loves; what we crave, the stars crave for us. So, when we read the *Odyssey*, our neurons come to feel that our inner yearnings are rooted in the outer laws of physics. Just as the sun will rise at dawn, so too will the objects of our desire bloom up from the soil, sating our heart with everything we want.

This gratifying experience made literary romances popular throughout the wine halls of ancient Greece and even more popular throughout the great chambers of medieval Europe. In romances from the eleventh-century French *La Chanson de Roland*, to the twelfth-century Spanish *El Cantar de Mio Cid*, to the thirteenth-century German *Willehalm*, to the fourteenth-century Castilian *Amadís de Gaula*, to the fifteenth-century English *Le Morte d'Arthur*, to the sixteenth-century Italian *Orlando Furioso*, songsmiths updated Odysseus into feudal knights such as the questing King Arthur, the faithful Amadís, the dashing Sir Roland, and the ingenious El Cid. Dragons were vanquished, maidens were rescued, banquets were guzzled, treasures were plundered, heavens were opened. And it was all a terrible disaster.

The disaster is chronicled in *Don Quixote*. The novel's title character has spent his days imbibing literary romances. And falling victim to
the brain-altering machinery of the Almighty Heart, the don looks out
his window and sees the world he *wants* to see: a chivalric fantasyland
where he is the second coming of El Cid. So, tossing aside his books, the
would-be knight sallies forth to save the damsels of his barrio La Mancha.

The don's reward for these wish-chasing heroics is gruesome physical hurt. Crashing into the hard knocks of life, he gets chewed by lions,
outmuscled by pilgrims, and thwacked by windmills, ending up bone
bruised in ditch after ditch. But thankfully, we, the don's readers, are
rescued from a similar fate by Cervantes's romance reengineer, which
dismantles the Almighty Heart and replaces it with a very different narrative technology:

> Our dapper new adventurer therefore set out, remarking to
> himself: "Who doubts but in coming ages, when the true history
> of my famous deeds comes to light, that the sage who pens my
> sally in the morrow will do so thus: *No sooner had rosy-cheeked
> Apollo stretched the golden strands of his beautiful hair over the face
> of the wide and spacious earth, and no sooner had the little birds
> tuned their tongues to sing in sweet and mellifluous harmony of the
> coming of the rosy Dawn, who deserted the soft bed of her jealous
> husband to show herself to mortals through doors and balconies
> across the La Manchan horizon, than the famous horse-rider Don
> Quixote of La Mancha, abandoning the idle feathers of his mattress,
> mounted his famous horse Rocinante and commenced to walk across
> the ancient and well-known field of Montiel.*" And it was true that
> he was walking there.

This is irony, the invention we unearthed in chapter 4. Piercing through
the imaginary fluff of romance—"No sooner had rosy-cheeked Apollo
stretched the strands of his beautiful hair"—to reveal the situation's actual truth—"And it was true that he was walking there"—the ironic
style of Cervantes's novel hoists us out of the don's earthly delusions,
restoring our wits to God's-Eye sobriety.

Don Quixote was instantly popular in Spain and was soon translated into Italian, German, English, French, Dutch, Portuguese, and more. Over the ensuing decades, it was shipped to Peru, camel-backed across the Sahara, and pirated by rogue booksellers in Boston. It would go on to sell a staggering half billion copies, becoming the second most popular book in history, behind only the Bible.

And *Don Quixote* wasn't just widely beloved; it was also profusely medicinal. During the seventeenth century, its pharmaceutical irony helped break the medieval spell of chivalry, making way for the methodological reason of René Descartes and the *Principia* of Sir Isaac Newton: "We moderns have endeavored to dismiss numinous forces and call back nature to mathematical law."

At long last, the delusions of the Almighty Heart were banished. The Enlightenment's clear gaze had triumphed over the dark ages of magical thinking.

Or so it seemed. Because in short order, the world relapsed. Descartes decided that wizardry was, in fact, a science: "The occult powers of sympathy and antipathy will be traced to mechanical causes." Newton forgot his calculus and joined the alchemists in their chase of the philosopher's stone: "This is the sphere of ♂ & the living gold."

And before long, the madness of literary romance re-erupted, more violent than before.

The Madness Returns

The madness officially returned in November 1740. It was then that the prudish London gazetteer Samuel Richardson published his first novel: *Pamela*. Despite the reactionary leanings of its author, *Pamela* was a remarkable literary innovation. It took the private letters and journal entries of Pamela Andrews—a fictional maid who seduced her sex-mad employer with her own chaste virtue—and *stretched* these personal revelations to an enormous 225,000 words. The result was a lyric of epic proportions; a bosom whisper that outdid the *Odyssey* in length. Or to put it scientifically: *Pamela* expanded the Secret Discloser, that love-stirring literary invention from chapter 2, until it became an original form of Almighty Heart, engineering a potent new combination of intimate disclosure and wish fulfillment that convinced our gray matter that the whole world was a sonnet teeming with amorous prospects.

Initially, this romantic enthusiasm didn't seem so very bad. In fact, it seemed cheerful, hopeful, even inspiring. But soon it became clear that *Pamela* was breeding a new species of Don Quixote. To these new Quixotes, every man was a dashing gallant; every woman, a would-be bride; every waking second, a summons to nuptial bliss.

So it was that the new Quixotes suffered a fate worse than the original. The original had merely gotten broken of body, but the new Quixotes got broken of heart. They dashed again and again into love—only to discover to their miserable shock that the world was not, in fact, filled with would-be spouses. It was populated instead with carnal con artists, polite uninterest, and mismatched affections. Over and over, the new Quixotes rushed into kissing too fast. And over and over, they got dumped at the altar, their dreams ending in tears.

This situation needed rectifying. The pain-causing nonsense of *Pamela* had to be dosed away with healing medicine. And as luck would have it, there was a literary doctor living in London, not too far from Samuel Richardson's print shop, who possessed a restorative prescription.

The doctor called himself Conny Keyber. But that was a pseudonym. The doctor's real name was Henry Fielding.

The Doctor Gallops to the Rescue

Henry Fielding was many things: a playwright, a newspaperman, a father of ten.

But most of all, Fielding was an avid reader of *Don Quixote*. As a twenty-two-year-old playwright, he drafted the comedy *Don Quixote in England*. And when he turned later to writing novels, he inked the subtitle *Written in Imitation of the Manner of Cervantes, Author of Don Quixote*.

So, when Fielding got hold of *Pamela*, he at once diagnosed the problem: an excess of romance, produced by epic-length intimate disclosure, leading to foolish sentimentality and broken-heartedness. And Fielding also had no doubt about the cure: irony. Irony had saved the chivalry-addled readers of *Don Quixote*, and it could now do the same for

Pamela's love-besotted readers. Thus in April 1741, a mere six months after *Pamela* premiered, Fielding published an ironic parody. Its title, naturally enough, was *Shamela*.

Shamela was a mild success, earning a second edition seven months later. Yet to Fielding's disappointment, it wasn't nearly as popular as *Pamela*. Its curative irony went largely unheeded by the literate masses, who continued to pervert their heads with further romance novels: *The Adventures of the Countess of XXX*, and *Letters from a Peruvian Woman*, and, most perverting of all, *Fanny Hill, or Memoirs of a Woman of Pleasure*: "Every part of me was open and exposed to the licentious courses of her hands, which, like a lambent fire, ran over my whole body, and thawed all coldness as they went."

Meanwhile, the unrepentant instigator of this hot madness, Samuel Richardson, kept toiling over his romance technology, extending its blueprint and adding new circuitry. Until at last, in 1748, he emerged from his workshop with a truly astounding creation: *Clarissa, or, the History of a Young Lady*.

Clarissa was a titanic novel. It very nearly reached a million words, and all of it in private letters, aflood with personal revelations:

> My heart is too full;—so full, that it may endanger my duty, were
> I to try to unburden it to you on this occasion: so I will lay down
> my pen.—But can—Yet positively, I will lay down my pen—!

The pen was not laid down. On the novel went, for five hundred letters further. This was intimate disclosure on a more than epic scale. This was the love poem colossus.

Inevitably, the reading public lost what remaining sense it had. Smitten by the amorous fictions of *Clarissa*, legions of new Quixotes swooned across Europe. Even the age's great titans of reason weren't immune. Denis Diderot, co-inventor of the encyclopedia, rhapsodized that he would not part with the novel under any circumstance; if his dear friends needed food, if his children needed schooling, he would sell all his library, but never *Clarissa*.

Instantly, Fielding knew that he had to act. He had to concoct a more effective prescription than the simple irony of *Shamela*. He had to be more gallantly doctorly than ever before.

So, Fielding took up a pharmacological stylus and withdrew into his apothecary chambers. And in a feat of medical heroism, he wrote *Tom Jones*.

The Medicine of *Tom Jones*

Tom Jones, like *Shamela*, was a mock romance.

But it wasn't just a mock romance. It was also a *genuine* romance, spinning the comically heartwarming tale of a young couple who, after tumbles and spills, eventually found their way to the chime of wedding bells.

Why was this sentimental love story written by Henry Fielding, that inveterate foe of romance novels? Had his wits gone soft with age? Had he decided to give up his scruples and make a quick shilling?

No. Fielding constructed *Tom Jones* as a love story because he'd gotten smarter. He'd realized why *Shamela* hadn't really worked: irony alone wasn't enough to doctor up the general public. To be healthy of heart, the public needed more than unremitting fantasy debunkment. It needed a little warmth, a little hope, a little joy. It needed, in short, a little romance.

When Fielding realized this, his opinion of the general public dropped. But then he remembered his marriage to the bonny Charlotte Craddock—and his subsequent marriage to the perhaps even more bonny Mary Daniel. And musing on his cheerful wedded hours, Fielding had an epiphany: there were two kinds of romance, bad and good. Bad romance recklessly inebriated us with delusional hope; good romance raised our spirits without intoxicating them.

But how to write a novel that conveyed good romance's sober uplift? How to translate the undrunken bliss of Fielding's matrimonial unions into literary form? There was no precedent that existed on all the world's bookshelves, so in *Tom Jones*, Fielding boldly invented a new blueprint, alternating between Almighty Heart ("It is impossible to conceive a more tender or moving scene than the meeting between the uncle and nephew") and lightly satiric narration ("Jones went up to Blifil's room, whom he found in a situation which moved his pity, though it would have raised a less amiable passion in many beholders").

The result was a mix of epic-length intimate disclosure and mock-epic irony, a back-and-forth between *Pamela* and *Don Quixote*, that elevated our heart while also restraining it.

Fielding's sentimental-ironic concoction was a great publishing success. *Tom Jones* dramatically outperformed *Shamela*, becoming a best seller and earning a place in many of the world's most level-headed libraries. Adam Smith turned its pages before crafting the materialist doctrine of *The Wealth of Nations*. Thomas Jefferson dallied in its paragraphs before drafting the self-evident truths of the Declaration of Independence. Edward Gibbon delighted at its droll amours before authoring his sagacious opus *The Decline and Fall of the Roman Empire*. And soon the novel would be plucked off a shelf by another discerning reader—indeed, a reader rather *more* discerning than Smith, Jefferson, and Gibbon, at least in literary matters.

That reader inhabited the greeny shire of Steventon, amid garden hedgehogs and dog rose blooms, about seventy miles southwest of London. Her mother, Cassandra Leigh, was a wit who'd adventured to see an almost-royal uncle, Theophilus, in his master's office at Oxford University. Her father, George Austen, was an Anglican rector whose sister, Philadelphia, had odysseyed to India in pursuit of a spouse.

And she, herself, in April 1776 was carried as her parents' seventh child to the quiet parish church beside the oaks, where she was baptized with the common name of Jane.

Jane Austen Diagnoses *Tom Jones*

When Jane Austen read *Tom Jones*, she was deeply impressed. And the more she reread it, the more impressed she grew. The novel was, she saw, a literary breakthrough. Its blueprint was ingenious—and it worked just as Henry Fielding had imagined, restraining romance without killing it off.

Yet as Jane Austen leafed through Fielding's triumph, she came to realize that there was a further breakthrough to be made. *Tom Jones* had been successful, no doubt, but it hadn't captured as vast an audience as *Pamela* and *Clarissa*. Those novels had sold in prodigious quantities, inspiring a horde of English duplicators such as Sarah Scott's *The History of Cornelia* (1750), Frances Sheridan's *Memoirs of Miss Sidney Bidulph*

(1761), Frances Brooke's *The History of Emily Montague* (1770), Charlotte Turner Smith's *Emmeline, the Orphan of the Castle* (1788), and Mary Robinson's *Angelina: A Novel in a Series of Letters* (1796). And Richardson's novels had also extended their influence far beyond the English shoreline: they'd been quoted in German sermons, prescribed by Spanish lawyers, transformed into Austrian operas, and imitated in the love letters of America's future first ladies.

Why hadn't the joyful tonic of *Tom Jones* enjoyed this same level of popular reception? Jane Austen couldn't say at first, but as she meditated on the matter, an answer hoved slowly into view: Fielding's strategy of alternating between sentimental and ironic narration had yielded a half romance and a half dose of medicine. That's why *Tom Jones* had proved only half as popular as *Clarissa*—and also why it had cured only half of the world's quixotic love. To reach the full readership of *Clarissa* and give that readership a complete hospital treatment, a novel couldn't go half-and-half like *Tom Jones*. Instead, every one of its pages would have to be entirely romantic and entirely ironic.

This, of course, was impossible. A novel could be a sonnet or a satire—or it could do a *Tom Jones* and flip back and forth between. It couldn't treat its readers to sentences that were simultaneously love stirring and disenchanting.

Except that, as Jane Austen realized, it *could*. All it would take was a new kind of literary technology. Or rather, all it would take was an *old* kind of literary technology that had been known to Fielding and generations of earlier ironists but that possessed a secret potential they had failed to grasp. Prior to Austen, this old technology was so disregarded that it didn't even have a formal name. But in the years after Austen made the technology famous, that slight would be corrected and the long-neglected nuts and bolts would gain a portentous scholarly appellation: free indirect discourse.

Free Indirect Discourse

Free indirect discourse was invented almost two thousand years before Jane Austen.

The inventors were ancient satirists who wanted a literary mechanism for combining irony with self-disclosure. Here's an early prototype from Horace's first satire, which wryly exposes Rome's golden age as less than golden:

> Why is no one happy anymore? "O lucky traders!" moans the sol-
> dier, his once-young limbs now busted-up with combat. While the
> storm-tossed trader sighs in response, "O to be at war! Where in
> one crowded hour, the whole issue is decided, for death or glory!"

This short passage might not appear so very extraordinary, but it per-
forms a remarkable sleight of tongue. It seems to contain three independent voices: the voice of the satirist, the voice of the soldier, and
the voice of the trader. But, in fact, all three voices are spoken by the
satirist; he imitates the voices of the soldier and the trader, ventrilo-
quizing them.

Why does this matter? Well, since the satirist is always talking, and
since the satirist is always ironic, every word of the passage is ironic. But
since the satirist parrots the inward emotions of the sailor and the soldier,
the passage also offers a glimpse into the hearts of two characters, mingling its constant irony with bursts of private sentiment.

As employed here by Horace, the technique is fairly crude. In fact, at
this stage in its development, it is not yet free indirect discourse; it's a pre-
cursor known as double voice. But Horace would refine the technique
into full free indirect discourse in his later satires, and that refinement
would enter English literature at its earliest morrow: Geoffrey Chaucer's
fourteenth-century story collection *The Canterbury Tales*.

The Canterbury Tales begins by introducing us to a procession of religious pilgrims, one of whom is perhaps not quite so religious:

> A Monk there was, a mighty one,
> Who rode about and loved to hunt.

This little couplet, like Horace's satires, is imbued with irony. Hunting
is not, after all, on the list of approved activities for monks; that list contains things such as prayer and manual labor and reading holy books,
not keeping hawks and chasing red foxes and arrowing bucks. And *The*

Canterbury Tales then continues its ironic lampoon by cheekily pretending to justify the monk's absurd lack of interest in monk work:

> Why should he scramble his brains all night,
> Poring over dry and dusty sermons?
> Why toil with his hands as Augustine bid?
> How then would the world be served?
> Let Augustine have his work for him reserved!
> And so he rode his horses hard.

This is all very amusing, when all of a sudden, something quite seriously astonishing occurs. You can detect the something in the second-to-last line: "Let Augustine have his work for him reserved!" Here we can actually hear the monk scoffing at Saint Augustine for working so hard: *What good did work ever do the world? Not as much good, surely, as me going on a fast hunt!*

But how do we hear the monk? The monk never actually speaks. There are no dialogue quotes; the only one speaking is the narrator.

The answer is that Chaucer is using free indirect discourse. In free indirect discourse, the voice of the parroted character isn't formally marked off with punctuation, as in Horace's first satire. Instead, the narrator dips freely in and out of the character's inner psychology, allowing Chaucer to give us a dash of the monk's interior sentiment while fully maintaining the narrator's ironic voice.

This technique is a marvel. It's one of the most extraordinary inventions in the history of literature. Its constant irony prompts us to snicker at the monk's ridiculousness, while its pivot into self-disclosure stirs us with an affable warmth for the monk's ebullient disobedience. In that instant of double consciousness, our brain feels wryly outside and emotionally inside the monk at the very same time. And although this outside-inside neural flicker lasts for only a moment in *The Canterbury Tales*, it opens up a remarkable literary possibility: an ironic romance that inspires us to care about its characters. Or in other words, a satiric love story that genuinely touches our heart.

So remarkable was this possibility that it never appears to have occurred to Horace or Chaucer. Nor is there any sign that it occurred to the many other satirists who dabbled in free indirect discourse, on and off, for almost two thousand years.

But it did occur to Jane Austen.

Jane Austen Goes Free Indirect

In 1811 a new novel appeared. It was published anonymously, its title page revealing only that it had been authored "by a Lady." It sold slowly yet steadily; after two years, all 750 copies of its first print run had been purchased, so a second printing was ordered.

The novel was *Sense and Sensibility*. And its secret author was Jane Austen.

Austen had begun drafting *Sense and Sensibility* in her late teens. Back then, she'd copied the blueprint of Samuel Richardson's epistolary romances, constructing her novel as a sequence of fictional letters exchanged between the Dashwood sisters, Elinor and Marianne. But when *Sense and Sensibility* finally appeared in bookstores, it didn't read like *Pamela* or *Clarissa*. Instead, it read like this:

> The prospect of four thousand a-year, in addition to his present income, besides the remaining half of his own mother's fortune, warmed [John Dashwood's] heart, and made him feel capable of generosity.— *"Yes, he would give [his sisters] three thousand pounds: it would be liberal and handsome! It would be enough to make them completely easy. Three thousand pounds! he could spare so considerable a sum with little inconvenience."*— He thought of it all day long, and for many days successively, and he did not repent.

Like the satires of Horace and Chaucer, this passage uses free indirect discourse to mock a clueless character. The clueless character here is Mr. John Dashwood, whose inner thoughts (marked in italics) reveal that he's a little too pleased with his own "generosity."

With her dig at Mr. John Dashwood, Austen became the first author to deploy free indirect discourse in a romance novel. And quickly, she began to innovate further. She gentled the free indirect discourse, making it feel less like a broad satiric caricature and more like a character's unique inner disclosures. Until in 1816, five years after *Sense and Sensibility*, Austen published *Emma*, which began its opening chapter with this:

> Sorrow came—a gentle sorrow—but not at all in the shape of any disagreeable consciousness.—*Miss Taylor married*. It was Miss Taylor's loss which first brought grief.

The free indirect speech marked in italics is Emma Woodhouse's inner voice. It's her consciousness, what's in her head. It could be read by us, if we wanted, in a slightly melodramatic tone. But it's not comically absurd in the way that Mr. John Dashwood's inner feelings are. And as *Emma* proceeds, this subtleness continues:

> [Emma] had not been there two minutes when she found that Harriet's habits of dependence and imitation were bringing her up too, and that, in short, they would both be soon after her. *This would not do*; she immediately stopped.

In *Emma*, there are hundreds of these light pivots toward Emma's personal sentiments. And the more of these pivots that we get, the more that our brain begins to experience something that literature had never made a brain feel before.

The Neuroscience of Austen's Novels

Prior to Jane Austen, no novels had drawn us into feeling irony and love at the same time. The most they'd done was to alternate between ironic detachment and sentimental romance, like *Tom Jones*.

But as Austen discovered, we're perfectly capable of experiencing irony and love simultaneously. That's because irony and love exist in different parts of our brain. Irony occurs in the perspective-taking circuitry of our outer cortex (see the introduction and chapter 4), while love dwells in the inner emotion zones of our amygdala. So, by focusing our cortex and our amygdala on different narrative objects, literature can inspire a neural mix of wry perspective and romantic feeling.

This division of our neural attention is what Jane Austen does in

Emma. Austen's ironic narrator focuses our brain's perspective-taking circuitry on one narrative object: the novel's storyworld. Meanwhile, her free indirect pivots focus our brain's emotion zones on a second narrative object: Emma.

The first half of this equation, the ironic focus on the storyworld, precisely reverses the effect of the Almighty Heart. Where the Almighty Heart lures our brain into feeling that the sky and the trees pulse with human sentiment, Austen's irony disenchants the world, reducing its laws of physics to Cartesian logic and Newtonian calculus.

The second half of this equation, the sentimental focus on a character, stirs our heart (or more precisely, our amygdala) with love for an individual. We care for Emma in the way that we care for Pamela, Odysseus, and the other heroes of romance.

The resulting cortex-amygdala blend draws us into experiencing an intimate human connection alongside a wry detachment from the greater world. Which is to say: it opens our heart to other people without duping us into mistaking our own desires for the laws of reality.

This neural duality is very healthy. It gives us all the psychological benefits of love—joy, energy, enthusiasm for life—while protecting us from the heartbreak suffered by romantic Quixotes. It helps us care— *with* care.

And this isn't the only neural benefit of reading Austen. As psychologists have recently discovered, the free indirect style of *Emma* fosters a very different kind of love than *Pamela* does. Richardson's love technology makes our brain feel that Pamela is an extension of our own feelings; Austen's invention encourages our brain to recognize that Emma loves different things, in different ways, than we do. That is, unlike Richardson's novels, Austen's novels don't motivate us to embrace other people as versions of ourselves. Instead, Austen's stylistic fusion of intimate disclosure and ironic detachment inspires us to embrace other people while acknowledging that those people have their own distinct needs and desires. So, when we read *Sense and Sensibility*, *Pride and Prejudice*, or *Emma*, our neural circuitry is guided into loving others for who they are, not for what we want them to be.

Such is the more generous love eventually discovered by Emma herself. At first, Emma is a romantic Quixote; convinced that her own feelings echo the world's Almighty Heart, she spends most of the novel meddling in the love life of her friend Harriet Smith. Harriet wants to marry Robert Martin. But to Emma, Robert Martin is a most unsuitable husband. He's not a man who touches the heart; Mr. Elton is *much* better. So, Emma chases away Robert Martin and pushes Harriet and Mr. Elton together.

Yet to Emma's surprise, wedding bells do not ensue. Instead, Harriet's romance with Mr. Elton collapses, leading Emma to suspect that Harriet will be happy only if she marries Mr. Knightley, the very man that Emma herself has fallen for. After all, if Mr. Knightley is right for Emma, then how could he *not* be right for everyone else as well?

Until finally, at the novel's end, Harriet reveals to Emma that the man she most desires is . . . Robert Martin. And as bewildering as this revelation is to Emma, she at last manages to free indirectly accept that Harriet desires the man that she herself does not:

> [Emma] had no sooner an opportunity of being one hour alone with Harriet, than she became perfectly satisfied—*unaccountable as it was!*—that Robert Martin had thoroughly supplanted Mr. Knightley, and was now forming all her views of happiness.

Emma has come to love Harriet while accepting that her friend's tastes are "unaccountable." And Austen's style has helped us feel the same about Emma, caring for her even when she does things we never would.

This way of caring is the gift of Austen's novels to our neural circuitry. And it is a wonderful gift. It improves the health of our relationships, eliminating the friction and resentment that come from expecting our loved ones to be perfectly in sync with our own desires. And you might even say that it carries us a step closer to true love. Because isn't that what true love is? Forgetting our self-involved fantasies to embrace a different heart?

Using the "Valentine Armor" Yourself

If you want more pure romance in your life, you can walk into almost any public library and find shelves full of Samuel Richardson's swoon-inducing offspring. Of them, none is more legendarily potent than

Charlotte Brontë's 1847 novel *Jane Eyre*, which updates Richardson's technology in two dexterous ways. First, it exchanges Pamela's fanciful catalogue of real-time letters for the more plausible fiction of a retrospective "autobiography." Second, it does away with Richardson's efforts to restrain romance; where Richardson constructs *Clarissa* as a tragedy and ends *Pamela* with a God Voice sermon against desire, Brontë crafts a judgment-free conclusion that keeps our heart open in full. But beneath these updates lies Richardson's original pulse-elevating blueprint: an epic-length self-disclosure. And indeed, so similar are *Pamela* and *Jane Eyre* that Brontë seems guilty at times of the most flagrant plagiarism: in both novels, a female servant cares for her master's illegitimate child. In both novels, a gypsy fortune-teller dispenses marriage advice. In both novels, the female servant returns to her master upon learning he's ill.

You can also find Richardson's technology in a wealth of modern romance novels, from Ann Patchett's *Bel Canto*, to Audrey Niffenegger's *The Time Traveler's Wife*, to Nicole Krauss's *The History of Love*, to André Aciman's *Call Me by Your Name*. So, should you ever feel your days bereft of ardor, you can get them re-aflutter with an extended literary confessional.

But should you instead find yourself suffering from the opposite affliction—an overromanticizing of life that Don Quixotes your heart— you can find a remedy in Austen. Read the opening line of *Pride and Prejudice* ("It is a truth universally acknowledged"), feeling the narrator's lightly wry tone. Then keep that tone going, through all the inner self-disclosures of Elizabeth Bennet and Mr. Darcy, so that you care for their individual hearts while accepting that they inhabit an unsentimental world.

And if you're not an Austen fan (or if you've read her so many times that you're ready for the same feeling in a new story), there are plenty of modern novels that use Austen's invention to inspire more sensible— and more generous—amours. Try Ian McEwan's *The Children's Act*. Or *The Marriage Plot* by Jeffrey Eugenides. Or "Brokeback Mountain" by Annie Proulx.

Their free indirectness will help you be wiser in romance and kinder too. So, the next time you dance with your own Tom Lefroy, you keep your heart safe—and help it love true.

TWELVE

Energize Your Life

Mary Shelley's Frankenstein, *Modern Meta-
Horror, and the Invention of the Stress Transformer*

D r. Frankenstein wanted a way to quicken the pulse. So, he "dabbled among the unhallowed damps of the grave" and "collected
bones from charnel houses." Until at last: "it breathed hard, and a con-
vulsive motion agitated its limbs."

Alive! It came alive!

The Invention of Dr. Frankenstein

In May 1816 a teenage Mary Wollstonecraft Godwin—soon to be known
to the world as Mary Shelley—journeyed with her lover and her infant
son to vacation on the slopes of Lake Geneva at a stately villa inhabited
by a lordly English occultist and his hired sleepwalking expert.

It was an overcast summer, the air murky from the faraway eruption
of Mount Tambora, a volcano that flung such quantities of ash into the
global atmosphere that hoarfrost formed in June. And late one afternoon, as dusk began to drop and shadows mingled with the lava haze,
Shelley and her companions retreated inside the villa's shuttered library,
where upon a cobwebbed shelf, they found the eerie Franco-German
tome *Fantasmagoriana*, or *Little Ghost Tales*. Turning its leathered pages,
they read about a man who dug up a talking head. And about a painting
that killed children with a kiss. And about a Death Bride who hunted

grooms. And about a young woman whose spirit warned her that she'd die that night at nine o'clock: *Ticktock, ticktock, ticktock* . . .

These tales, Shelley remembered later, "awaken[ed] thrilling horror . . . quicken[ing] the beatings of the heart." Energized by the feeling, she and her friends set about inventing their own little ghost tales. The sleep-walking expert ratcheted together the ghoulish saga of a skull-eyed lurker. The lordly occultist concocted one of the world's first literary vampires.

And Shelley? Well, Shelley failed. The creative pistons of her mind misfired, and instead of engineering a monster supernatural, they prompted Shelley to imagine a scientist, an un-monster entirely natural. Mortified, Shelley kept the mental miscarriage to herself. But although her lips stayed locked, she could not expel the scientist from her mind. And a few nights later, she was gripped by a vision of him at work upon a "powerful engine": "I opened mine [eyes] in terror . . . a thrill of fear ran through me."

This was a terror as powerful as any ghost story. And yet, its "thrill" was unlike the tales of *Fantasmagoriana*. It was a horror different.

The Horror Different

Horror stories give us a fictional scare that tricks our brain into an in-vigorating fight-or-flight response. Pumping our pulse with adrenaline speed and pouring feel-good endorphins through our spinal cord, they dose us with a physiological rush.

But not all horror stories rush us the same. Some provide a good rush that charges our mind, powering us to get more out of life, while others provide a bad rush that can damage our health.

The difference between these two kinds of rush has been traced by scientists to a weird anatomical structure that sprawls from our brain's hypothalamus and pituitary glands to the adrenal cortex of our kidneys. The structure is our HPA axis, and one of its regular functions is to reg-ulate cortisol, a hormone that stimulates wakefulness. Our blood levels of cortisol are dropped by our HPA axis during nighttime sleep, then boosted back up when our eyes open at dawn, reaching peak strength about a half hour after we roll out of bed.

This morning cortisol boost is meant to be our body's cup of natural coffee, delivering a kick of energy and heightened focus to buoy us through the day. But when we get spooked, the coffee dispensing kicks into overdrive. Our HPA axis generates more cortisol, which in turn works on our brain like extra caffeine, giving us the added energy and focus to outrun or outthink any chasing bogeymen.

That cortisol bump can be a lifesaver. But it's not without a potential cost. The same elevated cortisol that benefits us in the short term can damage our health in the long. It can cause insomnia and exhaustion; contribute to anxiety and depression; and increase our odds of diabetes, heart attack, and stroke.

These negative health effects of cortisol were discovered in the mid-twentieth century by another enterprising doctor: Dr. Hans Selye. Selye was raised amid the Roman watchtowers and medieval ruins of the Hungarian city of Komárom, a day west of Transylvania. In the 1920s, when Selye was training in Prague as a medical student, he noticed that some of his patients were eerily suffering from maladies with no obvious physical cause. And in the summer of 1936, after Selye had relocated to a neo-Victorian biochemistry laboratory in Montreal, he published a letter in the science journal *Nature* that warned of "a syndrome produced by diverse nocuous agents" such as "spinal shock." Or as the good doctor would more crisply summarize his finding: people were getting sick— and even dying—from "stress."

After Selye identified the dangers of stress, other doctors began recommending that we avoid anything that might elevate our blood cortisol: *Stay away from high-pressure environments—and don't read any more ghost stories!* Yet as Selye continued his weird anatomical research, probing ever deeper into the neurochemical mysteries of the HPA axis, he discovered that stress wasn't always harmful. And in his 1974 book *Stress Without Distress*, he dissected stress into two kinds. There was bad stress, or "distress." But there was also good stress, or "eustress."

Just like bad stress, good stress prompts our HPA axis to dose us up with cortisol. But unlike bad stress, good stress isn't associated with insomnia, anxiety, stroke, or diabetes. So, good stress gives us all the benefits of extra cortisol—increased energy and focus—without the drawbacks. (Except for exhaustion, which good stress does cause. We can't, unfortunately, get additional brain activity for free.)

The science of eustress seems almost too good to be true. And the science only gets better: psychology studies have revealed that the root difference between good stress and bad is simply our brain's perception of whether the stress is voluntary or not. Involuntary stress, triggered by a stalking predator, a tyrant boss, or a medical crisis, is bad. But voluntary stress, like embarking on a new career, venturing on a first date, or banking everything on a dream, is good. So, if we want an energizing kick of eustress, all we need to do is tackle a fresh challenge. And more miraculously still, if we want to eliminate our bad stress, all we need to do is *choose* to embrace it. If we decide to see a career setback, a romantic rejection, or even a cancer diagnosis as a chance for personal growth, then our distress will be converted into eustress, and we'll feel charged and focused instead of sleepless and anxious.

It's not easy to shift our perception in this way, of course. But as Mary Shelley discovered, literature can help.

The First Discovery

Mary Shelley's discovery was preceded by another.

We don't know who made the first discovery, but we do know that it had been made by the time of Jane Austen, who would publish her own debut novel in 1811, seven years before Shelley. Austen was stuck indoors one soggy afternoon when she decided to peer inside the world's first gothic novel, *The Castle of Otranto*, authored by Horace Walpole in 1764. And soon Austen found herself immersed in the tale of a most peculiar wedding day. Everything for the nuptial ceremony was ready: the bride veiled, the feast prepared, the guests expectant in the chapel. Yet when the groom began his walk toward the marriage aisle, he was suddenly squashed by a gigantic knightly helmet that tumbled from the sky. Stunned, the waiters spilled the drinks, while a palace servant shrieked, "Oh! the helmet! the helmet!"

This was meant to be chilling, and to many of Austen's contemporaries, it was. The Scottish novelist Walter Scott—a man of such luminous acumen that he would be commissioned to track down his nation's missing crown jewels—declared in 1811 that *The Castle of Otranto* engineered the same uncanny "sort of terror" that you got from noticing how the painted eyes of old oil portraits seemed to track you as you sauntered past.

But Austen felt no such ghoulish creep. Instead, she couldn't stop chuckling: *Oh! the helmet! the helmet!* And as peculiar as Austen's response might have seemed to Sir Walter, it's not uncommon for people to smile or even laugh when havoc occurs: a birthday cake candle accidentally ignites a dangling festoon of crepe paper decorations; an irascible pet goes berserk and violently attacks a hapless houseguest; a tourist peering at his phone collides with a carnival of stilt walkers, tumbling bodies everywhere. And instead of reacting to these scenes of mayhem with appropriate consternation, a few people in observance forcibly swallow grins or even snicker openly.

If you're one of those snickerers (or if you happen to be standing next to one right now), don't worry: it's not a sign of psychopathy; it's neurally normal. That's because, strange as it seems, our mental feelings of horror and *ha-ha-ha* share the same origin: our brain's perception of something odd.

This curious fact is why "funny" has a double meaning. We can have a funny feeling that makes us chuckle, or we can have a funny feeling that tingles the hairs on the back of our neck, filling us with nervous creep. Both kinds of funny begin when our brain's perception of something odd triggers our threat-detection network, which, as we explored back in chapter 6, is finely tuned to notice any anomaly in our environment. In response to the anomaly, our threat-detection network warns the decision-making apparatus of our frontal cortex: *There's something odd here!* Our frontal cortex then analyzes the something odd, deciding whether it's possibly dangerous, definitely dangerous, or not dangerous. If it's *possibly* dangerous, our brain pauses, experiencing an edging concern. If it's *definitely* dangerous, our brain gets scared and tells us to run. If it's *not* dangerous, our brain laughs.

The first two responses are stimulated by horror stories. Horror stories introduce us to weird anomalies—a dead head that talks, a piece of medieval armor falling from the heavens, an almost-human built from salvaged limbs—and make us feel like the anomaly is potentially, or definitely, dangerous. The more uncertain the danger, the longer the horror creep; and the more certain the danger, the harder the horror jolt.

So, horror stories can generate a protracted feeling of psychic unease—or a violent shock.

The third neural response to something odd is triggered by a very different literary genre: comedy. Comedy feeds us strange characters or eccentric schemes and then reveals them to be harmless, making us chortle. This, itself, seems a kind of oddity. Why is our brain configured to giggle at things that are weird but unthreatening? The biological answer seems to be that our brain's humor response evolved in part as a way of reversing the stress caused by our threat-detection network: one of laughter's physiological functions (as we saw in chapter 4) is to reduce our cortisol level, so when our HPA axis mistakenly boosts our blood cortisol, a laugh can flush out the error.

The shared neural origins of horror and humor have spawned legions of intentionally campy horror flicks, from *Attack of the Killer Tomatoes* to *Evil Dead II*. And they can also empower us to pull a Jane Austen when consuming serious ghost stories. If our bad stress ever spikes too high, we can snicker at the oddness of tales such as "The Legend of Sleepy Hollow" or *The Haunting of Hill House*. Then the weird becomes harmless, and our stress response converts to grins and titters, laughing away the dangers of insomnia and anxiety.

But as Mary Shelley would discover a few years after Austen, there's an even more empowering shift of mental perspective that we can make in response to horror fiction. That shift doesn't get rid of the spook-spawned cortisol in our system. It *keeps* the cortisol and transforms it into something good.

The More Empowering Discovery

The seeds of Mary Shelley's discovery were planted on the waking night when her own blood cortisol wouldn't let her rest. Into Shelley's insomniac brain fluttered the vision of the scientist. And she realized that his science struck her differently from the supernatural stuff of *Fantasmagoriana*. The supernatural stuff had felt imposed by higher powers, but the science felt like a voluntary thing of human making. The scientist *chose* to build his engine and peer into the secrets of life.

This feeling of choice, Shelley would later decide, was a delusion.

The scientist was, in fact, compelled by greater forces—desire, destiny—to pursue his own doom. But when it comes to the physiological effects of horror stories, what matters isn't the underlying reality of life; what matters is our brain's perception of reality. And as Shelley's midnight vision had revealed to her, one of science's peculiar powers is to excite our brain with the belief that we have the power to freely achieve anything: omnipotence, immortality, resurrection.

So, two years later, when Shelley decided to expand that midnight vision into her 1818 novel *Frankenstein; or, the Modern Prometheus*, she began by inviting her readers to imagine a scientific expedition to the North Pole:

> What may not be expected in a country of eternal light? I may there discover the wondrous power which attracts the needle; and may regulate a thousand celestial observations. . . . These are my enticements, and they are sufficient to conquer all fear of danger or death.

This is the Promethean dream of science. And because the power of the dream is to make us believe that we can be gods who engineer our own fate, the "danger" that awaits us on our scientific quest isn't a source of health-gnawing anxiety. It's a source of eustress. By imagining that "death" is our own free choice, we come to feel more alive.

To amplify this energizing feeling, Shelley then constructs the remainder of *Frankenstein* as a pulse-raising gothic novel, with one mad scientist twist: she inverts the distress-inducing blueprint of earlier gothic novels to generate eustress instead.

Earlier gothic novels had induced distress through reading immersion: a psychological experience of being engrossed in, and even swallowed by, a story. This experience had been engineered in *The Castle of Otranto* by a preface in which a translator explains how he'd stumbled upon the tale of the falling knight helmet "in the library of an ancient Catholic family." No such library ever existed. The translator and the library were both fabrications of the tale's actual author, Horace Walpole. Yet even so, the preface's make-believe has a real-world effect: it makes the following tale feel more immersive to our brain.

The immersiveness is generated by two features of the preface. First, the translator remarks that although the tale of the falling helmet is "evidently fictitious,"

> I cannot but believe that the groundwork of the story is founded on truth. The scene is undoubtedly laid in some real castle. The author seems frequently, without design, to describe particular parts.

This is a clever literary trick. Preemptively disarming our skepticism, it encourages us to suspend our doubts and peer deeper into the story, seeking authentic truths hidden beneath the surface preposterous.

Our reading immersion is then increased further by the preface's second feature: its use of a "Story in the Story," an ancient literary device (for some examples, see chapter 24) where a character in one story tells another story, transporting our brain into a second zone of fiction. This transport is a subtype of the *stretch* (see the introduction), and, like all *stretches*, it reduces activation in our brain's "self zone," dissolving the neural border between our consciousness and fiction. So, in *The Castle of Otranto*, when the story of the fake translator *stretches* into the Story in the Story of his "translated" novel, it softens our self-aware distance from the physical book in our hands, immersing our brain further in horror.

After Walpole, this basic blueprint of horror immersion was expanded by Ann Radcliffe's *The Mysteries of Udolpho* (1794), Matthew Gregory Lewis's *The Monk* (1796), E. T. A. Hoffmann's *The Devil's Elixirs* (1815), and other gothic novels that blur the line between their storyworlds and our mind, making us feel engulfed by the narrative on the pages before us. And so, in the decades following *The Castle of Otranto*, horror stories pulled our brain ever deeper into helpless terror, drowning us, suffocating us . . . until in 1818 Mary Shelley's *Frankenstein* flipped the blueprint, interrupting our reading immersion with self-conscious moments where we feel the power of our own volition.

Frankenstein Flips the Horror-Immersion Blueprint

The most ambitious element of Mary Shelley's blueprint flip is her reversal of Walpole's Story in the Story. Where Walpole's *Castle* uses its

preface to plunge us one way into an inner story, never appending a con-
cluding translator's note to lift us back out, Shelley engineers *Frankenstein* to include two Story in the Story exits.

The first of these exits occurs at the end of the novel's second volume,
which we spend submerged in the psyche of Dr. Frankenstein's monster:

> "My rage returned: I remembered that I was for ever deprived of
> the delights that such beautiful creatures could bestow. . . . I only
> wonder that at that moment, instead of venting my sensations in
> exclamations and agony, I did not rush among mankind, and per-
> ish in the attempt to destroy them."

Here the monster is absorbed in a profound feeling of horror until suddenly he gains a reflective distance: "I only wonder." And moments later,
the narrative provides us with that reflective distance too. The monster's
Story in the Story ends, and we're extracted to the outside story of Dr. Frankenstein: "The [monster] finished speaking, and fixed his looks upon me."

This pullout does more than just return us to the outside gaze of
Frankenstein; it also triggers an intense moment of self-consciousness:
"fixed his looks upon me." These five words break the "fourth wall" of
the story, like a monster staring right out of our television screen to lock
eyes with us. So, they prompt sharp activation in our brain's self zone,
undoing the neural effect of the Story in the Story *stretch*, and replacing
our lost-in-a-book flow with an abrupt consciousness of our own separate existence.

The same double rupture is repeated by *Frankenstein*'s second Story
in the Story exit, which occurs at the end of the novel's third and final
volume. There we're exited from Dr. Frankenstein's tale to the outer
narrative of the North Pole explorer. And when we exit, the first thing
we encounter is the explorer's declaration to his sister: "You have read
this strange and terrific story, Margaret; and do you not feel your blood
congealed with horror, like that which even now curdles mine?"

Once again, our immersion is doubly broken. First, we're made aware
that Frankenstein's narrative is a "story." And second, we're called upon
to self-consciously analyze our feeling of "horror," prompting renewed
activation in the fiction distancer of our neural self zone.

Through these double ruptures, Shelley replaces the deep immersion of earlier gothic novels with the opposite neural experience: a detached self-awareness. Which is to say: Shelley invents what we now know as meta-horror. Meta-horror does the reverse of engulfing us in a horror we cannot escape. It makes our brain conscious that the horror is a fiction that we've chosen to consume—and can keep choosing to consume if we wish.

Perhaps this feeling of choice is real. Or perhaps it's just another human fantasy. But either way, it has a true psychological effect upon our brain. Shifting our neural perception of Dr. Frankenstein's gothic nightmare, it provides us with the same experience of voluntary discovery that thrills the scientific explorer on *Frankenstein*'s opening pages. Just like the explorer, we don't feel that "danger and death" are chasing us; we feel as though we are chasing them. And so it is that Mary Shelley's meta-narrative invention keeps our adrenaline pulse elevated and our cortisol eye full open—transforming our stress from bad monster to good.

Using the "Stress Transformer" Yourself

At the end of *Frankenstein*, the North Pole explorer's ship becomes trapped in the ice. His sailors rebel, demanding that the expedition turn back. When suddenly Dr. Frankenstein bestirs himself from the ship's hold.

The doctor is dying, his health ruined by the monster's depredations. Yet for a brief instant, the old spark flies to Frankenstein's eyes, and, turning to the mutinous sailors, he cries:

> "Did you not call this a glorious expedition? And wherefore was it glorious? Not because the way was smooth and placid as a southern sea, but because it was full of dangers and terror; because, at every new incident, your fortitude was to be called forth, and your courage exhibited; because danger and death surrounded, and these dangers you were to brave and overcome."

With this speech, Frankenstein reminds the sailors that they chose to face danger and death. And it was a healthy choice, too, one that has filled the sailors' lives with vital energy, rousing their spirits and electrifying their minds.

Now another moment of choice has arrived: the sailors can decide to abandon the expedition, calming their minds back to normal. Or they can decide to feel more alive by embracing danger again.

So, what will you choose? Will you be a retreating sailor? Or a second Frankenstein? Will you turn your ship away from death, seeking warm harbor behind? Or will you chase the monster into dark poles beyond?

If you choose the latter, you'll get a jolt of eustress. And whenever you want more of that jolt, you can find it in the many works of modern horror that use Mary Shelley's meta-horror blueprint to give our brain a self-aware distance from the terror before us. This distance isn't an invitation to snicker; it's not comic, or campy, or ironic. It's an affectively neutral reminder that the terror is a fiction, and, as a fiction, something that we've made a conscious decision to watch. At any time, we can shut the book or turn off the screen, returning to our horror-free reality.

For a classic meta-horror energizer, try the epilogue of the 1983 film *The Twilight Zone*. For a more recent heart charger, try *The Cabin in the Woods*. For meta-horror more violently electric, try *Funny Games*. For meta-horror more lightly thrilling, try *Scream*. Or flip through your own favorite horror fictions and identify the ones that create a light neural separation without prompting the *full* separation that triggers laughter. Then convert your stress to healthy energy by choosing to run into death, danger, and the nightmare.

And feel alive.

Alive!

THIRTEEN

Solve Every Mystery

Francis Bacon, Edgar Allan Poe, and the
Invention of the Virtual Scientist

I n ancient times was writ the mystery of God creating light, and the
mystery of Noah's ark, and the mystery of a carpenter's son walking
on the Sea of Galilee.

When these biblical mysteries were read aloud at Sunday tabernacle, the congregation yearned to know, *How could that possibly have happened?* But the congregation got no answer. The point of the mysteries
was that they could never be fathomed. They defied all reason, humbling
the know-it-all mind and opening the soul to the saving grace of faith.

During the waning days of the Roman Empire, the Bible's faith-stirring
enigmas inspired the beginnings of a new literary genre: the mystery play.
The mystery play amazed crowds with the parting of the Red Sea, and
manna from heaven, and Sarah pregnant at ninety, and Jonah escaping
the whale's belly, and Daniel in the den of lions, and water turned into
wine, and Lazarus raised from the dead. Their marvelous scenes would
become the most popular theatrical entertainments of the European Middle Ages, staged in cities from Elche to York by bands of semiprofessional
actors clad in the robes of Moses, the fig leaves of Eve, and the thorn crown
of Jesus. Shakespeare likely saw them as a boy, and they may well have
inspired him to pen his own dazzlingly insoluble mysteries: the ghost of
Hamlet, the charm of Cleopatra, the magic of Prospero.

And so the mysteries extended further and further through history, until two centuries after Shakespeare, a storyteller asked himself: Why not write a work of literature where the mystery was solved? It was a most unorthodox idea—so unorthodox that there was no evidence that any author had conceived it before. But the storyteller was enough of a freethinker to give it a go. So, he imagined a pair of sleuths who encountered a mystery. And he filled his steel dip pen with ink to scribble down what happened next . . .

When suddenly he paused midscrawl, struck by an even more exciting idea: Why not go further than writing a story that contained detectives? Why not write a story that *trained* detectives?

Why not write a mystery that taught readers how to go forth and solve mysteries of their own?

The Solver of Mysteries

The origins of the mystery-solving blueprint lay in London, less than four years after Shakespeare's death. It was then, in 1620, that a voluminous manuscript of stylish Latin prose was handed to John Bill, the royal publisher at Blackfriars, by Sir Francis Bacon. Bacon was lord high chancellor of England, a position he'd achieved through a mixture of shrewdness and flexible ethics. His favorite philosopher was Machiavelli, and in a year's time, he'd be stripped of his chancel robes for the crime of "being twice paid"—a euphemism for accepting bribes.

Bacon's worldliness made him suspicious of priests and their chatter of insoluble mysteries. He brushed aside the importance of miracles, insisting that Jesus was more social reformer than magician. And to peel back the gauze of medieval superstition that clung to nature's atomic mechanism, Bacon devoted his spare hours to reading the publications of a crew of clear-eyed sleuths. The sleuths included astronomers such as Galileo, who was unriddling the mysteries of the heavens above; physicists such as William Gilbert, who was unriddling the mysteries of the world below; and anatomists such as William Harvey, who was unriddling the mysteries of the heart within.

How were the sleuths unriddling these mysteries? To find out, Bacon betook himself to his prodigy house at Gorhambury, where, amid great Doric columns and flint-built chambers, he spent hours poring over the sleuths' maverick works: Galileo's *The Starry Messenger*; Gilbert's *On the Magnet and Bodies Magnetic, Including That Great Magnet, the Earth*; and Harvey's 1616 Lumleian Lectures, *Prelude to a Complete Anatomy*. Until eventually Bacon devised an answer that he expounded in the voluminous 1620 manuscript that he gave to John Bill. The manuscript was titled *The Great Instauration*. And the answer was contained in the manuscript's almost as grandly titled second part: *Novum Organum Scientiarum (The New Logic of Sciences)*.

As signaled by that title, Bacon's answer began by taking a skeptical look at the "old" logic of sciences. The old logic was deduction, which employed *general* knowledge to draw conclusions about *individual* cases. So, let's say that you'd acquired the general knowledge that the only large, black birds living in the north of England were crows. And then, one Saturday on a pleasant stroll in Liverpool, you saw an individual large, black bird. Instantly, you'd deduce: *The bird must be a crow!*

This process of deduction was drilled into medieval European students from the eleventh-century University of Bologna to the seventeenth-century University of Turku. Students would begin by memorizing a few approved textbooks, such as the Bible and Aristotle's *Metaphysics*. Then they'd apply the general knowledge from these textbooks to individual questions: Why is there a moon? How much faster will a bucket of rocks fall than a bucket of air? What quantity of angels can stand upon a needle's point? The answers could be supplied by deduction. And if the answers couldn't be supplied, well, then God had intended for the answers not to be known.

For centuries, this seemed an entirely satisfactory system. It explained almost everything, while leaving just enough mystery to stir awe at God's divinity. But then, in the decades prior to Bacon's radical book, the system was violently disturbed by the sleuths. The sleuths wielded telescopes, scalpels, and other devices unknown in the universities. And those devices turned up very different answers than the old logic. Answers like: there's not just one moon; there are moons around Jupiter too. And: a bucket of rocks and a bucket of air fall at exactly the same speed. And: those tiny things on needles' points are actually unangelic bugs.

By themselves, these answers were startling enough, but they were only the prelude to an even more startling affair. For the sleuths then used these answers to contest the general knowledge that had been taught for generations in medieval schools. First, the sleuths challenged Aristotle, scoffing that his *Metaphysics* was bunk. Then they went further and dared to challenge the Bible itself. The Bible was quite clear that the earth sat still:

> The world also is stablished, that it cannot be moved.
>
> —Psalm 93:1

> Fear before Him, all the earth: the world also shall be stable, that it be not moved.
>
> —1 Chronicles 16:30

But this scriptural authority left the sleuths themselves unmoved. Waving their telescopes, they proclaimed: *"terram mobilem, Solem vero in medio universi immobilem constituit"*—"The earth moves, while it is the sun that sits unmoving at the center of the universe."

The university professors were naturally appalled. Challenge the Bible on the basis of some newfangled seeing tube? It was lunacy.

But it wasn't lunacy, at least not according to Francis Bacon. It had a perfectly sound logic: the new logic.

The New Logic of the Sleuths

The new logic, Bacon argued, was induction.

Induction precisely inverted deduction. Where deduction employed general knowledge to draw conclusions about individual cases, induction employed individual cases to form conclusions about general knowledge. So, let's say that on a pleasant Saturday stroll in Liverpool, you spotted a hundred white-bellied aquatic birds—and all those birds were cormorants. On the basis of those hundred individual cases, you'd posit a piece of general knowledge: "All the white-bellied aquatic birds in the north of England are cormorants." And there you go. You'd have performed an induction.

Induction was not, strictly speaking, a "new" logic. Aristotle himself had practiced it, and it had been known to university professors for centuries. But even so, induction had always been treated as a minor component of the medieval educational system. It was a method for confirming the general knowledge of Aristotle's *Metaphysics* and the Bible, not for making new knowledge. And it certainly wasn't a method for *overturning* the great philosophical truths that wise minds had accepted for hundreds, even thousands, of years.

Bacon disputed this. He claimed that induction, not deduction, was the foundation of learning. He urged the development of more powerful looking devices for gathering individual observations that could be transformed by induction into new general truths. And to promote this investigative revolution, Bacon authored his own literary yarn, *New Atlantis*, which imagined a futuristic utopia where sleuths rivaled biblical miracles, using the new logic to cure leprosy, recycle wastewater into delicious new wines, and create tele-visual illusions that dazzled the eye. Into this fictional story, Bacon then craftily slipped the technology of the Vigilance Trigger (see the blueprint in chapter 6), inducing the brains of his readers to question the old truths and seek fresh ones themselves.

In 1660, thirty-four years after Bacon's death, a dozen of those questioning readers founded the College for the Promoting of Physico-Mathematical Experimental Learning, later to be known as the English Royal Society. And its members—who would include luminaries such as Isaac Newton, Robert Boyle, and Robert Hooke—began filling books with new physics, new chemistry, new medicine, new biology. By the early nineteenth century, Bacon's inductive method had inspired the invention of the steamship and the locomotive, and as these powerful machines stretched England's empire across the world, the nation's sleuths followed in the wake. They studied plants in North America, perfumes in South Asia, and plate rocks in central Africa. Like the fictional utopians of *New Atlantis*, they spied into the minutest crevices of the world and spun vast new theories about the cosmos.

Until all of a sudden the sleuths realized there was a terrible problem: Bacon had got it wrong.

Bacon's Error

Bacon's mistake began to dawn on the sleuths in the eighteenth century. And by the 1820s, it could no longer be ignored.

The mistake was this: induction could never lead the sleuths to the truth. According to the laws of logic, the only way to reach the truth through induction was to study every individual case. Not just *many* cases, or *most* cases, but *every single one*. So, to reach the truth about cormorants, it was necessary to study every single cormorant; to reach the truth about atoms, it was necessary to study every single atom. And there was no human way to accomplish this. No mortal being, no matter how diligent, could examine all the white-bellied aquatic birds in the north of England, let alone all the microscopic molecules. Only an omnipotent, omniscient being could accomplish such vast acts of observation. Only God could possess the infinite eye needed for induction.

So, if induction were the only path to general knowledge, then there might as well be no path for the sleuths at all. The veil over nature was restored, and the mystery bloomed again . . .

Until, in a miracle of logical prowess, the sleuths were rescued. Their rescue was set forth in 1830 by the English astronomer John Herschel in his *A Preliminary Discourse on the Study of Natural Philosophy*. Despite its ponderous title, *Preliminary Discourse* became an instant best seller, capturing the imaginations of popular novelists such as Maria Edgeworth and sparking a "burning zeal" in young Charles Darwin. And among the book's many wonders, the most wondrous was a remedy to Bacon's mistake. For as Herschel explained, it was possible for us mere mortals to arrive at cosmic general truths if we gathered up "a great number of particular facts,—to make them a part of one system" that we then used "to *predict facts before trial.*"

Those italicized words—*predict facts before trial*—produced a sensation, for they suggested that Bacon was totally right and also totally wrong. How could this be? Well, according to those words, the sleuths' method followed two steps. In the first, the sleuths collected enough "particular facts" to posit a general "system" (that is, theory) of nature. In the second, the sleuths used this theory to "predict" a new fact. So, the first step was a rough induction; the basic technique enshrined by Bacon. But the second step was most certainly *not* an induction. It was a translation of a general theory into a hypothesis about an individual case, or in other words, a deduction, the medieval practice Bacon had rejected.

With this revision of Bacon, Herschel combined the old logic with the new. He showed how induction and deduction could be married into a method that established general truths by testing predictions through "trial." So, the method went: induction, deduction, experiment. Or more colloquially: gather facts, make a prediction, and test to see if the prediction panned out.

This method was a revolution. But Herschel explained modestly that it wasn't his invention. It was the method that the sleuths had used all along:

> It had been objected to the doctrine of Copernicus, that, were it true, Venus should appear sometimes horned like the moon. To this he answered by admitting the conclusion, and averring that, should we ever be able to see its actual shape, it *would* appear so. It is easy to imagine with what force the application would strike every mind when the telescope confirmed this prediction, and showed the planet just as both the philosopher and his objectors had agreed it ought to appear.

So it was that the sleuth revolution had begun. A sleuth had predicted the horns of Venus—and the prediction had been confirmed by an experiment.

In 1833, three years after Herschel published *Preliminary Discourse*, his friend William Whewell coined the term *scientist* to refer to the sleuths. Henceforth, the sleuth revolution became the scientific revolution, and Herschel's predict-then-test method became the scientific method. A new age of answers dawned. The old night of mystery ebbed away.

But the revolution wasn't complete just yet. Now that Herschel had uncovered the scientific method, it needed to be spread to all of the globe's curious minds, teaching them to look with mystery-busting eyes. And as Bacon had realized when he'd penned his *New Atlantis*, the most effective way to accomplish this teaching wasn't with a textbook; it was with a work of fiction. So, an updated *New Atlantis* had to be crafted. One that could train its readers to go beyond induction into science.

The New *New Atlantis*

In Philadelphia, 1841, a court-martialed cadet and university dropout by the name of Edgar Allan Poe discovered the scientific method in a book written by another of Herschel's friends, the Scottish kaleidoscope inventor David Brewster. The book was *Letters on Natural Magic*, and it advertised itself as a guide to solving mysteries: "It is lamentable to think how many minds rest contented with the most unphilosophical apology for ignorance, by designating the acts they do not examine [to be] wonders or mysteries."

Poe encountered these spell-breaking words during his own bit of sleuthing. While browsing through twopenny papers such as the *New York Spectator* and the *Daily National Intelligencer*, he'd stumbled upon the strange case of a Hungarian chess-playing robot. The robot was known as the "Mechanical Turk," and it had dazzled the world by checkmating everyone from Benjamin Franklin to Napoléon Bonaparte. So, immediately, Poe wanted to know: How did the robot work? What was the engineering secret beneath its miraculous achievements?

Brewster's *Letters on Natural Magic* promised an answer, so Poe cracked the cover. And scanning the pages inside, he lit upon a paragraph where Brewster employed the scientific method to unravel the Mechanical Turk's secret. The paragraph began by marshaling induction to come up with two general theories: "Upon considering the operations of [the Turk], it must have been obvious that the game of chess was performed either by a person enclosed in the chest, or by the exhibitor himself."

The paragraph then went on to use the second of these theories—"or by the exhibitor himself"—to make some deductive predictions. But when these predictions were put to the test, they failed, debunking the second theory and leaving only the first: "the game of chess was performed . . . by a person enclosed in the chest." This defied all reason, because "the smallest dwarf could not be accommodated within." Yet when put to the test, it proved true: there was indeed a tiny man inside the "robot."

Mystery solved. The Mechanical Turk wasn't a clockwork genius. It was a hoax.

Poe was captivated. And what captivated him wasn't simply Brewster's use of the scientific method. It was the way that Brewster's book *taught* the method by guiding readers, step-by-step, through inductive observations and deductive predictions. It was like an updated version of the old parable "Give a man a fish and you feed him for a day, but show him how to fish and you feed him for life." Brewster had gone beyond serving us a single meal of science. He'd trained us to be scientists who could forever sate our appetite for answers.

This was a remarkable achievement. But as Poe rifled through Brewster's book, he realized that the scientific method could be taught in an even more compelling manner: by giving readers an even more compelling mystery. The Mechanical Turk was a good puzzle, no doubt. But Poe could already imagine a better one. It would include events that seemed so impossible as to be supernatural: minds would be read, killers would vanish from locked rooms, bodies would be rent asunder with inhuman strength.

Witnessing these events, we'd think: *Surely some otherworldly creature is at work. Surely I've witnessed a demon from beyond.* But then a brilliant detective would stride onto the scene, and, like a scientist, he'd solve the mystery, introducing us to a method more powerful than any magical monster.

Inspired, Poe flew to his writing desk. And on a rag-pulp broadsheet, he dashed down a story titled "The Murders in the Rue Morgue."

Poe's New Blueprint

"The Murders in the Rue Morgue" is introduced by a most peculiar preface. It starts with some "random . . . observations" about the games of checkers and chess, remarking that checkers is vastly superior at training our brain in the "method" of mystery solving. At which point, it shifts unexpectedly to a discussion of the card game of whist, musing that the successful whist player "makes, in silence, a host of observations and inferences."

Why is the preface telling us this? Where's the gripping mystery and the brilliant detective? Why are we reading random stuff about games?

It's an enigma, indeed. So, let's use the sleuths' method and hypothesize an answer: Poe is employing the apparently arbitrary narrative of the preface as a secret training device, designed to guide our brain into thinking more scientifically. And to test that guess, let's now take a quick pivot into neuroscience to see if the facts about our brain support the case.

The Science of Learning

Our brain learns by making predictions that fail. The fail jolts our brain with unexpected negative feedback, prompting our neurons to hastily gather more intel and make another prediction. Or in other words, to perform a rough induction followed by a deduction.

This was the pedagogical secret discovered by David Brewster. His *Letters on Natural Magic* doesn't simply guide our brain to make inductions followed by deductions. It leads our brain into making an errant hypothesis—"the game of chess must have been performed by the exhibitor himself"—that's then debunked. The debunking of that hypothesis forces our brain to react by revising our earlier inductions and deductions, seeking out more comprehensive evidence and crafting more rigorous predictions. And that's when our brain learns like a scientist.

This technique of debunking a hypothesis is very effective at making our brain scientific. So effective, in fact, that it can work without the other component of Brewster's pedagogy: the modeling of how to induct and then deduct. That's because, as modern scientists have discovered, our brain innately knows the sleuth method; it's hardwired into our gray matter from birth.

The hardwiring has recently been uncovered by ophthalmic researchers who study our visual cortex. Our visual cortex contains neurocircuits that continually anticipate what our eyes are just about to tell us, imagining the outside world before we see it. Without this anticipation, we'd have to lurch our way forward, pausing every few steps to wait while our eyes scanned the terrain ahead. But with the anticipation, we can smoothly meet the world where we expect it to be.

The foresight of our visual cortex is remarkably accurate, but it's not perfect. It can misguess the future, making a prediction that fails. When that happens, our visual cortex slows down briefly to examine the unexpected eye data that it has received, using that data to form a fresh prediction that allows us to stride forth again. So, without ever thinking consciously, our brain uses the scientific method: it inducts, then deducts, and launches a trial—and when that trial fails, inducts then deducts more rigorously.

This is a wonder more extraordinary than a true Mechanical Turk: like an automated scientist, our brain robotically employs the same method of active anticipation that Copernicus used to prophesy the horns of Venus. But the neural miracle of our visual cortex also poses a neural mystery: If our brain is a natural scientist, then why did science need to be invented? Why wasn't our species building telescopes long ago?

The answer is that the automated circuits of our visual cortex are responsible only for a narrow slice of our learning. The rest of our learning occurs in other neural regions, many of which are linked to an antiscientific entity known as our ego. Our ego is a proud and fragile creature; like an insecure emperor, it hates to admit that it has made a mistake. So, from atop its lordly mount, our ego frequently circumvents a crucial part of the scientific method: the part where we acknowledge that our initial hypothesis was wrong.

Our ego's most brazen technique for pulling this antiscientific maneuver is to try to twist the facts into agreement with our flawed hypothesis. This is the neural foible known as confirmation bias, in which our ego cherry-picks, fudges, and generally manipulates data to support our original guess. But our ego also frequently disrupts our native scientific method in two other ways.

The first is by becoming intimidated at the method's difficulty. It's hard, after all, to translate unexpected data into coherent new models of reality; it requires us to be both sternly rigorous and flexibly imaginative, spinning unyielding evidence into creative theories. And faced by that challenge, our ego often balks. Not wanting to fail at science, it simply ignores its predictive error, pretending that nothing ever went wrong.

The second is to engage in magical thinking. Magical thinking is when we ascribe physical outcomes to *meta*physical causes such as fate, or karma, or God's will, or serendipity, or cosmic irony, or the power of the stars, or those cursed socks we wore. Since these causes exist outside the material domain of science, they cannot be tested by scientific experiment, a fact that greatly pleases our ego. If our magical thinking cannot be tested, then it cannot be debunked, so our ego can rest happy in the knowledge that it can never be proved wrong.

Magical thinking, intellectual insecurity, and confirmation bias are all powerful barriers to scientific discovery; they blocked the eyes of generations of astronomers before Copernicus. But as twenty-first-century researchers have discovered, these three barriers can all be demolished with a simple teaching trick: transporting our brain to an environment outside our own. That environment can be a nature preserve many miles from our home, or a computer-simulated Mars, or any other space that our ego doesn't associate directly with our health, social status, and material success. In that environment, our ego will be less inclined to take the failure of its predictions personally. Certainly, our ego may feel a little chagrined that its guesses about the nature preserve or Mars were wrong, but it was never really that invested in the guesses to begin with. Why should it care too much about things that have no bearing on its own fame or well-being? So, in that happy state of apathy, our ego is less likely to get data manipulative, mentally intimidated, or magically minded, leaving the rest of our brain free to abandon failed hypotheses and venture new ones.

This method of disarming our ego has proved highly effective at improving the scientific skills of students in college, high school, middle school, and even elementary school. When those students are transported into a field-trip forest, or a virtual-reality landscape, or some other place where the ego feels safe mucking around, they become significantly more likely to acknowledge their predictive failures, significantly more comfortable at making new predictions, and significantly more prone to make those new predictions physically testable. Liberated from the survival pressures of their daily lives, they become better at practicing the scientific method stamped inside their genes.

The same educational breakthrough is made by Poe in his preface to "The Murders in the Rue Morgue." That preface begins by transporting us into a zone of lowered stakes: chess, checkers, and whist are all, as the preface comments, "trivial occupations." They're not real work; they're games, things of inconsequence. So, why should our ego feel threatened if it draws erroneous conclusions about them? And having reassured our ego on this score, the preface then leads us into drawing just such an erroneous conclusion. By praising the sleuth-boosting powers of checkers, it invites our brain to guess: *This must have been written to encourage me to play more checkers.* Until abruptly, the preface debunks our prediction by instead praising the value of whist, prodding our brain to discard our old hypothesis and form a new one: *I'd have been quicker on the uptake if I played more whist.*

After giving our brain a taste of this scientific learning experience, Poe then ushers us out of the preface and into an even more educational setting: a storyworld set in nineteenth-century Paris. This storyworld is a faraway space, making it as unthreatening to our ego as a checkerboard or a whist table. But this storyworld is also more effective than checkers or whist at honing our use of the method. Unlike such games, nineteenth-century Paris doesn't arbitrarily make up all its rules of play; it's a virtual reality that obeys the physical laws of our actual world. So, it's an elegantly fictional yet fact-based environment in which we can hone our inducto-deductive circuitry, learning real science by playing the part of a "Virtual Scientist."

And to help us play that part, Poe has no sooner conveyed us into his virtual science lab than he does what effective science teachers do: he leads our brain into making predictive mistakes.

The Mistakes We Make

Our mistakes begin when we meet the world's first literary detective, Monsieur C. Auguste Dupin.

Dupin is introduced to us as a creature of "romance" who devours books in a "fantastic gloom" of "superstitions." Which is to say: Dupin is introduced as a young man who has read too many gothic novels, that literary genre we explored in chapter 12. He's crammed his brain with fictions about ghosts and vampires until it has become "diseased," acting like a thing of darkness itself.

Yet, of course, Dupin's brain cannot be a thing of darkness. Ghosts and vampires, we know, are idle fantasies. For unlike Dupin, we have not curdled our wits with paperback literature. We are enlightened sleuths of science!

And then our confident prediction is undone. Because just like a thing of darkness, Dupin turns and reads our mind. The mind reading occurs when we're walking with Dupin at midnight. We haven't spoken to him for a quarter hour, yet somehow he knows exactly what we're thinking. And what makes his knowledge all the more stunning is that we're thinking of something very, very specific: the curious case of a cobbler who became stage mad and tried to act the role of a Persian tyrant in Prosper Jolyot de Crébillon's 1714 tragedy *Xerxes*.

How on earth could Dupin have seen into our mind with such unerring detail? Does he have supernatural powers? Is he a ghost or a vampire after all?

No. Dupin is not. Our mind has once again leapt to the wrong conclusion. In fact, Dupin has read our mind by using the same scientific method as the successful whist player. And to prove it, he explains patiently and slowly, so that we can follow along and "comprehend all clearly." He begins by revealing that when he saw us look down at the street's pavement stones, he hypothesized that those stones would make us think of a particular star. Then moments later, lo and behold, our eyes turned skyward to that star, revealing to Dupin that he'd cracked the hidden logic of our brain. Through his predict-then-test method, he'd uncovered a general rule of our mental behavior.

Meanwhile, by interrupting our own predictions about Dupin, "The Murders in the Rue Morgue" has been training us in the same method. We're not, of course, quite as good at science as Dupin is. We can't yet predict his moves like he can predict ours. But maybe that's about to change. Because "The Murders" is going to give us one final mystery to solve—a mystery of such sublime perplexity that it verges on the Bible's ancient miracles.

So, can we observe, predict, revise, and predict again? Can we solve the mystery before Dupin?

The Solution to the Final Mystery

It would ruin "The Murders in the Rue Morgue" to explain its final mystery. To benefit from Poe's invention, you need to tackle that mystery yourself, spinning predictions from the facts you uncover—and then respinning your predictions when they propel you into error.

And if you reach the end of "The Murders" and want more opportunities to play the part of the Virtual Scientist, you can get plenty more of Poe's disrupt-our-predictions-about-fictional-environments invention from the Sherlock Holmes stories of Arthur Conan Doyle, the crime novels of Agatha Christie, and the thousands of other detective tales that now crowd our library shelves. And you can find even more of Poe's invention in the futuristic tele-visual contraption predicted by Bacon's *New Atlantis*, a contraption that brims with *Dragnet*, *Law & Order*, *Veronica Mars*, *House*, and dozens of other procedurals about the mysteries of criminal minds, crime scenes, and medical diseases.

So, thanks to Poe, the world is now filled with virtually-real sleuth stories that help us stow our antiscientific ego. And all these stories can be solved by the same mystery-busting method:

Gather the data at hand, then make a guess that you can test.

And when your test fails, more rigorously gather and guess.

FOURTEEN

Become Your Better Self

*Frederick Douglass, Saint Augustine, Jean-Jacques
Rousseau, and the Invention of the Life Evolver*

I t was July 4, 1854, the seventy-eighth anniversary of America's independence day. Most of the nation was commemorating the occasion
with fireworks. But the white abolitionist William Lloyd Garrison opted
for a less celebratory pyrotechnic display. At a picnic grove west of Boston, he stood beneath an upside-down American flag, raising aloft the
US Constitution. And, condemning it as a slave-holding pact, he set its
parchment alight with the touch of a phosphorous match.

"So perish [this] covenant with death, [this] agreement with hell!"
Garrison cried as America's founding document crumbled into char.
"And let all the people say, *Amen*!"

Watching Garrison's fire show with frank dismay was his old friend
Frederick Douglass. Not that Douglass denied the horrors of slavery.
He'd himself been born into those horrors on a sandy-soiled plantation near the Eastern Bay of Maryland, where he'd been degradingly
treated—at the mandate of the Constitution's Article One—as "three-
fifths" of a person. Nor did Douglass deny the hypocrisy of America's
freedom celebrations. Just two years earlier, in the "free city" of Rochester, New York, he'd mounted a podium at tall-windowed Corinthian
Hall to demand: "What to a slave is the Fourth of July?"

But still, when Douglass had posed the question, his answer hadn't been
to immolate the Constitution. Instead, he'd declared, "The Constitution is a

glorious liberty document. Read its preamble, consider its purposes. Is slavery among them? Is it at the gateway? Or is it in the temple? It is neither."

Don't cast away this glorious document, Douglass had urged. Change it instead. Change Article One. Change America into the realm of "liberty" that it had always claimed to be.

This was a vision too radical for Garrison. How was it possible for America, tainted from birth by the original sin of slavery, to be reformed? But Douglass had reason to believe that the United States could change. For he himself had changed, and indeed, changed profoundly. You see, not so very long ago, he'd been a second Garrison who had branded the Constitution as an agreement with hell.

And had called for it to burn.

Douglass's Original Point of View

It had been in 1845, seven years after Douglass escaped that Maryland plantation on a steamboat to freedom, that he'd called for the Constitution's destruction by fire. At the time, he'd been encouraged by Garrison to author an autobiography: *Narrative of the Life of Frederick Douglass, An American Slave*. This autobiography, as the last and first words of its title indicated, was marketed as a slave narrative, a popular genre in the first half of the nineteenth century:

Life of William Grimes, the Runaway Slave. Written by Himself

A Narrative of the Adventures and Escape of Moses Roper, from American Slavery

Chains and Freedom: Or, The Life and Adventures of Peter Wheeler, a Colored Man Yet Living; A Slave in Chains, a Sailor on the Deep, and a Sinner at the Cross

The Narrative of Lunsford Lane, Formerly of Raleigh, N.C., Embracing an Account of His Early Life, the Redemption by Purchase of Himself and Family from Slavery, and His Banishment from the Place of His Birth for the Crime of Wearing a Colored Skin.

The popularity of these narratives derived from their two-part literary blueprint: one, chronicle the horrors of slavery; two, chronicle the moral failings of slavers. The first part of the blueprint stirred empathy for the enslaved:

> For a young boy, it was too much for me to bear. . . . My heart was almost broke with grief. . . . I was born a slave—and many a time, like old Job, I've cussed the day I was born.

The second part of the blueprint incited outraged contempt for the enslavers:

> She would beat me until I could hardly stand. . . . They whipped me until I hardly had any feeling. . . . Master become a very devil—he 'bused me and other folks most all-killin'ly.

This was a potent literary combination of emotions, and it could have been employed to change the minds of readers. But it wasn't. Instead it was deployed to do the reverse: entrench readers in their preexisting beliefs. That's because slave narratives were intended to be read by abolitionists. And abolitionists all agreed, before they ever picked up a slave narrative, that slavery was wrong.

What, then, was the purpose of slave narratives? Why preach the gospel to the choir? The answer, Garrison explained, was "moral suasion." Moral suasion started from the pious premise that social reform came not from our mortal words or deeds, but from God and God alone. Yet despite this total demurral to God's omnipotence, moral suasion didn't absolve us from the responsibility of confronting evil. Instead, it called upon us to wade into the wickedness of the world, putting our faith to the test. The bluntest edge of that test was the naked violence threatened upon us by angry unbelievers; like the biblical martyrs of yore, we might be forced to stand strong while our loved ones were tortured and burned. But such overt assaults, Garrison warned, weren't the only part of the test. Our faith could also be challenged in a subtler and more common way: corruption. That corruption took root when the fallen invited us into their society, and it was then nourished by our Christian kindheartedness. Forgetting that God's sacred commandments could never be softened, we'd convince ourselves that it was charitable to tolerate sinners, so we'd mingle with them in shops and public greens, living under their laws, paying their taxmen, and gradually becoming more and more assimilated to their ways, until we'd betrayed our soul to their damnation.

It was to guard against this slow perversion that abolitionists read slave narratives. Slave narratives stiffened the spine and reminded the wavering mind that there could be no compromise with evil. To defeat the devil on earth, we had to stand stalwartly apart from slavers, the US Constitution, and hell's other institutions, like patient angels waiting for the Judgment Day, until God Himself reached down to burn the wickedness away.

This uncompromising virtue was what William Lloyd Garrison extolled each week from the crowded brick office in South Boston where he published his abolitionist newspaper, the *Liberator*: "No Compromise with Slavery!" And this uncompromising virtue was what Douglass espoused in his own *Narrative,* which explicitly celebrated Garrison's newspaper for wielding moral suasion's two-part literary blueprint:

> [The newspaper's] sympathy for my brethren in bonds—its scathing denunciations of slaveholders—its faithful exposures of slavery—and its powerful attacks upon the upholders of the institution—sent a thrill of joy through my soul, such as I had never felt before!

Like a fortifying slave narrative, Garrison's newspaper inspired compassion for slaves and contempt for slavers, hardening the righteous heart against iniquity. Thus it was that Douglass used his *Narrative* to repeat Garrison's sermon back to Garrison. And thus it was that Garrison reciprocated by penning a preface for Douglass's book that rerepeated the theology back again: "No Compromise with Slavery! No Union with Slaveholders!"

But then, in the years before Garrison made good on these words by setting the Constitution alight, Douglass did something that roused grave apprehension among the moral suasioners: he began to change.

Douglass's Conversion

Douglass's shift of mind was prompted by conversations he had with dissenting abolitionists who took a different view of moral suasion, one they'd acquired from their efforts to correct another constitutional injustice: the denial of women's right to vote.

Women in America had long agitated against this injustice. In 1756 a widow in Uxbridge, Massachusetts, had convinced the town fathers to let her cast a ballot as her dead husband's proxy. Then in 1776 New Jersey's "Petticoat Electors" had persuaded their state to grant them suffrage, so long as they were rich enough to own land. But such triumphs were rare and short lived, and by Douglass's day, women still had not gained the franchise. Instead, they'd been deflected by obstacle after obstacle, one of which was moral suasion.

Moral suasion taught that worldly compromise was wrong, so it condemned participation in politics—including voting. Voting was an exercise in choosing between imperfect political parties. It traded true virtue for the selection of the lesser evil, and like all forms of ethical bargaining, it was seen by moral suasioners as corrupting. Millions of justice-loving, early-nineteenth-century female abolitionists were therefore proud that their sex had never been besmirched by the ballot box. To them, casting a ballot wasn't the first step toward a less bad society; it was the beginning of the fast slide to hell.

But in the late 1840s and early 1850s, right after Douglass published his *Narrative of the Life*, a growing number of American women began to alter their view of the matter. They decided that they wanted to participate in democracy; they decided that they wanted to drive practical change. "Moral suasion is moral balderdash," one female reformer asserted in 1852. "This is a utilitarian age."

Other women nodded. It was time to exchange the high idealism of moral suasion for more "utilitarian" strategies of reform. It was time to abandon the behavior of angels and join men at the voting booth.

The voices of these feminist reformers moved Douglass. In 1847 he broke with Garrison's *Liberator* and founded his own newspaper: the *North Star*, in Rochester. And the more that Douglass ran this paper, the more he found himself talking with people who had differing points of view: "The responsibility of conducting a public journal . . . imposed upon me . . . the necessity . . . of meeting opposite views from abolitionists in this state."

Unlike Garrison, Douglass didn't view those opposite views as contaminating; he viewed them as an opportunity for mutual exchange—and then mutual change. So, Douglass began to change. And as he changed, he set his eyes on changing other things: his fellow citizens, his country, his Constitution.

But before Douglass could alter any of those things, he realized that he first had to alter something else: his story of his own life.

Douglass Writes a Second Autobiography

It was the early 1850s, less than a decade since Frederick Douglass had composed his autobiography. But he knew that he had to sit down and compose it again.

His original autobiography had been filled with literary technologies that were designed to stop its readers from changing. By inspiring moral suasion's righteous empathy and scorn, *Narrative of the Life* had tried to fix minds in place. Now Douglass wanted to shift course. He wanted to dispense a literary technology that could instead accomplish what his encounters with the opposite views of other abolitionists had achieved: the nurturing of healthy change.

Douglass didn't know what that change-nurturing technology was. But, eager to learn, he left his writing desk to scour the libraries of western New York, searching for the blueprint that previous autobiographies had used to foster personal growth. Yet on that course of self-improvement, Douglass made a surprising discovery: history's most compelling autobiographies didn't employ a single blueprint for personal growth. Instead, they employed two.

Blueprint number one dated back to the fourth century, when Saint Augustine had withdrawn from the jackal wilds of the North African coast into the ancient walled harbor of Hippo to craft his *Confessions*. Augustine's *Confessions* wasn't the first autobiography in history, yet it had become so legendary in the Christian West that it was frequently hailed as the first to matter. Before Augustine, diarists had merely recorded facts about their lives, but with Augustine, autobiography's unique literary power was unlocked.

That power had transformed many a reader in the same way that young Augustine had himself been transformed. In his teens and twenties, Augustine had walked in sin, stealing fruit, frequenting the theater, and fornicating with concubines. Until one day, Augustine had heard a mysterious cry: "Take up the book and read." Surprised, Augustine obeyed. He took up the nearest book, which turned out to be the Bible. And he read: "Let us walk honestly, not in rioting and drunkenness, not in sex and wantonness, not in strife and coveting. But put ye on the Lord Jesus Christ, and cast the lust of the flesh from your heart."

Those words converted Augustine, and to read the *Confessions* was to encounter a literary technology designed to prompt a similar conversion in us. The technology was self-irony, which had been devised eight centuries earlier when (as we explored in chapter 4) the Athenian philosopher Plato put a neural twist on regular irony. Regular irony makes us conscious that there's a truth that someone else doesn't know; self-irony makes us conscious that there's a truth that our *self* doesn't know. So, self-irony flips around the perspective circuits of our frontal cortex, humbling us with a God's-Eye glimpse of our own ignorance.

Augustine admired Plato; in the *Confessions*, he thanks God for guiding him to "certain books of the Platonists." And across his autobiography, Augustine relentlessly deploys Platonic self-irony to stir contempt for our earthly state: "My flesh stirred up steamy lust. . . . I was in the sixteenth year of my flesh. . . . O the blindness of flesh!" Strictly speaking, Augustine didn't claim this literary style as a source of personal amendment; he believed that only God could produce change. Yet even so, Augustine wrote the *Confessions* because he thought that God might choose to work through books, and as reader after reader opened the *Confessions* and was converted to Augustine's pious faith, it became clear that self-irony was a potent mind-altering force.

Douglass felt that force himself. And he knew it would be wise to incorporate Augustine's blueprint into his own revised autobiography. But at the same time that Douglass was appreciating the life-changing power of self-irony, he was also appreciating the power of the second blueprint for autobiography.

And that blueprint worked in exactly the opposite way.

The Second Blueprint

The second blueprint for autobiography was set down in the 1760s in a riverside farmhouse at the foot of the French Alps by Jean-Jacques Rousseau.

Rousseau titled his autobiography the *Confessions*. Not out of homage to Augustine's work, but because he wanted to efface it utterly with his own.

True to this ambition, Rousseau completely reversed Augustine. Augustine claimed that we could be redeemed only by God—while Rousseau claimed that we could redeem ourselves. Augustine advocated for the saving grace of the Bible—while Rousseau advocated for the saving grace of nature. Augustine viewed our heart's desires as the hook of sin—while Rousseau claimed them as the ladder of salvation.

So it was that Rousseau replaced Augustine's ironic self-disgust with a very different literary technology: intimate self-disclosure. (See chapter 2 for the blueprint.) From the opening pages of his own *Confessions*, Rousseau admits his boyish faults in cheerful detail: "I was a chatterbox, a glutton, and occasionally a liar too." He even acknowledges his love for romance novels: "I would read all night, unable to stop."

These self-disclosures inspire our reading brain with gentle affection for young Rousseau. We don't condemn him to hell for thieving sweets; we appreciate his honest nature. And because that nature is, in Rousseau's telling, our common human condition, it encourages us to feel affection for our own nature too. Such self-love had been condemned by Augustine as impiously complacent, but, once again, Rousseau believed the opposite. Wasn't it in the nature of acorns to grow into oak trees? And for eggs to grow into eagles? So, surely, the way to mature into our full potential wasn't to reject our nature; it was to *embrace* the desires and instincts of our flesh, feeding the appetites that transformed romance-reading boys into kindhearted men.

Douglass was deeply moved by Rousseau's *Confessions*. Like Rousseau, he believed that there was something inherently good in people, even if they'd never read the Bible. And like Rousseau, Douglass felt that it was in his nature to grow.

But Douglass also realized that Rousseau was the literary antithesis of Augustine. The two versions of the *Confessions* were clashing engines, forcing a choice between their competing mechanisms of personal transformation. Was Rousseau's technology of self-love the better blueprint for change? Or was Augustine's technology of self-critique? Did we grow more by embracing the good of our nature? Or by wryly ironizing our faults?

It was a difficult, difficult choice. So, in the end, Douglass did something that no autobiographer had ever done. He didn't choose between Augustine and Rousseau.

He chose them both.

The Origins of Douglass's Choice

The origins of Douglass's choice can be traced back to when he was roughly twelve years old. For it was then that a fateful decision was made by his Baltimore slave mistress, Mrs. Sophia Auld.

Mrs. Sophia Auld was a God-fearing woman who wanted Douglass to study the Bible, so she decided to instruct him on his alphabet letters—until her husband intervened in dismay, explaining that it was illegal to teach slaves to read. Happily for posterity, this husbandly intervention came too late; already Douglass had learned enough to keep teaching himself. And by the time he was thirteen, he'd secreted away the money, he recalled, "to buy what was then a very popular school book, viz: *the Columbian Orator.*"

The Columbian Orator was indeed "very popular." It could be found in hundreds of schools across New York and New England. And its underlying pedagogy was more popular still. For *The Columbian Orator* was a rhetoric textbook that drew upon an instructional method that had been taught to generations of literature students, from the second-century-BCE North African slave Publius Terentius Afer, to the sixteenth-century English schoolboy William Shakespeare, to the future sixteenth president of the United States, Abraham Lincoln.

This instructional method, as modern neuroscientists have since discovered, can do more than teach us rhetoric's art of public oratory. It can also support our personal growth by nurturing cognitive flexibility. Cognitive flexibility is our capacity to transition from one way of thinking to another. And that capacity is fed by rhetoric textbooks through two separate neural pathways.

The first pathway involves our mental action models. Those action models are recorded by our brain each time we learn to do something new. So, when we first learn to make a left turn, our neurons remember: *This is how we pivoted our feet.* That way, on the next occasion that we rotate left, our brain isn't re-inventing the foot wheel. It's cueing up a premade action loop that tells our toes how to spin untrippingly.

And crucially, our brain can do more than just store these action models. With the help of the memory circuits of our limbic system, our brain can *link* these action models to specific contexts. Without that linking, our head would contain only general models such as: *Always turn our feet like this!* But with that linking, our brain can remember: *At this place, we turn our feet left, and at that other place, we turn our feet right.* So, instead of sending us roundabout in endless circles, our brain's library of context-linked action models helps us navigate the varied roads of life.

Our brain's ability to house this library of local rights and lefts was known to the authors of rhetoric textbooks. The authors weren't, of course, aware of the limbic system or any of that. But they'd observed that in matters of public speaking, there was no general rule like "Always go left!" Every listening audience was unique, requiring its own tailored speech. So, rather than attempting to instill students with universal laws of effective oratory, rhetoric textbooks strove to nurture creative bend by providing a varied historical catalogue of rhetorical models. As the sixteenth-century pedagogical psychologist Juan Luis Vives remarked in his *On Education*: "The greater the number of rhetorical models, and the less likeness between them, the greater the student's growth." Or as *The Columbian Orator* explained: "The Author has preferred variety to system."

This variety built cognitive flexibility by enriching students' memory banks with eclectically different models for communicating, and it nurtured future flexibility by encouraging open-mindedness to other models that students might encounter on their travels. And so it was that when young Frederick Douglass turned the pages of his text-book purchase, his eyes were greeted with more than eighty speeches, including . . .

"Speech of an Indian Chief of the Stockbridge Tribe, to the Massachusetts Congress, in the Year 1775"

"Speech of a Roman General," by Caius Cassius

"The Oration on the Manumission of Slaves," by Reverend Samuel Miller

. . . growing Douglass's mental elasticity and encouraging him to keep brain-stretching further.

The second neural pathway through which rhetoric textbooks enhanced cognitive flexibility was self-irony—that neural God's-Eye we discussed earlier in the chapter. Its chastening gaze is snapped open by *The Columbian Orator*'s self-reflexive counsel of *caution, caution, caution*:

The like caution is to be used against the contrary extreme. . . . Caution should be used to not represent any argument of weight in a ludicrous way. . . . But here, as has been before observed, great caution should be used.

And to further activate our self-irony circuitry, *The Columbian Orator* includes several speeches by William Pitt, an eighteenth-century member of the British Parliament who modeled an array of rhetorical techniques for prodding our brain to consider itself humbly from without:

If I were an American, as I am an Englishman, while a foreign troop remained in my country, I *never* would lay down my arms. . . . In the sportsman's phrase, when you have found yourself at fault, you must try back.

Think of yourself as an American, Pitt urges his English audience. Leave your own perspective to inhabit someone else's. And be conscious that you can be "at fault." You can overrun your mark, forcing you to "try back."

William Pitt's self-irony-inducing speeches were well known to Douglass. In fact, of all the speeches in *The Columbian Orator*, they were his favorites: "I read them, over and over again, with an interest that was ever increasing."

This ever-increasing interest would later inspire the adult Douglass to infuse his own public talks with rhetorical inducements to self-irony. In hundreds of packed halls from Indiana to Ireland, he guided audiences to smile wryly at themselves, a phenomenon documented in 1881 by George Ruffin, a free black who paid his own way through Harvard Law School:

> Douglass is brim full of humor, at times, of the dryest kind. . . .
> You can see it coming a long way off in a peculiar twitch of his mouth. It increases and broadens gradually until it becomes irresistible and all-pervading with his audience.

With dry self-humor, Douglass encouraged his audience to take a lightly ironic view of their own situation, boosting their cognitive flex by opening their minds to truths outside their own.

So it was that *The Columbian Orator* helped young Douglass grow the minds of others. And when Douglass reached his late thirties, he realized that he could nurture even more of that growth. All he had to do was follow his rhetoric textbook's embrace of wildly different historical models. All he had to do was combine Augustine and Rousseau.

The Marriage of Growth Formulas

Augustine and Rousseau each contained an opposite half of *The Columbian Orator*'s growth-promoting blueprint. The first half, an eclectic catalogue of historical action models, was embodied by Rousseau's sentimental treasuring of the assorted behaviors of his past. The second half, a consciousness of our present faults, was embodied by Augustine's ironic attitude toward his fallen here and now. So, by mixing and matching

Rousseau's past-tense self-love with Augustine's present-tense self-irony (and by pruning out the elements of both *Confessions*, like Augustine's past-tense self-irony, which clashed with the *Orator*'s rhetorical blueprint), it would be possible to engineer an autobiographical style that doubly nurtured positive change, encouraging our brain to embrace the diversity of our previous life experiences while maintaining an awareness of our current shortcomings.

This mix and match is exactly what Frederick Douglass does in his second autobiography, *My Bondage and My Freedom*, published in 1855. The book begins in the voice of Rousseau, describing how Douglass's "heathen" childhood guided him to imitate a rich catalogue of "strange" models for behavior:

> Freed from all restraint, the slave-boy can be, in his life and con-
> duct, a genuine boy, doing whatever his boyish nature suggests;
> enacting, by turns, all the strange antics and freaks of horses, dogs,
> pigs, and barn-door fowls, without in any manner compromising
> his dignity, or incurring reproach of any sort. He literally runs
> wild . . . as happy as any little heathen under the palm trees of
> Africa.

Then, in its final chapter, *My Bondage and My Freedom* pivots to Augustine's technique of present-tense self-irony, offering wry acknowledgment of Douglass's extant limitations:

> As my experience, and not my arguments, is within the scope and
> contemplation of this volume, I omit the latter and proceed with
> the former . . . never forgetting my own humble origin.

Until at last, *My Bondage and My Freedom* leverages these two sources of personal growth into a profound transformation:

> I became convinced that . . . to abstain from voting, was to refuse
> to exercise a legitimate and powerful means for abolishing slav-
> ery; and that the constitution of the United States not only con-

tained no guarantees in favor of slavery, but, on the contrary, it is, in its letter and spirit, an anti-slavery instrument. . . . Here was a radical change in my opinions.

This "radical change" was a rejection of William Lloyd Garrison's moral suasion for the belief that voting could grow America into a better version of itself. And to read Douglass's revised autobiography from cover to cover is to feel a similar change taking root within our own mind, as we discover a hybrid style of life writing that encourages us to love the rich strangeness of where we came from, while opening ourselves to all the possibilities beyond.

Using the "Life Evolver" Yourself

In his third autobiography, *The Life and Times of Frederick Douglass* (1882), Douglass recorded the Constitution's own moment of change like so:

> President U. S. Grant, with his characteristic nerve and clear perception of justice, promptly recommended the great amendment to the Constitution, by which coloured men are to-day invested with complete citizenship—the right to vote, and to be voted for, in the American Republic.

Here we have the first half of Douglass's growth tonic: a past-tense love of history. And Douglass follows immediately with the tonic's second half. Pivoting into the present tense with a detached eye, he critiques his beloved Constitution for failing to treat women as equals:

> In this denial of the right to participate in government, not merely the degradation of woman and the perpetuation of a great injustice happens, but the maiming and repudiation of one half of the moral and intellectual power for the government of the world.

Douglass didn't live to see this "great injustice" overturned. But after American women at last gained the right to vote in 1920, the suffragist

Mary Church Terrell would remember how seventy-two years earlier, at the Seneca Falls Women's Rights Convention, no one had dared to support the resolution "that it is the duty of the women of this country to secure to themselves their sacred right to the elective franchise." The whole convention sat silent, ready to let the resolution die. When "Frederick Douglass . . . had the courage to arise in that meeting and second [the] resolution. . . . If Frederick Douglass had not, [then] it is anybody's guess how long the cause of suffrage for women would have been delayed."

If you want Douglass to do the same for you, speeding you on your way to positive change, pick up one of the many modern autobiographies that adopt his stylistic invention of past-tense self-love and present-tense self-irony. There's *The Autobiography of Malcolm X*, published posthumously in 1965, where Malcolm begins with fond memories of his boyhood nature . . .

I loved especially to grow peas. I was proud when we had them on our table. I would pull out the grass in my garden by hand when the first little blades came up. I would patrol the rows on my hands and knees for any worms and bugs, and I would kill and bury them. And sometimes when I had everything straight and clean for my things to grow, I would lie down on my back between two rows, and I would gaze up in the blue sky at the clouds moving and think all kinds of things.

. . . and builds his final chapter toward an ironic reflection on his current self:

I think that an objective reader may see how when I heard "The white man is the devil," when I played back what had been my own experiences, it was inevitable that I would respond positively; then the next twelve years of my life were devoted and dedicated to propagating that phrase among the black people.

And there's Michelle Obama's 2018 memoir *Becoming*, which elegantly sums up Douglass's two-part blueprint with its closing words:

There's power in allowing yourself to be known and heard, in owning your unique story, in using your authentic voice. And there's grace in being willing to know and hear others. This, for me, is how we become.

Or you can take the same approach as young Frederick Douglass himself: read widely in history, memoir, and autobiography, treasuring the uniqueness of every past life you discover while taking a lightly ironic view of your present self. That way, each dawn will bring a chance to celebrate history—and embrace future change.

Making every day your independence day.

FIFTEEN

Bounce Back from Failure

George Eliot's Middlemarch *and the
Invention of the Gratitude Multiplier*

E ighteen forty-eight seemed a year for revolution.
As the first buds of spring bloomed across Europe, millions
of potato farmers and factory workers uprose, to be joined by shoe
cobblers and street builders, housepainters and chimney sweepers, rye
growers and pottery makers. In Palermo and Paris, Vienna and Mu-
nich, Milan and Venice, Buda and Pest, Transylvania and Rome, Liège
and South Tipperary, people demanded more democracy, more freedom of the press, more food, more humanity. Barricades were flung
across ghetto streets; police garrisons were surrounded; great palaces,
stormed. The old military aristocracies tottered; a new age of liberty
dawned.

But over the following summer and winter, the revolution collapsed,
its ranks decimated by rebel infighting and government grapeshot. Its
inciters were beheaded on scaffolds, gunned down in markets, and
strangled in windowless prisons. "We have been unhanded, untongued,
scattered asunder," cried the French anarcho-pacifist Pierre-Joseph
Proudhon. "We have tasted defeat—and humiliation!"

That humiliation would ultimately prove the crushing blow. Most of
the revolutionaries survived the ensuing crackdown with their hands and
tongues intact, but so haunted were they by the aura of failure that they
huddled in shadows as freedom spun backward. In Prague, martial law

was imposed by the musket bayonets of the Prince of Windisch-Graetz. In the German Confederation, democratic clubs were abolished and the repressive Federal Assembly restored. In Russia, the screws of censorship were turned so tight by Emperor Nicholas I that imperial blue pens outnumbered published books.

And so 1848 became the great change that wasn't, "the turning point at which modern history failed to turn."

Witnessing the failed turn from the relative calm of the English West Midlands was twenty-nine-year-old Mary Ann Evans, later to be known by her pen name, George Eliot. Eliot found it impossible to agree entirely with the revolutionaries: they had too many different manifestos, espousing too many contradictory ideas. But still, she admired their drive for reform. Like them, she believed that Europe's "millions of unfed souls and bodies" were a human tragedy. And like them, she dreamed of a day when kings and queens would be placed in "a sort of zoological garden," where their lordly imperiousness could be peacefully exhibited alongside the daffodil flower and the red admiral butterfly.

So, when George Eliot saw the hopes of 1848 collapse into retreat, she felt a pained dismay. Surely, she thought, there had to be a more productive response to failure. Surely there had to be a way to leave our humiliation in the past and take a second try.

And although it took Eliot many second tries to find that better way of failing, she would herself succeed at last.

The First Try at a Remedy for Failure

Eighteen years after the unrevolution, George Eliot published her fifth novel: *Felix Holt, the Radical.* As its title announces, the novel details a radical uprising against the landed English gentry, but at the novel's heart lies a more personal conflict triggered by a letter. The letter is handed to one of the radicals: a preacher committed to reforming inequities of wealth. And it reveals the preacher's adopted daughter to be a secret heiress due to inherit the most massive fortune:

> Herewith we send you a brief abstract of evidence . . . the sole and
> lawful issue of Maurice Christian Bycliffe . . . the possession of es-

tates to the value, at the lowest, of from five to six thousand per annum.

These revelations leave the preacher so agog that he cannot speak. He has visions of his daughter leaving his small house at Chapel Yard to dally in a splendid world of silk sofa cushions, deep turf lawns, and dashing cavaliers. And suddenly the preacher is overwhelmed by a piercing sense of his own futility. Feeling that he's just lost his precious child to the corruptions of the idle rich, he retreats into his study, where he betakes himself to "prayer without ceasing."

That a preacher would pray in times of crisis is not so very notable. But what *is* notable is the particular way that this preacher prays. For his prayer "without ceasing" is inspired by one of the Bible's most astonishing passages: "Pray without ceasing. In every thing give thanks."

This short injunction from 1 Thessalonians is far more surprising than the letter that leaves the preacher speechless. For by directing us to give thanks to God for every thing, it doesn't just advise us to express gratitude for success and plenty. It instructs us to thank God for failure and hardship too.

Why? Why would we express gratitude for not getting what we wanted? In *Felix Holt*, the preacher's explanation is that failure is the will of God, and God is always good. But you don't need to be a Victorian preacher to think that there's deep wisdom in 1 Thessalonians. Neuroscience has given us an additional justification for the Bible's counsel to give thanks in times of setback: gratitude helps our brain rebound from disappointment and disaster.

Gratitude's rebound effect has been discovered by psychologists only in the past decade or so. And that's largely because it's so counterintuitive that they never thought to look for it before. Thanksgiving offers no obvious remedy to our stumbles. It doesn't put them in perspective or laugh them away. It doesn't encourage us to take heart or practice self-compassion. In fact, it doesn't do anything self-directed at all. It turns our eyes away from ourselves and onto others.

Yet as psychologists have discovered, it's this turning away that gives gratitude its therapeutic potency over failure and misfortune. Failure and misfortune cause psychic pain by triggering a neural process known as rumination: a brooding over the negative aspects of our lives. So, the best way to stop the pain is simply to stop thinking about ourselves. When we stop, the introspective brain regions that drive rumination—like the potent worry circuits of our dorsolateral prefrontal cortex—gradually relax. As that happens, our mishap ceases to be a source of anxiety, self-disgust, and despair. It recedes into being just another event in our life, one that we can mine calmly for insight—or gradually forget.

Because rumination is interrupted by a looking away, any looking away will help alleviate it. But psychologists have discovered that acts of gratitude are particularly effective. Gratitude has enabled middle schoolers to recover from poor test performances and helped adults bounce back emotionally from cancer diagnoses. It has lowered the occurrence of suicidal ideation among bullied teens, reduced rates of depression among the survivors of terror attacks, and nurtured resilience among displaced Syrian refugees.

Although this therapeutic salve has come to psychologists' attention only recently, it goes back long before our present day. So ancient is gratitude's neural action that its biological origins can be traced to chimps and even capuchin monkeys, suggesting that it evolved in the simian brain tens of millions of years ago. And the healing boon of gratitude was discovered long ago by human cultures too. In times more distant than modern historians can see, our ancestors learned the value of gratefulness. They invented expressions of thanks such as the Old Norse *þokk* and the Sanskrit *dhanyavaadaha* and the Hebrew *todah*. And then our ancestors went further: they took gratitude's natural healing salve—and used literature to boost it artificially.

That artificial gratitude booster can be found in the world's oldest known literary text, *The Kesh Temple Hymn*: "Was there ever a mother greater than Nintud, mother of the world?" And it can be found, too, in the biblical scriptures that precede 1 Thessalonians:

> O give thanks unto the Lord. To him that by wisdom made the heavens. . . . To him that stretched out the earth above the waters.

Both these texts employ the same blueprint: express gratefulness for a world creator such as Nintud or the biblical God. That expression of gratefulness takes our natural biological gratitude for a single kind act and *stretches* it into a spiritual gratitude for everything we see. Like all literary *stretches*, this one imbues our brain with wonder. (See the introduction for why.) And since wonder makes us less conscious of our self, it amplifies thanksgiving's therapeutic turn-away. Enriching gratitude's other-love with its own self-dissolve, it doubly relieves the introspective gnaw of rumination.

The effectiveness of this ancient theological combo of wonder and gratitude has been confirmed in twenty-first-century science labs, where it has been shown to significantly increase the healing effects of thanksgiving. And it's the remedy delivered by the prose of 1 Thessalonians. The provenance of 1 Thessalonians is uncertain, but it seems to have been composed by the Apostle Paul around the year 50 CE, an era of great difficulties for the Christian faithful. They'd suffered famines, been excommunicated from their Jewish birth communities, and seen their leaders perish. And as they cast their eyes toward the sky, waiting for their savior to fulfill his promise of return, the days stretched into months and years, until the faithful began to fret: *Is Jesus really coming back? Did I throw away my life upon the wrong messiah? Have I made a terrible mistake?*

It was to ease such painful broodings that 1 Thessalonians dispensed its healing salve: "In every thing give thanks." This medicine helped the beleaguered revolutionaries of early Christianity forget their initial adversities and keep laboring on—until, in time, their diligent gospel touched almost every acre of the world.

Yet as potent a curative as 1 Thessalonians proved to be, it wasn't the final breakthrough in literature's gratitude technology. Ninety generations after 1 Thessalonians, the Bible's therapeutic action would be improved again by a tribe of revolutionaries.

And among that tribe was George Eliot.

Improving the Gratitude Technology

George Eliot was left unconvinced by 1 Thessalonians. In her novel *Felix Holt*, the prayer "without ceasing" doesn't salve the preacher's mental hurt; instead, his rumination is ended only by the ringing of the dinner bell.

This light jab at 1 Thessalonians reflected Eliot's own doctrine of social affection, summarized by her as: "Love excludes gratitude." Love was true affection between equals; gratitude was the groveling appreciation of a lowly mortal for his almighty Lord. This inequality, Eliot believed, undermined the sincerity of gratitude. When we thanked God, we weren't doing so purely out of gratefulness; we also felt compelled by submissive fear and dutiful obligation.

Eliot was right about gratitude, at least from a scientific perspective. The healing power of gratitude is weakened by feelings of dependence or inferiority. These feelings return our brain's negative gaze to itself, retriggering our worry circuits, and dragging us back into the self-gnaw of rumination. So, from the vantage of human psychology, the design glitch in 1 Thessalonians is that its creator-god amplifies the natural benefits of thanksgiving—yet also diminishes them. Like the Lord Himself, it giveth and taketh away.

For many thousands of years, from the time of *The Kesh Temple Hymn* to the age of George Eliot, this glitch seemed irreparable. Since the very same feature of the creator-god—the god's immense power—generated both the gratitude boost of wonder and the gratitude diminisher of inferiority, there was no evident way to disentangle the benefit of the former from the drawback of the latter. The maximum benefit of gratitude appeared to have been reached.

And then in the mid-nineteenth century, the glitch was fixed. The fixer was an unemployed cultural anthropologist who lived in the pastoral heights of Bavaria, supported by his wife, Bertha. His name was Ludwig Feuerbach, and in 1841 he published a two-volume treatise with a disarmingly conventional title: *The Essence of Christianity*. But when readers turned past the book's title page, they were surprised to discover that in Feuerbach's opinion, the essence of Christianity was not Christ. Christ, according to Feuerbach, was just an ordinary man. All of Christ's miracles—including the five loaves at Bethsaida, and the walking on water, and even the Resurrection on the third day—were literary fictions devised by Matthew of Galilee, Luke of Antioch, and the other gospelists.

The same claim had been made six years before by one of Feuerbach's friends, the University of Tübingen scholar David Strauss, in a provocative book titled *Das Leben Jesu (The Life of Jesus)*. But Feuerbach went much further than Strauss. Feuerbach didn't merely suggest that Christ's life was a fiction. He suggested that *God Himself* was a fiction.

This seemed to be a wholesale rejection of religion, but discerning readers realized it was not. Feuerbach was, in fact, founding a new faith that would become known as humanism. Humanism acknowledged that God was a literary myth, but denied that the sacred virtues of God—vast love, vast kindness, vast creativity—were also myths. Those virtues really existed in us, the human species. As Feuerbach explained through a topsy-turvy retelling of the book of Genesis, Adam and Eve had long ago fashioned God in their own image, inventing a goliath Human Good in the sky. And successive generations of humans had then proceeded to worship that make-believe theocrat, bowing to a king who never was instead of giving due credit to themselves: "The Christian worshipper . . . is thankful, grateful to God, but unthankful to man."

This upside-downing of traditional religion amazed George Eliot. In fact, it amazed her so much that she didn't just read Feuerbach's book in its original German; she translated it into English. And in 1854 her translation was published by the youthful doctor-editor John Chapman at his inky boardinghouse at 142 Strand, from whence it uplifted readers all across London with Feuerbach's eucharistic creed of gratefulness toward humanity:

> Think, therefore, with every morsel of bread which relieves thee from the pain of hunger, with every draught of wine which cheers thy heart, of the God who confers these beneficent gifts upon thee, – think of man!

This was a major psychiatric breakthrough. By inspiring wonder at the vast gifts of humanity, it preserved the gratitude augmenter of 1 Thessalonians while removing the gratitude limiter of the creator-god, delivering an even more potent salve for failure and adversity than biblical scripture.

Yet Feuerbach's breakthrough didn't have the revolutionary effect on public health that Eliot had hoped. Instead, its unorthodox doctrine of humanity as God was widely denounced. First, it was denounced by the

Catholic Church as the rationalist fruit of the Protestant Reformation; then it was denounced by Protestant Reformers as a descent into atheism; and finally, it was denounced by atheists such as Max Stirner and Karl Marx for not being atheistic enough. So, across all of Europe, there arose not one solitary church for worshipping humanity.

Observing this second unrevolution, Eliot began to wonder: Was there another way for her to spread Feuerbach's therapeutic innovation? Could she go beyond translating the doctrine of humanism into English—and translate its healing benefits into the minds of readers who recoiled from its ideological content?

Yes, Eliot knew, she could. For Feuerbach himself had already pointed out a way: literature. Literature had created *The Kesh Temple Hymn* and the other original songs and stories that had inspired us to give thanks to creator-deities, so surely literature could create new works that inspired us to give thanks to humanity. Those new works could multiply our natural gratitude with wonder for a greater human goodness, and because the multiplier would be a fictional tale instead of a theological tract, it wouldn't require us to alter our religious beliefs. Even if we were as piously committed to God as the author of 1 Thessalonians, or even if we were as unspiritual as Karl Marx, a literature of humanism could enhance our well-being with a practical scientific remedy.

Excited by this idea, George Eliot turned to her library for the literary technology that she'd need to put it into action. But as she scanned her capacious shelves, she made an unwelcome discovery: the technology for dispensing humanism didn't exist. In fact, the most updated books that Eliot owned were filled with precisely the opposite circuitry.

The Opposite Circuitry of Modern Literature

The newest literary technology in Eliot's library was the novel. And the novel's own newest and most popular genres were modern romance and modern tragedy.

These two genres were intended to capture the fullness of human experience by dividing it between them. Our hopes and desires fell under romance; our doubts and fears, under tragedy. But despite this effort to include the whole of our psychology, modern novels had, Eliot saw, paid short shrift to one of our mind's essential faculties: gratitude. For instead of nurturing a healthy appreciation for others, romances and tragedies groomed us only to worship our own selves.

This feature of modern romance was diagnosed by Eliot in an 1856 essay for the *Westminster Review*, where she wryly portrayed the rampant self-regard of the typical romance hero: "She has a superb contralto and a superb intellect; she is perfectly well dressed and perfectly religious; she dances like a sylph, and reads the Bible in the original tongues."

And if modern romance was an ego puff for its readers, modern tragedy was worse. Back in the 1830s, the French author Honoré de Balzac had sworn to engineer an alternative to modern romance in his novel *Le Père Goriot:* "Behold! This Tragedy is no fiction, no Romance." But instead of undoing modern romance's self-centeredness, the modern tragedy of *Le Père Goriot* had only intensified it. The novel culminated with the burial of its title character, Father Goriot, a kindly pasta merchant who'd spent all his wealth to keep his daughters happy. Yet the daughters were too self-involved to attend Father Goriot's funeral, and even the priest himself wasn't interested; after reciting the short prayer he'd been paid to perform, he fled the scene unceremoniously. Soon there remained only one mourner, young Eugene Rastignac, to shed a melancholy tear. But when Rastignac shed that tear, he shed the last of his innocence too. Stepping away from the graveside, he turned toward the honeyed pleasures of Paris, declaring, "*À nous deux, maintenant!*"—"It's between us, now!" And, determined to be the victor of the contest, Rastignac set off into the city to seduce his way to the top, starting with a daughter of Father Goriot.

This scene troubled George Eliot deeply. On October 25, 1859, she confessed in her notebook that she found it "hateful." It forsook the model of ancient tragedy, which had emphasized the fragility of even the mightiest lives, to instead stoke admiration for the strong and contempt for the weak: Eugene Rastignac's heroic cynicism was celebrated as the scientific mode of life, while Father Goriot's generous love was despised as sentimental foolishness.

And as Eliot returned *Le Père Goriot* to its shelf, scanning the hundreds of other literary volumes that she'd gathered beside it, she came to realize that the self-centeredness of modern literature extended even further than modern tragedy and modern romance, reaching into the very circuitry of the novel itself. For unlike theater, oral poetry, and other earlier forms of popular literature, the novel wasn't built to be consumed as part of a large audience of strangers; it was instead made to be absorbed in reading isolation through our private imagination. In that immersive solitude, we became all and everything, self-sufficient in ourselves, so we had no need of gratitude for others—and to whom would we be grateful, anyway? We the novel reader sat alone as we watched the narrative unfold, like a creator-god observing life's grand story from our solitary throne.

So, if Eliot wanted to introduce readers to the medicine of humanism, she'd have to do more than reform the strutting egoism of contemporary fiction. She'd have to invert the entire technology of the novel, upending its lordly aloofness with a humble togetherness.

Reconjuring the spirit of 1848, she'd have to start a revolution of her own.

George Eliot's Revolution

At the age of fifty, Eliot picked up a portable writing desk. And, settling herself upon a couch in the roomy two-story abode where she lived at London's Regent's Park, she began drafting a new novel that would become known as *Middlemarch*.

Middlemarch tells a story of failure. It begins by brooding about all the individuals who could have been extraordinary, yet never were. Those individuals "found for themselves no epic life wherein there was a constant unfolding of far-resonant action; perhaps only a life of mistakes."

In the chapters that follow, *Middlemarch* then recounts one such life "of mistakes": that of a woman who failed so completely that she's been forgotten by history, existing now as "a foundress of nothing." This character sounds very much like Father Goriot. And, indeed, she is. She too is loving and generous, and she too vanishes into an unvisited grave. Yet even so, she moves us very differently from Goriot, for her familiar character is paired with an innovation to another story element: the narrator.

The narrator of *Le Père Goriot* had begun by chatting to us in the first-person-plural *we*: "Don't we all like to feel our power over others?"

But the narrator had then abandoned this inclusive *we* voice to grow aloof; so aloof that he vanished altogether at Father Goriot's burial, leaving us to think what we would.

The narrator of *Middlemarch* follows the opposite arc. She starts at a lofty remove, but when we drift toward Eugene Rastignac's contempt for other people's suffering, she comes down from her sky mount to whisper:

Pity the laden one; this wandering woe
May visit you and me.

These words arrive in *Middlemarch* as the epigraph of the seventy-third chapter. Their narrative substance replaces modern tragedy's self-centeredness with ancient tragedy's caring community of mutual "woe." And to help us enter that community ourselves, their narrative style does something extraordinary: it deploys the phrase "you and me."

"You and me" occurs rarely in literature, and for good reason. It has a shorter and more elegant synonym: *us*. The author of *Middlemarch* could have said, "May visit us," and she'd have meant the same thing. But even though "you and me" is uncommon in literature, it does have a practical use in daily speech: it helps our brain bond to other people. Unlike "us," which accepts that we're already bonded, "you and me" stimulates the neural feeling of a physical connection coming into being. In cases when we're not bonded yet, that feeling wraps our consciousness around a new coalition; in cases when we're bonded already, it renews our sense of the union. That's why "you and me" appears most frequently in the conversation of children. When we're children, we're still very much negotiating our place in society, making new friends and exploring fresh partnerships, so we feel the specialness of coming together. That coming together isn't an assumed fact of life, and it needs to be *emphasized* to make sure that the parties involved understand.

Because "you and me" occurs in the daily speech of children and the occasional bonding adult, it does pop up here and there in the dialogue of literary characters. But it almost never occurs in the speech of narrators—and when it does, it occurs only in first-person narration. Prior to *Middlemarch*, in all of known literature, "you and me" never drops from the mouth of an omniscient third-person narrator. Such narrators are the literary descendants of the God Voices deployed in *The Kesh Temple Hymn* and the world's other holy scriptures. (See chapter 1 for the blueprint.) So, they're not equals, on our level, trying to establish a feeling of coming together; they're lordly superiors striving to humble us with awe and fear.

The same lordly God Voice is deployed in the opening sentence of *Middlemarch*, where the narrator booms omnisciently about "time" and "the history of man." But when the narrator pivots to the voice of "you and me," she abandons the up-aboveness of scripture. Descending to join her *me* to our *you*, she triggers our brain to feel another person alongside us, infusing our readerly solitude with a neural experience of togetherness.

This third-person narrative infusion of togetherness was a revolution in novel writing—and in spirituality too. Across all the verses of the Bible, there's just a single instance of "you and me." And it doesn't fall from the heavens. It's uttered by the author of 1 Thessalonians in a moment of loneliness: "I long to see you . . . that I may be comforted together with you by the mutual faith both of you and me."

Here we have another very surprising biblical passage. Instead of looking directly to God for relief, a holy author expresses gratitude for a "mutual" humanity. Yet as surprising as this passage is, it's still conventional in two crucial respects. First, the "you and me" is spoken by a first-person narrator: "*I* long to see you." Second, the "you and me" is followed by a pivot of thanksgiving to God:

> For it is the power of God unto salvation to every one that believeth. . . . Praise the Lord, all ye Gentiles; and laud him, all ye people.

Both conventions are shattered by *Middlemarch*. In the novel's final sentence, its all-seeing narrator returns once again to the voice of "you and me." And instead of following 1 Thessalonians in subordinating itself to an up-above Lord, the voice of "you and me" *stretches* out across horizons of time and space to thank a forgotten humanity:

The growing good of the world is partly dependent on unhistoric acts; and that things are not so ill with you and me as they might have been, is half owing to the number who lived faithfully a hidden life, and rest in unvisited tombs.

This is the humanism of Feuerbach, fashioned into literary experience. The "you and me" pulls the God Voice from the heights, revealing its almighty to be one of us. And at the same time that this revelation imbues our brain with a feeling of equal togetherness, the togetherness is flung outward into world-spanning gratitude for "the number who lived faithfully a hidden life." The result is a neural experience of vast and awe-soaked thanksgiving that dissolves our self with wonder while enriching our mind with love for a billion other lives.

In that double release from ourselves, our own disappointments vanish from mind. And freed from rumination's backward clog, we feel a human possibility beyond.

Using the "Gratitude Multiplier" Yourself

In the 1930s, the Great Depression struck. Unemployment in America soared to almost 25 percent, and the birthrate shrank by nearly as much. Failure and self-doubt were everywhere.

And everywhere, too, was a radio song: Kate Smith's 1938 rendition of *God Bless America*. It was a religious song of thanksgiving, so it was propitious for the times. It lifted sunken minds from their brooding introspection, bestowing the healing touch of gratitude for a creator-god.

Yet the song irked one man: Woody Guthrie. Like George Eliot, Guthrie felt a clash between an up-above God and the free expression of gratitude. And like George Eliot, Guthrie found a resolution to that clash in humanism. As he later explained his own personal rendition of Feuerbach's faith:

God Is Love. . . . It was those three words that made not only religion, but also several other sorts of superstitious fears and hatreds in me meet one very quick death. . . .

Love makes this wonder then, in fifty thousand billions of un-counted trillions of life's forms, shapes, patterns, in every step and in every stage of life . . . and in the same plain ways all through the moves and the actions, the very thoughts, of every human being that travels here in plain view of our eyes.

Inspired by this humanistic creed, Guthrie decided in 1940 to rewrite "God Bless America." Replacing its higher God with "every human being that travels here in plain view," he transformed it into an anthem of submission-free gratitude that he titled "This Land Is Your Land."

From California to the New York island . . .
This land was made for you and me.

For "you and me." Love made this land for you and me.

Whenever you'd like more of that grateful soul heal, you can find it all across your library. For such is the marvel of George Eliot's invention that you can carry it into every novel that you read. All you need to do is pause when the novel is done—and think of all the nameless acts of love that helped create it.

Think of all the people who gave their hours to provide the novel-ist's bread. Think of all the hands that built the schoolrooms where she learned. Think of all the strangers who labored in shadow to give her pen and ink and paper, strangers whom she'd never see.

Then think of her, wrestling against confusion and self-doubt and endless false starts to carry her narrative to its last shining word.

And all of it for readers whom she'd never see.

All of it for you and me.

SIXTEEN

Clear Your Head

"Rashōmon," Julius Caesar, *and the Invention of the Second Look*

On a pleasant January day in 1913, just across from the lake wisteria of Tokyo's Hibiya Park, the Japanese Imperial Government filed into a temporary wooden structure of Teutonic-shogunate design to await the new emperor. The old emperor, Meiji the Great, had just been buried in Kyoto, bringing an end to an industrious fifty-year reign: copper mines had been drilled into the ancient Ashio peaks, samurai daughters had been put to work at silk mill spindles, steam-driven motorcars had beeped their way past Okayama Castle, and the twelve-inch guns of the world's mightiest battleship, the *Mikasa*, had sunk Russia's navy at the Battle of Tsushima.

Outside the wooden structure, a rumble of two-cylinder engines announced the new emperor's arrival. Accompanied by a few nervous orderlies, he strolled to the front of the Imperial Government, a prepared speech in hand. With painstaking care, he began to roll up the speech. And once he'd finished rolling, he lifted the speech to his eye, peering through it like a telescope. First, he studied the glittering chest medals of Prime Minister Katsura Tarō. Then he panned across the room, discovering new stars.

In just a moment, we'll explore what happened next in Tokyo. But before we go any further, let me ask you: Did you believe what you just read about that pleasant January day? Did you believe that the Imperial

Government was housed in an odd wooden building across from Hibiya Park? Or that the new emperor used his lecture papers as a looking tube?

Yes. You did believe. Maybe you're not completely believing anymore. Maybe you've just started to question whether my story was true. But you did believe it all at first.

Why? Why did you believe? Why didn't you question my words when you read them?

You might think that you believed because of some special ingredient of my story. You might think that I used a secret literary invention to catch your gullibility. But that's not it at all. There wasn't anything special about the story I told. Instead, the reason that you believed is simply this: because of the way that your brain evolved, you believe every new thing that you read.

You're having a hard time accepting this biological fact about your brain, I know. That's because I've just made you suspicious. But I can be trusted, you'll see: if you open almost any history of early-twentieth-century Japan, you'll discover the curious tale about how the new emperor, Emperor Taishō, rolled up his speech into a telescope. So, I didn't make up the story; I just repeated what most people believe—and what I believed when I first heard it too. And after I've explained why our brains all believed that story, I'll then explain what I did to make you suspicious.

Because that's the real literary invention here.

The Neuroscience of Our Gullibility

When the brain first evolved, in wormlike animals that emerged more than half a billion years ago in the nitrogen-thin shallows of the Ediacaran Era, its simple purpose was to process sensory information about the surrounding world. It detected light or food and directed the body: *Swim to that light! Quick, eat that food!*

The brain, in other words, emerged without a filter. It didn't question whether the light or the food was real. It trusted all its primary perceptions.

This system was crude yet effective. After all, most of the sensory data that arrived in the brain were reliable. The light existed, as did the food. In fact, so effective was this crude system that it's still used by many animals today. Bugs all over the world continue to exist without questioning their senses. Their brains just accept what their retinas see.

Eventually, however, more complex brains emerged. And these brains discovered that there could be advantages to questioning. One of the advantages, rather ironically, was to offer protection from other complex brains. Complex brains could lie and deceive, duping their targets with elaborate fictions. So, over time the complex brain evolved the capacity to skeptically evaluate the things it saw—and judge whether or not those things could be believed.

But even as the complex brain evolved new neural circuits that enabled it to judge, it didn't rewire itself completely. Instead, it patched its new circuits onto the old neural hardware that it had inherited from its ancient worm ancestors. Which meant that the brain continued to accept everything it saw—and then judge after the fact what was actually true.

Our brain continues to work this way. Rather than deciding what to believe, it decides what *not* to believe. It doesn't inspect every new idea and tag it as "true" before admitting it into our belief system. Instead, it accepts every idea into our belief system—then sifts through our belief system, retroactively tagging ideas as "false."

This makeshift method isn't necessarily bad. It allows us to react faster to things that pop up, and it keeps our mind permanently open. But like anything biological, it does have its drawbacks. One of those drawbacks is that we tend to be biased toward first impressions. We accept unthinkingly—and later have to work to change our mind. Another drawback is that we turn into easy dupes if we're tired or overwhelmed. Since it takes effort to *not* believe, we become more credulous in times of stress, allowing powerful regimes or predatory corporations to brainwash us with images when we're deprived of sleep.

Our brain is full of that brainwashing now. You and I believe all sorts of nonsense spewed by politicians, businesses, media pundits, and other exploiters who take advantage of our natural gullibility (and our increasing state of modern exhaustion) to slip misinformation inside our skulls.

Yet the brainwash doesn't need to stay inside our head forever. Literature has an invention to wash it back out.

The Origins of the Un-Brainwashing Invention

The earliest known version of the invention is an ancient rhetorical trick that's gloriously illustrated by Shakespeare's *The Tragedy of Julius Caesar*.

Julius Caesar recounts the tale of a Roman cabal that assassinates the play's title character. When this assassination happens onstage, we have no doubt that it's meant to serve the public good. It is, after all, initiated by the senator Brutus Marcus Junius. And Brutus, as we've learned from even his enemies, always acts with the noblest of intentions.

But then, at Caesar's funeral, Caesar's friend Mark Antony addresses the Roman people with this speech:

> The noble Brutus
> Hath told you Caesar was ambitious:
> If it were so, it was a grievous fault,
> And grievously hath Caesar answer'd it.
> Here, under leave of Brutus and the rest—
> For Brutus is an honourable man;
> So, are they all, all honourable men—
> Come I to speak in Caesar's funeral.
> He was my friend, faithful and just to me:
> But Brutus says he was ambitious;
> And Brutus is an honourable man.
> He hath brought many captives home to Rome
> Whose ransoms did the general coffers fill:
> Did this in Caesar seem ambitious?
> When that the poor have cried, Caesar hath wept:
> Ambition should be made of sterner stuff:
> Yet Brutus says he was ambitious;
> And Brutus is an honourable man.

Again and again, Antony utters the phrase "Brutus is an honourable man." And the more that he repeats it, the more we start to ask ourselves: *Is Brutus, in fact, so very honorable?*

Antony's repetition incites this question for a simple reason: it creates a light sensation of déjà vu that makes our brain self-conscious. In that self-conscious state, our brain is pulled out of its passive viewing experience and prompted to take an active second, third, and fourth look at our internalized belief that Brutus is an honorable man. And as our brain goes back and reviews, and re-reviews, and re-re-reviews, we have to decide, and re-decide, and re-re-decide: *Do I tag this belief as true or untrue?* So, a belief that initially slipped inside our head without resistance becomes a repeated object of our conscious judgment.

Antony's use of verbal repetition to prompt self-conscious introspection is a simple neuro-literary trick. But it's effective. It has prompted many audiences to take a skeptical re-look at their prior beliefs about Brutus. And among those audiences was a young student at Tokyo Imperial University, a few miles north of the odd wooden structure at Hibiya Park.

The student was Ryūnosuke Akutagawa. In his Imperial University classes, Akutagawa was studying with professors such as the famed British Japanologist Basil Hall Chamberlain, who in 1912, the year of the old emperor's death, took aim at the samurai code of bushido:

> Bushido was unknown until a decade or two ago! *The very word appears in no dictionary, native or foreign, before the year 1900. . . .* The accounts given of it have been fabricated out of whole cloth, chiefly for foreign consumption.

So, when young Ryūnosuke Akutagawa read *Julius Caesar*, he did what Antony's audience had done to Brutus and what Professor Chamberlain had done to bushido: he paused to re-look.

Seeing Even Clearer

In 1915, two years after the new emperor's peculiar visit to the Imperial Government, the result of Akutagawa's re-look appeared as the short story "Rashōmon."

"Rashōmon" was printed by a jobbing letterpress inside Tokyo Imperial University. And it greeted its university readers with a picturesque opening sentence: "That nightfall, a servant crouched beneath Rashōmon gate, waiting for the rain to pass."

This sentence is a gentle homage to the *Konjaku Monogatarishū* and other collections of medieval Japanese folktales that styled the Rashōmon gate as a place where magical spirits revealed themselves to ordinary folk. Yet in the story's following paragraphs, no such spirit appears. Instead, what appears is the story's own narrator. And the narrator doesn't sweep us to a magical realm. Instead, he carries us back to revisit his earlier remarks:

> A few moments ago, I wrote that the servant was "waiting for the rain to pass," but in fact the man wasn't really waiting; he'd been dismissed several days ago by his master and had nowhere to go. So, rather than writing that the servant was "waiting for the rain to pass," it would have been better to write: "a servant crouched beneath Rashōmon gate, homeless and lost."

In this extraordinary passage, the narrator reveals that he got it wrong. The servant was not, in fact, doing what the narrator originally said. The truth of the matter was entirely different, prompting the narrator to return to his opening sentence—and rewrite it.

This is the "Second Look." It's the rhetorical technique used by Shakespeare's Mark Antony, amplified. Now, instead of being deployed by one character within a story, it's deployed by the narrator relating the whole of the story. So, it jars our brain into self-consciously reviewing everything we've learned since we started reading. And as our brain undergoes that self-review, we experience the mental state known as alienation.

Alienation is the neural inverse of paranoia, the emotion we explored in chapter 6. In paranoia, we come to distrust the narrative voice guiding us through a story. But in alienation, we don't feel that distrust: our brain believes the narrator at the start of "Rashōmon," and our brain believes him when he interrupts to correct. Rather, what our brain starts to question is *itself*. Aware that it mistakenly accepted the narrator's first statement, it starts to worry, *What other false data have I allowed in?*

This worry activates a different region of our brain from the region activated by paranoia. Paranoia occurs in our threat-detection system, a system so ancient that paranoia is almost certainly experienced in some basic form by rats and dogs. But alienation occurs in the cutting-edge self-reflexive circuitry of our frontal cortex, a neural zone found only in humans and a few close primates. That self-reflexive circuitry doesn't make us leery of outside threats. Instead, it trawls through our brain's *inside* beliefs, tagging more of them as potentially false.

Such self-scrutiny can feel uncomfortable; our brain doesn't like to think of itself as mistake prone. (See chapter 13 for why.) And because self-scrutiny occurs in our brain's newer circuitry, it's more neurally fragile than paranoia's primal suspicion of others. So, to help keep our alienation going, "Rashōmon" proceeds to treat us to another Second Look. The Look begins when the servant slips inside the gate, where he finds an old woman stealing hair from corpses to sell as a wig. Appalled, the servant chastises the old woman. But she responds defiantly:

> "Yes, yes; it's immoral, perhaps, to pluck the hairs from the dead. But these particular dead didn't treat their lives as sacred. Take the woman whose locks I now hold—she used to cut up snake meat and sell it to the royal guard as fish. I don't think that was immoral. She had to feed herself somehow. She didn't have a choice. And I think that she'd understand that I don't have a choice either. I think she'd understand why I'm robbing her hair."

With this eloquent self-defense, the old woman reveals herself to have a thoroughgoing ethics of life—the same one promoted, in fact, by Japan's most celebrated early-twentieth-century novelist, Natsume Sōseki. Over the decade that preceded "Rashōmon," Sōseki had cast a wry eye over the mystic spiritualism of the old Japanese folktales, suggesting that our best chance at happiness was to instead acknowledge our physical nature, committing ourselves to forming a society where we supported one another's material needs.

This tolerant naturalism is a world away from bushido and medieval magical thinking—just the sort of ethics needed in our modern world. And then "Rashōmon" makes us take a Second Look. After the old woman has finished her speech, the servant agrees with her, and to show how deeply he agrees, he declares: "You'll understand, then, why I need to rob you. I don't have a choice; I have to feed myself somehow." At which point, the servant violently disrobes the old woman and vanishes with a triumphant cry into the darkness.

This is a shocking moment—and also a moment of repetition. Just like Antony when he repeats our belief "Brutus is an honourable man," the servant repeats back the old woman's disenchanted naturalism—"I don't have a choice . . . I don't have a choice"—knocking our brain into self-review: *Why did I accept the old woman's belief so unthinkingly? Why didn't I see that it would leave her naked with the dead?*

In this self-review, we experience a new depth of introspective questioning, deeper even than we experienced when the narrator corrected his picturesque opening sentence. Back then, we wondered how our brain could have been duped into a rosy, old medieval fantasy. But now we're starting to question whether even our acceptance of modern materialism is sound. And as our brain is touched by this doubt, it asks itself: *Is there anything reliable in my head? Do I believe anything true at all?*

Using the Second Look Yourself

In 1950, twenty-three years after Akutagawa died by suicide, "Rashō-mon" was made into the film *Rashomon* by the celebrated director Akira Kurosawa.

Or that's what you'd think from the film's title, anyway. In fact, the plot of Kurosawa's *Rashomon* is based primarily upon a different Akutagawa short story, "In a Grove."

But even though *Rashomon* is a departure from "Rashōmon," it does borrow the short story's deep architecture for its own narrative frame. Exchanging Akutagawa's servant for a commoner and Akutagawa's woman for a woodcutter, the film has the woodcutter tell the story of a samurai's death. And after the woodcutter finishes his telling, the film then retells the story of the samurai's death in a contradictory way, before going on to retell the story two more times, with each version contradicting all the ones before.

This storytelling technique has often been misunderstood as a device for stirring our distrust in Kurosawa's narrative or even in reality itself. But like Akutagawa's original short story, the effect of Kurosawa's film isn't paranoia. It's alienation. Far from seeming less and less trust-worthy as it goes along, the film's narrative seems constantly believable. Each retelling of the samurai's death is witnessed with our own two eyes, striking our brain as instantly true, and prodding us to take Second Look after Second Look at the previous retellings lodged inside our memory. Until finally, the film returns to the event that concludes Akutagawa's story: the commoner/servant commits a self-interested theft in front of the woodcutter/woman, prompting our brain to wonder why we ever believed the woodcutter/woman's tarradiddle about a greater human nature. This is the disenchanted ending we were anticipating from the film's title; this is Akutagawa's culminating Second Look.

But then Kurosawa prompts us to look again. He engineers one last story beat, entirely of his own devising, where the woodcutter gener-ously adopts a needy infant, inspiring a hopeful sun to banish the rain at Rashōmon gate. This unexpected happy ending jars our brain, and, in fact, jars our brain so intensely that Tokyo film critic Chiyota Shimizu once accused Kurosawa of getting the ending "wrong."

The ending is not wrong, however. It alters the details of Aku-tagawa's earlier story conclusion to preserve the deeper innovation be-neath: a Second Look. In this *second* Second Look, our earlier certainty that *Rashomon* was a venture into postmodern skepticism is challenged by our new certainty that the film has all along been a revival of pre-modern sentimentalism. And as our brain stares in disbelief at our two opposed certainties, we become alienated from the contents of our own psyche, realizing that somewhere along the line, we've believed the un-believable.

Since this alienated feeling is less neurally durable than paranoia, our brain can often slip, like Chiyota Shimizu, from questioning itself into reproaching others: *You're what's wrong here!* But a life where we reject alienation for paranoia is a life where we miss the chance to ex-amine our own thoughts. And to help us make more of that chance, authors post-Akutagawa have filled our global library with literary works that use narrative repetitions, revisions, and retellings to inspire déjà vu moments of self-inspection: James Joyce's *A Portrait of the Artist as a Young Man*, Nella Larsen's *Passing*, Bertolt Brecht's *Mother Courage and Her Children*, Chinua Achebe's *Things Fall Apart*, Kurt Vonnegut's

Slaughterhouse-Five, Philip Roth's *Portnoy's Complaint*, Ama Ata Aidoo's *Our Sister Killjoy*, Timothy Mo's *The Redundancy of Courage*, J. M. Coetzee's *Disgrace*.

So, if you don't want ideas that aren't your own, try clearing your head with an alienating book. You may be doomed to believe everything you see, but with fiction's paper looking tube, you can take another look.

SEVENTEEN

Find Peace of Mind

Virginia Woolf, Marcel Proust, James Joyce, and
the Invention of the Riverbank of Consciousness

L ondon, 1922.

The Great War was over. The guns across Europe were silent. The killing fields had been replanted with apples and wheat. Yet still Virginia Woolf could not find peace. In her redbrick room at Hogarth House, she was experiencing flashbacks: "These fine December nights . . . keep sending through me such shocks from my childhood." And on the gray-paved walks of Bloomsbury, she was caught in runaway feelings: "A certain melancholy has been brooding over me this fortnight. . . . The feeling so often comes to me now."

Woolf confided these facts to her diary. It would be better for her husband not to know. If her husband knew, he'd take her to see the doctor. And Woolf loathed the doctor. He was "tyrannical." He was stone hearted. He had provoked Woolf to bitterly remark: "Really, a doctor is worse than a husband."

The doctor in question was George Savage, a friend of Woolf's father, and a most eminent psychiatrist. He was the cofounder of the *Journal of Mental Science*. He was profiled in *Vanity Fair*. He was knighted by the king.

When Sir George Savage had first examined Woolf, he'd instantly diagnosed the source of her mental turbulence: it was a classic case of "nerves." Nerves, in the doctor's view, were common ailments in women.

Women had fragile nervous systems that were easily overstimulated, and such overstimulation, as the doctor had explained learnedly in many an asylum, was routinely caused by just the sort of "useless book learning" that Woolf insisted on doing:

> If a . . . girl is allowed to educate herself at home, the danger of solitary work and want of social friction may [cause] insanity. It is in this manner that the results of defective education become often apparent in the case of the weaker sex now-a-days.

Reading. Writing. Thinking. These were risky activities for the "weaker sex," and there could be no doubt in George Savage's mind that Virginia Woolf's troubles resulted from her incessant intellectual activities. She had frayed her nerves with literature; she had overexcited her brain with novel writing. To Dr. Savage, the cure was thus obvious: Woolf must rest. She must be confined to bed. And in bed, she must have nothing to do with books: "You shant read this . . . You shant write a word . . . You shall lie still and drink milk."

So, Woolf was forced to lie still, for day after day. Yet no matter how much Woolf rested, the flashbacks and the runaway emotions persisted. Until at last, she decided to escape George Savage and invent a new cure.

The First Step Toward Woolf's New Cure

On a warm Sunday evening in May 1924, Virginia Woolf delivered a lecture to the Cambridge Heretics Society on the scientific revolution underway in modern psychology.

The revolution had first caught Woolf's attention as a way of innovating "character in fiction," and her interest had been piqued further by a conversation she'd had recently with another Cambridge heretic: the flamboyant British logician Bertrand Russell. Russell had taught at Cambridge University's most distinguished college, Trinity, until in 1916, at the height of the Great War, he'd been publicly expelled for pacifism.

After the war, Woolf and Russell became acquainted through mutual friends. The two peace seekers sat together at dinners, chatting about

"the Spirit of the Age," and prompting Woolf to note the contrast between Russell's impressive intelligence and his rather-less-so physique:

> His luminous, vigorous mind seems attached to a flimsy little car,
> like that on a glinting balloon. . . . He has no chin. . . . Nevertheless,
> I should like the run of his headpiece.

Among the many vigorous luminosities running through Russell's headpiece at that time, there was one that could not fail to interest Woolf, for it
put a liberating spin on modern psychiatry. Modern psychiatry had begun
its emergence in the eighteenth century when the English physician William Battie had walked into the asylums of London and stared in horror at
the two main treatments being meted out. The first was to shackle patients
in foul-smelling rooms where they were visited by a daily slop bucket and
the occasional priest. The second was a regime of vein slicing, hellebore,
and antimony, a combination that compelled patients to bleed, vomit, and
defecate until they fainted from dehydration and shock.

These "cures" were motivated by the archaic medical belief that
mental illness was caused either by malignant spirits or by imbalances in
the humors, four bodily fluids that doctors had blamed since antiquity
for depression, mania, and other psychic ailments. The malignant spirits
could be treated only by locking up patients and hoping for a visitation
from God; the imbalances only by forced expulsion of the offending humors, via leechcraft and emetic toxins.

Battie thundered against this outdated physic in his 1758 manifesto *A
Treatise on Madness*. The true cause of mental illness was not, he scoffed,
mystical spooks or mythical liquids. It was the physical nerves that made
up the human brain. To cure madness it was therefore necessary to treat
these nerves, which could be done, Battie suggested, by prescribing small
amounts of wine, or mineral waters, or mild narcotics such as henna
flower—or even just waiting for the patient's nerves to calm down over
time.

Battie's "nerve theory" improved the lot of the mentally ill. It gave
hope to patients who'd been chained up in dark holes as forever incur-
able. It eliminated the bleedings and the medieval drugs. Yet as Woolf
was to discover, Battie's program of reform had its own ugly conse-

quence. By emphasizing the physical treatment of nerves, it failed to acknowledge that there was more inside the patient's head than just a nervous system. There was also hope, and pain, and love, and memory, and fear. There was, in short, a mind.

Nerve theory's neglect of the mind meant that the suffering mental patient found herself attended by physicians who cared for her body while disregarding her psyche. Psychiatry had forgotten the root of its own name, and it was this memory lapse that led in the later decades of the nineteenth century to the rest cure. The rest cure literally reduced patients to inert piles of flesh, lavishing all its nursing on the body, which was plied with endless medicates of butter and milk, while the conscious mind was forced to surrender in silence. The result could only be dehumanizing. The old, sadistic psychiatry had at least acknowledged that patients had minds—even souls. The new, kinder psychiatry dispensed with all that ennobling fluff. The brain was a tub of nerves; the mind an accidental attendant to the gut.

So it was that in 1908, the renowned rest-cure advocate Dr. Silas Weir Mitchell could remark offhandedly in America's premier medical journal: "You cure the body and somehow find that the mind also is cured." It never occurred to the good doctor that the "somehow" might be relevant to psychiatric treatment. No, to Silas Weir Mitchell, the somehow was just a somehow, so, like his patients' volitions, it was briskly ignored.

The disturbing effects of this clinical attitude were graphically evidenced in 1887 when Mitchell imposed the rest cure on American author Charlotte Perkins Gilman. "Never touch pen, brush, or pencil," the doctor warned her ruthlessly, "as long as you live." This prescription failed to heal Gilman. Instead, her "mental torment" deepened to the point that she felt herself losing her mind: "I made a rag baby, hung it on a doorknob, and played with it. . . . I would sit blankly moving my head side to side." Woolf's experience was similarly grotesque. "I resent," she informed her husband, "being kept with my head on a platter, like some gigantic sow."

Woolf's husband registered her complaint—and sighed. He had no desire to force his wife to rest. He had no desire to force her to do anything. But what else could be done? Woolf's nerves were clearly overagitated. They needed to be calmed. Physical rest was the only solution.

Yet as Woolf was to learn from Bertrand Russell, there was, in fact, another solution. It had been devised many years earlier, more than a decade before Silas Weir Mitchell imposed rest on Charlotte Perkins Gilman. Mitchell himself might have learned it if he'd had a curious mind.

But Silas Weir Mitchell did not have a curious mind. The doctor who did was William James.

William James and the Problem of Nerves

William James was born amid the human bustle of a New York City hotel in 1842, and from a young age, he was fascinated by the cosmopolitan diversity of people's minds. The fascination was one shared by his younger brother, Henry, who'd go on to author novelistic character studies such as *The Turn of the Screw*. (See chapter 24 for its blueprint.) But William James's interest in the variousness of human psychology wasn't the only reason that he would invent an alternative to the rest cure. There was another, even more personal reason: James had his own long struggle with mental health.

When James was in his twenties, he suffered bouts of depression that included thoughts of suicide. Seeking help, he saw a psychiatrist and was informed that he had "neurasthenia," the medical term for nerves. The treatment prescribed to James was the more masculine version of the rest cure: physical exercise. Work the body, rest the mind. Take a break from school, the doctor advised. Go to the Amazon. Go to Europe. Get fresh air and athletic stimulation. Stop reading so many difficult, mind-buzzing books.

James tried to follow the treatment. He postponed his medical studies. He traveled. Yet against the doctor's orders, James continued his reading. And in April 1870, while James was perusing a quirky philosophical essay by the French recluse Charles Renouvier, he discovered the inspiration for his own psychiatric innovation: "I finished the first part of Renouvier's second 'Essais' [including] his definition of Free Will—'the sustaining of a thought *because I choose to* when I might have other thoughts.'"

The moment that James read this "definition of Free Will," he felt better. By inspiring him to believe in his own psychic liberty, it lightened the symptoms of his neurasthenia. So, James decided to see whether he could eliminate his symptoms entirely by continuing down this mental path: "My first act of free will shall be to believe in free will. For the remainder of the year, I will . . . voluntarily cultivate the feeling of moral freedom, by reading books favorable to it."

With this promise to himself, James flipped the old psychiatry of William Battie and Silas Weir Mitchell. That old psychiatry had been mechanistic—and deterministic. It had insisted that our mental life was dictated by the outside power of the attending physician. It had refused to countenance the possibility that we might use the *inside power* of our mind to participate in our own recovery.

James opened himself to this alternate possibility. He decided to see if his mind could heal itself by making healthy choices. And to encourage those choices, James committed to stocking his library with books that were "favorable" to his belief in his own volition. Books, he concluded, weren't the menace that his doctor had told him. No, books were part of the remedy.

So it was that James became his own psychiatrist. He discontinued the rest cure. And he prescribed himself a dose of positive reading.

James Develops His New Medicine

There were many reasons to doubt James's new medicine. But the main one was that it seemed more mystical than scientific.

James's therapy had no basis in scientific experiment, and neither did the idea of free will. Unlike nerves, which were physical things with measurable electric charges, free will was a vaporous, undetectable entity that might as well have been a spook or a spirit. So, surely, free will was a matter for priests, not physicians. Otherwise, medicine was doomed to lapse back into the theological superstitions that had made earlier generations perceive mental illness as a demonic visitation.

James agreed with these cautions. He agreed that free will fell under the purview of metaphysics, not science. He agreed that psychologists and psychiatrists had no tools in their labs or their medical kits for probing the mystery of human volition.

Yet even so, James was certain that his new treatment was scientific. After all, his treatment didn't depend on the existence of free will. It depended merely on a *belief* in free will. That belief could be ascertained empirically; you simply needed to ask patients whether they held it in mind. And the effects of that belief could also be scientifically evaluated: if the symptoms of neurasthenia were alleviated in patients who believed in free will, then that would show that the belief's power was real, regardless of whether or not free will was too.

The first experimental trial of this new treatment could be conducted by James himself. He could adopt a belief in his own mental power and see whether his psychic health improved. So, that's exactly what James did. He consumed a steady diet of books "favorable" to his own volition, and gradually he felt his dark emotions lift. By 1872, the lift was so complete that James declared his "soul sickness" gone. And becoming increasingly confident in his self-made medicine, he changed careers. Leaving behind the old asylum training of Battie and Mitchell, he joined the faculty of Harvard University, where he helped found the new field of modern psychology.

At Harvard, James promoted his psychiatric innovation through his own favorable writings, one of which was the best-selling *The Principles of Psychology*. Published in 1890, this groundbreaking textbook noted that our mind experienced a "feeling of effort" when making certain logical decisions. Was that feeling free will? It was impossible to know, but the feeling suggested that our mind at least believed in its own volition. Six years later, James then wrote another book, encouragingly titled *The Will to Believe*. In its lucid pages, he pointed out that in order to empirically test the power of a belief, we first needed to believe in that belief. Which was to say: if we wanted to see whether we could be our own doctor, we had to take a leap of faith. We had to *will* ourselves to believe in our power of self-healing, kick-starting our return to health with an act of free-willed positive thinking.

Over the first decade of the twentieth century, this empowering new approach to mental health was embraced with growing enthusiasm in America. In Europe, the interest in James's ideas developed more slowly, but the tide began to turn after the psychologist's death. In 1921, eleven years after James had passed away, one of England's leading philosophers published a short textbook titled *The Analysis of Mind*. And in its next-to-last chapter, the textbook casually assented to James's psychological definition of free will:

> James, in his *Principles of Psychology*, chapter 26, maintains that the only distinctive characteristic of a voluntary act is that it involves an idea of the movement to be performed. . . . I see no reason to doubt the correctness of this view.

The distinguished author of this passage was forty-nine-year-old Bertrand Russell, the man who was so impressing Virginia Woolf with his "headpiece."

Woolf Aligns Herself with William James

The same year that Bertrand Russell published his textbook, George Savage died.

He was seventy-eight, and he went to the grave a wealthy, lauded man. The *British Medical Journal* published a long obituary declaring that Dr. Savage might be departed, but his work endured: "His textbook, *Insanity and Allied Neuroses*, was deservedly popular with students and practitioners, and is now in its fourth edition."

George Savage's death should have been a relief to Woolf. But unfortunately for her, the *British Medical Journal* was right: the doctor's influence lived on. His view of Woolf as a mindless lump of tissue led her melancholy to be diagnosed as a symptom of dental bacteria, and she was duly strapped into a chair to have her offending teeth removed. Yet to the amazement of the attending dentist, the treatment failed. As Woolf bleakly observed on June 11, 1922, "I have lost three teeth in vain."

Woolf's ups and downs would remain with her for the rest of her life. Unlike William James, she never felt like she'd discovered the deep secret to alleviating her soul sickness. Four summers after her tooth operation, she would record in her diary: "everything insipid, tasteless, colourless . . . no pleasure in life whatsoever."

But over those four years from 1922 to 1926, Woolf would nevertheless make a breakthrough. She would invent a new literary style that
provided peace to other suffering souls. And she would do so by embracing two of William James's beliefs.

The first belief was that our mental health could be improved by favorable books. In the summer of 1926, Woolf observed that her return
to health originated with a mental spark: "sense of physical tiredness,
but slight activity in the brain. Beginning to take notice. Making one or
two plans." Among those plans was a trip to the poets on her bookshelf:
"Read some Dante & [Robert Seymour] Bridges, without troubling to
understand, but got pleasure from them." Woolf was now certain that
George Savage had got it backward: bookishness wasn't the source of
her mental distress. It was the cure.

The second belief that Woolf came to share with James was seemingly more obscure. But in short order, it would produce a revolution in
the therapeutic power of literature.

It was the belief in "the stream of consciousness."

The Stream of Consciousness

In January 1884 William James was forty-two. He was still just an assistant professor of philosophy. But he was soon to earn a promotion, both
at his university and in the eyes of the world.

James earned that promotion by publishing an article in the international psychology journal *Mind*. The article began with the startling
claim that the great English psychologists had all mangled their object
of study. They'd taken the special essence of human psychology—that
mysterious psychic experience known as consciousness—and crudely
"chopped [it] up in bits."

This chopping had never been admitted by the great English psychologists, but it was nevertheless evident in the way that they'd described
consciousness as a "chain" of ideas or a "train" of thought. These metaphors, which were everywhere in psychology journals and textbooks,
suggested that consciousness clattered along in discrete chunks, like railway cars upon a track. When, in fact, as James observed, consciousness
was something else entirely:

It is nothing jointed; it flows. A "river" or a "stream" are the metaphors by which it is most naturally described. *In talking of it hereafter let us call it the stream of thought, of consciousness, or of subjective life.*

After James made this declaration, the great English psychologists scratched their heads. What was the assistant professor going on about? Why did it matter whether consciousness was a "train" or a "stream"?

It mattered a great deal. As James pointed out, if our consciousness wasn't a stream, then our ideas would be painfully disorientating to us. They'd arrive suddenly in our awareness—and then vanish—with no indication of why they'd arrived or where they were going. Our whole mental experience would consist of disconnected jolts, or as James later termed them, "nervous shocks." Like a soldier in a battle trench, we'd be bombarded with constant pops of light and sound that came and went without any greater logic, leaving us in rattled bafflement.

This was not how our brain worked at its best. When our brain was focused on a good book or some other business of life, it operated calmly and fluidly. It was the opposite of a wartime trench. It was at peace.

That neural feeling of peace revealed that our consciousness was more than a train of ideas. It was also the *connections* between ideas. Those liquid connections conveyed the origins and purpose of our ideas, helping us understand *why* each one arrived in our awareness—and *where* it was carrying us. As James described poetically:

> Every definite image in the mind is steeped and dyed in the free water that flows round it. With it goes the sense of its relations, near and remote, the dying echo of whence it came to us, the dawning sense of whither it is to lead. The significance, the value, of the image is all in this halo or penumbra.

This was a stunning new way of thinking about the mind. But as James pointed out, it was not really original to him. It had already been discovered by literary authors.

Literary authors? The English psychologists were now really scratching their heads. What did literary authors know about human consciousness? Yet James was right. When authors picked up their pens, they did so to share something that they had in mind. They wrote, that is, to communicate a piece of their own consciousness. And to succeed in that communication, authors had learned long ago that they couldn't just write out a train of ideas, one after the other, separated into atomistic sentences by the plunking down of periods. They had to include the transitions *between* ideas. Those transitions could be crafted in all sorts of ways, but on a basic level, as James noted, they took the form of linking words such as *and* and *but* that established the "relation" between each idea and the next.

So, thousands of years prior to James, authors had noticed the importance of the stream of consciousness. And soon, authors would go further. Picking up James's belief in the stream, they would incorporate that belief into a new kind of novel.

The Stream-of-Consciousness Novel

In 1917 Dorothy Richardson's novel *Honeycomb* startled the literary world by presenting the mind of its nineteen-year-old governess, Miriam Henderson, like so:

> A vision of spring in dim rich faint colours, with the noisy real rushing spring still to come . . . a thing you could look at and forget; go back into winter, and see again and again, something to remember when the green spring came, and to think of in the autumn . . . spring; coming; perhaps spring was coming all the year round.

This was so unlike anything in previous English literature that the *Saturday Review of Literature* promptly diagnosed it as a case of neurasthenia. The author clearly had frail nerves, and she'd overexcited them by writing. She needed a stiff dose of bed rest.

But five months later, a very different review appeared in the modernist periodical the *Egoist*. This review was by the poet, suffragist, and Ambulance Corps volunteer May Sinclair, who observed that in *Honeycomb* there is no drama, no situation, no set scene. Nothing happens. It is just life going on and on. It is Miriam Henderson's stream of consciousness going on and on. . . . In identifying herself with this life, which is Miriam's stream of consciousness, Miss Richardson produces her effect of being the first, of getting closer to reality than any of our novelists who are trying so desperately to get close.

So, Richardson was not, in fact, mentally unwell. Quite the opposite. She was "the first" English writer to convey what it felt like to have a functioning mind. She'd developed a new literary technology for capturing our inner "stream of consciousness."

In 1919 Woolf wrote her own review of Richardson's next novel, *The Tunnel*. The novel didn't satisfy Woolf: "sensations, impressions, ideas and emotions glance off [the narrator's consciousness], unrelated and unquestioned, without shedding quite as much light as we had hoped into the hidden depths." But even so, Woolf was intrigued by Richardson's stream-of-consciousness style. And three years later, she became still more intrigued when she discovered that Richardson's breakthrough had been inspired by an earlier French novel: Marcel Proust's 1913 *À la Recherche du Temps Perdu (In Search of Lost Time)*.

In that novel, Proust had placed a madeleine sponge cake in his mouth and

All of a sudden, a memory appeared to me. This taste, it was the taste of the little piece of madeleine on a Sunday morning in Combray (because on that day I did not go out before mass), a piece that when I went to bid good morning to her in her room, my Aunt Léonie offered me after having soaked it in her tilleul tea. The sight of the little madeleine hadn't sparked my memory before I tasted it; maybe because, having often seen madeleines since, without eating them, on the shelves of pastry chefs, their image had left those days of Combray to bond with other images more recent . . .

. . . and on the memories went, connected in the flow of remembrance.

Proust's *In Search* amazed Woolf, filling her with a calm she'd never found in literature before. By pulling her along in its stream of consciousness, its style had lightly soothed her nerves, generating the psychological serenity that William James had described as the "free water" of the healthy mind.

This was the feeling of rest that the rest cure had promised yet never delivered. And instantly, Woolf knew that it was what she wanted to provide in her own fiction too. She wanted to write like Proust. She wanted to imbue the psyches of her readers with a gliding tranquility . . . until suddenly Woolf realized that she could do more. She could take Proust's stylistic innovation and increase its therapeutic action, generating an even deeper experience of mental peace.

Woolf was struck by this epiphany because of a second stream-of-consciousness novel that she discovered in that summer of 1922. The novel was *Ulysses* by James Joyce. And Woolf did not enjoy reading it at all. She griped:

> Oh what a bore about Joyce! Just as I was devoting myself to Proust—Now I must put aside Proust—and what I suspect is that Joyce is one of those undelivered geniuses, whom one can't neglect, or silence their groans, but must help them out, at considerable pains to oneself.

If *Ulysses* caused Woolf all this dismay, then what could she possibly have learned from turning its pages? How could she have discovered a way to deepen the peace of *In Search of Lost Time*?

Let's compare Joyce and Proust closely, so we can see.

The Stylistic Differences Between Joyce and Proust

In *Ulysses*, the thoughts of its main character run like so:

> Ineluctable modality of the visible: at least that if no more, thought through my eyes. Signatures of all things I am here to read, seaspawn and seawrack, the nearing tide, that rusty boot. Snotgreen, bluesilver, rust: coloured signs. Limits of the diaphane. But he

adds: in bodies. Then he was aware of them bodies before of them coloured. How? By knocking his sconce against them, sure. Go easy. Bald he was and a millionaire, *maestro di color che sanno.* Limit of the diaphane in. Why in? Diaphane, adiaphane. If you can put your five fingers through it, it is a gate, if not a door. Shut your eyes and see.

This excerpt from chapter 3 of *Ulysses* is exactly the same length as the "madeleine" excerpt from Proust. But it takes our brain longer to read— so long that our brain often just gives up and starts skimming the words in incomprehension. Why has a "rusty boot" appeared abruptly? Who is the "bald" millionaire? And what does the bald millionaire have to do with an Italian quote?

These questions interrupt our reading for a simple reason: *Ulysses* doesn't include what William James refers to as the relations between ideas. Instead, the novel simply presents a mind's ideas, leaving us to work out the relations ourselves:

> The rusty boot must have been washed onto the beach alongside the "seawrack."

> The millionaire must be Aristotle, the bejeweled philosopher who claimed that we perceive the substance of "bodies" before we perceive their "color."

> The Italian quote must be from Dante, who describes meeting Aristotle on his poetic descent through hell.

This work of deducing the relations is why Woolf felt such "considerable pains" at reading *Ulysses*: because *Ulysses* lacks the connections between ideas that make consciousness into a fluid stream, it arrives instead as a series of jolting railway cars or (to use William James's term) nervous "shocks," an effect heightened by Joyce's preference for short sentences that constantly stop-start the narrative flow.

Proust's style is the opposite. It incorporates long sentences that can run fluidly for fifty words or more. And it also carefully includes the *re-*

lations between ideas. On a technical, stylistic level, these relations come from narrative referents. *Ulysses* is conspicuously lacking in referents: the chapter 3 excerpt gives us a *he* without telling us that *he* refers to Aristotle; and gives us a phrase of Italian without telling us that the phrase refers to Dante's *Inferno*; and gives us *seaspawn* and *seawrack* and a *rusty boot* without telling us that they refer to Sandymount Strand, a patch of shore outside Dublin. *In Search of Lost Time*, in contrast, is filled with meticulously crafted referents. When Proust introduces "her," he explains four words later that "her" is "my Aunt Léonie." When Proust introduces his memory, he explains that his memory is of a Sunday morning in Combray. And when Proust introduces his ideas of the tilleul tea and the pastry chefs, he refers them back to a single source: the madeleine sponge cake. That cake triggers a "taste" (which in turn inspires a memory of Aunt Léonie's tilleul tea) and a "sight" (which in turn inspires a reflection on the shelves of pastry chefs).

So, unlike Joyce, who restricts himself to providing the atomistic dots of a character's thoughts, Proust connects the dots, producing a flow of epic-length sentences and linking referents that pour like water from a spout. This liquid consciousness is what gives Proust's style its therapeutic effect. It immerses our brain in the stream of a free-flowing mind, gentling away our own nervous shocks.

Yet as Woolf realized, Proust's style still limits our brain's experience of "free water" in one crucial way: it confines us to a single mind. It puts us in Proust's individual stream of consciousness and keeps us there, restricting our experience of mental liberty.

Joyce's novel breaks out of this restriction. Instead of adopting *In Search of Lost Time*'s autobiographical first-person style, *Ulysses* uses an outside third-person style that flows in and around different characters. This enables *Ulysses* to leap between minds, and at the end of chapter 3, that's just what the novel does. It jumps out of the rusty-boot mind and into another character's mental stream:

> Boland's breadvan delivering with trays our daily but she prefers yesterday's loaves turnovers crisp crowns hot. Makes you feel young. Somewhere in the east: early morning: set off at dawn, travel round in front of the sun, steal a day's march on him. Keep

it up for ever never grow a day older technically. Walk along a strand, strange land, come to a city gate, sentry there, old ranker too, old Tweedy's big moustaches leaning on a long kind of a spear. Wander through awned streets. Turbaned faces going by.

This second stream of ideas is as choppy as the first. It has the same short sentences, the same missing referents. But still, it hit Woolf like a revelation. It made her realize that if a novel combined the stream feeling of Proust with the multiple minds of Joyce, it would unite William James's two psychiatric innovations. Marrying a calm state of neural flow to a therapeutic experience of mental freedom, it would create an even deeper psychic peace than *In Search of Lost Time*.

So, in June 1923 Woolf opened a notebook and began writing the novel that would be published two years later as *Mrs. Dalloway*.

Virginia Woolf and the Streams of Consciousness

Mrs. Dalloway takes place on a single June day in 1923. Over the course of that day, the novel's title character, Clarissa Dalloway, buys flowers for a party, worries about her daughter, meets her old flame Peter Walsh, and learns about the suicide of the Great War veteran Septimus Smith.

So, like *Honeycomb*, *In Search of Lost Time*, and *Ulysses*, Woolf's novel "is just life going on and on." But unlike these novels, *Mrs. Dalloway* presents the goings-on in Woolf's uniquely therapeutic style, one that you can feel from the very first page, when Clarissa Dalloway steps through an open door into the morning air:

What a lark! What a plunge! For so it had always seemed to her, when, with a little squeak of the hinges, which she could hear now, she had burst open the French windows and plunged at Bourton into the open air. How fresh, how calm, stiller than this of course, the air was in the early morning; like the flap of a wave; the kiss of a wave; chill and sharp and yet (for a girl of eighteen as she then was) solemn, feeling as she did, standing there at the open window, that something awful was about to happen; looking at the flowers, at the trees with the smoke winding off them and the rooks rising, falling; standing and looking until Peter Walsh said, "Musing among the vegetables?"—was that it?—"I prefer men to cauliflowers"—was that it? He must have said it at breakfast one morning when she had gone out on to the terrace—Peter Walsh. He would be back from India one of these days, June or July, she forgot which, for his letters were awfully dull; it was his sayings one remembered; his eyes, his pocketknife, his smile, his grumpiness and, when millions of things had utterly vanished—how strange it was!—a few sayings like this about cabbages.

She stiffened a little on the kerb, waiting for Durtnall's van to pass. A charming woman, Scrope Purvis thought her (knowing her as one does know people who live next door to one in Westminster); a touch of the bird about her, of the jay, blue-green, light, vivacious, though she was over fifty, and grown very white since her illness. There she perched, never seeing him, waiting to cross, very upright.

In the first paragraph, the technical influence of Proust's style is everywhere:

Like Proust, Woolf uses long sentences; there's one that stretches to almost a hundred words.

Like Proust, Woolf includes referents. She no sooner introduces a memory than she reveals the memory's emotional origin: "a girl of eighteen." She no sooner utters, "He must have said," than she clarifies, "Peter Walsh," just as Proust clarified: "my Aunt Léonie."

Like Proust, Woolf refers every idea back to a single source. The winding smoke, the cabbages, the terrace, India, letters, eyes, a pocketknife, grumpiness, breakfast, a smile—all of them are referenced back to Peter, just like all of Proust's mental associations are referenced back to the madeleine sponge cake.

But Woolf doesn't only write like Proust; she also writes like Joyce. In the second paragraph, Woolf makes a Joycean leap into another mind, leaving the stream of Clarissa's consciousness to plunge into the stream of Scrope Purvis:

> (knowing her as one does know people who live next door to one in Westminster); a touch of the bird about her, of the jay, blue-green, light, vivacious, though she was over fifty, and grown very white since her illness.

By hopping into this other consciousness, Woolf enriches Proust's liquid style with a Joycean flow of multiple minds. And it's an enrichment that Woolf repeats again and again. Over the following pages of *Mrs. Dalloway*, Woolf leaps from the stream of Clarissa to the stream of Scrope, to the stream of Septimus Smith, to the stream of Septimus's wife, Lucrezia—and on and on she keeps leaping, into new streams and back into old. She leaps many more times than Joyce had ever leapt in *Ulysses*—and into many more streams.

By leaping so often and so widely, Woolf hoped to create a feeling of being "at large beneath the sky." Like William James, she wanted us, her readers, to know the psychiatric benefit of experiencing our own "freedom." And she succeeded. As modern neuroscience has revealed, the style of *Mrs. Dalloway* can indeed create a sensation of psychological freeness that provides the therapeutic peace that Woolf herself was seeking.

The Neuroscience of Woolf's Style

Twenty-first-century psychiatrists have speculated that Woolf suffered from manic depression. Did she? We can never know for sure. Woolf's individual mind, her unique stream of consciousness, vanished with her death in March 1941, putting it forever beyond the reach of today's psychiatry.

But even though Woolf's mind is gone, the symptoms described in her diaries remain with us in our own mental streams, tumbling through the pages of the American Psychiatric Association's *Diagnostic and Statistical Manual of Mental Disorders*: involuntary and intrusive memories, abnormally elevated activity, apprehensive expectation, recurrent thoughts of death, upsetting dreams, strong and persistent distress upon exposure to cues, excessive worry.

These symptoms are broadly referred to by psychologists as instances of heightened "cognitive reactivity." It's a clunky term, but it means what it says: our mind overreacts to a wave of its cognitive stream. A memory sends us into a panic, a sight pitches us into gloom, an idea dashes us into stampeding thoughts.

Heightened cognitive reactivity can be a feature of mania, depression, posttraumatic stress, complicated grief, and other psychiatric conditions. (For more on these conditions, see the introduction and chapter 8.) And it's also a common result of stress, tiredness, overstimulation, and other conditions of ordinary life. At one time or another, almost all of us will experience the unpleasant ripples of cognitive reactivity. We'll find ourselves agitated by an unexpected image, plunged into sadness by a recollection, or unable to sleep as thoughts buzz through our head. Sometimes the unpleasantness will pass on its own, but on other occasions, it will persist and even compound, scrambling our mind and disrupting our peace.

To help us recover, modern psychiatrists have identified a range of practical therapies. The most popularly known is mindfulness, but there are many others that carry less familiar names: cognitive defusion, cognitive distancing, decentering, detachment, metacognitive awareness, metacognitive mode, self as context, self-distanced perspective. These therapeutic approaches are different in important ways, but they share a common goal: to encourage us to feel a slight separation from our consciousness, as if we're observing our own ideas from without. So, instead of being dragged along by a rushing river of moods, memories, and impressions, we stand free on the riverbank, watching our mental waves lap past.

This feeling of psychological distance reduces brain activity in emotion and memory-processing regions such as our cortical midline structures and insular cortex. And that reduction in turn lowers our cognitive reactivity, gentling the symptoms of even depression, mania, generalized anxiety, and posttraumatic stress. In one recent clinical study, psychiatric patients were given the therapy and then placed in a brain scanner as they watched heart-wrenching films. The patients reported being very sad, yet their brains physically expressed less emotion, so the patients were conscious of a deep sorrow they didn't actually feel.

Woolf's style provides the same therapeutic effect. As it guides us through the consciousnesses of character after character after character, it gradually attunes our brain to a greater consciousness: the third-person perspective of the novel itself. That perspective weaves us in and out of the minds of Clarissa, Scrope, Septimus, and all the rest, enabling us to simultaneously experience inside feelings and outside distance. The resulting blend of emotional perception and cognitive separation mimics the modern psychiatric treatment for heightened cognitive reactivity. Filling our consciousness with mental flow, yet reducing the neural activity of our cortical midline structures and insular cortex, it allows us to experience emotional torrents while remaining free of their undertow.

In this therapeutic state, we can be conscious of Clarissa's "shock of delight" and Septimus's desperate suicidal thoughts without being shocked or desperate ourselves. We can know the river's deepest currents while feeling calm upon the shore.

Using the "Riverbank of Consciousness" Yourself

Mrs. Dalloway begins its new therapy by rejecting the old.

In the novel, that old therapy is doled out by the psychiatrist Dr. Holmes, who examines Septimus for shell shock and instantly diagnoses it as a case of nerves: " 'headaches, sleeplessness, fears, dreams—nerve symptoms and nothing more,' he said." And so it is that Holmes dispenses the same medicine to Septimus that Woolf had received from George Savage: "rest in bed; rest in solitude; silence and rest; rest without friends, without books."

This portrait of military psychiatry wasn't a novelistic flight of fancy. The prescription of bed rest for shell shock dated all the way back to Silas Weir Mitchell himself. Mitchell had served as a physician during the American Civil War, where he'd noticed soldiers become wildly agitated by combat. Such soldiers, Mitchell would later opine, had suffered "nerve wounds" that made them "hysterical." *Hysterical* was a medical term derived from *hystera*, the ancient Greek for uterus, and, in the view of Silas Weir Mitchell, a man suffering from combat trauma might as well have had a uterus. Such a man was as fragile, nervous, and over-emotional as the "weaker sex," so there could only be one cure for him. Like a woman who'd read too many books, he needed a long stay in bed.

In *Mrs. Dalloway*, this treatment proves as damaging to Septimus as it proved to Woolf: he leaps to his death out a window, like Woolf had herself attempted to do in 1904 after her initial treatments by Savage. So, to provide us with an alternative to Savage's rest cure, the novel treats us with Woolf's stream-of-consciousness style. That style deepens our calm the longer we read, until at last, the novel flutters toward Clarissa's old flame Peter and draws to a close with these final words:

> "I will come," said Peter, but he sat on for a moment. What is this terror? What is this ecstasy? He thought to himself. What is it that fills me with extraordinary excitement?
>
> It is Clarissa, he said.
>
> For there she was.

For a moment, we're in Peter's mental river: *What is this terror? What is this ecstasy?* And then the tense shifts, gliding us from Peter's inside "is" into the novel's outside "was." From that outside perspective, we witness Peter's consciousness from a gentle distance, perceiving its ups and downs without being rattled by its nervous clatter. So when the novel's last line gives us Peter's glimpse of Clarissa—"For there she was"—it doesn't agitate our thoughts with Peter's "terror" or his "ecstasy." Instead, it fills us with a wider peace.

Whenever you'd like more of that peace, you can find the innovations of Woolf and Proust in a wide range of modern fiction. If you'd like a sci-fi mystery, try Colson Whitehead's *The Intuitionist*. If you'd like a voyage through the mind of a neurosurgeon, try Ian McEwan's *Saturday*. If you'd like a dip into sixties-style hallucinogenic paranoia, try Thomas Pynchon's *The Crying of Lot 49*. If you'd like a love story, try Jojo Moyes's *Me Before You*.

Choose whichever novel seems most favorable to you. Then turn its pages and feel the war inside your nerves relax as the flow of rivers rushes past.

EIGHTEEN

Feed Your Creativity

Winnie-the-Pooh, Alice in Wonderland, *and the Invention of the Anarchy Rhymer*

I n winter's gray of 1689, the world's imagination died.

The death stroke was delivered by the English philosopher John Locke in his *An Essay Concerning Human Understanding*, which despite its title's modest first word, was rather more ambitious than your typical essay. It spanned four books and almost four hundred pages, exploring abstruse topics that had previously seemed beyond all understanding, human or otherwise: Innate speculative principles. The simple modes of the idea of space. The thoughts of children, idiots, etcetera.

The essay's erudite musings on these recondite matters made it a best seller. It was read in coffeeshops across London. It was debated in the high courts of Wetzlar and Constantinople. It wended its way to Java and Jamaica, the Vatican and Virginia, the Bahamas and the Bay of Bengal—even the wildy outback of New York. And wherever it went, it inspired lofty conversations about that loftiest of topics: the human mind. The essay's main claim was that the mind was born entirely blank. We arrived in the world with an empty canvas in our head. So, upon that canvas could be painted anything—literally *anything*. The wildest fantasies, the most outlandish creations, the most impossible imaginings; any of it could bloom inside.

The thought of this filled Locke with great alarm. Healthy minds, he believed, contained only one thing: reason. Reason fostered cool morality, sober restraint, and industrious prosperity. Without it, life was all "defects" and "errors" and "madness." So, to ensure that no such unreasons were brushstroked on our nascent blankness, Locke used his *Essay* to promote a new method for "educating young children." In the past, those children had been told creative fictions about "goblins and sprites." But no more. In the future, they would be drilled only in the "association of ideas" that possessed "a *natural* correspondence." Children would, in other words, be taught the laws of physics. From the cradle to the schoolhouse, they would be told that ice was cold and fire hot; that money bought things and dreams did not.

This rational program of education was adopted by hundreds of teachers in eighteenth-century England, France, Germany, Holland, Switzerland, and the Americas. And more important even than Locke's direct influence was the broader trend that his reforms portended. Before Locke, a child's education was haphazard and spontaneous, filled with gaps and free time for random imagining. After Locke, a child's education became increasingly regimented, formal, and serious. Children were placed in rows of desks, where they memorized rules about counting and grammar. They were taught that playtime was for organized games and sports with rules; they were assigned homework to discipline their hours out of school. And so it came to be that in school districts across the globe, idle daydreaming was replaced by practical life skills, logical decisions, and prudent forward planning.

It was all very sensible, or so it seemed. Because then, in the late twentieth century, scientists made a startling discovery: daydreaming wasn't a menace, a defect, or a time-wasting indulgence. Daydreaming was good for the mind.

The Discovery

The discovery was random. So random that it wasn't meant to be a discovery at all.

It happened in the mid-1990s, after scientists had invented a fantastical brain surveyor: the positron emission tomography (or PET) scanner. The PET scanner was a donut-shaped hub of whirring electronica that used radioactive fluorine-18 to map the human brain's consumption of glucose; the more glucose consumed by a particular neural region, the more think-work its gray matter was doing.

This new contraption was installed in the School of Medicine at Washington University in Saint Louis. And to calibrate it, scientists loaded in a young woman, instructing her, "Relax and stop thinking." The young woman nodded, but her brain didn't stop consuming glucose. Part of it kept on thinking and thinking and thinking.

The scientists frowned and repeated their instruction: Relax. Relax. Relax.

"I'm relaxed already," the young woman responded happily. "I'm feeling lovely in this big machine. So white and spacey, like a tunnel through a star."

Naturally, the scientists decided that there was something amiss with the young woman, so they replaced her with a respectable elderly gentleman. But to their great surprise, the same thing happened. The gentleman claimed to relax, but part of his brain kept on thinking and thinking and thinking. And as the scientists stared at that brain part in growing astonishment, they realized that it couldn't be found in *The Big Brain Atlas*, or *Functional Neuroanatomy*, or any of their other clinical textbooks. It was a previously undiscovered neural network that stretched from the front of the brain, up the top, along the back, down the bottom, and across both sides.

What could this enormous network be? The scientists weren't sure. They had all sorts of wild, gigantic, unfounded hypotheses about it. They had all sorts of remarkable, creative, original ideas. But they didn't want to embarrass themselves by voicing anything too fanciful. So, on the advice of one of their members, the bespectacled former US Air Force surgeon Dr. Marcus E. Raichle, they sagaciously opted to name their discovery the "default mode network." The network, they reasoned, was the brain's default mode. When the brain wasn't engaged in any particular task, the network went active. It took advantage of the brain's free time to engage in some mysterious activity.

And as it turns out, that activity isn't so mysterious. It's the same thing that we generally do with time off from work.

We play.

The Science of Mental Play

Mental play is a kind of anarchy.

Anarchy oozes with bad connotations: chaos, violence, the end of civilization. But anarchy simply means that no one's in charge. We're all free to make up our own rules—and change them, if we'd like, as we go along.

That's how children play. Their games can often seem unstructured, but they follow rules—rules that have no authoritative source and can evolve at any time. And our brain plays the same way. It abandons the strict top-down regulations that govern our mental processes during work. And instead, it allows for emotions, memories, and other neural stuff to bottom-up freely, triggering anarchic streams of thought.

The scientific term for this haphazard head play is mind wandering. Mind wandering isn't entirely arbitrary. Pure randomness is an elusive thing, and nothing in nature may ever achieve it. Yet even so, mind wandering can have the randomness of tumbling dice or a lottery-ball machine. The ideas in our brain can jumble about, bouncing off one another to form associations with no master logic.

Mind wandering has been linked with myriad psychological benefits. It can nurture creativity. It can inspire fresh solutions to nagging old problems. And it can also just be fun, increasing our well-being and making us more cheerful at life. So, even the most solemnly sober of scientists recommend that we make a little time for mind wandering today. A little time to dream original. A little time to freshen up our glee.

Our mind will often do that wandering spontaneously. When not engaged in a focused task, it will start to drift, rambling through memories or dreaming new plans. So, the most basic way to encourage mind wandering is simply to relax. Clear your head of work. Close your eyes so that your attention isn't focused on the world outside: *Relax. . . . Relax. . . . Relax. . . .*

If you just tried that, and your mind didn't wander far, you're not alone. The simple procedure once used by our ancestors isn't always enough in our day and age. The more that we've filled our youth with educational toys and practical pursuits, the more that our brain has become conditioned in certain grooves of thought. Even when our thoughts wander, they wander along familiar tracks, retrenching themselves in the same old ruts.

But don't fret. You can still get all the ancient mental benefits of being a child. As scientists have discovered, there's a method to get our inner arbitrary popping, energizing our default mode network and escaping our tired mental furrows. And in fact, the method is so effective that it can go beyond restoring our natural mind-wandering abilities. It can *increase* those abilities, inspiring our mind to wander like no human minds have ever wandered before.

This mind-wandering booster is known as artistic improvisation, or "improv." It takes all sorts of forms, and, of course, you can always improvise more. But the form most studied by scientists is musical improv. Musical improv is used by classical flutists, freestyle rappers, and jazz pianists to gin up free-flowing original jingles and lyrics. And when improvising musicians have been placed inside brain scanners, those scanners have revealed that improv is linked with two separate neural networks. The first network, as you might expect, is the default mode network. The second network, more surprisingly, is a rule-following network that involves authority figures such as our medial prefrontal cortex.

The interplay between these two neural networks is due partly to the loosening influence of mind wandering upon our mental regulations. But it's also due to influence in the opposite direction: our disciplined brain regions facilitate improv by providing a scaffold of musical structure. This scaffold is light and flexible; like the anarchic rules of children's games, it can bend and evolve over time. But also like those rules, the scaffold facilitates creativity by focusing our mind around a set of generative constraints.

To experience this interplay between spontaneity and structure, we can train for years to become flutists, rappers, and pianists. Or we can take a shortcut and read literature. Because there's a special kind of literature that's designed to imbue our brain with musical improv.

It's called the nursery rhyme.

The Nursery Rhyme's Musical Improv

The nursery rhyme is a remarkable invention. It dates, we think, from an age long before Locke, although we can't trace its origins with any certainty. Like other forms of oral literature, its earliest days are lost to time. It wasn't until the later eighteenth century, about nine decades after Locke, that the first nursery rhymes were published in songbooks such as *Mother Goose's Melody*, which became a pulp best seller, first in Britain, then in America, gorgeously adorned with illustrations by Thomas Bewick, a free-dreaming woodblock engraver.

What makes the nursery rhyme so remarkable is that it encourages mental play. Most other early forms of children's literature were designed to do the opposite. They were meant to *scare* us with tales of big bad wolves who'd eat us if we strayed too far from our parents. They were meant to *imprint* us with adult ideas of right and wrong, so we'd behave like good little children and do as we were told.

Meanwhile, nursery rhymes were doing this:

Hey diddle diddle,
The Cat and the Fiddle,
The Cow jump'd over the Moon;
The little dog laugh'd to see such Craft,
And the Fork ran away with the Spoon.

What is a diddle? Why is a cat with a fiddle? How is a cow vaulting through space? And where is the spoon planning to go?

Our brain doesn't know. But our brain doesn't melt in confusion or grind to a halt to figure it out. Our brain keeps nodding along because it feels a musical pattern beneath the verbal nonsense. *Diddle* rhymes with *fiddle*, *craft* rhymes with *laughed*, *moon* rhymes with *spoon*, and the whole is tied together with a syncopated metrical beat.

This song structure is how "Hey Diddle Diddle" gets our brain to loosen our strictures of reason and enter a space where cutlery can elope and cattle go astral. And by guiding our brain into that space, the nursery rhyme introduces our neural circuitry to improv's deep rule: the rule of "Yes, And."

The rule works like this. When we hear a random association, we don't say "No." Or "But." We say "Yes." Then we say "And."

The *yes* embraces the random association. The *and* extends it. So, we don't shut down ideas that seem arbitrary or even nonsensical; we encourage them. All of which makes "Yes, And" a very unusual sort of rule. Unlike regular rules, it doesn't promote right or wrong or "Do what you're told." It promotes anarchy instead.

"Yes, And" seems an easy rule to follow. But it's not. (You see, I just broke it.) That's because the rule goes against our brain's natural inclination to say "No" and "But." *No* and *But* are safer. They slow down life and keep things familiar. So, *No* and *But* are prized by the mighty fear regions of our brain as sources of self-preservation.

To escape the "No, But" conservatism of those mighty fear regions, we need to practice, practice, practice, *practice*, Yes-Anding into strange terrain. Which is what "Hey Diddle Diddle" helps our brain do. The rhyme and the rhythm provide just enough structure to make our fear regions feel safe suspending their Nos and their Buts, allowing the rest of our brain to frolic audaciously into the unknown.

And now that we've reached the end of that brave little gambol, we can look back at "Hey Diddle Diddle" and see that it has carried us beyond associating words, images, and objects. It has gotten us to associate *events* such as the cow jumping and the dog laughing and the spoon running. And this event associating is tremendously, enormously, spectacularly exciting. Because if we can get our brain to "Yes, And" from event to event to event, then we can mind wander new afternoon plans, new midnight schemes, new plots for transforming tomorrow.

"Hey Diddle Diddle" doesn't get us very far down this narrative road. But in nineteenth-century England, nursery rhymes began inspiring children's literature that did.

The New Kind of Children's Story

Nineteenth-century England was not the funnest place to be a child. If you were poor, you began working at the age of five or earlier. You were sent into coal mines, textile factories, gasworks, and shipyards. Your only protection was a flimsy parliamentary act that banned you from more than ten hours of daily labor. If you were wealthier, things were less dire, but not much more merry. You were drilled in Victorian society's twin principles: reason and morality. You were taught to be eminently prudent and to hew devotedly to God's commandments.

None of this afforded much room for imaginative play. So, in 1846 the painter-poet-pianist Edward Lear tried to loosen up things with a limerick anthology: *The Book of Nonsense*. Then in 1871 Lear got even looser, escaping the limerick's metrical narrows to compose a wildly inventive children's poem:

> The Owl and the Pussy-cat went to sea
> In a beautiful pea-green boat,
> They took some honey, and plenty of money,
> Wrapped up in a five-pound note. . . .
> They dined on mince, and slices of quince,
> Which they ate with a runcible spoon;
> And hand in hand, on the edge of the sand,
> They danced by the light of the moon,
> The moon,
> The moon,
> They danced by the light of the moon.

This poem is "The Owl and the Pussy-cat." Like "Hey Diddle Diddle," it's a catalogue of "Yes, Ands" with a musical structure of rhythm and rhyme. And, yes, it also goes *further* than "Hey Diddle Diddle" by giving us a more intricate plot. That plot carries us on a story of sailing with honey, picnicking on Asian pears, and dancing along lunar-lit beaches, stretching our brain with long improv flights into the narrative unknown.

These flights delighted many a Victorian reader, and they prompted one Victorian author to wonder: Could the "Yes, And" be stretched even further? Could the plot go on and on and on?

Lewis Carroll's "Yes, And" Stories

In 1865 Lewis Carroll published *Alice's Adventures in Wonderland*. The book began as a piece of creative whimsy, spun for the ten-year-old daughter of a friend. Like "The Owl and the Pussy-cat," it has a musical quality, and it even includes its own "Yes, And" songs:

"Will you walk a little faster?" said a whiting to a snail,
"There's a porpoise close behind us, and he's treading on my
    tail.
See how eagerly the lobsters and the turtles all advance!
They are waiting on the shingle—will you come and join the
    dance?"

And yet unlike "The Owl and the Pussy-cat" and "Hey Diddle Diddle," Lewis Carroll's novel also includes vast nonmusical stretches of plot. Stretches without meter or rhyme. Stretches where a young girl named Alice follows a waistcoated rabbit down a hole, finding herself in a world of cakes that make you grow enormous, caterpillars that smoke hookahs, and queens that play croquet with mallet flamingoes.

These associations stretch our brain's narrative improv skills to spectacular lengths—and also raise a question: What's the structure? What's holding all this anarchy altogether? Now that the music and the rhyme and the rhythm are gone, why aren't the fear regions of our brain stopping or scowling?

The answer is that Lewis Carroll has replaced the musical structure of "Hey Diddle Diddle" with a *narrative* structure. That narrative structure is character: specifically, the character of Alice. Like the tuneful meter of a nursery rhyme, Alice's emotions and personality stay consistent throughout the story. And like all sources of structure, Alice provides boundaries by saying "No." She begins her adventure by saying, "No, it will never do to ask," and ends it by saying "No" again: "I won't! You're nothing but a pack of cards!"

By revealing that a structuring character like Alice could be used to create an extended "Yes, And" narrative, *Alice in Wonderland* threw open the mind-wandering possibilities for children's literature. The nursery rhyme could be expanded into an endless vista of short stories and novels. So long as we were accompanied by a stable character, our brain could go on the wildest improv adventures.

Those adventures would hatch many, many innovations for boosting our improv abilities. And the most basic and important would be made by a little stuffed bear.

In Which We Are Introduced to an Improv Booster and Some Bees

The little stuffed bear got his start in A. A. Milne's nursery rhyme "Teddy Bear," published in *Punch* magazine in February 1924:

> A bear, however hard he tries,
> Grows tubby without exercise.

This tubby bear was Winnie-the-Pooh. And quickly, Winnie-the-Pooh began to make up his own silly songs:

> Isn't it funny
> How a bear likes honey?
> Buzz! Buzz! Buzz!
> I wonder why he does?

As in *Alice in Wonderland*, these musical moments are folded into larger plots: Winnie humily-bumbles ahead, carrying our brain on "Yes, And" adventures to hunt down Woozles, deliver late birthday presents, and abscond with baby kangaroos. Yet Winnie-the-Pooh is different in one crucial way from Alice. Unlike Alice, Winnie-the-Pooh isn't a creature of regularity and Nos; he's a bear of consummate whimsy.

So, from where does the light scaffold of structure come in *Winnie-the-Pooh*? What's the narrative replacement for rhythm and rhyme? Well, that replacement is the *world* of the story. The world of *Winnie-the-Pooh* isn't the mind-wandering world of dream. It's the world of Christopher Robin. And Christopher Robin is a sensible boy. In Christopher Robin's world, if you walk north, you don't end up in a land of Mad Hatters. In Christopher Robin's world, if you walk north, you reach the North Pole.

So, in other words, the literary blueprint of *Winnie-the-Pooh* is the inverse of *Alice in Wonderland*. In *Alice in Wonderland*, a sensible character goes on an adventure in an anarchic storyworld, while in *Winnie-the-Pooh*, an anarchic character goes on an adventure in a sensible storyworld.

This innovation removes the one big psychological obstacle to "Yes,

And" in *Alice in Wonderland*: the sense of danger. That sense of danger comes from our being dropped by Lewis Carroll into a landscape of unstable rules. Things bigger than us suddenly turn grotesque—and alarming—such as the Queen of Hearts, whose arbitrary tyranny is less the happy fun of play and more the sinister result of legal volatility.

A. A. Milne's invention creates an entirely different neural experience. Rather than plunging us into a lawless geography where we always feel a little unsafe, *Winnie-the-Pooh* invites us into a snugly consistent realm where even the most guarded parts of our brain can relax, Yes-Anding along with a mind-wandering bear.

Here's how it works in the bear's first adventure: "In which we are introduced to Winnie-the-Pooh and some bees." The adventure begins when Pooh looks up to the top of a tree and spots a bees' nest brimming with honey. Honey, as every Pooh knows, is good for the tummy, so this particular Pooh tries to climb the tree's branches, only to crash-bang back down in a spectacular tumble. At which point, the first thing to pop into Pooh's head is: *I wonder if Christopher Robin has such a thing as a balloon about him.*

This, you will notice, is a rather random idea. Why a balloon? And why would Christopher Robin possess one? Pooh's brain has no answers. It contains only fluff. So, we might be inclined to respond to Pooh's idea with a "No, But." We might suggest that Pooh instead seek out something more prudent. Like a tree-climbing ladder. Or some bee-free honey. Or one of John Locke's educational pamphlets.

Pooh's brain, however, remains free of these mindful cautions. Instead, Pooh's brain says "Yes, And," prompting his legs to toddle off to find Christopher Robin.

Now, as it turns out, Christopher Robin *does* have a balloon. Yet being the sensible lad that he is, he immediately points out a problem with Pooh's plan of ballooning up the tree: even if the bees don't notice the balloon, they're sure to notice the honey-hungry Pooh bear dangling beneath.

Does Pooh respond to this sensible caution by abandoning his plan? (I'd respond with a "No," except that would break the whole improv flow we've got going here, so let's just glide over my authorial incompetence and ignore the question, shall we? Yes, let's do that, and . . .)

Agreeing with a Yes to Christopher Robin's point that the bees will notice him hanging under the balloon, Pooh then goes with the first And to pop into his mind: Why not roll in the mud, disguising himself as a little black raincloud?

This "Yes, And" doesn't work. The bees are skeptical of Pooh's masquerade, suspecting that he's not the meteorological phenomenon he pretends. Yet once again, Pooh doesn't stop or go back on his plan. Instead, he comes up with two more "Yes, Ands." The first is to have Christopher Robin fetch an umbrella. That will make the bees think that Pooh is full of rain! And the second is to improve his cloud disguise by singing a song:

How sweet to be a Cloud
Floating in the Blue
Every little cloud
Always sings aloud.

So it is that Pooh's improvisations carry us along an ever-growing chain of playful connections until we have a bear, disguised as a storm nimbus, dangling from a balloon and rhyming nonsense verse while a boy walks under with his rain deflector.

It's as random as anything in *Alice in Wonderland*. And instead of giving us a reason to quake at the imagination's wilds, it treats our brain's fear regions entirely to fun.

Using the "Anarchy Rhymer" Yourself

Two and a half centuries after Locke's *Essay*, there was another revolution in children's education. This one was instigated by John Hersey, a world-wandering journalist who published a 1954 *Life* magazine article in which he railed that the textbooks in American schools were all filled with "abnormally courteous, unnaturally clean boys and girls." Where, Hersey demanded, were the messy, rule-breaking textbooks that served "to widen rather than narrow the associative richness" of students' minds? Where were the textbooks that fed children's imaginations?

Hersey's article was passed along to a fellow by the name of Theodor

Geisel, or, as he was more commonly known then, Dr. Seuss. Dr. Seuss had achieved money and fame by writing *If I Ran the Zoo* and other entertaining children's stories. So, was he now perhaps interested in writing a textbook that made children more imaginative? If he was, then he'd have to follow some very strict rules. He'd be given a list of four hundred words, and the whole book would have to be writ from that list. No adding new words. And certainly no making words up. But within the list's confines, Dr. Seuss could have total freedom to create. He could dream up anything, no matter how dotty or daffy or haphazardly new. Would that arrangement suit Dr. Seuss?

Yes, Dr. Seuss said. That suited him fine. And what he then improvised was this:

> Something went *bump*!
> How that bump made us jump!
> We looked!
> . . . And we saw him!
> The Cat in the Hat!

Like Pooh, the Cat in the Hat is an anarchist in a storyworld of rules and order. And like "The Owl and the Pussy-cat" and "Hey Diddle Diddle," his story is a nursery rhyme. So, just imagine how far it can wander your mind.

And whenever you'd like more of that education revolution, you can find A. A. Milne's invention of an improv character riffing through a logical storyworld in Astrid Lindgren's *Pippi Longstocking* (1945), Leo Lionni's *Frederick* (1967), Wes Anderson's *Bottle Rocket* (1996), and stacks of other children's literature. So, go take a break from long-windedly erudite essays like this. Go feed your creativity (and your fun) by returning to the shelf you stocked with books when you were young.

Then say "Yes."

And . . .

NINETEEN

Unlock Salvation

To Kill a Mockingbird, *Shakespeare's*
Soliloquy Breakthrough, and the Invention
of the Humanity Connector

On February 8, 1958, an article appeared in the *Gospel Messenger*, the bicolor newspaper printed each week in Elgin, Illinois, by the Church of the Brethren. The article was titled "Out of the Long Night," and it made the astonishing claim that hate could be conquered by love. No matter how cruel the hate, no matter how mighty its empire, it could be overcome with kindness.

The Brethren had a long history of embracing such astonishing claims. Two hundred years earlier, they'd astounded all of Christendom by agreeing with Alexander Mack, an eighteenth-century emigre to Philadelphia's Germantown neighborhood, when he'd distilled the entire Bible to Jesus's paradoxical Sermon on the Mount: "Blessed are the poor in spirit, for theirs is the kingdom of heaven." But even for the Brethren, the article was hard to accept. How could love, as the article asserted so confidently, solve America's "real crisis in race relations"? How could "reactionary elements" such as segregationist White Citizens' Councils or militant supremacists such as the Ku Klux Klan be won over with "friendship and understanding"?

To allay the Brethren's doubts, the article's author, a twenty-nine-year-old Baptist minister by the name of Martin Luther King Jr., reached into his library for a quote: "The arc of the moral universe is long, but it bends toward justice." If there was ever a quote to make the readers of the *Gospel Messenger* believe that patient charity could conquer hate, this was it. For the quote was a remarkable quote with its own long arc, stretching from the most revolutionary drama of the English Renaissance to the most consciousness-expanding novel of Martin Luther King's own lifetime . . .

. . . and all of it bending the mind toward justice, love, and a salvation beyond.

The Quote

The quote originated on the tongue of Theodore Parker, an abolitionist preacher raised in early-nineteenth-century northeastern Massachusetts. Parker's parents were subsistence farmers, their wedding so poor that the plates were wood, their land so pestilent that half their twelve children perished from a devil's mix of cholera, typhoid, and tuberculosis.

Parker later remembered this existence as a "valley of tears." But its hardships did not disillusion him; from his earliest days, he had an eagerly interested spirit. He would scurry through his farm chores—digging potatoes, laying stone walls, toting Grandmother her afternoon punch—so that he could busy himself in bee glades with books: Homer's *Odyssey*, Plutarch's *Lives*, Warren Colburn's *Algebra*, Charles Rollin's *Ancient History*, Jedidiah Morse's *Geography Made Easy*.

Parker's self-schooling nurtured his independent habit of mind, and when he turned preacher in his late teens, he veered quickly off the beaten path, denying biblical miracles and expressing misgivings about the historical truth of Jesus. These unorthodox forays were flatly condemned as blasphemous by mainstream Baptist, Methodist, and Evangelical clergy, and they ultimately got Parker ejected from his ministerial post in the Unitarian Church. The Unitarian Church was famously tolerant of unconventional beliefs; its members had gone so far as to question Jesus's virgin birth. But even they couldn't countenance Parker's doubts, which seemed to voyage beyond reasonable questioning to abandon faith entirely.

Yet the Unitarians misunderstood Parker. As skeptical as he was, he hadn't forsaken all belief; he retained an absolute conviction in justice. And so mighty was that conviction that it gave him the strength to continue preaching without a church. He stood up in market squares, in crowded city streets, in public halls. And he called for slavery to be abolished, for women to be granted equality, and for poverty to be stamped out.

The force of Parker's preaching amazed his listeners. He seemed another biblical prophet, a second John the Baptist dispatched to cry truth. But when those listeners spoke to the wild preacher after his sermons, they discovered that his mighty belief had a literary source: the bookish spiritual movement known as transcendentalism.

Transcendentalism dated to September 8, 1836, when a rogue trio of Unitarian ministers and a thirty-three-year-old poet met amid the "orchards, gardens, and pleasure grounds" of Cambridge, Massachusetts, to start a new club. A new club, they decided, would be better than a new church. It would be more inviting to skeptics, doubters, and free questioners. And anyway, the world had churches enough.

The club's most public advocate became that thirty-three-year-old poet, Ralph Waldo Emerson. Emerson had attended the chimney-bricked and liberally minded Harvard Divinity School, where he'd tried, and failed, to become a minister. He was simply too ambivalent about organized Christianity. But like Parker, Emerson continued to hold fast to his personal spiritual beliefs. And two of those beliefs emerged as foundational to transcendentalism.

The first belief, as jotted down by Emerson in his journal, was: "the infinitude of the private man." Emerson's phrasing was poetic. But his meaning was simple: the cosmos had a human soul. All the good inside us—our love, our hope, our charity, our joy—was shared by the universe around.

The second belief was that we could discover this universal human soul through intuition. Intuition was a sort of sixth sense that differed from both reason and emotion. Unlike reason, intuition wasn't bound by the laws of logic, so it was invulnerable to skepticism. And unlike emotion, intuition didn't originate in the heart, so it couldn't be seduced or misled.

With these two foundational beliefs, transcendentalism enlarged humanism, that spiritual faith we explored in chapter 15. Humanism connects us to a soul that links every person on earth; transcendentalism *stretches* that soul to include every tree, every star, everything in the galaxy.

Transcendentalism was heavily based on the writings of Immanuel Kant, Johann Gottfried Herder, and other eighteenth-century and early-nineteenth-century German idealists and Romantics. But Emerson decided that these philosophical writings weren't the most effective way to access the power of intuition. Philosophy was, after all, largely an exercise in reason. So, instead, Emerson went to his bookshelf and plucked down a work of literature.

That work was Shakespeare's *Hamlet*.

Emerson and *Hamlet*

Hamlet triggered an astonishing intuition in Emerson. Turning its pages, he came to perceive a "living Hamlet" that bound all existence into a greater soul:

> Now, literature, philosophy and thought are Shakespearized. His mind is the horizon beyond which, at present, we do not see.

Emerson's phrasing was once again poetic. And once again, his meaning was simple: we were all Hamlet—and Hamlet was everywhere.

This intuition strained credulity at the time, and it has come to seem only more outlandish in the many generations since. For we are plainly *not* all Hamlet. Hamlet is a medieval Scandinavian prince who talks to a ghost, assaults his mother, makes spectacular speeches, murders casually, and uses his dying breath to gasp an off-beat joke: "The rest is silence." Which is to say: Hamlet's culture is distant, his behavior startling, his humor idiosyncratic, and his life history unique.

Yet as patently counterfactual as Emerson's belief in our universal Hamlet-ness seems, that belief was not misplaced. Against all reason, Shakespeare's play has convinced a great many of our human brains that we are indeed Hamlet. And it has done so because it contains a remarkable literary breakthrough.

The breakthrough was forged by Shakespeare out of two long-standing theatrical devices: monologue and dialogue. In monologue, one character voices his personal sentiments; in dialogue, two characters talk back and forth. Both these devices had been invented by ancient playwrights, and for two thousand years, from fifth-century-BCE Athens to sixteenth-century Renaissance Europe, they'd seemed to be the only ways for characters to speak. But then Shakespeare had a thought: What if a character had a conversation—with himself? What if a character came onstage and voiced two different inner perspectives, combining dialogue and monologue into a dialogic monologue?

That character might express one sentiment, like: "To be." And then he might express the opposite, like: "Or not to be." And from there, he might go on to wrestle:

That is the question:
Whether 'tis Nobler in the mind to suffer
The Slings and Arrows of outrageous Fortune
Or to take Arms against a Sea of troubles,
And by opposing, end them?

The character who speaks this back-and-forth is Hamlet. His new speech invention of a dialogic monologue is the soliloquy, a verbal dramatization of a character's inner conflict. And through that new speech invention, Hamlet shares his inner conflict with us all. Should he do the pious thing and forget his father's murder, trusting heaven to punish it? Or should he do the honorable thing and die in a bold attempt to take vengeance?

To do the first is to be a person of faith—but perhaps also a coward who shirks from death. To do the second is to be a person of courage—but perhaps also a fool who forsakes God for hell.

So, what's better? To trust in a divine justice that may not exist? Or to fight for a worldly justice that might be a sin? To be—or not to be?

These are extraordinary questions. And they have an extraordinary neural effect. They make our brain feel: *I am the character asking the questions. I am Hamlet.*

The Neuroscience of Hamlet

To understand why we identify with Hamlet, we need to start with a more basic question: Why do we identify with our self?

This might seem like an odd question. Don't we always and automatically identify with our self? No, in fact, we don't. To identify with our self, we need to experience self-awareness (or as it's termed by neuroscientists, metacognition). We need to be aware of our self as a distinct entity, separate from the world.

Most of the time, our brain doesn't possess that self-awareness. Most of the time, our brain is just in the flow of life. It's acting (or reacting) unself-consciously, pulled along by the sights of the world outside or by the streams of thought inside. So, our brain sees, without thinking: *It's me that's seeing*. And our brain thinks, without thinking: *I just thought that thought—me, me, me*.

Life is more efficient this way. If we were self-aware all the time, we'd act and think slower—and we'd use up more neural energy too. So, our brain's default setting, even while we're awake, is not to be aware of itself.

For our brain to exit this default setting and become self-aware, one of two things has to happen. First, we can choose to be self-aware. We can direct our brain, right now, to start thinking about itself. And it will. (Whether or not this is actually a choice is debated by scientists. It's possible that the choice is something that bubbles up from the other source of self-awareness. Which is . . .)

Second, we can be made self-aware by a part of our brain known as the salience network. The salience network monitors our brain for internal conflicts. Those conflicts might involve a clash between the emotions of our amygdala and the plans of our ventral tegmental area. Or a disagreement between the long-term memories of our hippocampus and the current perceptions of our visual cortex. Or even a collision between the reading immersion of our middle temporal gyrus and the immersion interrupter of *We can direct our brain, right now, to start thinking about itself*. But whatever the internal conflict is, it prompts our salience network to shout out a warning to our medial prefrontal cortex: *Hey! You're fighting with yourself! You need to sort out which part of you is right!*

This warning rouses our self-awareness, reminding us that we're not part of the undivided flow of life. We're a distinct entity with our own individual drives and needs, and those drives and needs could be compromised if we don't resolve our inner conflict by figuring out whether it's better to trust our emotions or our plans, our memories or our perceptions. Biologically speaking, self-awareness is thus a tool of self-preservation. It makes us aware that we *have* a self so that we can protect that self by stepping back from life's flow to act more coherently.

This ancient neural process is hacked by Hamlet's cutting-edge soliloquy. The hack begins by posing a problem: "To be or not to be?" As that problem enters our brain, it sets off an internal conflict. On one side of the conflict is our primeval justice network, which, as we saw in chapter 3, feels very strongly that *Yes, we should sacrifice ourselves to punish injustice*. On the other side of the conflict is the big-picture network of our frontal brain, which feels oppositely: *No, no, no—rushing into a hasty revenge is going to make things worse for everyone*. And then the fray is joined by other neural entities, such as our guilt about the dead, our fear about dying, our hope that heaven holds a future justice, our questions about whether heaven really exists, our courage of sacrifice, and our conscience against killing.

Because our brains are all different, the collision among these different neural entities won't take a universal form. Some of us will be more conflicted between guilt and doubt; others, between courage and conscience. But since Hamlet's question strikes at a profoundly complex and difficult question—*What's right?*—almost all of us will feel a neural conflict of some kind. And because of that conflict, we'll have our salience network triggered.

This triggering, by itself, is nothing extraordinary. It's the traditional effect of stage drama. All the way back to the first known dramas in history, the stage had posed thorny questions of wrong and right. Was it right, in the *Oresteia*, for a son to avenge his father by killing his mother? Was it right, in *Antigone*, for us to love our families more than we loved our fellow citizens?

Yet as old as these sorts of theatrical conundrums are, *Hamlet* still interacts with our brain in a revolutionary new way. Previous plays such as the *Oresteia* and *Antigone* had triggered our salience network with conflicts *between* characters. One character was for "To be" and the other for "Not to be." This meant in turn that the characters were different from us; we experienced an inner conflict that the characters did not.

Hamlet does something radically new: it uses a soliloquy to trigger our brain with a conflict *within a single character*. So, when that triggering makes us self-aware, we become self-aware of Hamlet's problem. Our sudden flash of self-identification is a moment where the mind's eye of our medial prefrontal cortex identifies our self with Hamlet's inner struggle.

This is logically impossible. How can we self-identify with the self of someone else? But it's psychologically possible because of our brain's wiring. That wiring makes us self-aware of whatever internal conflict enters our salience network. So, if the internal conflict is "To be or not to be," we experience a self-awareness of Hamlet.

Since this self-awareness occurs at the threshold of our consciousness, we may not say to ourselves explicitly: *I am Hamlet!* But our brain nevertheless experiences a flicker of identification that has the feel of what Emerson describes as an intuition, something we perceive to be true without necessarily being able to explain why. Even if we don't perceive Hamlet's conflict in precisely the same way as his original audience, and even if we resolve that conflict in our own unique fashion, the sheer experience of being mentally torn between "To be or not to be" will make our brain feel that part of us is Shakespeare's prince.

This self-awareness hack was an extraordinary innovation, ushering in what would become the most distinctive feature of modern literature. In the ancient days before *Hamlet*, we had felt *for* Achilles and Antigone; but from now on, we would identify *with* Jane Eyre and Holden Caulfield. Drawn in by the neural power of the soliloquy, we would go beyond caring about characters—and we would *become* them.

And as writer after writer copied Shakespeare's breakthrough, they didn't just copy. They added their own breakthroughs too.

The Next Breakthrough

On a frosty Paris night, twenty-one years after Shakespeare's death, the legendary beak-nosed actor Montdory stepped onto the converted tennis courts of the Theatre du Marais. He was playing the title role in Pierre Corneille's new drama *The Cid*. And at the end of the play's first act, he uncorked a long soliloquy in which he struggled to resolve his inner conflict between the honor demanded by his father and the love demanded by his betrothed:

> My father or my betrothed? Love or honor?
> Duty's harsh bonds or the heart's sweet tyranny?
> Either my happiness dies, or my name is ruined;
> One is bitter, the other unthinkable.

These lines were delivered in the voice of an eleventh-century Castilian knight to a paying audience of seventeenth-century French weavers, watchmakers, and wood sellers. The voice and the audience had nothing apparent in common. Yet the early modern merchants at the theater found themselves identifying powerfully with the medieval nobleman onstage. So powerfully that many of them purchased tickets to see him again the next night. And that next night, when Montdory launched into his soliloquy, they stood upon their gallery seats and chanted perfectly in unison: "My father or my betrothed? Love or honor? Duty's harsh bonds or the heart's sweet tyranny?"

The audience had literally become the character. Their lives had fused with his.

This was an unprecedented event, and the civic authorities became perturbed. Fearing that *The Cid* might herald a social revolution, the king's chief minister, Cardinal Richelieu, censored the play for being a dangerous novelty. Chagrined, the playwright repented, and no new soliloquies appeared at the theater for the remainder of the seventeenth century.

But already, *The Cid*'s soliloquy had shown that Shakespeare's invention was bigger than *Hamlet*. *The Cid*'s soliloquy was written in a different style and staged within a different story land. And it also expressed a different psychological back-and-forth: instead of "To be or not to be," it was "love or honor." Yet the soliloquy had still triggered identification, revealing that Shakespeare's invention could be translated into new genres, new characters, new internal conflicts.

With this breakthrough, the soliloquy became more *flexible*. And before long, another breakthrough would make the soliloquy more *powerful* too.

The Soliloquy in the Novel

The breakthrough became known as the novel.

The novel, as its name implied, was beyond classification. Its defining characteristic was simply its newness, its experimentalism, its breaking old rules. So, over the eighteenth and nineteenth centuries, the authors of novels innovated relentlessly. And one of those innovations was to engineer the blueprints of *Hamlet* and *The Cid* into a profusion of new soliloquies:

> There was the soliloquy in Daniel Defoe's *Robinson Crusoe* (1719), where Crusoe was torn between his hunger for adventure—and his aspiration to settle down, work hard, and enjoy a life of honest prosperity.
>
> There was the soliloquy in Johann Wolfgang von Goethe's *The Sorrows of Young Werther* (1774), where Werther was torn between his love for Charlotte—and his admiration for Charlotte's betrothed.
>
> There was the soliloquy in Mark Twain's *Adventures of Huckleberry Finn* (1884), where Huck was torn between his wish to save himself by acting like an angel—and his desire to save his friend Jim by lying, cheating, and stealing.

Like the soliloquies of Hamlet and the Cid, these conflicted inner dialogues trigger our salience network with the deep question *What's right?* But they also do something new, creating an even stronger feeling of identification than the soliloquies of the theater.

That increased feeling of identification has a simple neural origin: when we watch a play, our brain is conscious of a physical separation between our body and the soliloquizing character, so at the same time that our brain is thinking, *I am Hamlet*, it's also thinking, *Hamlet is standing over there*. This identification-disrupting second thought vanishes when we read a soliloquy on a novel's printed page. On the page, there's no embodied actor, so we can enter into the character's inner conflict without experiencing an intervening whisper of *The character is standing over there*. Instead, our brain thinks only: *I am Robinson Crusoe. I am young Werther. I am Huck Finn.*

Thus it was that novels upgraded the soliloquy by accident. Their authors didn't craft a new literary mechanism to insert into *Hamlet*; they simply deleted the stage and the persons upon it. But as blindly unintentional as this soliloquy innovation may have been initially, its effect was profound and enduring. By eliminating the physical element that disrupted the soliloquy's identification effect, the novel added via subtraction.

The novel's mechanism of more from less suggests that we can achieve a similar state of increased identification if we read Hamlet's soliloquies instead of viewing them. And this is, in fact, exactly what occurs. The phenomenon was recorded in 1811, when the British East India Company accountant Charles Lamb observed with a sigh: "It is difficult for a frequent play-goer to disembarrass the idea of Hamlet from the person and voice of Mr. K." To see *Hamlet* onstage is thus to see an actor—the tall, precise Mr. John Philip Kemble—playing Hamlet. But to pick up an edition of Shakespeare's play, Lamb goes on to observe, is to discover an entirely different neural experience: "While we read [the play], we see not [the character], but we are [the character],—we are in his mind."

Emerson, too, noted a version of this phenomenon, remarking to his friend Edwin Whipple:

> I see you are one of the happy mortals who are capable of being carried away by an actor of Shakespeare. Now, whenever I visit the theatre to witness the performance of one of his dramas, I am carried away by the poet . . . actor, theatre, all vanish . . .

Like Edwin Whipple, most of us lack this ability to mentally delete whole theaters. But thanks to the novel, we can still experience what Emerson experienced. In the pages of *Robinson Crusoe* and *Huck Finn*, we can discover soliloquies that work more potently on our brain than the stage performances of Mr. K. or Montdory, conveying us effortlessly into identifying with a literary character.

And then, in the middle years of the twentieth century, a novelist discovered how to make the soliloquy even more potent.

The Innovation

In 1960 the Philadelphia medical textbook publisher J. B. Lippincott printed the first novel by thirty-four-year-old law school dropout and former airline ticket clerk Nelle Harper Lee.

The novel was *To Kill a Mockingbird*. Despite its unassuming origins, it became a literary sensation, winning a Pulitzer Prize, selling forty million copies, and establishing itself as a staple of high school literature courses across America. And at the root of all the sensation was a soliloquy innovation.

Like *Robinson Crusoe*, *The Sorrows of Young Werther*, and *Huck Finn*, Lee's novel begins by introducing us to a first-person voice that pivots here and there into soliloquies. That particular voice belongs to Scout Finch, a six-year-old who lives in Maycomb, Alabama—and who is, like Hamlet, of two minds about things. Should she ignore her classmate Cecil's racist taunts, like her father has asked? Or should she prove to Cecil that she's not a coward?

These soliloquies aren't as theatrically spectacular as Hamlet's "To be." But they touch on the same deep question: *What's right?* So, they encourage our brain to feel an intuitive identification with Scout. We may not be six, or from Maycomb, or taunted by Cecil. But because Scout's soliloquized conflicts trigger our salience network, they make us feel that she is us.

Having dusted off Shakespeare's old gadget of the dialogic inner monologue, Lee then adds her own innovation: she has Scout observe other characters as *they* soliloquize. At which point, Scout identifies with those characters, prompting our brain, through Scout, to identify with them too.

Of those characters whom we identify with through Scout, the two most prominent are Scout's attorney father, Atticus, and Scout's reclusive neighbor, Boo Radley. Atticus's soliloquized struggle is between his love for his hometown and his horror at its racial prejudice. As he articulates it to Scout:

> We're fighting our friends. But remember this, no matter how bitter things get, they're still our friends and this is our home.

Boo's inner struggle is more primal, dramatized not by grand speeches but by wordless actions. He's torn like a child between curiosity and fear, between wanting to connect with the world—and wanting to retreat to his house and never come out.

Atticus's and Boo's internal conflicts are profoundly different, yet as we watch their soliloquies through Scout's soliloquy, we come to identify with both. Until at last, Scout observes:

> Atticus was right. One time he said you never really know a man until you stand in his shoes and walk around in them. Just standing on the Radley porch was enough.

In this remarkable moment, Scout realizes that she's come to identify with two other people. She sees through her father's eyes—*Atticus was right*—as she stands in Boo's "shoes." Her medial prefrontal cortex is now perceiving two minds in one.

Meanwhile, our medial prefrontal cortex has reached an even more mind-expanding state. It has come to identify with Scout as she identifies with Atticus and Boo. Which is to say: our brain is now experiencing three minds in one.

This is multiple times the identification provided by *Hamlet*. It's Emerson's greater soul, expanded, giving us an intuition of the humanity beyond . . . and beyond . . . and beyond.

Using the "Humanity Connector" Yourself

Lee's invention has a potent neural effect. Like the Almighty Heart (see chapter 1), it prompts our brain to feel that our humanity stretches everywhere. But where the Almighty Heart conveys this experience as a neurochemical warmth, Lee's soliloquy-in-a-soliloquy communicates it in a cortical leap that feels like a numinous sixth sense. So, what we see in the human beyond is not our fleshly desires, but the more rarefied elements of our consciousness: higher meaning, eternal truth, universal justice.

The intuition of these cosmic values can give our brain purpose in times of peace and strength in times of disaster. And it can even encourage our brain to do a little of what Martin Luther King preached: respond to hate with love. After all, it's easier to love people when our brain identifies with them. We don't need to overcome our biological fear, pride, or anger; we can give to the other lives that are actually us.

And when we extend that love, one last wonder occurs. As modern psychologists have learned, nothing boosts our neural happiness more reliably, more deeply, or more enduringly than acts of generosity. So, by giving our love to others, we really do receive ourselves. Like Theodore Parker and the transcendentalists, we find connection to a greater human soul.

If you ever lose faith in that soul, walk to your bookshelf and take down a soliloquy. Since *Hamlet*, the literature of the world has grown abundant with them. Anytime that you notice yourself identifying with a character who seems nothing like you, the blueprint of a dialogic monologue is probably there, either articulated through an explicit verbal soliloquy (like Atticus's) or implied more subtly through conflicted behaviors (like Boo's).

And if the world's soliloquies don't give you intuition enough, try Lee's up-powered invention of the soliloquy in a soliloquy. Like Hamlet's original, Lee's invention has come to exist in its own branching variants. There are third-person variants, such as Marilyn French's *The Women's Room* (1977). And comic variants, such as Sue Townsend's *The Secret Diary of Adrian Mole, Aged 13¾* (1982). And romance variants, such as Robert James Waller's *The Bridges of Madison Country* (1992). And cinematic variants, such as Pixar's first *Toy Story* (1995).

But inside them all lies the same literary technology: a "To be or not to be" that triggers your brain to connect with *her* and *him* and everyone—bending humanity's long arc toward you.

TWENTY

Renew Your Future

Gabriel García Márquez's One Hundred Years
of Solitude, *Franz Kafka's* The Metamorphosis,
and the Invention of the Revolution Rediscovery

C hange came to Colombia in 1959. For it was then that rebel peasants escaped into the mountain outback of the Andes to found the Marquetalia Republic.

The republic was a wonder, quilting freedom and justice with monsoon rain forests and avalanche peaks. And although its size was modest, its hundreds of inhabitants had a bold plan to expand. They'd erase the old system of monied power and rescript civilization, building utopia.

But abruptly, in the late spring of 1964, utopia was ended. The Colombian government descended with sixteen thousand soldiers backed by US Huey choppers rattling angry in the sky. Ambushed, the rebels were forced to abandon the republic, grabbing machetes and petrol bombs as they fled for the heights. Up in those heights, the rebels formed the Revolutionary Armed Forces of Columbia, and for the next sixty years, that guerilla army waged an increasingly violent resistance against global capitalism. Its soldiers kidnapped government ministers, extorted coffee farmers, and trained eight-year-olds to fight with Kalashnikov rifles. Until at last, the revolutionary forces tore themselves apart in bitterness and blood.

Yet despite the republic's ugly demise, the hope of change endured in a rundown barrio many miles to the northwest, where there sat another Colombian rebel: Gabriel García Márquez. Márquez admired the republic's world-transforming ambition, but he anticipated its doom from the start. For before the republic, the same plan to break with the past and rewrite Colombian society from scratch had been attempted by General José María Melo in the coup d'état of 1854, and by the radical Liberals in the Thousand Days' War of 1899, and by General Gustavo Roja Pinilla in the coup d'état of 1953. Each time, the people of Colombia had been promised a whole new way of life. And each time, they'd gotten carnage, misery, and chaos instead.

So, as Gabriel García Márquez pondered this history of failed change, he decided to attempt a different revolutionary road. Instead of trying to escape the past, he would revisit it—anew.

The Beginnings of the New World

It was in July 1965, just over a year after the death of the Marquetalia Republic, that Márquez was transformed by the memory:

> In a flash, I realized: I had to tell the story the way that my grandmother told hers, starting from that afternoon when the boy is taken by his father to discover ice.

Out of that "flash" came the first line of a novel published in 1967 as *Cien Años de Soledad*—*One Hundred Years of Solitude*: "Many years later, as he faced the firing squad, Colonel Aureliano Buendía was to remember that distant afternoon when his father took him to discover ice."

This stunner of an opening sentence would dazzle millions of global readers, helping to earn Márquez the Nobel Prize for Literature. And its extraordinary brilliance culminates with the ending that Márquez glimpsed from the beginning: "to discover ice." Those three words are so calmly matter-of-fact—and so brain twisting. How is it possible to discover ice? Isn't ice something that the world already knows?

The answer is that Colonel Aureliano Buendía and his father didn't really discover ice. They *re*discovered it, just like when we first savor a guava or learn of the Marquetalia Republic, we're rediscovering something that other people have discovered before. And, in fact, this is what we're doing when we start reading *One Hundred Years of Solitude*. At the same moment that the colonel is remembering his rediscovery of ice, we're rediscovering that rediscovery. We're learning for the first time something that the colonel already knew.

This experience of rediscovery occurs again and again in the initial pages of *One Hundred Years*. First, we rediscover how the colonel's father rediscovered the world: "The world was so recent that many things lacked names, and in order to indicate them, it was necessary to point." And then more rediscoveries ensue:

> Every year during the month of March, a family of ragged gypsies would set up their tents near the village, and with a great uproar of pipes and kettledrums they would display new inventions. First they brought the magnet.

The magnet is a discovery so ancient that it was known to the junk-sailing traders of the Han dynasty in the second century BCE. Yet to the colonel's father, it's a marvelous "new invention." And his rediscovery of its marvel is followed in short order by his rediscovery of the telescope, the astrolabe, the compass, and the sextant. All of these old navigational technologies are new finds to the colonel's father, and with them, he makes another astonishing rediscovery: "The earth is round, like an orange." For all his previous years, the colonel's father had dwelt on a flat earth. But now he's re-found our spherical world.

Why does *One Hundred Years of Solitude* lead us through all of these rediscoveries? Why does it relentlessly present and re-present the old world as new? It all goes back to that "flash" where Márquez rediscovered his grandmother's storytelling way. Because in that flash, something special happened to his brain.

The Science of Rediscovery

Our brain is capable of a strange feat known as relearning.

Relearning makes use of our ability to forget, which is the neural not-quite-opposite of learning. Learning occurs when our neurons extend new synaptic connections, and forgetting happens when those connections shrink. Yet curiously, our brain forgets at a more staggered rate than it learns: the first synaptic connections can wither in minutes, while the last ones can remain for years, hanging on to scattered fractions of long-ago life lessons.

Why do our neurons work like this? Why don't they choose to remember—or choose to forget? If our neurons think that a memory might have future importance, why don't they hold on to it intact? Or if they think that a memory no longer matters, why don't they erase it completely? Why does our brain maintain a library of books with half-vanished pages?

There's no answer to this mystery. Our brain emerged blindly through natural selection, so it doesn't (and never did) know. But even though the rationale behind our neural method of forgetting is nonexistent, it does have its advantages. By not forgetting all the way, we can save time: it's faster to relearn riding a bicycle than to learn from scratch. And relearning has another benefit too: it allows us to learn differently on the second go-round. In relearning, our neurons reach out fresh connections that come to coexist with the still-remaining connections from before, producing a blend of past learning and new. And sometimes that hybrid leads to a creative breakthrough: we devise a different way of bike riding than our old brain knew.

So, by forgetting and then relearning, we create an opportunity for a special kind of discovery that brings wisdom from the past but also fresh eyes from the present. If we'd never learned in the first place, we'd have nothing more than our current perspective to guide us. If we'd never forgotten, we'd repeat our history in an endless loop.

This process of relearning enriches each day of our life. If you'd like a quick taste of it now, just go to your bookshelf and grab a novel you read years ago. As you start to turn the pages, you'll feel your brain entwining old details it remembers with new ones it never grasped before, mingling nostalgia with epiphany, and making the novel feel novel once more.

And relearning isn't just something that we do individually. It's also something that we do collectively. Something that can change our world.

Relearning Together

Each generation has to relearn the know-how of the generation before. And anthropologists have discovered that this social process mimics the relearning in our brain. Each generation acquires the existing know-how faster, helped by the guidance of the generation before. But each generation also brings new perspectives that can yield original discoveries.

One of those discoveries was made with the very same stargazing tools—the astrolabe and sextant—that the colonel's father rediscovers in *One Hundred Years*. The tools were wielded in a sixteenth-century northern Polish town by Nicolaus Copernicus, an astronomer who spent his nights studying the positions of the constellations. Three hundred years earlier, these positions had been recorded by Arab astronomers in a big book, *The Alfonsine Tables*, that Copernicus consulted carefully each evening. But as Copernicus took up his own astrolabe and sextant to reiterate the sky measurements of the past, he experienced an unprecedented epiphany: the earth wasn't at the center of the cosmos, as the Arab astronomers had thought. No, the earth was spinning around the sun.

This was an astonishing insight—so astonishing that Copernicus waited for more than twenty years, until the very last moments of his life, to publish: "I realized what a strange declaration it would seem to those who knew that the wisdom of centuries had placed the earth motionless at the center of the universe, if I, to the contrary, asserted that the earth moves."

And what made Copernicus's discovery seem especially strange was that it wasn't based on any new evidence: the constellations were in exactly the same place as the Arab astronomers had seen centuries before. The only thing different was Copernicus's perspective. For centuries, astronomy had been caught in a rigid habit of mind: *The earth sits still . . . the earth sits still . . . the earth sits still.* But by relearning the old star tables, Copernicus ushered in a new world.

A world that flew.

Copernican Rediscovery in *One Hundred Years of Solitude*

One Hundred Years of Solitude originated in Gabriel García Márquez's own Copernican rediscovery: "I had to tell the story the way that my grandmother told hers."

By relearning his grandmother's old style of storytelling, Márquez began telling a story unlike any before. And that story brims with its own Copernican rediscoveries, like the one where the colonel's mother, Ursula, journeys to the lands outside the village of Macondo. To make this journey, Ursula follows the earlier footsteps of her husband. Yet unlike her husband, she doesn't return empty-handed. She comes back with a crowd of people who look familiar yet not:

> They came from the other side of the swamp, just two days away, where there were towns that received mail every month in the year and where they were familiar with the implements of good living.

Like Copernicus, Ursula has followed the old route to the old place— and found a new world.

This is the most hopeful moment of Márquez's novel. Slowly, the mood of rediscovery will ebb away. The characters will forget more and more of the past, dooming each subsequent generation to repeat history instead of relearning it. But even though the characters of *One Hundred Years* end up going round and round to nowhere, the novel itself keeps change going by teaching us Ursula's revolution blueprint.

The teaching is provided by a literary invention that originates in another retracing of steps, this time back to the ancient literary discovery that poetic language is not quite the same as regular language. Regular language is: "a blue flower." Poetic language is: "a flower blue."

Why does poetic language work like this? Why does it put words in unusual places? The poets, perhaps driven by the same blind evolutionary forces as our brain, have not explained. But two centuries ago, the English lyricist Samuel Taylor Coleridge hypothesized in his opium-tinged memoir *Biographia Literaria* (1817) that poetic language rearranges usual speech in order "to re-create." If the poets had simply written "a blue flower," we'd hurry on past, melding the flower into all the blue flowers that we'd seen before. But because the poets wrote "a flower blue," our eyes see the flower in an original light, re-creating its beauty in our mind.

Psychologists have since confirmed that Coleridge was right: poetic phrasings release a brain-slowing burst of dopamine wonder that mingles our existing memories with a new mental perspective. The mingling breaks our prior habits of reading, defamiliarizing things that we've come to see as boringly ordinary, and inspiring us to see fresh details, fresh points of emphasis, fresh opportunities for discovery.

This poetic prompt for relearning can be found throughout *One Hundred Years of Solitude*. From the novel's opening page, the prose bursts with unexpected phrasing: "A river of waters diaphanous" . . . "stones white and enormous, like prehistoric eggs" . . . "sparrow hands" . . . "the learned alchemists" . . . "the desperation of nails and screws."

And this old invention isn't just rediscovered by *One Hundred Years of Solitude*. It's revolutionized too.

The Revolution of *One Hundred Years of Solitude*

A generation before Gabriel García Márquez, an Argentinian short-storyist by the name of Jorge Luis Borges was rereading Franz Kafka's 1915 novella *The Metamorphosis*. And as Borges reread, he noticed that Kafka had taken the old invention of poetic language and reinvented it as poetic narrative. Poetic narrative followed poetic language in bending an old rule. But where poetic language bent a rule of grammar, poetic narrative bent a rule of story.

The particular bending of story effected by Kafka could not be simpler. *The Metamorphosis* takes a familiar happening—a young man living at home with his family—and turns the young man into a giant bug. Like the rearrangement of "the blue flower" to "the flower blue," no explanation is given for this rearrangement of *man* to *bug*. Its purpose isn't to logically establish new laws of narrative; it's to surprise us into reconsidering the old. That old law, in the case of *The Metamorphosis*, is family love. In the past, we'd been taught by moral parables, sentimental novels, and other traditional tales that family love was selflessly generous. But when the insectoid young man of *The Metamorphosis* repulses his parents and retreats heartbroken into his room to die, we relearn that family love can be very conditional indeed.

After Kafka's surrealist invention was rediscovered by Jorge Luis Borges two decades later, he used it to engineer dozens more poetic narratives, including:

"The House of Asterión," in which a man raves insanely that he cannot escape his house of doorless corridors . . . only to then reveal himself as the entirely sane Minotaur of Daedalus's labyrinth.

"Pierre Menard, author of *Quixote*," in which a scholar immerses himself so thoroughly in *Don Quixote* that he becomes its author, rewriting it word for word.

"The Bibliotheca of Babel," in which we enter a library filled with books that contain every possible arrangement of typewriter keystrokes, producing endless rooms of gibberish, but also the tantalizing prospect of a tome that reveals all the secrets of God.

Like *The Metamorphosis*, these narratives rearrange a single element of a familiar story to help us see it afresh. The legend of the Minotaur is rearranged by delivering it from the minotaur's perspective. The classic novel about a man who becomes intoxicated by chivalric romances is rearranged by swapping the chivalric romances for the classic novel. The biblical story of Babel is rearranged by trading ancient tongues for modern texts. And as we re-see the old plots, original possibilities emerge. We escape the labyrinth; we stop rewriting the same pages. We leave the babble books upon the shelf.

And we experience a "flash" of new narratives ahead.

One Hundred Years of Solitude Rediscovers Borges

"The House of Asterión" is a short story of less than 850 words. *The Metamorphosis* is a brief novella of about 19,000 words. *One Hundred Years of Solitude* is an epic of more than 144,000 words.

This epic length clues us in to Gabriel García Márquez's ambition to re-rediscover the poets' old discovery yet again. In the beginning, the poets discovered rewording. Then Kafka and Borges discovered re-*worlding*. Now Márquez will go further. He will use the old inventions of poetic language and poetic narrative to craft the new invention of po-etic *history*, rearranging our collective memory to help us relearn where we came from—and where we could go differently.

This rearranging begins with the first sentence of *One Hundred Years* and grows in scope over the opening chapter, which propels us into a se-quence of "hallucinating sessions." In those sessions, we force "the limits of . . . imagination to extremes," witnessing a gypsy potion of invisibility, a pig-tailed boy, and a carpet that flies, filling our brain with dopamine's light buzz of possibility.

After the buzz begins, *One Hundred Years* then presses our brain into active rediscovery, carrying us along with the colonel's father as he hacks his way through a tangle of ferns to find a Spanish galleon sitting on dry land. This is clearly another hallucinating session. And yet . . .

> Many years later, Colonel Aureliano Buendía crossed the region again, when it was already a regular mail route, and the only part of the ship he found was its burned-out frame in the midst of a field of poppies. Only then, convinced that the story had not been the product of his father's imagination, did he wonder how the galleon had been able to get inland to that spot.

When the colonel rediscovers his father's original discovery, we're our-selves prompted to pause over it with fresh eyes. And in that pause, we re-ponder the old laws of gravity, opening our mind to a voyage that seemed impossible before.

A voyage sailed through jungle green, upon an orange world.

Using the "Revolution Rediscovery" Yourself

Long before Gabriel García Márquez, authors encouraged us to imag-ine new worlds. In 360 BCE Plato depicted the mythic realm of At-lantis; in 421 the reclusive Chinese landscape poet Tao Yuanming described the idyllic lost land of *The Peach Blossom Spring*; and in 1888 the Massachusetts journalist Edward Bellamy kicked off the modern craze for utopian sci-fi with the speculative worldbuilding of his novel, *Looking Backward*.

But these works and their heirs differ from *One Hundred Years* in one crucial respect: they don't prompt us to rediscover our past; they prompt us to delete it. Sometimes the deletion is explicit: an armageddon occurs, wiping away the old world with earthquakes or plagues or nuclear bombs. Other times, the deletion is implicit: the story leaps ahead in time, or hops to a fresh geography, allowing a new community to bloom free of the world's existing taint. Yet either way, the writers follow the same radical blueprint as the Marquetalia Republic: they erase the previous social order, attempting to reboot the globe from zero.

Gabriel García Márquez's innovation is to bring the past along. In *One Hundred Years*, he poetically retells a rough century of Colombian history, from the 1854 coup of General José María Melo to the 1953 coup of General Gustavo Roja Pinilla. And by guiding us to relearn that history, *One Hundred Years* breaks the tragic cycle that has doomed utopias from Atlantis to Marquetalia. Mingling old roots with green branches, his invention organically renews our future.

In the decades since *One Hundred Years*, Márquez's creation has itself been rediscovered by Toni Morrison's *Beloved*, Haruki Murakami's *A Wild Sheep Chase*, Laura Esquivel's *Like Water for Chocolate*, Guillermo del Toro's *Pan's Labyrinth*, Alfonso Cuaron's *Roma*, and many other books and films. So, if you ever find yourself caught in a life that keeps repeating the mistakes of times gone by, try feeding your mind a history poetic.

Re-seeing a hundred yesteryears you knew.

And spinning revolution in a circle—new.

TWENTY-ONE

Decide Wiser

Ursula Le Guin's The Left Hand of Darkness,
Thomas More's Utopia, *Jonathan Swift's* Gulliver's
Travels, *and the Invention of the Double Alien*

I n the fall of 1948, college students from Manhattan, New York, to Westwood, Los Angeles, dutifully commenced the ritual of reading Alfred L. Kroeber's *Anthropology*, the classic textbook introduction to the study of human cultures. But this year, the ritual went differently. For the old classic had been revised to include a new element: a list of "Simultaneous Inventions."

Telescope: Jansen, Lippershey, Metius, 1608

Steamboat: Jouffroy, Rumsey, Fitch, Symington, 1783–88

Telegraph: Morse, Steimhill, Wheatstone and Cooke, 1837

Photography: Daguerre and Niépce, Talbot, 1839

Surgical Anesthesia: Jackson, Liston, Morton, Robinson, 1846

Telephone: Bell, Gray, 1876

Phonograph: Cros, Edison, 1877

The telescope, the camera, the phone—all these devices had been invented in two, three, or even four places at the very same time. Yet their inventors had possessed no knowledge of one another. They'd converged independently on the identical world-changing blueprints.

The list of simultaneous inventions made a great impression on students—so great that the list was still being reprinted many years later, after most of the textbook's other ideas had been abandoned and the author himself was deceased. And the list made an especially great impression on one particular student: the author's daughter, Ursula.

Ursula Kroeber was herself in college when the list was published, but she'd learned of the list a few years earlier when her father was still at work on his textbook revisions. Back then, in their cheerfully honeysuckled home in Berkeley, California, her father had explained that the list was more than a list. It was itself an invention with its own special purpose: to free readers from a mental bias. Ursula's father called that bias the "great man theory of history." Today, modern psychologists know it as the "fundamental attribution error." It's our brain's tendency to overcredit individuals for their failures and successes, discounting the greater life contexts that hindered or helped.

Ursula was deeply intrigued by her father's invention. But as she pored over its blueprint, she came to realize that it hadn't quite worked. It might have eliminated the old bias, but in doing so, it had promoted a new one. After all, by emphasizing the importance of external circumstance to the invention of telescopes, cameras, and phones, the list had upheld the founding assumption of her father's career: that individuals were shaped by their culture. Which is to say, it had perpetuated modern anthropology's self-serving bias.

When Ursula noticed this, she wondered: Had her father's engineering deed been doomed from the start? Were we fated to forever think that we were becoming more and more objective, when we were really falling prey to egocentric bias, confirmation bias, blind-spot bias, and a mob of other mental gremlins? Or was it possible to fix the flaw in her father's invention? Was there a way to go backward to a time in human life before our errant judgments began, undoing the source of our biases and restoring our brain to its original state of neutrality?

Curious to find out, Ursula decided to seek out that original state.

Putting aside her father's modern textbook, she slipped into the brick colonial library of Radcliffe College, and, in the sun-glow of high windows, she prowled through musty wooden shelves, gathering up armfuls of the world's oldest printed works of anthropology.

And what Ursula discovered in those works was a special kind of literature: a literature for busting bias.

A Literature for Busting Bias

The world's earliest known forays into anthropology are ancient and medieval travel writings such as Herodotus's fourth-century-BCE musings on Egyptian circumcision; Fan Chengda's twelfth-century geographies of the painted towers of the southern Song dynasty; and Ibn Battuta's fourteenth-century guides to the fruited rivers of Persia, the pickled pepper pods of Zanzibar, and the seed-eating wizards of the old Mughal Empire. These travelogues all contain eyewitness accounts of different cultures, intermixed with suppositions about what makes human life universal—or not.

And then in the early sixteenth century, the thirtysomething English royal counselor Thomas More was seized by a notion: *Why not write a fake travel narrative? Not as a fraud or a hoax, but as a work of literature.* The notion seemed a little whimsical to More's friends, but he had a most unwhimsical purpose in mind. He wanted to use his fake travelogue to better convey one of travel's real benefits: the busting of bias.

Travel's bias bust had been observed by More on his diplomatic excursions through stone-towered Calais, spice-heavy Bruges, and other overseas European locales where he'd found himself becoming less provincial, shedding his home-born preconceptions for a broader view of human culture. And in our own day and age, More's observation has been extended by global neuroscientists. Those neuroscientists have discovered that travel can indeed bust bias by stimulating our brain's anterior cingulate cortex, or ACC, a talon-shaped error detector that tracks our mental expectations and alerts us when they're not met. The alert comes in the form of a self-conscious awkwardness that stalls us midaction, preventing our mouth and our limbs from carrying through on our incorrect preassessments and providing our senses with time to scan for new data that we can use to fashion more accurate opinions.

This self-conscious awkwardness occurs all the time when we visit unfamiliar realms. Nothing in those realms aligns with our expectations. The food, the geography, the weather—all of it surprises. So, our ACC goes active continually, pausing our automatic behavior and prompting us to study our environment more closely. This frozen state of intel gathering can feel uncomfortable and even overwhelming, but it can deliver rich psychological rewards. The most frequently celebrated is the wonder-infused sensation of learning that our brain gains from globe-trotting: *Wow, I'd never have guessed that.* And the ACC pause of travel can also convey other less popularly known yet equally remarkable rewards—rewards that were first detected twenty-three centuries ago by a Greek who lived upon the western Peloponnese.

The Greek was Pyrrho of Elis. In his young adulthood, Pyrrho undertook a long course of international travel: he journeyed eastward for thousands of miles, by foot, by mule, and by raft, past the Black Sea, over the Phrygian deserts, and along the fertile crescent of Mesopotamia, meeting the Zoroastrian Magi of Achaemenid Persia and the vegetarian gymnosophists of the Ganges River Valley. Those foreign encounters triggered Pyrrho's ACC, stalling a part of his mind that he referred to as his "judgment." And during the stall, Pyrrho experienced a remarkable tranquility, leading him to conclude that if he could suspend his judgment completely and forever, he'd attain *ataraxia*, or total mental peace.

Pyrrho acknowledged that it was very hard to reach *ataraxia*, and modern neuroscience has deemed it to be impossible. To get up in the morning (or even to stay in bed) requires our brain to make a judgment, conscious or cognitively automated. Yet even so, twenty-first-century scientists have discovered that Pyrrho was partially correct: travel can guide us into *some* suspension of judgment.

For starters, science has revealed that there are a number of judgments that we can suspend permanently, including most of our judgments about other people. Our brain is constantly making such judgments. It looks at strangers on the street—and judges them. It looks at celebrities in magazines—and judges them. It looks at family members and colleagues and friends in homes and offices and restaurants—and judges them. These judgments feel instantly good to our neurons; they deliver pleasant microdoses of emotional superiority. But in the long run, they make us anxious, incurious, and less happy, so we can improve our long-term mental well-being if we suspend them.

And even when we can't suspend our judgments about other people indefinitely, science has revealed that there's still a benefit to be gained from suspending our judgments for as long as we can. For the longer we suspend our judgments, the more accurate our subsequent verdicts become. This valuable fact has been uncovered by researchers who've spent decades probing the mechanics of better decision-making, only to discover that the key is simply more time and more information. Which is to say: reserving our judgment until the last possible moment.

Travel helps us do this. Travel challenges our expectations not only about cuisine and landscapes but also about people. Like the Magi and the gymnosophists that Pyrrho encountered, the humans we meet on our journeys don't conform smoothly to our prior mental models. Their clothing, their customs, and their speech are different from anything in our memory banks. So, they prompt our ACC to delay our snap judgments, improving both our mental well-being and the accuracy of the judgments that we do eventually make. And such is the force of this ACC delay upon our brain that its benefits persist even after travel is done. As psychologists have found, the more fully that we immerse ourselves in faraway cultures, the more that our brain delays its judgments about others when we return home.

Because travel has these bias-busting benefits, you'd naturally expect travelogues to convey them too. By immersing our brain in foreign lands that frustrate our anthropological expectations, the travel narratives of Herodotus, Fan Chengda, and Ibn Battuta seem engineered to trigger our ACC. But as Thomas More realized back in the early sixteenth century, traditional travelogues weren't doing a very good job of mimicking the bias bust of travel. In fact, far from curbing our prejudice, they often entrenched it.

The Problem with Traditional Travel Narratives

The travel narratives of Herodotus, Fan Chengda, and Ibn Battuta seem very different. They convey us through wildly diverse lands, and they're thick with idiosyncratic viewpoints:

In those deserts live ants bigger than foxes and faster than horses.

I doubt the common wisdom that the Qutang gorge cannot be ascended when its rapids swell with white waters.

When I met the Shaykh of Tabríz, I could not but covet his grand cloak of goat fur.

Yet beneath this diversity of narrative *content* lies a sameness of narrative *form*. The travelogues of Herodotus, Fan Chengda, and Ibn Battuta are all told in the voice of a single author who presents himself as a trust-worthy set of eyes; the sort of experienced guide whom we might hire on a real trip to show us around. This style of writing sets our brain on autopilot. Even when the travelogue introduces us to people who act unexpectedly, it supplies us with a constant source of social cues: the nar-rator. The narrator never gets flustered, so neither do we; we just flow along with his easy prose.

This autopilot feature of travelogues isn't intrinsically bad. In fact, it has one psychological advantage over physical travel: it boosts the won-der. With our self-consciousness stowed, our brain is free to gape, drink-ing in the diversity of life beyond our door. But the autopilot experience of travelogues does make them far less effective than actual travel at treating our bias. Our ACC is rarely jolted by a traditional travel narra-tive. Even when we're surprised by what the narrator reveals, our brain always knows what to do: keep reading. There's never a need to pause, flag our biases as unreliable, and come up with a new action plan.

Thomas More decided to change that. So, he abandoned the tradi-tional travelogue format. And he tinkered up a fresh style of travel writ-ing that felt more like actually leaving our home.

Thomas More's New Travel Style

In 1516 Thomas More published his fictional travelogue, *A Book of Solid Gold, as Healthy as It Is Fun, About the Best Kind of Society and the New Island of Utopia.*

The "new island" of Utopia couldn't be found on any map; its name meant "no place" in pseudo-ancient Greek. Yet despite the realm's non-existence, it caused a sensation among its initial readers. Those readers were mostly scholars, and like scholars everywhere, they suffered from overconfidence bias, so they were used to knowing just what to think. But they quickly found their thoughts flummoxed by the many contradictions of Utopia:

Utopia was free of hunger or poverty, because all property was distributed equally. Yet despite this egalitarian ethos, everyone in Utopia also owned slaves.

Utopia possessed astonishing technologies, like egg incubators that hatched infinite chickens. Yet, weirdly, it lacked the basic instruments of seaborne navigation.

Utopia seemed more Christian than even Christian Europe; like Jesus himself, its people threw away wealth to embrace a life of honest simplicity. Yet those same people also countenanced the most bizarrely unchristian practices: euthanasia and, even worse, divorce.

Ordinarily, such contradictions in a travelogue wouldn't have been too disconcerting. The narrative would have flowed along with the author acting as a steady guide, and at the end, readers would have gone on with their lives, not bothering to ponder the journey further. But More's book wasn't written in the format of an ordinary travel narrative. Instead of having an author who acted as a steady guide, it had *two* authors. And those authors disagreed.

The main author was Thomas More, or at least his fictional representative. That "Thomas More" starts the narrative by relaying the story of his trip to Flanders and its cinnamon harbors. But in those harbors, he encounters a second author, Raphael Hythloday, who proceeds to give an account of his voyage across the Atlantic to Utopia. Utopia, in Hythloday's view, is an ideal society, much better than the societies of Europe. Yet "Thomas More" dissents. He confesses that he finds many things about the Utopians to be absurd.

So, who's right about Utopia? Hythloday or "Thomas More"? The book refuses to say. It starts by taking both sides in its title, *About the Best Kind of Society and the New Island of Utopia*, which includes a strategic *and* that leaves us free to judge whether "the best kind of society" and "Utopia" are the same or not. And the book ends with this ambiguity intact. "Thomas More" concedes that he might be biased against Utopia by his Eurocentrism, and he remarks that there are some things about Utopia that he'd like to import to England. Are those things the communal eating halls—or the golden shackles for criminals? The six-hour workdays—or the enforced dress code? The tolerance for atheists—or the bans against free movement? "Thomas More" never says. He just announces his plans to talk more on the subject. And promptly stops the narrative.

The unresolved dual authorship of *Utopia* requires our brain to decide: *Whose judgment about the Utopians do I follow: that of Hythloday or "Thomas More"?* Ordinarily, such a question would elicit a snap decision from our brain, which has been conditioned by millions of years of natural selection to decide—and decide fast. Better to dash into an adequate answer than to dally in pursuit of a perfectly accurate one, losing a meal, or worse, getting eaten ourselves. This biological pressure to make rapid judgments is why bias exists in our brain in the first place. Bias is a way of arriving at quick conclusions. It keeps us from pausing too long in a state of nature, where the reward for deep reflection is to lose out to the mob of animal appetites. To our brain, bias thus isn't lazy stereotyping; it's sensible shortcutting that improves our odds of seeing tomorrow.

But then our brain encounters More's book, and all of a sudden the need for shortcutting is lifted. Since Utopia is a fictional no-place, there isn't any immediate life pressure to make a decision about which narrator's social cues to follow. We can pause our judgments about Hythloday and "Thomas More" and the Utopians for minutes, for hours, for days—even forever. We can do what *Utopia* does in both its title and its two-author structure. We can inhabit a neutral in-between, suspended forever like Pyrrho of the western Peloponnese, at least as far as More's book is concerned.

Yet as it turns out, most of us don't do that when we read *Utopia*. Instead, our brain overrules More's clever invention, forcing judgment.

Our Brain Forces Judgment—and Gets a Comeuppance

Here's how we know that Thomas More's invention didn't quite work: the word *utopia* hasn't retained its original judgment-free meaning of "no place." Instead, it's become a synonym for "the best kind of society." That's because Thomas More's original readers decided that *Utopia* had only one true author: Hythloday. The "Thomas More" fellow, they reasoned, was a satirical gag, so they compressed *Utopia*'s unique two-author structure into a traditional one-author travelogue. Then they closed the book's cover and merrily judged their way through the rest of their day.

This response to *Utopia* is exactly what you'd expect the human brain to do. The human brain isn't going to junk millions of years of hard-earned experience about the value of bias because of one work of fiction, no matter how clever the fiction's engineering. No, the human brain is going to primitively overrule that engineering, unsuspending our judgment so that we can crash on with surviving adequately. But even so, More's brave sally against human biology wasn't entirely for nothing. A few human brains were open-minded enough to take note of More's innovation. And two centuries later, one of those brains made a breakthrough.

The breakthrough was Jonathan Swift's *Gulliver's Travels*, published in 1726. Just like More's utopian fiction, *Gulliver's Travels* was a fake travel narrative; its subtitle was *Travels into Several Remote Nations of the World*. But unlike *Utopia*, Swift's fake travel narrative didn't have two authors. Instead, it offered a different literary innovation: it took the one trustworthy narrator of traditional travelogues and replaced him with one *untrustworthy* narrator.

That untrustworthy narrator was the surgeon-captain Lemuel Gulliver. If you happened to be a perceptive reader in 1726, you might have noticed that "Gulliver" derived from the word *gullible*, but you'd probably have trusted Gulliver anyway. That, after all, is what you'd done seven years earlier when you'd read the enormously popular fictional travelogue *Robinson Crusoe* by Daniel Defoe. From *Robinson Crusoe*'s opening page, you'd seen that its titular narrator was an imperfect man, prone to immaturity and flights of fancy. But still, you'd trusted Robinson, and he hadn't let you down. Over his journeys, he'd come round to Jesus, bestowed civilized names upon cannibal savages, and constructed "two plantations" where he'd cultivated corn, barley, butter, cheese, and even raisins. And thus had all your chauvinistic biases about the Protestant industry of your fellow Europeans been pleasantly confirmed.

So, you had no reason to suspect that an author would write a novel containing precisely the opposite sort of narrator: one who dragged you further and further away from your comfortable cultural preconceptions, until you felt utterly lost. Yet this is precisely what Gulliver does. Over his travels, he goes on multiple adventures. And on each adventure, the same thing occurs: Gulliver sees absurd people—and is gullibly impressed. He sees the tiny, petty folk of Lilliput—and is gullibly impressed. He sees the pompous giants of Brobdingnag—and is gullibly impressed. He sees the absentminded scientists of Laputa's sky island—and is gullibly impressed.

This pattern of adventure reaches its climax in the novel's final book, where Gulliver arrives in the land of the Houyhnhnms. The Houyhnhnms are such a strange people that they're not people at all. They're horses. Yet still, Gulliver admires them. And how could he not? The Houyhnhnms aren't just any horses. They're *ultra-rational* horses who never lie, who treat women as equal to men, and who cherish the virtues of temperance, exercise, and cleanliness.

This, to Gulliver, is almost utopia. It has just one imperfection: a breed of domesticated animals, known as Yahoos, who are so stupid, vile, and craven that Gulliver agrees enthusiastically when the Houyhnhnms decide to exterminate them. There's just one complication: Gulliver himself is a Yahoo. You see, Yahoos are humans. So, by idolizing the Houyhnhnms, Gulliver has entangled himself in a bizarre contradiction: he's come to hate his own species.

Gulliver's disgust at humanity creates a weird neural experience for us as readers. Are we meant to agree with Gulliver? Are we meant to loathe ourselves? And then the neural weird gets weirder. Gulliver is expelled by the Houyhnhnms as part of their eugenics program, forcing him to return to his English life among the Yahoos. And when his wife embraces him joyfully at the doorway of his old home, he falls "into a swoon for almost an hour." As Gulliver explains, most matter-of-factly, he had "not been used to the touch of that odious animal for so many years."

Gulliver's declaration that his wife is an "odious animal" wobbles our brain. If our ACC wasn't already agitated by Gulliver's enthusiasm for humanicide, it's agitated now. And then our ACC gets agitated further. To avoid having to "smell" his own children, Gulliver shoves tobacco and lavender up his nose. After which he races out to purchase a pair of horses and proceeds to spend "at least four hours a day" chatting to them.

With this bonkers conclusion, *Gulliver's Travels* upgrades the bias bust of More's fake-travelogue blueprint. In More's blueprint, our brain had been presented with two narrators and asked to decide: Which one is better? That choice wasn't easy, but it was at least a choice, and since our brain has been conditioned by evolution to make hard choices, that's what our brain did.

Gulliver's Travels does something more devious—and more psychologically potent. Instead of giving us a hard choice, it lures us into an easy choice—*trust the narrator*—that turns out to be spectacularly misguided. This error trips up our fast-judging neural transistors with their own hasty momentum, so that at the end of *Gulliver's Travels*, our brain isn't calmly contemplating: *Which of these two narrators is more reliable?* Instead, as we witness Gulliver discoursing with horses and stuffing flora up his nostrils, our brain short-circuits in bafflement: *What the . . . ?*

Having deposited us in this mental stall, Swift's novel then denies us an exit. There's no alternative narrator to Gulliver, no "Thomas More" or Hythloday that our brain can turn to now that our main travel guide has voyaged into lunacy. So, our brain sticks in its stall, grasping for an eject lever that *Gulliver's Travels* doesn't provide.

This was a powerful literary blueprint for judgment suspension. So powerful that it drew Swift's readers closer and closer to the threshold of *ataraxia*'s mental peace—until abruptly, their judgments unsuspended. Reader after reader decided that *Gulliver's Travels* was the opposite of *Utopia*: where *Utopia* had been uniformly idealistic, *Gulliver's Travels* was being uniformly satiric. In the Houyhnhnms and the Yahoos, Swift's novel was ironically portraying the two faces of our own mortal folly: heartless rationality and senseless passion. Really, then, the purpose of Swift's book wasn't to stop us from doing a Gulliver and judging too fast. No, no, the purpose of Swift's book was to encourage us to judge everyone in the whole world instantaneously and simultaneously, smirking at all of humanity.

This consensus dismantled Swift's clever innovation. Once again, millions of years of evolutionary bias had triumphed over literary engineering. Yet even in defeat, *Gulliver's Travels* wasn't a failure. It had demonstrated that More's original bias-busting blueprint could be amplified. So, perhaps there was a way to amplify it again.

Perhaps there was a way to pause our judgment longer.

The Way to Pause Our Judgment Longer

In 1968 *The Left Hand of Darkness* was penned by Ursula Le Guin.

Ursula Le Guin is the married name of Ursula Kroeber, the professor's daughter from our chapter's beginning. And like *Utopia* and *Gulliver's Travels*, *The Left Hand of Darkness* is a fictional travelogue. This time the fictionalized travel occurs roughly three thousand years in the future, carrying us from the earth to Gethen, a planet that is home to humanlike but not quite human peoples.

The encounter with these peoples is narrated by Genly Ai, a human who stocks his account with a detailed investigative report on the physiology of the Gethen people, a rendition of a Gethen creation myth, and even entries plucked from a Gethen diary. Yet despite all this scientific, sociological, and personal research, Genly Ai pulls his own Gulliver. He wildly misjudges the people of Gethen, making prediction after prediction that turn out to be wrong. So, once again, we're lured by a narrator into making erroneous judgments about other cultures, activating our ACC when our expectations are then disrupted. Until at last, *The Left Hand of Darkness* builds to a scene that's torn right from the last pages of *Gulliver's Travels*. In that scene, Genly Ai ends his long immersion in Gethen culture to reunite with his own people:

They all looked strange to me, men and women, well as I knew them. Their voices sounded strange: too deep, too shrill. They were like a troupe of great, strange animals. . . .

I managed to keep myself in control. . . . When we got to the Palace, however, I had to get to my room at once.

Just as Gulliver recoils from his "animal" wife, hastening to escape her in his stables, Genly Ai feels so overcome with revulsion at the "animals" of his own species that he flees to escape them in a separate room.

But then *The Left Hand of Darkness* goes a step beyond *Gulliver's Travels*. After Genly Ai hurries away from humanity, he visits the family of a Gethen friend. In that family, he meets a typical Gethen child, born of the incestuous coupling of two androgynous brothers. And at the thought of this coupling, Genly Ai is immediately overwhelmed with "strangeness," feeling as shockingly repelled by the Gethens as he does by humans.

With this narrative twist, Ursula Le Guin doubles the innovation of *Gulliver's Travels*. It's as though Gulliver ended by swooning in horror at his wife—then swooning in horror at the horses in his stables. The double swoon delivers twice the ACC stall of *Gulliver's Travels*, and it also eliminates the stall exit that our brain had forcibly made in *Gulliver's Travels*. That exit had been to reverse our decision to trust the narrator. By jumping back from Gulliver, we'd been able to extricate ourselves from his shocking behavior, gaining the wider, ironic view of the situation that our brain needed to return to fast decisioning: *Gulliver is crazy, the Houyhnhnms are crazy, everyone is crazy, crazy, crazy* . . .

But in *Left Hand*, our neural reverse out of the narrator's Gulliver swoon at humans is counteracted by the narrator's anti-Gulliver swoon at Gethen sexuality. That second swoon reveals the narrator to be half like us: he, too, feels the strangeness of androgynous incest. So, rather than allowing us to follow the readers of *Gulliver's Travels* in rocketing out of the narrator's orbit, *Left Hand* interrupts our thrust away, suspending us in a state of half repulsion and half agreement . . .

Genly Ai is crazy—and he's sane. He's so strange—and he's just like me . . . our judgment hung in space indefinitely.

Using the Double Alien Yourself

On the last day of August 1911, Alfred L. Kroeber was ensconced in his research lab at San Francisco's Museum of Anthropology, meticulously dusting artifacts with a horse-bristle brush, when he received a most unusual phone call.

The call came from the Northern California town of Chico, where a few days earlier, a fifty-year-old man had wandered out of the wilderness. The man was garbed in a peculiar handmade smock and was babbling in a language that no one could understand. Naturally, the man had been arrested, but it soon became clear that he was peaceful and intelligent, so now the people of Chico were stuck. It wouldn't do to lock up a man who wasn't a criminal, but then again, it wouldn't do to allow a man to wander around speaking gobbledygook. Was there, by any chance, someone at the museum who could solve this anthropological predicament?

Kroeber was then still a young professor. He wouldn't draft his list of simultaneous inventions for almost forty more years. Yet even so, he was California's foremost academic expert on human languages, and he'd teased out the meaning of many a seemingly unintelligible utterance. So, he answered bravely: "Yes. Yes, I think I can help."

The fifty-year-old man turned out to be the last member of the Yahi people. The Yahi had once inhabited the canyons of the Sierra wild, gathering elderberries and bow-hunting quail. But in the late 1860s, following the wake of the California Gold Rush, they'd been massacred by settlers, until finally, there was just the lone survivor left.

The lone survivor never introduced himself to Kroeber. It was not the place of a Yahi to introduce himself; introductions were made on his behalf by relatives. And since the survivor had no relatives anymore, his name remained a mystery to Kroeber and the museum staff. They simply called him Ishi, which in the Yahi tongue meant "Man."

For five years, Ishi stayed at the museum. He lived amid anthropological relics that belonged to other peoples. He spoke to strangers who treated him kindly but referred to him endlessly by not-his-name. He existed in an endless border zone—a man without a home.

It was a strange, self-conscious feeling. But Ishi displayed such preternatural calm that Alfred L. Kroeber later remarked: "He was the most patient man I ever knew. I mean he had mastered the philosophy of patience, without trace either of self-pity or of bitterness to dull the purity of his cheerful enduringness."

Could this possibly have been the therapeutic state sought all those centuries ago by Pyrrho of the western Peloponnese? Could Ishi's perpetual in-betweenness have guided his brain into the impossible peace of *ataraxia*? Or was the truth quite different? Had Kroeber misunderstood Ishi, reading his own assumptions onto a person whom he never really knew? Or are we the ones misreading both Ishi and Kroeber? Have we fallen back into one of our old biases or maybe even plunged into a new one, undiagnosed as of yet by scientists?

Perhaps it's best to refrain from deciding, at least for now. Perhaps. Perhaps. Perhaps.

If you'd like a life with more of that perhaps, you can find Ursula Le Guin's bias-busting blueprint in Paul Theroux's *The Great Railway Bazaar: By Train Through Asia* (1975), Marjane Satrapi's *Persepolis 2: The Story of a Return* (2000), and many other modern travelogues. Or if you'd like to take the next step into science fiction and discover how new narrative technologies can manipulate our expectations, try playing the video game Bioshock (2007).

Then rush ahead, on full autopilot. And give your ACC a jolt.

Suspending your judgment. Maybe for good.

TWENTY-TWO

Believe in Yourself

Maya Angelou's I Know Why the Caged Bird Sings *and the Invention of the Choose Your Own Accomplice*

T he birth was easy, and then the boy was hers. A thing of gold he was, chasing off the Oakland gloom.

But soon the nurses left. And panic came. What now? She'd never raised a child before. She was only seventeen herself. So, for hours, she lay awake, fright climbing in her heart. Until in the exhausted dark, she heard a voice:

"You don't have to think about doing the right thing. If you're for the right thing, then you do it without thinking."

Calmed by the voice, she closed her eyes. And when she woke at dawn, she did right without thinking, greeting the day by cradling her son.

That young mother was Maya Angelou. The voice belonged to her own mother, Vivian. And many years later, when the boy born in Oakland, California, was happily grown, Maya Angelou decided to give us all the gift that her mother's voice had given her: the gift of trusting ourselves.

The Origins of Self-Trust

The gift started back in Africa, five thousand years ago. There, on the clay-silt banks of the Nile River, lived a dynasty of mighty engineers.

Those engineers dug intricate canals to irrigate a hundred thousand lentil fields; they hauled limestone ton-blocks up to the pyramidal peaks of Giza; and finally, on a dented workbench beneath a palm-leaf roof, they took up a thin reed brush and crafted *The Wisdom of Ptahhotep*.

The Wisdom of Ptahhotep is a tremendously ancient work of literature. Just how ancient, we cannot be sure. Its prose style suggests that it might have been composed in the twentieth century BCE, during the twelfth dynasty days of the white-crown queen Khenemetneferhedjet. But its title suggests that it dates from many centuries earlier, back to when the royal vizier Ptahhotep oversaw the construction of the fifth dynasty's green-gold tombs at the Memphis necropolis.

However old *The Wisdom of Ptahhotep* may be, its continued existence is remarkable. It is the oldest surviving work of literature to be preserved on the fragile paper of papyrus. The older works before it have been preserved instead in stone or clay. Those older works endured, that is, because of the strength of the material that they happened to be printed on. But *The Wisdom of Ptahhotep* endured because of the strength of its words:

> The strength of my words is their truth.
> They live on in mouths and in minds
> Because of their worth.

Such was the worth of these words that generations of scribes brushed them again and again onto fresh scrolls, preserving them before their old paper could decay; and, indeed, such was the worth of these words that Ptahhotep claimed that they predated even his original papyrus. He was the first to record them with mineral inks, but they'd come to him from voices before, stretching perhaps to the very beginnings of human time, before canals were dug or pyramids dreamed.

Why was *The Wisdom of Ptahhotep* this lastingly valuable? How did it prove as durable as stone? What secret technology exists inside its teachings, keeping them alive inside our mind when a million other wisdom works have vanished with the years?

The answer is this:

For as long as you live, follow your heart.
Waste not a moment chasing anything else.
Follow your heart. Follow your heart.

Can you feel the power in those words? Can you feel the engineering breakthrough that they made?

The Engineering of Wisdom

When we're given words of wisdom, we rarely listen. No matter how wise the words, our brain typically dismisses them.

Why? Why doesn't our brain accept the sage counsel of our elders? Why don't we eagerly embrace the hard-earned lessons of the lives before?

Long ago, a clever parent discovered what science has more recently confirmed: the wisdom of elders threatens our self. Our self likes to believe that it's strong and independent. And, in fact, our self *needs* to believe that it's strong and independent; otherwise, we'd be overwhelmed by the world's vast toughness, losing heart and giving up. It's to avoid such emotional capitulation that we're so headstrong when we're young. We require a spirit of self-belief to face life's trials and carry on.

This needed self-belief is undermined by sage advice. Whatever the particular advice may be, its underlying message is: *You don't know as much as you think.* So, when our elders dole out the fruits of their wisdom, it creates an impossible choice for our brain: either we ignore the wisdom and crash into disaster, or we heed the wisdom and erode the self-belief that we need to brave the day. Both ways, we lose.

But then the long-ago parent discovered a third option; a way to dispense enlightened counsel that nurtures self-belief. That way is to tell our child brain: *What you're doing is really creative. And it might work even better if you tried doing it like so.* This style of advice redirects our outward behavior while supporting our inward belief in our self. It says: *I admire you for wanting to do things in your own original way; now let's make good on that desire by tweaking your approach.*

Neuroscientists refer to this method of advice as self-affirmation. The term is a little misleading; it makes it sound like we're affirming ourselves. But self-affirmation includes any statement that supports our self, including a statement made by another person. It's synonymous with "affirmation of our self."

The most effective way to affirm our self is to praise our values. We can have all sorts of different values—creativity, family, fun, work, health, kindness, fairness, intelligence, love, daring—but whatever our values may be, they sit right at the core of our self. And when they're commended, two zones go simultaneously active in our brain. The first is a parietal zone that's associated with mental representations of our self. The second is a ventral striatum zone that's associated with valuing objects. So, self-affirmations such as "I respect your *kindness*," or "People will remember your *work*," or "You're right; nothing's more important than *love*" literally encourage our brain to treasure our self as though it were gold.

This self-treasuring has been shown by psychologists to make our brain more receptive to prudent counsel. Normally, when we're given such counsel by doctors and nurses, our brain nods politely and does nothing to amend its ways. But when the same medical professionals mingle their guidance with an affirmation of one of our core values—"Think how happy your *family* will be to have you around for a few extra years"—our brain is dramatically more likely to start exercising, stop smoking, and eat more vegetables. And as studies have shown, a single dose of self-affirmation can make those healthy changes stick for months and even years.

Such was the neural secret that Ptahhotep discerned millennia ago: "Follow your heart. Follow your heart." This dose of self-affirmation is why generations of ancient Egyptians heeded Ptahhotep's recommendations to dispense grain to the hungry, to be forgiving to neighbors, and to refrain from boasting like a crocodile. Such counsel, no doubt, was very sound. But it wouldn't have endured if Ptahhotep had not been wise enough to whisper, "The core of you is right and true."

And Ptahhotep's wisdom was only the beginning. Because then literature became even more self-affirming.

The Next Invention of Wisdom

You can feel the breakthrough here:

> Every dawn, tell yourself, "Today I will encounter selfish, schem-
> ing, stealing men. But I know goodness—and its beauty. And be-
> cause I know, nothing can harm me. So, I will love the men who
> act in ugliness toward me."

This speech comes from *The Meditations of Marcus Aurelius*. Authored
in the second century by the last emperor of the Pax Romana, *The Meditations* became revered as a guide for the wisest of minds, consulted by
readers from the tenth-century archbishop Arethas of Caesarea to the
twenty-first-century US Marine Corps general James Mattis.

The Meditations follows the basic two-part blueprint of Ptahhotep.
One, give solid advice: "Be generous and strong." Two, mix in self-
affirmation: "You know goodness." And then *The Meditations* adds in the
breakthrough, which is to get us to literally speak the self-affirmation to
our self: "Every dawn, tell yourself, 'I know goodness.'" With this out-
loud statement, we affirm our core values in our own voice. Or to put it
in more clunky sciencespeak, we perform self-self-affirmation.

Self-self-affirmation is even more potent than self-affirmation. When
struggling middle school students were asked by psychologists to write
a fifteen-minute essay about why their personal values were important,
their test scores in math, English, and social science improved by an average of 5 points. That simple self-self-affirmation also halved the number
of students receiving Ds and Fs. And its booster effect persisted for years.

Long before neuroscience, long before even Marcus Aurelius, this
benefit of self-self-affirmation was uncovered by literary authors. Hints
of its neural tonic can be found as far back as 1950 BCE, in the Egyptian
Middle Kingdom's *Loyalist Teaching*, which pivots into the first-person
we to make us feel like we're giving advice to ourselves: "We live through
work. Without work, poverty comes."

We haven't, of course, really issued this industrious counsel; we've
simply been duped into parroting our elders' words. But still, the *Loyalist Teaching* is a clever literary ruse. And it appears to be as far down

the road of self-self-affirmation as literature can go. Literature is necessarily an outside voice, after all. If we wanted true self-self-affirmation, we couldn't ever get it from reading. Like those middle school students, we'd have to pick up a pen ourselves.

Or so it seemed, anyway, for thousands of years.

Maya Angelou's Discovery

Four years after Maya Angelou birthed her son, she experienced a grim epiphany:

> I had a visitation of my mortality. I suddenly realized that I wouldn't live forever, and it so frightened me that I may have gone through a mild breakdown.

In this "frightened" state, Maya Angelou was unable to sleep. She brooded on the end of her life, wondering whether it would come in a month, a week, or even tomorrow. Until she realized suddenly: if death came tomorrow, that didn't make today nothing. It made today *everything*.

> Every moment is precious. You bring all your equipment to everything, holding back nothing because that might be the last moment. I am constantly aware of that, which makes me existential in a very strange and serious way.

This same basic commitment to valuing the present can be found in the ancient speech of Ptahhotep:

> If a woman revels in the moment, don't cast her away. Let her enjoy life. Joy is the sign of deep waters.

Yet even so, there was a radical originality to the "strange and serious" way that Maya Angelou valued the present, an originality we can glimpse in her use of the word *existential*. For this was a term that, at the very moment that Maya Angelou was grappling with her own mortality, was being popularized by Jean-Paul Sartre, Simone de Beauvoir, and a group of mid-twentieth-century French authors as an alternative to all the wisdom of the ancients.

The ancients had always rooted wisdom in gods, or reason, or some other universal; even Ptahhotep's "Follow your heart" had been based in the belief that the human heart was implanted with Maat, the eternal virtue of the cosmos. But the French proponents of the existential held no such belief. On October 29, 1945, just months after Angelou gave birth, Sartre declared himself an "existentialist"—and then promptly denied the existence of Maat, God, and all the rest: "We are all born for no reason and die through collision."

This was a grim conclusion, as grim, perhaps grimmer, than Maya Angelou's vision of her own mortality. But even as Sartre abandoned faith in a greater logic of things, he didn't surrender to despair. Instead, he found an extraordinary hopefulness in the existence of his own self:

> In despair is the start of true optimism: the optimism of knowing that nothing good is coming to us—and the joy of relying on ourselves alone to bring good to everyone.

Such self-wrought "joy" was the meaning of life. And since all we had of life was the now, now, now, every heartbeat was to Sartre an urgent invitation: "I seize each second, sucking it dry."

Sartre's existentialism matched Maya Angelou's own experience of life, a life filled with unreason and chance collision—and constant opportunity to seize the joyful now. Angelou had taken that opportunity when she'd become pregnant at sixteen, and when she'd married a Greek sailor-turned-electrician, and when she'd danced the calypso in the nightclub basement of San Francisco's Purple Onion, and when she'd met Martin Luther King in 1960 and organized the *Cabaret for Freedom*. It was all so absurdly haphazard. It was all so joyfully meant.

And then after Maya Angelou discovered existentialism, she had another haphazard collision. This time with a new kind of art.

The Strange and Serious Art of Existentialism

The existentialists created a style of theater that came to be known as the theater of the absurd.

In America, the most famous example of this theater was a translation of French existentialist Jean Genet's 1959 *Les Nègres, clownerie—The Blacks: A Clown Show.* The play began with a group of blacks who reenacted the crime of murdering a white. After which the reenactors turned to a jury of blacks in whiteface—and sentenced them to death.

This bizarrely enigmatic spectacle was a runaway hit in New York City. *The Blacks* opened on May 4, 1961, and continued for more than 1,400 performances. It was the longest-running off-Broadway play of the decade, and Maya Angelou knew all about it. Not because she'd seen it. No, because she'd starred in it.

Her role had been one of the whiteface jurors, the White Queen, who had lines such as:

I'm sculpting myself into a ruin—a ruin eternal. And it's not time or tiredness that wears away at me. It's death that does my shaping.

Those words teemed with meaning, but what exactly did they mean? How could ruin be sculpted? What crumbling body lasted forever? Why did the Queen claim to be her own sculptor, only to then assert that death held the chisel?

No answers are provided by the play. So, the answers must come from us, the audience. We have to declare, "This is what the White Queen's words mean to me." And with that declaration, we create our own moment of significance, becoming existentialists.

Or to put it scientifically: *The Blacks* encourages us to engage in self-self-affirmation. Its suggestive but incoherent performance throws us into a chaos of meaning that prompts our brain to reach for stability in our own core values. So, if one of those values is family, we might think: *That White Queen is rather like my sister.* Or if one of those values is justice, we might think: *What's happening to that White Queen is only fair.* Or if one of those values is daring, we might think: *I have no idea what that White Queen is going on about, but at least this playwright took a risk.*

By prompting these neural responses, *The Blacks* reveals that it's possible, after all, for literature to guide us into genuine self-self-affirmations. To do it, literature simply has to make the counterintuitive move of *removing* core values from its narrative. Instead of following *The Wisdom of Ptahhotep* and *The Meditations of Marcus Aurelius* in providing universal verities for us to regurgitate, literature has to delete bits of the cosmos, drawing us into actively filling in the blanks with our own personal beliefs.

In the hot New York summer of 1961, this existentialist literary breakthrough profoundly inspired Maya Angelou. But as she walked onstage as the White Queen night after night, she began to see that the performance didn't have the same self-affirming effect on everyone. Many audience members were just baffled, while others veered toward Maya Angelou's own pre-existentialist experience of "breakdown," finding despair without hope.

The reason for these mixed responses was obvious: *The Blacks* didn't simply invite us to assert a single belief; it *forced* us to assert *all belief*. By plunging us into a narrative absent of any stable meaning, it demanded that we imagine a whole new galaxy of private truth. And if we could not rise instantly to that enormous challenge, we found ourselves engulfed by confusion or dismay.

This prompted Maya Angelou to wonder: What if she could create a more self-affirming introduction to existentialism? What if, instead of hurling us straightway into the infinite depths of no-God and no-Maat and no-reason, she could give us a chance to teach ourselves to swim within the shallows? What if she could take the literary technology that the theater of the absurd used to encourage self-affirmation—and combine that technology with a gently steadying hand?

It was a transformative idea, but also seemingly unachievable. How could there be an existentialist literary work that provided a "steadying hand"? Wasn't the whole point of existentialism that no such outside guides existed? At first, Maya Angelou had no answer to this conundrum. But over the next few years, she would arrive at the right answer for her: the steadying hand could be the wisdom gained from many long years of joyful collision with the now, now, now. The wisdom, that is, of one individual's existential life.

With this personal answer in mind, Maya Angelou checked into a London hotel and removed all the previous art from the walls. Then she reached into her suitcase and retrieved a Bible, a thesaurus, a deck of cards, and "some good, dry sherry." And plumping herself on the bed with a yellow legal pad, she began to write her memoir.

The Existential Ptahhotep

Maya Angelou begins her 1969 memoir *I Know Why the Caged Bird Sings* with a prologue that throws us into an instant where we're less aware of what we know than what we don't:

> "What you looking at me for?
>   I didn't come to stay . . ."
>   I hadn't so much forgot as I couldn't bring myself to remember.
> Other things were more important.
>   "What you looking at me for?
>   I didn't come to stay . . ."

As we learn a few moments later, young Maya Angelou is experiencing a similar befuddlement: she's flailing to recite a poem to her church on Easter Sunday. But before we can get our bearings on what this flailing means in the grand scheme of things, the memoir's narrator abruptly pulls us into a back-and-forth about a "lavender taffeta" dress:

> As I'd watched Momma put ruffles on the hem and cute little tucks around the waist, I knew that once I put it on, I'd look like a movie star. (It was silk, and that made up for the awful color.) I was going to look like one of the sweet little white girls who were everybody's dream of what was right with the world.

So, first, the dress is dreamily "cute," even Hollywood. But then the narrator interrupts herself to confess its "awful" color; after which, she swings into a sarcastic jab at racial prejudice, before continuing on through further tonal shifts, until at last, the taffeta-dressed Maya flees from church with a bladder full to bursting:

I tried to hold, to squeeze it back, to keep it from speeding, but when I reached the church porch, I knew I'd have to let it go, or it would probably run right back up to my head and my poor head would burst like a dropped watermelon, and all the brains and spit and tongue and eyes would roll all over the place. So, I ran down into the yard and let it go. I ran, peeing and crying, not toward the toilet out back but to our house. I'd get a whipping for it, to be sure, and the nasty children would have something new to tease me about. I laughed anyway, partially for the sweet release; still, the greater joy came not only from being liberated from the silly church but from the knowledge that I wouldn't die from a busted head.

The first sentence is matter-of-fact—until it veers grotesque: "brains and spit and tongue and eyes would roll all over the place." Then Maya is peeing and crying—and laughing. Laughing because she's free from that "silly" church. But also because her head didn't detonate like a urine watermelon. So, in rapid succession, the narrator's voice sweeps us from whimsy to tragedy to farce to worry to ridiculous victory.

The tonal volatility of this scene is a technique Angelou borrows from existentialist art. Like a performance of *The Blacks*, Angelou's preface whips chaotically from one mood to the opposite, prompting us, the readers, to supply the narrative transitions—wistful or cynical, ironic or solemn, hopeful or antiheroic—that hang together life's greater logic. But unlike *The Blacks*, Angelou's preface doesn't abandon us to this daunting existentialist task on our own. Instead, right after the church-peeing episode, it extends a "steadying hand":

If growing up is painful for the Southern Black girl, being aware of her displacement is the rust on the razor that threatens the throat.

It is an unnecessary insult.

Here the narrator's voice shifts dramatically; the first-person voice—"I," "I," "I"—of the preceding Easter church scene is replaced with a third-person voice: "the Southern Black girl," "her displacement," "the throat," "It is." This third-person voice, like the third-person voices of Ptahhotep and Marcus Aurelius, feels bigger than our individual first person, so it steadies us amid the memoir's tonal chop. But this voice also differs in one crucial respect from the voices of the ancient sages. Those voices brim with the eternal know-how of yesterday and tomorrow; this voice arrives entirely in the present tense: "is painful," "is the rust," "is an unnecessary insult."

By speaking in this present-tense *is*, Angelou's third-person voice bequeaths an existential wisdom that, like everything existential, subsists only in the now, now, now. So it stabilizes us briefly without confining us lastingly. It doesn't tell us what has been foreordained from times immemorial or what necessity will in our future be. It simply gives us a heartbeat of assurance, like a mother's voice from the dark—*If you're for the right thing, then you do it without thinking*—providing a temporary support that helps us venture on our own into all the nows to come.

This literary method of interspersing tonally unstable first-person historical narrative with grounding moments of third-person present is Maya Angelou's invention. And she continues to use it throughout *I Know Why*:

> The fact that the adult American Negro female emerges a formidable character is often met with amazement, distaste, and even belligerence. It is seldom accepted as an inevitable outcome of the struggle won by survivors and deserves respect if not enthusiastic acceptance.

The result is a double-existentialist style where omniscient-present interjections buoy us through past-tense tonal shifting, marshaling self-affirmation to support self-self-affirmation.

Or to put it more plainly: Angelou deploys her hard-earned life wisdom to assist us in hard earning our own. So, like *The Blacks*, Angelou's memoir offers us an existential journey into the "strange and serious." But unlike *The Blacks*, Angelou's memoir never forces us to make a cosmic meaning out of nothing. Instead, by deploying Angelou's life example to help us assert our own personal truths, it empowers our freedom to choose.

Using the "Choose Your Own Accomplice" Yourself

When psychologists first began studying self-self-affirmation, they worried that the more we affirmed ourselves, the more smugly self-content we'd become, until at last, we'd arrive at the opposite of hard-earned wisdom: blissful ignorance.

This concern proved unfounded. As psychologists have discovered, when we affirm our values, we gain an inner poise that increases our willingness to shift our outward behaviors, making self-self-affirmation a powerful tool for personal change. It boosts our curiosity and our courage to try new things. It makes us more open-minded and more willing to embark on fresh challenges. It nurtures learning and lifelong growth.

You can witness all those benefits of affirming yourself in *I Know Why* and its sequels: *Gather Together in My Name* (1974), *Singin' and Swingin' and Gettin' Merry Like Christmas* (1976), *The Heart of a Woman* (1981), *All God's Children Need Traveling Shoes* (1986), *A Song Flung Up to Heaven* (2002), and *Me & Mom & Me* (2013). Over their hundreds of pages, Maya Angelou transforms and transforms again, earning scholarships, becoming the first black female cable-car conductor in San Francisco history, learning modern dance, teaching herself Shakespeare, writing poems, recording albums, singing opera, studying languages, fund-raising for the civil rights movement, broadcasting for Radio Ghana, directing films, teaching at universities, earning a Tony Award nomination, and even moving to the land of Ptahhotep to edit the Cairo newspaper *Arab Observer*.

All of which means: a little personal treasuring won't make you anything other than your most vivid self. And if you want more of that self, why not create your own version of Angelou's existential invention? Start by getting a hotel room and taking all the art off the walls. Then write out your earliest memory of self-worthlessness—and interrupt it with the present-tense wisdom that you've learned since.

Affirming yourself. And seizing the now.

TWENTY-THREE

Unfreeze Your Heart

Alison Bechdel, Euripides, Samuel Beckett,
T. S. Eliot, and the Invention of the Clinical Joy

The ancient Greeks left behind many mysteries. But none more mysterious than the tragedies of Euripides.

Euripides was the last of the three famed Athenian tragedians, after Aeschylus and Sophocles. Yet where Aeschylus and Sophocles became renowned for writing classic tragedies—*Agamemnon, Oedipus, Antigone*—Euripides earned a reputation for infusing his tragedies with comic elements that surprised audiences with smiles and even joy. The result was a collection of theatrical oddities—*Alcestis, Iphigenia Among the Taurians, Ion, Helen*—that were sorrowful, yet amusing; fatalist, yet uplifting.

None of these "tragicomedies" seem to have won the ivy crown at Athens's annual theater festival, the City Dionysia. Nor were any of them, with the lone exception of *Alcestis*, chosen by ancient Byzantine schoolmasters for inclusion in the "selected" editions of great tragedies that would be diligently analyzed by the literature students of antiquity. Instead, they survived through a strange fluke: an unknown Euripides devotee, living in a dark age of history, possessed both the patience and the hand strength to transcribe the playwright's ninety-plus plays into an alphabetic ten-scroll compendium. And of that compendium, a solitary scroll somehow escaped the library fires and Peloponnesian wars and casual neglect that destroyed almost two hundred plays of Aeschylus and Sophocles.

So, even in the classical world, the tragicomedies of Euripides were a bit of a quirk in the system. And when they resurfaced in later ages, they posed a curious puzzle: What was their purpose? The purpose of tragedy, as everybody knew, was to purge our mind of sorrow; and the purpose of comedy, as everybody equally knew, was to refresh our spirits with merriment. But what good could come from stranding us in a downy-uppy state between?

Valiantly, scholars did their best to explain:

Euripides was a skeptic who didn't believe that true tragedy was possible.

Euripides was a psychological realist who perceived how horror and humor blur in the mind.

Euripides was a postmodern who discerned the deepest tragic irony: our pain is absurd.

But none of these high-minded theories gained much purchase with audiences, so for century after century, Euripides's invention remained a literary idiosyncrasy. Traditional tragedies flooded into the world as medieval sermons, Renaissance dramas, and modern novels. But tragicomedy never went further than a niche pursuit. In the early seventeenth century, Shakespeare experimented with one—*King Lear*—that prompted such widespread bewilderment that it was rewritten in 1681 as a romantic comedy. In the mid-twentieth century, the avant-gardist Samuel Beckett revived the form again, only to prompt millions of baffled spectators to wonder, *Who is Godot? And why have we sat here for three hours waiting?*

Whatever tragicomedy was doing, it was lost on most people. And then in the twenty-first century, people were lost no more. An American cartoonist, Alison Bechdel, figured it out.

Bechdel's Solution to the Mystery of Tragicomedy

Bechdel's solution began with her own mysterious difficulty, which loomed into view on the day that she hurried home from college to the faded central Pennsylvania town of Beech Creek. Her father had unexpectedly killed himself, and Bechdel, wearing her best skirt, stepped toward the funeral casket, her brothers solemnly suited behind. Yet when Bechdel saw her father's corpse, she couldn't feel anything. Not grief, or anger, or shock, or guilt, or even relief. And as she watched her family weep, she mused: "If only they made smelling salts to induce grief-stricken swoons, rather than snap you out of them." It was a funny thought but also grim, because Bechdel knew that part of her had stopped working. Her emotions had frozen, leaving her numb.

This numbness was such a weird experience that Bechdel blamed it at first on the weirdest part of her childhood, growing up in a funeral home: "It was usually after school, in a melancholy fading light, that we found ourselves up there unwrapping caskets." But in reality, Bechdel's condition was caused by a far more common childhood experience: chronic abuse. Like millions of American children each year, she had suffered a mix of emotional neglect and physical harm; her father had bullied her, controlled her, shamed her, and hit her. So, like many other victims of chronic abuse, Bechdel had coped by going numb. Her emotions had shut down, sparing her from fear and loneliness but also trapping her in a state of deadened feeling that persisted into adulthood.

And, unfortunately for Bechdel and the millions of survivors like her, there existed no medical cure for this condition. In fact, when doctors tried to help, they only made things worse.

The Doctors Mis-Cure Numbness

When the doctors of the twentieth century tried to treat numbness, they made an honest mistake. The mistake began when psychiatrists observed that numbness originated in chronic trauma. This led them to diagnose it as a symptom of posttraumatic stress disorder, or PTSD. At which point, they recommended PTSD's standard treatment: exposure therapy.

Exposure therapy was devised in the early 1950s by the University of Cape Town psychologist James G. Taylor as a remedy for phobias and anxiety. Over the following decades, it was then adapted by the renowned behavioral psychiatrist James Wolpe to treat combat veterans suffering from "war neurosis." And in our own time, it has been refined and expanded into many clinical varieties: prolonged exposure, in vivo, virtual reality, flooding, systematic desensitization, implosive therapy, imaginal exposure.

All these varieties share the same basic therapeutic approach: they "expose" patients to objects, images, and stories that trigger memories of the original trauma. Patients with germ phobias would be led by James G. Taylor into filthy rooms; veterans who'd returned from urban warfare overseas with the crippling feeling that snipers lurked in every window were encouraged by James Wolpe to imagine themselves walking in broad daylight through the streets of New York.

Such treatments can seem less therapy than torture, but because the exposure is performed in controlled settings where patients can feel physically safe and psychologically empowered, it has a track record of being helpful for many trauma survivors. Bechdel herself attempted to engineer a version of it:

> For years after my father's death, when the subject of parents came up in conversation, I would relate the information in a flat, matter-of-fact tone. . . . "My dad's dead. He jumped in front of a truck" . . . eager to detect in my listener the flinch of grief that eluded me.

But unlike Taylor's and Wolpe's patients, Bechdel didn't gain any relief from this exposure. Her numbness persisted unabated. And in the early 2000s, after both Taylor and Wolpe had died, psychiatrists discovered why: there's not one kind of PTSD. There's two.

The more common kind is characterized by a hyperarousal of emotion: overwhelming sadness, panic attacks, traumatic flashbacks. The other kind is less common but hardly rare, accounting for roughly one in every three cases of PTSD. And its symptoms are precisely the reverse of traditional PTSD: not overactive emotions, but *under*active emotions. Or in other words, numbness.

So divergent are these symptoms that the two types of PTSD can seem wholly unrelated. But both trace their origins to the same part of our brain: the limbic system. The limbic system is the source of our fears, joys, and other strongly instinctive responses to life's threats and opportunities. Normally, those strong responses are tempered by the emotion "brake" of our brain's prefrontal cortex, allowing us to register the limbic system's emotional warnings and excitements without becoming engulfed by terror or ecstasy. But when our emotion brake is subjected to chronic stress, it can fail. The more obvious way that the brake can fail is by losing its grip, which is what leads to the runaway feelings of traditional PTSD. But the brake can also fail by locking on. When that happens, our prefrontal cortex clamps down preemptively on our limbic system, repressing the source of our feelings. So, instead of experiencing little bursts of fear or joy, our brain doesn't feel anything. It responds to life like a machine, running dispassionately through the motions.

This state of mechanical numbness is dissociation. Our brain *dissociates* from itself, coming to feel robotically detached. Dissociation has various subtypes, but the most common are depersonalization and derealization. In depersonalization, our thoughts and memories feel unreal; they're like ghosts inside our mind. In derealization, it's the world outside that seems less genuine, like a dream we're drifting through.

Depersonalization and derealization are common symptoms of chronic childhood abuse. And they can also originate in adulthood. Adults who suffer from dysfunctional relationships, hostile work environments, or long hours spent in hospitals, prisons, or war zones, can gradually lose feeling. Psychiatrists estimate that more than 150 million people worldwide suffer from chronic numbness, and many more of us will experience a short-term variety at some point in our lives.

Because dissociation originates from precisely the opposite neural mechanism as traditional PTSD, it cannot be treated in the same way. And if it is, it can worsen. The therapies that are designed to help our emotion brake grip harder are no good for us when the brake is already gripping too hard.

That's why Alison Bechdel didn't get any relief from her own foray into exposure therapy. And that's why when clinical psychiatrists discovered the second type of PTSD in the early 2000s, they began pioneering a new treatment.

Except that, as it turned out, the treatment had already been pioneered—by Euripides, twenty-four centuries before.

Euripides's Pioneering Treatment

Prior to Euripides, stage tragedy had engineered an ancient literary version of exposure therapy. Classic tragedies such as Aeschylus's *Seven Against Thebes* and Sophocles's *Ajax* expose us to war, child abuse, suicide, and other traumatic events in a safe physical space where we can be supported by loved ones and fellow trauma survivors, helping to strengthen our brain's emotion brake. (For more on this treatment, see the introduction.)

But to treat us for the opposite problem, the excessive braking that causes dissociation, literature needs to dispense the reverse of exposure therapy. Which is what Euripides's tragicomedies do.

Euripides's earliest known and most historically popular tragicomedy is *Alcestis*. The play opens with the funeral of its title character, but the lamentations are quickly put on hold when Apollo intercedes from heaven, swearing to retrieve Alcestis from the god Death. This divine intervention shifts the mood from tragedy toward happiness—when abruptly, the plot veers again. Death scoffs at Apollo, calling him a deity of "empty words" and then spiriting Alcestis away.

So, will Apollo make good on his promise, or will he indeed prove to be of "empty words"? Will Alcestis be saved, or is she doomed after all? Nobody at the funeral knows, and a servant runs manically through the palace, weeping: "Alcestis is alive and dead."

Then the mood gets even stranger. Without warning, the demigod Hercules barges into the proceedings. And, unaware that a funeral is taking place, he gets merrily drunk, laughing while the children of Alcestis mourn. This bizarre incongruity drops our brain into an emotional quandary: Is Hercules's inappropriate behavior comic—or tragic? Awkwardly funny—or uncomfortably disturbing? It's hard to say. So, we pause in a state of heightened self-consciousness, studying the characters onstage and surveying our own emotional responses, attempting to puzzle through *what* we should be feeling—and *why*.

This detached analysis of emotion wasn't what Athenian audiences had come to expect from tragedy. But it's a first step toward treating the numbness of type 2 PTSD. To alleviate that numbness, we need to relax our emotion brake, which, as psychiatrists have discovered recently, can be accomplished by a two-step therapy:

Step one is for us to look at photographs of people experiencing emotions—and to explain what the emotions are for: "That's grief; it helps people process trauma. That's fear; it helps keep people safe from danger. That's hope; it helps people stay positive in dark times. That's joy; it helps people celebrate their lives."

This procedure turns us into a kind of psychiatrist, diagnosing emotions from a clinical remove. And because the clinical remove occurs in our prefrontal cortex—the same brain region that's suppressing our feelings—its neural effect is to calm our overactive emotion brake. Our prefrontal cortex learns, from a safe distance, that emotion isn't an alien threat to our existence. It's something we can understand.

Step two is to engage in an activity that stimulates love, gratitude, awe, or another positive emotion. This fills our brain with pleasurable feelings that demonstrate to our brain that emotions aren't inherently bad. They bring psychological benefits that our neurons can experience firsthand.

The same two-step therapy is provided by *Alcestis*. The first step—the clinical analysis—is encouraged by the tragicomic tone, which prompts our brain to ask: *What am I feeling? And why?* So, unlike a classic tragedy, which triggers raw emotion in our limbic system, Euripides's tragicomedy inspires meta-feeling in our prefrontal cortex, jumping over our locked brake to loosen the frozen neural circuitry behind.

The second step—the positive emotion—is prompted by the play's happy ending, which begins when Hercules is shaken out of his oblivious revelry by a servant who informs him that he's desecrating a house of mourning. Mortified, Hercules decides to atone by rescuing Alcestis from hell, transforming her funeral into a joyous onstage reunion that seeps into the thawing circuits of our brain's prefrontal cortex, gently releasing our emotion brake.

It's not clear whether Euripides engineered this treatment intentionally. If he did, then there would be an enormous elegance to the historical evolution of Greek tragedy: after Aeschylus and Sophocles had devised a popular treatment for type 1 PTSD, Euripides focused his attention on those survivors suffering from type 2. But whatever Euripides might have been thinking when he engineered tragicomedy, it's clear that later generations didn't grasp the purpose of his new technology. For century after century, through later antiquity, the Renaissance, and the dawning of modernity, Euripides's tragicomedies remained on theater's fringe. They were never associated—even by the scholars who praised them—with any special medicinal effect.

And then as the twentieth century reached its midpoint, there was a revival of interest in the therapeutic power of *Alcestis*. In 1949 Euripides's innovation was resuscitated—twice.

1949 Euripides

Why 1949?

It's not entirely clear. But the recent horrors of the Second World War had left millions of survivors struggling with posttraumatic stress, encouraging the therapeutic innovations of James G. Taylor and James Wolpe, and prompting a strong demand for traditional literary trage- dies. In February 1949 Laurence Olivier, Vivien Leigh, and London's Old Vic Theatre Company staged a popular revival of Sophocles's *Anti- gone*. Later in the year, Arthur Miller's *Death of a Salesman* won a Tony Award on Broadway.

And alongside these classic remedies for trauma were birthed a pair of others more curious: T. S. Eliot's *The Cocktail Party* and Beckett's *Waiting for Godot*, both completed in early 1949. The two plays were so idiosyn- cratically different that audiences missed their shared roots in Euripides. But the roots were there. In 1951 Eliot revealed: "No one of my acquain- tance . . . recognized the source of my story in the *Alcestis* of Euripides. In fact, I have had to go into detailed explanation to convince them."

The "detailed explanation" can be found in Eliot's book *On Poetry and Poets*, but the brief explanation is this: Eliot updated Euripides for mod- ern sensibilities by replacing the supernatural back-from-the-dead of a deceased wife with the more realistic back-from-the-dead of a lifeless marriage. Beckett, meanwhile, was less coy about his debt to Euripides's ancient invention. The subtitle to *Waiting for Godot* is: *A Tragicomedy in Two Acts*.

After these two modern playwrights had availed themselves of Euripides's old tragicomic technology, however, they proceeded to deploy it in opposite directions:

> Beckett discarded the second stage of Euripides's invention to focus on the first: the meta-analysis of feeling. Like Alcestis, Beckett's characters in *Waiting for Godot* exist in a life-death twilight zone, talking about trauma in ways that seem simultaneously disturbing and amusing: "One daren't even laugh anymore" . . . "What about hanging ourselves?" . . . "Let's hang ourselves immediately!"

> Eliot did the reverse. He muted the first stage of Euripides's invention to emphasize the second stage: the pivot into positive emotion. Transforming a couple's divorce into a restored marriage, *The Cocktail Party* refits tragedy with a happy ending.

Both these half versions of Euripides made an impression on audiences. *The Cocktail Party* ran for more than four hundred performances on Broadway and earned a 1950 Tony Award, while *Godot* became an avant-garde sensation. Yet by splitting Euripides's therapy between them, the two plays also implied that the therapy could no longer be dispensed in full. In our modern world, we could have a realistic play with a believably happy ending, like *The Cocktail Party*. Or we could have a dissociative break from reality that never ended, like the eternal waiting, waiting, waiting of *Godot*. But we couldn't go back to the days of Euripides and have both the dissociative break and the believably happy ending. We couldn't have a character literally die—and then swing back to rescue us in a deus ex machina, like Godot appearing at the final moment to save us all from purgatory.

Except that as Alison Bechdel discovered, we could.

Completing the Therapy

In 2006 Alison Bechdel published her graphic memoir *Fun Home: A Family Tragicomic*.

Living up to its subtitle, *Fun Home* begins by interspersing a comic game of airplane with tragic meditations on the mythological death plummet of Icarus from the sky. And the memoir's following pages teem with further tragicomic devices. There are surreal moments that seem both horror and farce, such as the revelation that Bechdel's father was killed by a Sunshine bread delivery truck. There are wry juxtapositions of life and death, as when Bechdel relays the amusing story of how her father once got stuck in a muddy field—only for her to remark sardonically after his funeral that he's "stuck in the mud for good this time." There are shocks that arrive without warning and pass without resolution, like Bechdel's father suddenly striking his children or calling his wife a bitch.

After using these *Alcestis* devices to generate a mood of dissociation in our brain, Bechdel then leverages the dissociation into therapy by drawing ironic parallels between her real-life narrative and famous literary masterpieces. In one typical moment, Bechdel's character reads a line from Oscar Wilde's comic play *The Importance of Being Earnest*—"I have lost both my parents"—while she's enduring that very tragedy in her actual life. The resulting meta-literariness guides our brain into a detached analysis of the characters on the page before us. Like a psychiatrist studying a patient from a clinical remove, we trace the abusive behavior of Bechdel's father back to his own painfully repressed homosexuality. We diagnose his self-loathing. We map the geography of his suicide.

This work of dispassionate analysis dispenses the first part of the numbness remedy. Mimicking the meta-feeling of *Waiting for Godot*, it slowly loosens our brain's emotion brake. And on and on the therapy continues, right up to the final pages of *Fun Home*, where in a surprise twist, Bechdel gives us a happy ending.

The Twist into Happiness

To twist tragedy into happiness, *Fun Home* copies Euripides's narrative blueprint: a voyage into death that redeems a lost soul. But to suit this ancient myth to our modern sensibilities, Bechdel follows T. S. Eliot in making it eminently realistic. The voyage into death isn't a physical decent into the Greek underworld; instead, it takes the form of Bechdel imaginatively traveling back through the hellscape of her past.

That voyage leads Bechdel to uncover the startling irony that her father's tragic destruction was her own redemption. Partly, the irony is a "literal" fact: "If my father had 'come out' in his youth, if he had not met and married my mother . . . where would that leave me?" But more profoundly, her father's closeted self-loathing is what prompts him to admire Bechdel's own openness about being gay. That admiration stokes Bechdel's self-confidence, making her feel like the parent to her father's lost child. And it leads to the uplifting reversal of the memoir's last scene:

BUT IN THE TRICKY REVERSE NARRATION THAT IMPELS OUR ENTWINED STORIES, HE WAS THERE TO CATCH ME WHEN I LEAPT.

This scene treats our brain to two happy emotions: wonder and gratitude. (For their blueprints, see the introduction and chapter 15.) The wonder comes from a mind-bending *stretch*: Bechdel's father, the frustrated Icarus-author, tragically plunges into the sea . . . where he comically catches his Daedalus-child, the artist who will create the literary work that he could not. Meanwhile, the gratitude comes from Bechdel's heroic generosity: Bechdel *thanks* her father, inviting us to thank him too.

The resulting cocktail of sentiment carries us into the therapy's second phase. Steeping our brain in positive emotion, it encourages our prefrontal cortex to lighten its grip on our limbic system, thawing numbness with the good of feeling.

Using the "Clinical Joy" Yourself

In 1997, archeologists were excavating a cave on the south side of Sala-mis, an island roughly ten miles west of Athens, when they discovered a little clay pot. The pot was very old, dating back to the days of the last Greek tragedies. And it was engraved with the name Euripides.

Could this have been the same Euripides who authored *Alcestis*? If so, it would confirm a legend, recorded by the ancient historian Philo-chorus, that Euripides wrote his tragicomedies in a lonely island cave. It was said that Euripides was driven there, in anger and in anguish, after the Athenian public rejected his theatrical innovations. Year after year, the playwright would premiere an extraordinary new literary device at the City Dionysia. Yet unlike Aeschylus and Sophocles, who took home dozens of ivy crowns between them, Euripides saw his plays dismissed repeatedly by audiences. Until finally, he gave up, abandoning Attica to die amid the northern wilds.

But that unhappy ending wasn't the story's final act. Because in a surprise twist, a freshly inked playscript was found inside the cave of the departed Euripides. The playscript was titled *The Bacchae*. And when it was performed posthumously at the City Dionysia, it won the ivy crown. Like Alcestis, Euripides had returned from beyond the grave. His trag-edy of cave-island detachment had ended with a pivot into happiness.

If you'd like more of that pivot yourself, you can use Bechdel's blue-print to engineer your own literary remedy for numbness. Start by se-lecting a story with a happy ending. The story can be any genre: from memoir, to comic book, to novel, to film. Then read the story clinically. Pretend you're a psychiatrist analyzing the characters. Jot down each negative emotion—and speculate on its origins. Observe each positive emotion—and mark down its benefits. And when the ending arrives, set down your doctorly notes to embrace the sentimental uplift.

If you don't experience that uplift at first, don't abandon the tragi-comic therapy. The more you analyze the feelings of literary characters, and the more you open yourself to the cheerful finales of literature, the more your inner emotion brake will loosen.

Gently thawing out the heart and resurrecting buried joy inside.

TWENTY-FOUR

Live Your Dream

Tina Fey's 30 Rock, *a Dash of
"Supercalifragilisticexpialidocious," and
the Invention of the Wish Triumphant*

I n a tumbledown castle on the drylands south of Madrid, a wish dwindled to dust.

The wish had been wished by Alonso Quixano, a fiftyish Spanish gentleman with such an appetite for fiction that he pawned his estates and dined frugally on lettuce so that he could afford to purchase every adventure book then in existence. All day (and all night, when he couldn't sleep), Quixano would turn the woodcut pages of his precious books, losing himself amid dragons, enchantresses, and creatures fantastic. Until one sunny afternoon, the fantastic came real: Quixano heard a rumble of feet across the arid plain beyond his plaster battlements. And instantly, he knew: *Those feet are the feet of giants!* So, he rushed out from his library, and there in the kitchen, where his crockery had been, he saw a suit of hand-forged armor. Donning it, Quixano then flew to his stables, finding a horse, eyes bright with courage. And next to the horse, a squire bowed deep, extending a lance of whitest steel: *This is your weapon, my good knight, Don Quixote*.

For many fine days, Quixano was known to the world as the good knight Don Quixote. He rode hard, battled monsters, and defended the weak. Until at last, Quixano was informed by a priest that he'd imagined it all. His dashing horse was really a nag, his youthful squire was really a middle-aged fool, and his giant foes were really agricultural machinery. Disenchanted, Quixano repented his happy hours of heroism. He swore off the books that had led him to dream, and he died, clear eyed, beneath the sheets of a rickety bed.

This journey out of wish is recounted in Miguel de Cervantes's seventeenth-century novel *The Ingenious Knight, Don Quixote of La Mancha*, which is now regarded by many wise scholars as the greatest novel in history. And like those wise scholars, you can celebrate the disenchantment of Alonso Quixano. You can give up your books and die in your bed.

Or, if you'd rather not, you can use the technology of *Don Quixote* to do the opposite: you can make your fantasy come true instead.

The Technology of *Don Quixote*

To prevent us from repeating Alonso Quixano's mistake of confusing fantasy and reality, Cervantes infuses *Don Quixote* with an ingenious literary technology: the Story in the Story.

The Story in the Story was not Cervantes's invention. It had existed from literature's earliest days. But prior to Cervantes, its narrative gearings had always been used to transport us from one storyworld into another:

> The ancient Egyptian *Westcar Papyrus* uses a Story in the Story to convey us from the court of Pharaoh Khufu into the fifth dynasty's magical-musical future.

> The Sanskrit *Mahābhārata* uses a Story in the Story to carry us from a fragrant Ashoka rain forest into the fire temples of the kingdom of Kuru.

Cervantes's innovation is to hitch up the transportation. Instead of ushering us smoothly into a different narrative geography, he rejiggers the Story in the Story to keep returning our focus to the moment of transition, making us conscious of the line between two realities and prompting our brain to wonder: *Is one reality more real? Is one more fictional?*

The most dramatic example of Cervantes's innovation occurs in part 2 of *Don Quixote*, which went to press in 1615, ten years after part 1 had become a best seller. Hewing faithfully to this actual publishing history, part 2 begins with the don being informed that part 1 of his adventures is for sale in nearby stores. The don is astonished but soon finds that it's true: he keeps running into folk who've read about him in Cervantes's first book.

This is a mind bender, not just for the don but for us. A fictional character is riding around the world where his fictions have been published—which is to say, a fictional character is riding around the factual world. So, is the don real? Or is the real world a fiction? Our brain flutters back and forth, inspecting both possibilities, trying to sort out the meta-textual puzzle.

When suddenly the puzzle becomes more intense: as the don is trotting about, he hears that the readers of part 1 are so eager for more of his story that they've begun consuming a counterfeit sequel. This sounds like a prank on the don, but in actual fact, the counterfeit existed. In 1614, a year before Cervantes handed the official part 2 to his printer, a fraudulent part 2 had been published under the pseudonym Alonso Fernández de Avellaneda.

That untrue sequel by a sham author is attacked by a fictional Cervantes in the true preface to the actual 1615 sequel. And when Don Quixote himself stumbles upon the fake sequel, he becomes furious. "Books are better, the truer they are," he angrily informs his imaginary squire.

Determined to expose the pseudonymous work as a fiction, the don then makes a valiant decision: he will consciously depart from the plot of the bogus part 2. In that unauthorized plot, Don Quixote had journeyed east to the basilica-city of Zaragoza, as he'd implied he was doing at the end of the actual part 1. But now the Don Quixote of the true part 2 will go instead to Barcelona. When he appears there, everyone will see with their own two eyes that the other Don Quixote is a fraud.

This is one of the most involuted literary mind twisters in history: an unreal character sets out to disprove a false fiction by revealing himself in the real world through a genuine fiction.

And yet as complicated as the mind twister is, it does something simple to our brain.

Our Brain on *Don Quixote*

When we're born, we're all like Don Quixote: we can't tell fantasy from reality. But a few years later, we begin to tease the two apart. Children as young as three will insist, "Dragons aren't real!" And by the age of four, most children are committed to distinguishing between pretend and truth.

This doesn't mean that four-year-olds always make the distinction accurately; monsters lurk under their beds, and imaginary friends follow them everywhere. But the same holds true for us adults. We too have our superstitions and our magical thoughts. The important thing is that we know that there *is* a clear line between fantasy and reality, even if we don't always enforce it correctly.

Our awareness of this line is made possible by our brain's mental model of the world. That model is elastic enough to grow over time, enlarging our understanding of what life can contain, and it can also encompass local variants that enable us to transition from the rules of one environment to the next. But to provide us with a stable footing for action, there's a limit to how much the model can flex. And when the model is flatly contradicted by something we see—such as a green sun, or a ten-legged cat, or a talking eye—it triggers our brain's anterior cingulate cortex (or ACC), that error detector we learned about in chapter 20, to send out a warning: *Hey! We're hallucinating!*

After our ACC sends out this warning, it usually relaxes and lets the decision-making portions of our brain take care of things. If it didn't, we could never enjoy novels about magic or other fantastical things; our error detector would incessantly yell, *That's fake! That's fake! That's fake!*, making it impossible for our brain to get engrossed. But even though our ACC usually goes quiet after one warning, there is one variety of fantasy novel that keeps agitating it. That variety is the *badly executed* fantasy novel. The badly executed fantasy novel keeps breaking its internal story rules: characters act inconsistently, and spells violate their own laws of sorcery. Each time one of these contradictions occurs, our error detector cries out, *This couldn't really happen!* Until at last, we toss aside the book as poorly imagined hackwork.

This same incessant ACC shouting is triggered by *Don Quixote*. Like a ham-fisted fantasy novel, *Don Quixote* keeps contradicting the rules of its storyworld: fictional things keep showing up in factual places, and factual things in fictional. Yet even as our ACC bellows again and again at us, continually rupturing our experience of fantasy immersion, the decision-making portions of our brain realize, *This novel isn't hackwork. The scholars were right: it's quite clever, actually!* That realization stops us from chucking away the novel, even as our ACC keeps alerting us to further violations. So, the overall effect of reading *Don Quixote* is to be reminded again and again of the line that separates reality from fantasy, ramping up our awareness of the distinction between fact and fiction.

This heightened awareness is the neural elixir engineered by Miguel de Cervantes. Its sensible purpose is to keep us from ending up like poor Alonso Quixano; hence its glamorous reputation among scholars, all of whom have learned from books that it's dangerous to trust the things that we read.

But this de-Quixoting of our brain isn't the only thing that the literary technology of *Don Quixote* can do. In addition to making us *less* like the don, it can also transform us into the *more successful* version of the don—making us the don whose dreams are realized.

The More Successful Don

For us to achieve our dreams, we need to appreciate the line between truth and make-believe. Without the line, we'd make the don's error of believing that our fantasies are already true, charging deludedly ahead until hard reality wakes us up. But with the line intact, we can engage in a dream-come-true technique known as counterfactual thinking.

Counterfactual thinking, as its name suggests, is thinking that runs counter to the facts of life. To perform it, our brain imagines an alternate world in which a few of those facts are tweaked, allowing us to conduct a thought experiment to see how the tweaks cash out. If the cash-out is good, then our brain stops the thought experiment and returns to our actual existence, determined to make those same tweaks in reality.

Counterfactual thinking is an inborn ability of our brain, but it can be honed through practice. To practice, we need to focus on adjusting small details of our world, one at a time. That way, instead of impossibly reimagining life to suit our fancy, we learn how to construct plausible dreams that we can export more readily to the life beyond.

As scientists have discovered, there's a literary technology that can facilitate this practice. The technology is derived from the Story in the Story, and it has two parts, the first being the ancient invention known as the "Comic Wink."

The Comic Wink and Its Ancient Origins

Comedy began in Athens as an exercise in counterfactual thinking: *What would happen if we consumed more classic literature?* Or: *What would life be like if women ran the government?* The first of these thought experiments is played out in the 405 BCE comedy *The Frogs*, in which a god brings back a venerated author from the dead. The second is played out in the 411 BCE comedy *Lysistrata*, in which the women of Greece rise up to put an end to war. Both ancient comedies open our mind to alternate ways of living, and since alternate ways are often threatening, the two comedies try to relax us with jokes and physical buffoonery. *This counterfactual thinking is just a bit of fun*, the comedies assure us. *So, let's smile along and see what happens next.*

The counterfactual thinking encouraged by comedy was important to Athenian democracy, which depended for its survival on an openness to new ideas. But even when new ideas were presented in a lightly unserious format, they remained too unsettling for many would-be democratic minds to entertain. So, to tease open those minds, playwrights invented a potent reality-suspending device: the Comic Wink.

The Comic Wink is any moment where an actor breaks the stage's fourth wall to assure us: None of this is really real. A Comic Wink can be as simple as a wordless glance or as intricate as this speech, delivered by the slave character Pseudolus in the Roman comedy that bears his name:

> I know, I know. You're thinking that I'm a two-bit charlatan. But I assure you, all my impossible promises will come true. What kind of a comedy would this be if they didn't?

Comic Winks such as this comfort our brain: *Don't worry! The play knows that it's just a thing of make-believe. That's why it winked! It's not actually trying to make us consume more classic literature or put women in charge! It's just a big ha-ha spectacular.* And once our brain is thusly comforted, we can then slip into the play's alternate reality, exploring a world unlike our own and imagining what it might be like if we did things differently.

Since the days of *Lysistrata* and *Pseudolus*, the Comic Wink has remained an integral part of mind-expanding comedy. It was incorporated into modern American television with the 1950s sitcom *I Love Lucy*, which gently raised all sorts of alternative possibilities for mid-century America—What if women had jobs? What if marriages were inter-ethnic?—within a winking theatrical frame that insisted upon its own playfulness.

And as effective as the Comic Wink has proved at getting human brains to open themselves to outside ways of thinking, it's only the first half of the dream-come-true technology that modern authors have derived from the Story in the Story.

The second half is the invention known as the "Reality Shifter."

The Dream Come True, Part 2

The Reality Shifter also traces its origins to the ancient comic stage, but this time to the exaggerated yet still-believable worlds of Greek and Roman New Comedy. As the invention's name suggests, its power is to make the fantastic seem real. But unlike the books in Don Quixote's library, the Reality Shifter doesn't entirely *remove* the line between fantasy and reality. Instead, it more subtly *moves* the line.

To accomplish this, the Reality Shifter reverses the Story in the Story mechanism of the Comic Wink. The Comic Wink starts in a fantasyland—and then breaks the fourth wall to gesture *out* to the reality beyond. The Reality Shifter starts in the real world—and then drifts *in* to fantasy, gently pulling the boundary of reality with it.

You can experience this boundary pull by reading part 2 of *Don Quixote*, which starts in the real world, where the don's adventures have been published in a book, before edging us into a "real world" where that book is thumbed through by the don. And after *Don Quixote*, the Reality Shifter's blueprint was tweaked and expanded by Cervantes's many literary imitators, until eventually it became the basis of a major new genre of fiction: modern fantasy.

Modern fantasy, like traditional fantasy, encourages our brain to imagine things unreal. But where traditional fantasy wildly rewrites reality, flooding our neurons with spellcrafts and beings enchanted, modern fantasy is more restrained. It takes our real world precisely as it is, and then folds in one or two lightly fantastic elements that seem like they *could* be real. So, instead of providing a grand, imaginative escape from reality, modern fantasy provides a slight, imaginative *enrichment* of reality, encouraging us to ponder a world that might actually be.

This new fantasy genre began to take hold in the nineteenth century with works such as E. T. A. Hoffmann's short story "The Sandman" (1816), which opens with a realistic sequence of letters in which a young man reveals that when he was a child, he believed that he'd witnessed the experiments of a murderous alchemist. These letters are set in a world just like the world of E. T. A. Hoffmann and his contemporaries, so they make us think: *Of course, that's exactly the way life is. When we're children, we have wild imaginations about alchemists and other nonsense stuff.*

But then the letters end, and a narrator arrives to tell us that after the young man finished his correspondence, he caught sight of the alchemist once again. And giving chase, the young man discovered that the alchemist had now constructed a windup girl of such mechanical intricacy that she seemed to be an actual person of flesh and blood.

With this, the story catches our brain in a Reality Shifter. We've slipped from the real world of the young man's letters into a "real world" that has a single counterfactual tweak: a girl with a hidden clockwork heart. So, when we put down the story to return to our own "reality," our brain is nudged to wonder: *Are some of the people around me intricate machines? Have they been engineered so elegantly that they've tricked me into thinking that they're human?*

The Paired Effect of the Comic Wink and the Reality Shifter

The Comic Wink and the Reality Shifter guide our brain through the two separate actions of counterfactual thinking.

The Comic Wink ushers us into a world of make-believe where we can tweak reality to see what happens. The Reality Shifter allows us to carry a make-believe tweak back into the actual world, where we can put the tweak to use. So, to convey our brain through the full action of counterfactual thinking, literature simply needs to combine these two inventions, giving us a Story in the Story that alternates between wink-winking and reality shifting.

This feat was pulled off in the twentieth century by the Marx Brothers' *Horse Feathers*, Disney's *Mary Poppins*, Joss Whedon's *Buffy the Vampire Slayer*, and other lightly fantastic comic works that made our brain go: *What if?* And then one day in the early twenty-first century, the comedy author Tina Fey wondered, *What if I went further? What if I maximized both the Comic Wink and the Reality Shifter by pushing the worlds of reality and fantasy to their extremes?*

The result of this counterfactual What-if was the television sitcom *30 Rock*, aired from 2006 to 2013 on NBC network. To maximize the authentic feel of its real world, *30 Rock* abandons the old sitcom standby of three cameras on a soundstage, opting instead for a single camera that roams freely through the actual streets of New York City. And to maximize the imaginative possibilities of its fantasy world, *30 Rock* constructs its Story in the Story as a sketch-comedy stage, providing an infinitely flexible alternate reality that can be used for endless thought experiments.

Once *30 Rock* has established its two worlds, it proceeds to carry us back and forth between them, using Comic Winks to ease us into fantasy and Reality Shifters to then lightly budge the fantasy-reality boundary. This double action begins with the pilot episode's opening shot, which reveals our hero, Liz Lemon, standing in line at a New York hot dog cart . . . when all of a sudden an impatient jerk cuts the line, prompting Liz to thwart the jerk by taking out her credit card and buying all the hot dogs first.

Immediately, our ACC goes active: *No one would ever really do that credit card thing! It's just a fantasy that people have!* Heeding this warning, our brain starts to think about grabbing the remote; it doesn't want to waste its precious time on a poorly constructed fiction that pretends to be the true New York but isn't.

Yet before we can change the channel, our brain is relaxed by a

Comic Wink: Liz Lemon sweeps through the streets in a meta-theat-rical musical number where she goofily hands out unwanted hot dogs to the residents of the five boroughs. With this Comic Wink, *30 Rock* reassures us: *That whole bit with the credit card was meant to be absurd; this televised comedy is a little make-believe break from reality.* And our brain, persuaded that the show's creators know what they're doing, forgets the warning from our ACC and crosses the line into fantasy.

The instant our brain crosses the line, it's greeted by a Reality Shifter. The Reality Shifter begins when *30 Rock*'s main camera focuses on a sec-ond camera that's filming a comedy sketch. This camera-on-camera mo-ment budges the fantasy-reality border by telling our brain: *The world of the main camera is more real than the world of the second camera.* At which point, the main camera pulls back to introduce us to Kenneth Ellen Parcell.

Who is Kenneth Ellen Parcell? Well, he's a tour guide at 30 Rock, the real-life headquarters of the real TV network NBC. So, is Kenneth Ellen Parcell real too? He certainly seems real to our brain. After all, he's filmed by the main camera. But, really, Kenneth Ellen Parcell is *not* real. He's a comic character who's not fully equipped for modern existence. In his own words:

> "Sir, you sound like the mall Santas when they come back from lunch."

> "I don't drink hot liquids of any kind. That's the devil's tempera-ture."

> "What is happening to me?"

Kenneth Ellen Parcell may not be as over the top as the sketch-comedy caricatures on the second camera. But he's just nudged our brain's sense of reality one degree into fantasy.

This Comic Wink–Reality Shift combo is then followed by more, like the one where our hero meets her new boss, Jack Donaghy. Jack Donaghy immediately seems too ridiculous to be real. He kicks down a wall, announcing that the old boss is "dead," and sparking our ACC to go active: *This is <u>not</u> the true NBC. It's a lie, lie, lie.* So, once again, *30 Rock* calms down our brain with a string of meta-theatrical Comic Winks that culminate with Jack Donaghy's Story in the Story pitch for the General Electric Trivection oven:

> The GE Trivection oven cooks perfect food five times faster than a conventional oven. . . . With three kinds of heat, you can cook a turkey in twenty-two minutes.

Donaghy punctuates the word *turkey* by looking almost directly into the camera with an ebullient grin. Moments later, he's cartoonishly introducing himself as "the new vice president of East Coast television and microwave oven programming."

These Comic Winks prompt the decision-making portions of our brain to relax our ACC: *It's okay. This television show isn't attempting to deceive us; it's just some comic fun.* So, once again, we slip into fantasy—at which point, we're hit by another Reality Shifter: our hero Liz Lemon lies down, explaining, "Sometimes when I have these stress dreams, if I go to sleep in the dream, I come out of it." But our hero doesn't wake up; the stress dream goes on. And since our hero is real, and since she's in the dream, everything in the dream also comes to seem a little more real. Making us wonder: Could Jack Donaghy really exist? Is it possible that GE, which does, after all, own a controlling stake in NBC, would send an appliance executive to turn an NBC show into an oven advertisement?

Yes. It is possible. Maybe it hasn't happened yet, but it could. Or at least it seems so to our brain. Because now we've started counterfactual thinking. We're suspending fact and then shifting it, exploring imaginative possibilities.

All of this pausing and moving reality is a big mental workout. But it's a healthy workout. Because it's helping our own dreams come true.

The Science of Making Dreams Come True

To make a dream come true, our brain needs two things. One, it needs the will to work at the dream. And two, it needs a plan that can turn fantasy into reality.

Our brain gets both these things from practicing counterfactual thinking—*even when the counterfactual thinking has nothing to do with our specific dreams.*

How can this be? Well, for starters, neuroscientists have shown that counterfactual thinking of all kinds makes our brain believe that it's possible to change reality. And that belief in turn increases our willingness to try living our dreams.

Belief alone, of course, is not enough to make a dream come true; just remember the fate of poor Alonso Quixano. But scientists have also shown that exercises in counterfactual thinking can boost our ability to imagine creative ways to translate fantasy into reality. In one ingenious experiment, scientists handed people three items: a candle, a box of tacks, and a book of matches.

Then the scientists asked, "Can you affix the candle to a corkboard wall in such a way that the lit candle doesn't drip wax on the table below?"

Most people can't solve this puzzle on their first try. Less than 10 percent do. But if you use Tina Fey's invention, then the odds are that you *will* solve the puzzle. In fact, scientists have discovered that a little counterfactual brain exercising increases your odds of solving the candle problem by about 900 percent. Imagine that: a few minutes spent viewing *30 Rock* can make you dramatically more likely to achieve the dream of keeping a table wax-free.

(And if you can't do that viewing right now, don't give up on the dream; the author of this excellent chapter has himself watched *30 Rock* dozens of times, and, having thusly become a grandmaster of counter-factual thinking, he will soon reveal the candle solution to you.)

So, by leading our brain through the two steps of counterfactual thinking, *30 Rock* increases our belief in our ability to change the world; *and* it improves the problem-solving skills we need to make change a reality. It gives us the will and then gives us a way.

Using the "Wish Triumphant" Yourself

The first episode of *30 Rock* doesn't dispense one Comic Wink and one Reality Shifter. It doses us up again and again, culminating with the one-two injection of the episode's last scene. This scene opens with the wink-wink of an absurdly fake cat lady sketch. And it then focuses its main camera on the reality-shifting Tracy Jordan.

Tracy Jordan is a washed-up movie actor who not so very long ago was a neglected foster kid with nothing but his dreams. And when Tracy Jordan arrives on *30 Rock*'s TV soundstage, he continues to have nothing but his dreams. He possesses no script, no prepared comic routines, no plan at all. All he's got is a fantasy of making the "real" studio audience cheer.

And lo and behold, that fantasy comes to pass. In seconds, Tracy Jordan has the audience yelling, "We love you, Tracy!" And they really do. They roar with approval at whatever he does. He takes off his shirt, he dangles his arm, he writhes his naked abdomen, and the audience goes wild.

Could this really happen? Could a former foster kid barge onto a prime-time TV set and make the world love him, simply by being him-self? Yes, our brain thinks. It *could* happen. After all, that's what dreams do. With a wink and a shift, they come true.

If you'd like more of that dream coming true, get your own brain counterfactual thinking. Warm it up with some classic Comic Winks, such as Steven Sondheim's *A Funny Thing Happened on the Way to the Forum* or Mel Brooks's *Blazing Saddles*. Then feed it a few Reality Shift-ers, such as Edgar Allan Poe's "The Black Cat" or Henry James's *Turn of the Screw*. And once you've got the two halves of your neuro wish fulfiller humming, combine them by watching all 130 episodes of *30 Rock*—or by dipping into a few other meta-comic modern television shows such as *Miranda* or *My Crazy Ex-Girlfriend* or *Broad City*.

You'll know you've got your head wink-shifting when it can solve all the world's candle problems . . .

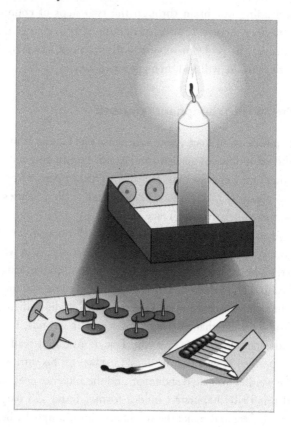

. . . just like the good knight Alonso Quixano would do.

TWENTY-FIVE

Lessen Your Lonely

Elena Ferrante's My Brilliant Friend,
Mario Puzo's The Godfather, *and the*
Invention of the Childhood Opera

O n a black cobblestone street in the old heart of Naples, Italy, lies a pink-walled museum fronted with palm trees. And inside that museum, in a sun-splashed great hall that once stabled the cavalry of Italian kings, sits a cracked marble sculpture of a writer who never existed.

The nonexistent writer's name was Orpheus. He was dreamed into being by ancient Indo-European nomads on the steppes between the Black Sea and the mountains of the Balkans. And in that distant age, he became a legend for his loneliness.

The legend went like this: Orpheus had fallen in love with the oak nymph Eurydice. But on the day of their nuptials, Eurydice was slain by a viper's bite, berefting Orpheus of his eternal partner. So terrible was that separation to Orpheus that he wrote a lament that broke the hearts of the gods themselves. All the wild beasts wept, and the forests did, too, and even the sun. And for millennia, the world continued to weep for Orpheus. His legend was retold in antique poems, in Renaissance operas, and in that modern pink-walled museum, where for year after year, tour guides would dutifully repeat the sculpture's tragic story: "This is Orpheus's last look at his love before she slips into the underworld, leaving him forever in loneliness."

Until one day in Naples, the loneliness was cured.

The cure came from a woman who was born less than three miles from the museum's palm trees, in a scorched orange ghetto that bristled with Fascista tenements and iron-barred balconies. The name of that woman was Elena Ferrante. In her teens, she heard the legend of Orpheus in a faded linoleum classroom at the Liceo Classico Garibaldi. And she learned that she had many things in common with Orpheus.

To begin with, she was also a writer—who never existed. You see, "Elena Ferrante" was the pen name of a Neapolitan novelist who preferred to stay hidden, shrouded in whisper and myth.

But that wasn't the most important thing that Elena Ferrante had in common with Orpheus. Their deepest, most profound connection was that they both realized the power of music. Orpheus had used that power to make hearts sick with loneliness.

Elena Ferrante would use that power to invent the remedy.

The Power of Music

Across the gladed vales of Greek antiquity, everyone knew that Orpheus's secret to stirring the tears of beast and god had been to set poetry to melody, creating the world's first musical literature: "O myth-made Orpheus, father of song, son of the harp of Apollo." Over the ensuing centuries, as Greece was conquered by Rome, and as Rome itself collapsed, the enchanted tunes of Orpheus vanished into myth, never to grace mortal ears again. Yet Orpheus's underlying invention wasn't lost forever. It would be rediscovered during the twilight of the Italian Renaissance.

In those dusky days, Florence opened its gates to a famed tenor and keyboardist whose birthname was Jacopo Peri but who preferred to style himself as Il Zazzerino—"the little shock of hair." At the turn of the seventeenth century, Il Zazzerino collaborated with a local poet to write *L'Euridice*, a play about the tragic lament that Orpheus sang for his soulmate, Eurydice. And drawing inspiration from that tragic lament, Zazzerino imbued his play with music. Harpsichords and lutes played ritornellos between the scenes, and Orpheus stepped onstage to lift his voice in aria: "Death has quenched the light, and now I'm in hell's shadows, cold and alone."

At the sound of that aria, the hearts of Florence ached with loneliness, and so potent was the ache that Il Zazzerino's audience declared that he'd outdone even the original Orpheus. He'd invented a new genre of musical literature, one of such soulful grandeur that it would henceforth be known simply as "the Work."

Or in its original Italian: *opera*.

The Innovation of Opera

L'Euridice is the world's oldest surviving opera. And it is indeed an innovation.

What makes opera an innovation isn't simply that it mixes music and theater. It's the way that opera does the mixing. Prior to opera, music and theater had been mingled by ancient stage plays and Renaissance masques, yielding melodic narratives such as the choral chants of Greek tragedy and the pageant songs of Shakespeare's *A Midsummer Night's Dream*. But in those earlier works, the music had worked in unison with the dramatic performance: a melancholy flute strain would usher in a character's lament or a rousing chorus would punctuate a couple's bliss, joining with the main plot to emphasize one common note of feeling.

Opera's innovation was to add a second note. Instead of orchestrating choirs that sang in unison, Il Zazzerino composed characters who voiced rival arias and choruses that crooned conflicting chords. His music didn't lilt a single tune; it clanged in warring twos.

These discordant clangs allowed Il Zazzerino to do something unprecedented in a musical drama: use music to tell its own story. Story emerges from conflict; conflict between (or within) characters is the engine that drives plots ahead. So, by establishing musical conflicts, Il Zazzerino was able to engineer musical stories that arced from inciting cymbal crashes into melodic harpsicord conclusions, enriching his drama's overall narrative with acoustic mini-journeys of agitation into harmony.

What was special about these musical stories within the story? What could their aural narratives add to the theater's overall plot? Il Zazzerino wasn't quite able to say. But a few years later, another Italian composer figured it out.

The Power of the Musical Story in the Story

Il Zazzerino had been too timid. Such was the epiphany that struck Claudio Monteverdi, another early-seventeenth-century Florentine musician. Monteverdi had an active mind and a talent for stringed instruments. And as he was listening to *L'Euridice*, he realized that he'd heard all its clashing notes before.

Those clashing notes had been standardized by earlier generations of Italian musicians (such as the monkish organist Gioseffo Zarlino and the fur-merchant-turned-madrigalist Giovanni Pierluigi da Palestrina) as acceptable discords; abrasive but not *too* much. So, when audiences listened to *L'Euridice*, they recognized all its clangs. And they knew exactly how long the clangs would last before resolving into standard harmonies.

This old-fashioned approach muted the power of Il Zazzerino's innovation. Like a tale that telegraphed its ending, it dampened the music's dramatic tension, diminishing the suspense and surprise of its sonic storytelling. So, Claudio Monteverdi decided to take Il Zazzerino's innovation and innovate it again. He would startle audiences with original clangs. And he would stretch out the clanging far longer than Il Zazzerino had dared.

With these bold resolutions in mind, Monteverdi wrote a new opera about Orpheus, entitled *L'Orfeo*. And when the opera premiered in 1606, it immediately made the audience wince. Their eardrums were bombarded with unfamiliar musical crashes, strangely sour notes, and arias that shattered together like glass. On and on the cacophony went, until the audience began to think that harmony was forever departed. There would be no sweetly fluted resolution, only the horror of sound gone awry.

Monteverdi, it seemed, had gone too far, spoiling music into noise. But then something most extraordinary happened. The audience stopped wincing and started smiling. They found themselves liking Monteverdi's clang-ridden opera. No, more than that, they found themselves *bonding* with Monteverdi's clang-ridden opera. They felt connected to it in a way that they'd never felt connected to a story before.

Monteverdi had accomplished an operatic breakthrough—and a scientific breakthrough too.

The Science of Monteverdi's Musical Method

As Monteverdi discovered, music can make friends with our brain. The befriending occurs when the pleasant sounds of musical harmonies trigger our brain's caudate nucleus to prime and then fire dopamine neurons in our nucleus accumbens, dosing us up with neurochemical sweet. That sweet shares its basic flavor with nicotine, heroin, and cocaine. And it's why we get hooked on our favorite songs. We miss their company when the music stops—and feel less lonely when it fills our ears again.

The befriending touch of music was discovered in prehistoric times: bone flutes date to at least forty thousand years ago, and long before that, early humans discovered the heart charm of birdsong. And such was the comfort bestowed by these musics upon the lonely heart that archaic composers set out to identify a few agreeable harmonies that could banish the pain of solitude forever.

As we now know, this archaic search for a musical panacea has a biological flaw: our brain doesn't release more and more dopamine sweet when it's given more and more of the same perfect harmony. Instead, our brain gets bored and releases no sweet at all. That's because our brain has been conditioned by hundreds of millions of years of global change to evolve into an insatiable seeker, always on the hunt for the next good thing. So, once we get ahold of something that we want, our brain stops wanting it as much. Which is why the first bite of desert always tastes the best. And why the same harmony played again . . . and again . . . and again starts to sound increasingly dull.

The dullness of harmony repeated was quickly discovered by composers. So, for thousands of years before Monteverdi, they focused on finding *new* harmonies. All across the ancient world, the Middle Ages, and the early Renaissance, composers expanded the range of pleasant-sounding chords, inventing ever-fresh tunes with which to befriend our brain. But as creative as all these endeavors were, they missed the real neural secret to increasing the bonding power of music. That secret isn't to satisfy our brain's appetite for fresh harmonies; it's to *defer* satisfaction, making our brain wait.

When our brain is made to wait for something it wants, it doesn't move on to wanting the next good thing. Instead, our caudate nucleus primes more and more dopamine neurons, increasing our ache for the something withheld. This ache is what we feel when a song uses musical dissonances to defer harmony. Deep in our brain, we start to crave the delayed harmony with a hunger that grows deeper and deeper the longer that the musical dissonances clang on. But still, the music withholds, feeding us new sonic discords that trigger further dopamine neurons to prime. Until at last, the harmony arrives, and our primed neurons all fire together, saturating our brain with dopamine ecstasy and bonding us profoundly to the song.

There are limits, of course, to this bonding technique. Some musical clangs can be so harsh that we cover our ears. Some dissonances can persist for so long that we slowly tune out, no longer perceiving the music as music. And all of our brains have their own internal range of tolerances; what seems mild to a punk guitarist might feel unbearable to a classical violinist. But as a general rule, music that pushes our neural limits, feeding us more sonic tension than we're expecting, will deliver more payoff. It will give us a bigger kick of dopamine when the harmony finally arrives.

Monteverdi figured this out. He realized that our connection to music is intensified by neural agitation and delay. That's why he had his Orpheus sing: "Love feels sweeter when it follows sadness." And that's why he crammed *L'Orfeo* with strange trombone clashes and lute harmonies deferred, stirring up his audience's hearts—and winning their love through discord.

Monteverdi called this operatic innovation the second method. And, following the success of *L'Orfeo*, the second method enjoyed its own encore. Its technique of encouraging emotional bonding through musical clangs was expanded by successive waves of opera composers, culminating in the nineteenth century with masterworks of sonic tension such as Giuseppe Verdi's *Rigoletto* (1851) and Richard Wagner's *Tristan und Isolde* (1865).

And the operas of Verdi and Wagner weren't the only groundbreaking nineteenth-century works born of Monteverdi's second method. In the mid-1840s, at the very moment that a youthful Verdi was composing his first fugues and canons, the second method inspired a literary breakthrough that accomplished the seemingly impossible feat of transporting the bonding experience of opera off the stage and onto the printed page, bringing the comfort of musical companionship to hearts that dwelt in silent solitude.

You'd think that sort of breakthrough would have made its inventors famous. But, alas, it had the opposite result: it made them infamous instead.

The Path to Infamy

The first known author to make the breakthrough was the thirty-five-year-old Englishman Thomas Peckett Prest.

Prest had trained in his teens as a singer, and although he never made it into the great opera houses of Italy, he did manage to earn a billing in the gin palaces and slum saloons of London's East End. Alongside another singer or two, young Thomas would perch upon a makeshift stage and hoist his voice into the same intricate arias, duets, and ensembles that echoed through the courts of Venice and Milan.

In those grungy, drink-soaked years, Prest learned dozens of operatic songs that borrowed Monteverdi's innovation of clashing into harmony. And because Prest was eager to make a little extra cash when he wasn't bel cantoing through the midnight hours, he began publishing those operatic songs (and numerous original compositions of his own) in serial chapbooks such as *The British Pocket Vocalist* and *The Singer's Penny Magazine*.

Those penny songbooks turned a minor profit. But soon Prest was to learn of a richer sort of penny publication. That publication's technical name was the penny periodical. But it was more popularly known as the penny dreadful.

Targeted at street urchins, coal cabbies, rat catchers, costermongers, and other members of the Victorian poor and barely literate, the penny dreadful offered up weekly serial installments of long romantic sagas, supernatural horror tales, and true crime adventures. Printed on cheap paper that quickly yellowed into dust, it was the forerunner of pulp mags like *Weird Tales,* comic books like *Batman*, and cable TV series such as *The Sopranos*.

Just as the first operas were impugned as crass debasements of traditional theater, so too were penny dreadfuls impugned as crass debasements of traditional literature. Traditional literature had birthed the *Odyssey*, *Antony and Cleopatra*, and *Pride and Prejudice*. The penny dreadful responded by hatching *Varney the Vampire*, *Adventures of a Notorious Burglar*, and *The Blue Dwarf*. Yet the penny dreadful had its own hidden literary virtue. Like Dr. Frankenstein's lab (see chapter 12), its outsider status allowed it to serve as a lawless kitchen where the most outrageous experiments could be attempted. And among those experiments was one that would find its way in time onto almost every bookshelf on the globe.

The experiment began when Thomas Peckett Prest dismembered opera, cutting out Monteverdi's technique of startling dissonance and grafting it into fiction.

Opera in Fiction

In 1845 Thomas Peckett Prest and his coauthor, James Malcolm Ryder, penned the first issue of *Varney the Vampire*.

Varney is famous now as one of the earliest vampire stories in English literature. Along with works like John William Polodori's 1819 short story "The Vampyre," it helped create the market for *Dracula*, *Twilight*, and *Let the Right One In*.

But *Varney* did more than stir the modern craze for vampire fiction. In its first issue, it took Prest's operatic training and engineered that training into this:

> With a sudden rush that could not be foreseen—with a strange howling cry that was enough to awaken terror in every breast, the figure seized the long tresses of her hair, and twining them round his bony hands he held her to the bed. Then she screamed— Heaven granted her then power to scream. Shriek followed shriek in rapid succession. The bed-clothes fell in a heap by the side of the bed—she was dragged by her long silken hair completely on to it again. Her beautifully rounded limbs quivered with the agony of her soul. The glassy, horrible eyes of the figure ran over that angelic form with a hideous satisfaction—horrible

profanation. He drags her head to the bed's edge. He forces it back by the long hair still entwined in his grasp. With a plunge he seizes her neck in his fang-like teeth—a gush of blood, and a hideous sucking noise follows. *The girl has swooned, and the vampire is at his hideous repast!*

This short passage deploys all the innovations of Monteverdi's second method. There's the "sudden" and "[un]foreseen" dissonance as a hell creature grabs an angelic tress of hair. There's the polyphonic clanging of voices, as the vampire's lustful howl clashes with his victim's awful scream. And there's even Monteverdi's use of *concitato*, or "angry" repetition of a single note, over and over, with building intensity and speed: "Shriek followed shriek in rapid succession." Again and again, we hear the same clanging sound, raising our pulse in crescendo as the wicked yells of the vampire clash against the holy cries of heaven, jangling our ears and agitating our heart—until at last, the moment of conflict is over, and the gruesome resolution arrives: *"The girl has swooned, and the vampire is at his hideous repast!"*

This repurposing of Monteverdi's musical technique had a wildly potent effect on the brains of readers. It ravished their caudate nuclei—and then rewarded them with a long, sweet jolt of dopamine. The result was a breakthrough in popular storytelling. Earlier mass-produced fictions had reeled in audiences with wonder, curiosity, empathy, and suspense. (For the blueprints, see the introduction and chapters 3 and 5.) But *Varney* grabbed hold of readers in an entirely new psychological way: it *befriended* them. Bonding their hearts to the penny fiction in their hand, it convinced them that *Varney* was their boon companion.

And then that feeling of underworld partnership became even more powerful. Because the authors of *Varney* ventured beyond Monteverdi's second method to add their own penny dreadful innovation.

The Innovation of the Penny Dreadful

The publishers of penny dreadfuls didn't want us to read and reread the same chapter of *Varney the Vampire*, like it was our lifelong friend; they wanted us to dash out and buy the next newsstand issue, handing over all of our pennies. So, to induce us to hunger after *Varney's* next installment, its authors adapted Monteverdi's second method into an ingenious new literary invention: the "Partial Dopamine."

Like the second method, the Partial Dopamine agitates our neural circuitry with dissonance and clang. But unlike the second method, the Partial Dopamine doesn't resolve that tension into full harmony. It resolves the tension only partway, treating us to half a neurochemical kick—while making us crave the rest of the dopamine still primed to fire in our brain.

This crafty invention increases the intensity of our bond with fiction. We don't just feel a connection with what we're reading. We feel a need for *more* connection. We ache to go on further adventures with our new friend.

Here's how it works in the first issue of *The Demon Barber of Fleet Street*, which was written by some combination of Thomas Peckett Prest and James Malcolm Ryder one year after they'd created *Varney the Vampire*. Toward the issue's end, the demon barber Sweeney Todd is preparing to shave a new client by the name of Mr. Grant, when Todd's young assistant, Tobias Ragg, reveals inadvertently that the last man to get such a shave has just passed into oblivion, leaving only his dog behind. At which point

> Todd [said], "Will you excuse me a moment, Mr. Grant? Tobias, my lad, I just want you to lend me a hand in the parlor."
>
> Tobias followed Todd very unsuspectingly into the parlor; but when they got there and the door was closed, the barber sprang upon him like an enraged tiger, and, grappling him by the throat, he gave his head such a succession of knocks against the wainscot, that Mr. Grant must have thought that some carpenter was at work. Then he tore a handful of his hair out, after which he twisted him round, and dealt him such a kick, that he was flung sprawling into a corner of the room, and then, without a word, the barber walked out again to his customer, and he bolted his parlor door on the outside, leaving Tobias to digest the usage he had received at his leisure, and in the best way he could.

When he came back to Mr. Grant, he apologized for keeping him waiting by saying, "It became necessary, sir, to teach my new apprentice a little bit of his business. I have left him studying it now. There is nothing like teaching young folks at once."

"Ah!" said Mr. Grant, with a sigh, "I know what it is to let young folks grow wild; for although I have neither chick nor child of my own, I had a sister's son to look to—a handsome, wild, harum-scarum sort of fellow, as like me as one pea is like another. I tried to make a lawyer of him, but it wouldn't do, and it's now more than two years ago he left me altogether; and yet there were some good traits about Mark."

"Mark, sir! did you say Mark?"

"Yes, that was his name, Mark Ingestrie. God knows what's become of him."

"Oh!" said Sweeney Todd; and he went on lathering the chin of Mr. Grant.

This is a tour de force of agitated dissonance. Sweeney Todd steps calmly into the parlor, where, without warning, he subjects his "unsuspecting" assistant to a brutal assault: choking him, hammering his skull against the wall, half scalping him, and finishing him off with a boot to the back. The surprising discord excites our caudate nucleus, so that when harmony is restored a few moments later by Todd's gracious apology to Mr. Grant, we get a small dopamine kick.

Yet even as we enjoy that neurochemical sweet, we don't get the full dose primed inside our brain. After all, the tension roused up by Todd's parlor assault hasn't been totally resolved. Todd may have stopped pummeling his young assistant, but he's revealed his penchant for unannounced displays of violence. And as Todd places his razor against Mr. Grant's throat, he's given reason to get violent again.

That reason is Mr. Grant's mention of Mark Ingestrie. Mark Ingestrie was a friend of Sweeney Todd's previous client, the one whom the assistant has just been battered for mentioning. Which can only make us wonder: Is Sweeney Todd about to go on the rampage again? Is he about to do something terrible with the blade now held within his hand?

The Next Installment of the Penny Dreadful

To enjoy the rest of the dopamine stirred up in their brain by Sweeney Todd, readers had to buy the next issue. So, they did. And then they kept buying more. Like a narrative cigarette, the Partial Dopamine hooked readers on its friendship, bringing them back for issue after issue, year after year. In fact, the Partial Dopamine was so potent that it kept bringing readers back after the penny dreadful itself was gone.

The penny dreadful reached the end of its print run in the early twentieth century. But before it dwindled out, it inspired a wave of cheaply printed serial magazines that collectively became known as pulp fiction. Pulp fiction enlarged the basic offerings of the penny dreadful, adding new genres of adventure, horror, and crime—*Thrilling Wonder Stories, Spicy Detective, Black Mask*—that all retained the core invention of the Partial Dopamine. So, just as *Varney the Vampire* had done the century before, pulp fiction's periodicals agitated our brain with sudden discord that was stretched out through continual half-harmony resolutions.

This bonding blueprint made pulp fictions very popular. During the 1930s and 1940s, their total monthly circulation stretched into the millions. And in the years after World War II, pulp fictions enlarged their circle of friends even further. Riding out of the literary shadows, they merged with the novel and went mainstream, finding their way into America's public libraries and white-picket homes.

To go mainstream like this, pulp fiction had to shed some of its roughness. Its choppy prose, wooden characters, and improbable plots had to be replaced with polished storytelling that made the luridly outrageous feel emotionally authentic and immanently real. Yet even as pulp fiction got more polished on the surface, it still roughed up its readers' hearts underneath. It still surprised them with discord, just like the penny dreadfuls of yore.

This blend of old rough and new polish spawned triumphs such as Mario Puzo's 1969 pulpy novel *The Godfather*, which was so emotionally gripping that it became more popular than even Monteverdi's opera, selling at the astonishing rate of a book every eight seconds for more than two years. By 1971, a copy could be found in one of every seven US living rooms.

This remarkable success was due to Puzo's masterful use of the Partial Dopamine, which he introduces in *The Godfather*'s opening chapter. To lay the groundwork, the chapter begins with the promise of a harmonious resolution: the immigrant Amerigo Bonasera has seen his daughter harmed, and he's come to a New York City courtroom to have the injury repaired.

> Amerigo Bonasera sat in New York Criminal Court Number 3 and waited for justice; vengeance on the men who had so cruelly hurt his daughter, who had tried to dishonor her.

Yet instead of providing justice—or any resolution to Bonasera's perturbation—the novel's opening chapter becomes an exercise in loud and repeated emotional dissonance:

> There was something false in all this.
> Animals. Animals.
> His beautiful young daughter was still in the hospital with her broken jaw wired together, and now these two *animales* went free?
> Out of control, Bonasera leaned forward toward the aisle and shouted hoarsely, "You will weep as I have wept—I will make you weep as your children make me weep."
> Wild visions of buying a gun and killing the two young men jangled the very bones of his skull.

Like a tide of mismatched musical notes, Bonasera's agitated private thoughts and violent public outbursts roil our reading mind, stirring up a mood of turbulent discord. This is the first ingredient of the Partial Dopamine, and the chapter ends by adding in the second: a note of partial resolution.

> Bonasera turned to his still uncomprehending wife and explained to her, "They have made fools of us." He paused and then made his decision, no longer fearing the cost. "For justice we must go on our knees to Don Corleone."

This decision by Bonasera treats us to a little dopamine sweet. It resolves the chapter's jumbled emotions into a closing note of harmony. It assures us that we will see justice done after all.

But the harmony of this moment is not total, because Bonasera has not received his justice yet. Justice will come only after Bonasera has paid "the cost" to Don Corleone. Until then, our agitated feeling will persist. So, to get the complete kick of the neurochemicals primed in our brain, we need to follow Bonasera into the following chapter. There, full harmony will be restored by the don. There, we'll meet our new best friend.

With this opening, *The Godfather* launches into opera. Like Monteverdi's *L'Orfeo*, it co-opts the friend-making technology of music, banishing our lonely hours with a hungry feeling of page-turning companionship. And in just a moment, we'll learn Elena Ferrante's brilliant device for making that feeling even more hungry.

But before we go any further, let's pause to address a doubt that might be nagging at your mind: Why would we want to be best friends with the don? How could that friendship possibly be good for us? Wouldn't it be better to get a different companion—or just live alone?

That is a very prudent doubt. Certainly, in real life, it might be best to avoid the company of gangsters. But not in fiction. In fiction, the don's friendship is healthy for our brain.

Improving Our Health with *The Godfather*

The first healthy thing about befriending *The Godfather* is that it wards off loneliness.

Loneliness depletes our quality of life, making us sleepless, sad, and irritable. And loneliness isn't just unpleasant; it's also dangerous. Chronic loneliness disrupts our HPA axis, an anatomical system that (as we explored in chapter 11) adjusts our blood levels of cortisol, a hormone that operates analogously to caffeine. At sunrise, our HPA axis spikes our cortisol to get us going with a "coffee" jolt, and at sunset, it drops our cortisol so that we can sleep. But when we suffer from chronic loneliness, our HPA axis stops working normally. Instead of cycling our cortisol up and down, it flatlines the hormone at a marginally elevated level, making us feel lightly wired all day and all night.

The likely biological reason for this flatline is that we humans are social animals whose survival depends upon being part of a greater group. That group supports us through our daylight labors and safeguards us through the shadows of midnight. So, when our brain feels apart from a group, it tries to protect us by never totally relaxing: it drips cortisol at a steady rate into our bloodstream, caffeinating us into a constant state of wakefulness.

Such wakefulness may have kept our lonely ancestors alive long enough to find their way back to society. But in our here and now, it can quickly become harmful. By depriving us of deep sleep, it contributes to anxiety, mood depression, bad judgment, and mistakes. It raises our blood pressure, increasing our likelihood of heart attack and stroke. And through complex physiological pathways, it can elevate our risk of type 2 diabetes, atherosclerosis, and neurodegeneration. In fact, it's so harmful that it has been found to increase our odds of early death by about 30 percent.

Thirty percent. That's an extraordinary, terrifying number. It means that being lonely is as harmful to our health as smoking two cartons of cigarettes a month.

But happily, these dangerous effects of solitude can be reduced by literature, even though they are material facts and it is itself an immaterial fiction. This is because, as we discovered in chapter 11, the action of our HPA axis can be influenced by our perception of reality. What matters to our HPA axis isn't the objective truth that there are people around; what matters is our subjective feeling of distance from others, which is why we can feel a restless loneliness even when we're at a bustling party or living in a crowded city.

When we connect with a book, we can ease that feeling of aloneness. Even though no one is physically with us, our emotional connection to the narrator's voice or to the lives of the story characters makes our brain feel like we're in friendly company, easing the psychological gnaw that contributes to abnormal cortisol. And with pulp fiction, gaining this bonding benefit from literature is easy. The libraries of the world are packed with adventure novels, detective fictions, and romance paperbacks that deftly use the Partial Dopamine to connect with our brain, tiding us over until our flesh-and-blood friends come knocking.

And if it feels like you've been waiting for that knock . . . and waiting . . . and waiting, don't abandon hope. Such is pulp fiction's concern for your health that it can help the knock arrive faster.

That's right. The Partial Dopamine can do more than provide you with an endless supply of paperback friends. It can also enrich your life with real human companions.

The Friend-Making Power of Literature

Neuroscientists have discovered a part of our brain that helps us make friends. It's the dorsal raphe nucleus, a broccoli-shaped region tucked in our brain stem, beneath the caudate nucleus.

The dorsal raphe nucleus contains a cluster of dopamine neurons that are primed by short periods of loneliness. Those primed neurons then fire when we next come into contact with people, encouraging us to be sociable and shake off our solitude.

But that's only half the story of the dorsal raphe nucleus. The other half is that its friend-making neurons don't stay primed forever. If our isolation drags on for days or weeks, the priming fades, and our brain hunkers down in isolation, becoming less sociable again. So, to get the most friend-making power out of the dorsal raphe nucleus, we need to prime it—and frequently re-prime it. When our solitude has persisted for so long that it has come to feel normal, we need to give our dorsal raphe nucleus a little jolt, waking up its hibernating neurons.

The Partial Dopamine can do that. It can prime and re-prime our friend-making neurons by bonding us to a story—and then interrupting the story before the bond is complete. This two-step process is what generates the sudden feeling of loneliness we experience when we finish an episode of a pulpy TV serial such as *24* or *Orange Is the New Black* or *Fleabag*. And while that loneliness can induce us to cue up another episode, binge-watching till dawn, it can also encourage us to be more social. Our brain is now primed to reward us for interacting with the next person we meet. It will feel good to strike up a conversation, and the conversation will lightly bond the two of us together.

To help that conversation happen, all we have to do is make some time to attend a viewing party for a pulpy television show. Even if we don't know any of the other partygoers, even if we've lived like a hermit for so long that our dorsal raphe nucleus has given up, the pulpy show can make us feel more social. It can re-prime our defeatist neurons, enticing us to chat with a new *amico* once the TV clicks off.

And on certain occasions, the Partial Dopamine can work an even greater feat than making us new friends. It can connect us with the most emotionally elusive people in the world. I'm speaking, of course, of our family.

Maybe our uncle is weird. Maybe our children are too cool for us. No matter: after a mutual watching of *Homeland* or *Stranger Things*, we'll be gabbing away like old buddies.

That's the power of the Partial Dopamine. It can create brand-new friendships or make us more friendly with the strangers already living in our house. And if the power of the Partial Dopamine still isn't working for you, don't quit on literature yet. There's one other literary invention out there that can help you conquer loneliness.

It's more powerful than *L'Orfeo*. More powerful than *Varney*. More powerful than even the Godfather himself.

The Invention of the "Childhood Opera"

Maybe you've sampled some pulp fiction and found it . . . lacking. Maybe its true crimes, vampires, and superheroes felt a bit too gonzo or insubstantial for your taste. Maybe you enjoyed it in the way you enjoy a kooky, casual acquaintance. But it didn't strike you as your deepest friend.

Elena Ferrante can help. She's devised a literary invention that can provide all the psychological benefits of pulp fiction, yet in a form that feels more authentic and emotionally rich. The invention uses the same basic operatic technique as penny dreadfuls and pulp fictions, from *Varney the Vampire*, to *Batman*, to *The Godfather*. But it adds its own innovation: giving us the opera from the eyes of a child.

This seems like a small innovation. But it unlocks a huge, untapped potential in pulp fiction. Pulp fiction, like opera, is focused on adult lives. And indeed, pulp fiction is even more adult than opera. Just take a glance at its tables of contents: *The Corpse Pays Cash! The Human Rocket Murders! Some Curves Are Dangerous! Mistress of the Blood Drinkers!*

Money, violence, lust, depravity. This is the adult material that pulp fiction uses to stimulate the friendship circuits of our brain. Yet here's the thing: our most powerful friendships don't usually begin when we're adults. They start much earlier, in childhood.

Elena Ferrante taps into this power of childhood friendships in her 2011 novel *My Brilliant Friend*, which chronicles the bond between two girls, Elena and Lila, in 1950s Naples. Thinking back later on the intensity of that time, Elena muses:

> Children don't know the meaning of yesterday, of the day before yesterday, or even of tomorrow, everything is this, now. The street is this, the doorway is this. . . . This is the day, this the night.

In other words: as children, we know only what's in front of us. And so it is that our childhood friendships can consume us utterly. They can have all the passion of adult romances. And they can be infused with a vast range of emotions—from wonder, to curiosity, to jealousy—that catch up our whole psychology.

To capture this all-consuming experience, *My Brilliant Friend* treats the relationship between Elena and Lila as a kind of pulp fiction serial: "It was time to go home, but we delayed, challenging each other, without ever saying a word, testing our courage." Like an issue of *Spicy Mystery* or *Terror Tales*, Elena and Lila agitate each other's heart. Immersing themselves in half-released dopamine, they form an ever-hungry bond that connects Elena and Lila for life; even their lovers and their families fall away.

And *My Brilliant Friend* does more than just show us the bond between Elena and Lila. It pulls us *into* the bond, allowing us to experience its potency firsthand.

Roughing up our emotions, like the two girls do to each other, the novel makes us feel part of their childhood gang.

We Join the Gang

To draw us into the same hungry friendship as Elena and Lila, Ferrante's novel dishes up a simple recipe: pulp fiction dissonance from the perspective of a child. The pulp fiction dissonance does its usual work of priming our dopamine neurons. Meanwhile, the childhood perspective increases the intensity and emotional range of the dissonance, making our dopamine bond to the novel feel deeper and more psychologically complete.

Here's how it works in the novel's first chapter. Five-year-old Elena marches up a flight of stairs toward the lair of an "ogre." And as she marches, she fills our heart with a child's agitated imaginings of violence:

> A long knife, the kind used for slicing open a chicken breast.

> Put me in the pan of boiling oil, the children would eat me.

Until suddenly the chapter ends with a sharp emotional twist:

> At the fourth flight, Lila did something unexpected. She stopped to wait for me, and when I reached her she gave me her hand. This gesture changed *tutto per sempre*—everything forever.

In an instant, the mood of terror is banished. Our heart no longer pulses in fear at the pulp fiction ogre lurking above. And yet the horror isn't resolved into emotional calm. Instead, it's replaced by another intense moment of unresolved feeling: the wonder prompted by Lila's offer of her hand. Like Sweeney Todd's parlor assault, Lila's offer is "unexpected." And also like that assault, Lila's offer throws open an uncertain future: "This gesture changed *tutto per sempre*—everything forever."

Everything has changed between Elena and Lila. But how, exactly, has it changed? What will the new forever be? For now, we cannot tell. All we know is that the chapter's ending has resolved one excited emotion by abruptly stirring up another. So, even as our brain gets a burst of dopamine from the terror turned to harmony, we feel more dopamine neurons primed to fire by the unresolved chords of Elena's and Lila's new togetherness.

Through this technique of resolving one stirred-up feeling with another, Ferrante's novel bonds to our brain at the same moment that Elena's and Lila's hearts bond to each other, prompting us to turn with them to the next page of their friendship. And to deepen and enlarge that friendship, the following chapter deploys the same technique again. It begins by extending the feeling of Lila's gesture into a mood of communal *we*:

> We played ... We liked that place ... we chose without explicit agreement ... we liked the bars ... We didn't trust the light on the stones ... We imagined the dark corners ... we attributed everything.

But just when this *we* bond seems about to resolve Elena's fears into a note of harmony, the chapter ends on a dissonant surprise:

> Lila knew that I had that fear, my doll talked about it out loud. And so, on the day we exchanged our dolls for the first time— with no discussion, only looks and gestures—as soon as she had [my doll], she pushed [it] through the grate and let [it] fall into the darkness.

Lila has once again "challenged" Elena. Pushing her treasured doll into the darkness, she stirs up Elena's heart—and ours—with agitated feeling.

This technique is repeated continually by *My Brilliant Friend*. Again and again, we get close to emotional harmony—only to be startled by a new emotional agitation at the chapter breaks. Those chapter breaks come in fast and loud *concitato*, like the pounding notes of Monteverdi's opera. In the novel's opening section, Childhood, they arrive at nearly the rate of every thousand words—and can come as quick as every five hundred. The result is constant bursts of almost harmony followed by newly agitated feelings. And because these feelings range over childhood's rich palette of emotions—hope, wonder, fear, love, shock, shame, envy, courage, anger, shyness, pride, curiosity, empathy, guilt—they connect with a vast span of our psyche.

Like childhood, they feel like everything. And like childhood, they feel intensely incomplete.

Bonding to us like our oldest friends.

Inventing Tomorrow

By the sixth-century age of King Arthur and the young Prophet Muḥammad, Aristotle's *Poetics* survived on only a single papyrus scroll shelved somewhere in the battle cauldron between the javelin battalions of Roman Byzantium and the war elephants of the Sasanian Empire. And even that lone scroll was, itself, no longer whole. It broke off in the middle, promising more chapters that never arrived.

No one knows what happened to those chapters. Maybe they burned to ash at the midnight hour of March 1, 86 BCE, when the mulberry-cheeked Republican general Lucius Cornelius Sulla sacked Athens with fire. Maybe they went the way of most papyrus and crumbled gently into fiber dust. Maybe they endure in some sand-buried Arabian archive, visited only by scorpions and the jird mouse.

Yet whatever the fate of the scroll's lost chapters, there's one more secret left to learn from the chapters that we have. That secret is how to go beyond finding literature's past inventions—and create its *future* ones.

The secret begins with Aristotle's observation that the origins of literature lie in imitation. By imitating birdsong, our ancestors fashioned the first music of poetry. By imitating mortal yearnings, our ancestors fashioned the first characters of epic myth. By imitating life's laughs and losses, our ancestors fashioned the first plots of comedy and tragedy.

So, if we want to fashion new literary inventions, then we need to imitate an inventor. And of all the world's inventors, one has invented like no other. That inventor has crafted a billion billion things original. That inventor has crafted miracles that fly, that see, that dream.

That inventor is Nature.

Nature's secret for inventing was discovered in the mid-nineteenth century, when Charles Darwin unriddled the mystery of evolution by natural selection. But long before Darwin, the authors of literature also discovered the secret. And roughly two millennia ago, their discovery was recorded by the famed writing instructor Quintilian of La Rioja in a massive but sprightly instructional manual titled *Institutes of Oratory*.

The *Institutes* went on to become perhaps the most influential textbook in history. It was studied by thousands of schoolchildren from Britain to Babylon, and it birthed a hundred later writing guides, from Thomas Wilson's *The Arte of Rhetorique* (which sat in Shakespeare's grammar school) to Caleb Bingham's *The Columbian Orator* (which remained with Frederick Douglass throughout his life). And in the *Institutes*, Quintilian lays out three invention-making techniques, all borrowed from Nature, that our literary pens can imitate.

The first technique is to embrace happy accidents. Such accidents lie at the root of all of Nature's inventions, every one of which has been engineered through evolution's blind process of lucky mutation and fortuitous environment. What built the marvels of the hummingbird heart and the dragonfly eye was chance. And so it was, too, with many, if not all, of the literary inventions included in this book. They came about through happenstance. An author meant to make one thing, and noticed only later what she'd actually created. As Quintilian puts it: "It's easier to stumble into accidental innovations than to intentionally write the thing that you were after."

The second technique is to splice together two old blueprints. This is what Nature stumbled onto with the invention of sexual reproduction. It's what Euripides did when he merged tragedy and comedy (see chapter 24); what Douglass did when he autobiographically wedded Augustine to Rousseau (chapter 14); what Virginia Woolf did when she combined the styles of James Joyce and Marcel Proust (chapter 17); what Shakespeare did when he Hamlet-ed together monologue and dialogue (chapter 19). And it's what led Quintilian to counsel, "Copy many models, not just one."

The third technique is to focus on what works, not on what's "right." This is how Nature has produced all of life's intricate astonishments; natural selection knows no higher reason, only the wing that lifts and the brain that thinks. This empirical method, too, is how modern medicine and psychology have developed all their useful tonics, antidotes, and remedies. And it's why Quintilian remarks, "Your writing needn't always be true; it just has to do what you want it to do."

For whatever the power of truth may be, literature's own special power has always lain in fiction, that wonder we construct.

It is the invention that unbreaks the heart.

And brings us into hope, and peace, and love.

The Secret History of This Book

T ossed across the coves and white-sand islands of the Eastern Mediterranean some twenty-five centuries ago was a loosely democratic
web of fishing villages and trading outposts: Ceos, Akragas, Abdera,
Elis, Chalcedon. And drifting through those salt-fumed ports, mingling
with voyagers Egyptian, Persian, Hebrew, and Phoenician, was a group
of teachers who knew all of literature's inventions.

For a little silver, the teachers would share their knowledge with you.
They'd show you poetic devices that could bewitch the heart with love,
mythic gizmos that could steel the soul with bravery, and plot contraptions
that could bless the eye with cosmic vision. These inventions seemed a kind
of sorcery, but with a grin, the teachers would reveal the machinery beneath
the magic trick. In those nuts and bolts, you'd see how literature was built.
You'd learn its hidden blueprints, unlocking every secret power for yourself.

The teachers from the coves and white-sand islands are gone now.
Their smiles, their wit, their wisdom—all vanished into ether. But still,
their teaching has endured, preserved in the invention-finding method
that we've used throughout this book. So, to honor what the teachers
have given us, the following pages will chronicle their forgotten story,
delving into how they came to be, how they perished utterly—and how
we can reclaim their island dream.

The Vanished Teachers

The teachers disappeared so completely that not one of their original
lesson plans endures. Yet even so, a few clues about their teachings have

been preserved in the writings of a rival group of instructors: the philosophers.

The philosophers were also tossed across the Eastern Mediterranean, but unlike the teachers, they tended to associate with more authoritarian regimes. There was the philosopher Thales (born c. 625 BCE), who spent his days under the electrum despots and nautical oligarchs of purple-flowered Miletus. There was the philosopher Heraclitus (born c. 535 BCE), who lived among the monumental architectures of Ephesus when it was ruled by satraps of the Achaemenid Empire. And most famously to later generations, there was the philosopher Plato (born c. 425 BCE), who approved of the theories (if not always the tactics) of the Thirty Tyrants that overthrew Athenian democracy.

This penchant for political absolutism reflected the philosophers' conviction that the world itself was governed by one doctrine, absolute. To find that doctrine, Thales demonstrated mathematically that life was hatched from holy water, Heraclitus marshaled paradox to prove that the root of peace was war, and Plato used an archeology of memory to excavate an inborn knowledge of eternal forms. Then, to sort among these competing credos, the philosophers and their disciples argued vigorously, slamming together different ideas in the belief that flawed opinions would break in the collision, leaving just the stronger stuff of truth behind.

As the philosophers debated one another, they also debated their educational rivals, including the teachers. And during the first half of the fourth century BCE, the philosophers' debates with the teachers were dramatized by Plato in pseudo-historical treatises that bore titles such as *The Sophist* and *Gorgias*. These treatises cannot be said to be objective; they were written expressly to besmirch the teachers as vapid, slick, and grifting. Yet even so, they contain some revealing details, including the fact that the philosophers referred to the teachers as Sophists and rhetoricians.

Sophist is an Attic Greek synonym for "the wise." And *rhetorician* is a synonym for "speaker," or "debater," or even "arguer." So, the names that the philosophers used to describe the teachers come very close to describing the philosophers themselves: seekers of wisdom who know how to argue. And indeed, the etymological root of *philosopher* is quite literally *Sophist*. A philosopher is a "lover" (*philos*) of "wisdom" (*sophia*), or in other words, an ardent Sophist.

What the teachers would have thought of these names, we cannot say. But still, the names are intriguing. Because the names suggest that perhaps the philosophers weren't just the teachers' adversaries.

Perhaps they were the teachers' students too.

The Teachers' Students

There's no doubt that the philosophers got their intellectual start in literature. Their earliest schooling was in verse epics such as Homer's *Iliad* (perhaps recited to the melodies of tortoise lyres and double-reeded pipes) and Hesiod's *Theogony* (perhaps at a cultic sacrifice, danced amid the lapis lazuli blue of colonnaded temple groves). And from those festival beginnings, enjoyed beside their parents and their siblings, the philosophers then undertook some secondary form of literary study, scratched down on wax tablets under the watchful gaze of slave tutors or done in public library vaults to the sesame glow of oil lamps, that rippled through their later scholarship. Heraclitus stitched his proverbs thick with metaphor, Plato crafted his Socratic masterpieces as theatrical dialogues, and the lone text to survive from Thales and his students is an alliterative scrap of prose-poetry: "The tomb of time is also its womb."

The philosophers thus knew at least a few of the teachers' secrets. And if the philosophers were indeed the teachers' academic descendants, then the lost history of the teachers might run something like this:

First, there were the students of literature. On gentle coves and white-sand islands, the students dedicated themselves to learning all about poem and myth, and in time, they discovered so much that other students came to the islands to learn. Then the original students became teachers. And they were given the name Sophists to honor their wisdom.

For many years, these Sophists and their students studied literature's technology, sharing the secrets of how it enriched human life with love and courage and other psychological uplifts. Until one day, a group of students made a discovery: literature could be weaponized. The inventions devised by poets to move hearts could be inserted into arguments, enabling lawyers and politicians to sway juries and princes.

The students who wielded literature in this way became known as rhetoricians. They went around to law courts and legislative assemblies, disputing over justice and civic policy. And they got very good at convincing people that their arguments were right. So good that, at last, a band of concerned citizens arose, accusing the rhetoricians of reducing right and wrong to literary wordplay.

These concerned citizens called themselves philosophers. Vowing to restore the Truth, they retreated into cloaked gardens, where they stripped the rhetoricians' words of literary embellishment, uncovering the pure arguments beneath. And once the philosophers had refined those arguments to deadly sharpness, they turned upon the rhetoricians and the Sophists.

Wounding the rhetoricians.

And driving the Sophists out of existence.

The history of the teachers cannot, of course, be this simple. The past is always more complicated than any narrative can suggest. Yet still, the narrative is a useful way to sort out three related groups of ancient teachers:

1. *The Literary Sophists.* This group taught the secrets of literature.

2. *The Rhetoricians.* This group combined the secrets of literature with the secrets of argument.

3. *The Philosophers.* This group turned away from the secrets of literature to focus on the secrets of argument.

At some point in antiquity, the literary Sophists were wiped out. Unlike the other two groups, they didn't specialize in arguments, so they couldn't (or wouldn't) defend themselves. Like poets on a battlefield, they died.

But the other two groups kept on. In fact, they flourished. Rhetoricians and philosophers bustled from the ancient world, to the Middle Ages, to the Renaissance, to the Enlightenment, to our modern age. Today almost all of us learn rhetoric and philosophy in some form when we're teens in school. And most big universities have separate departments for both.

This state of affairs has been good for the rhetoricians and the philosophers. But it's all but replaced the Sophists' literary ethos with the thing that destroyed it: the study of arguments. In our modern literature classes, from elementary school all the way through college, we concentrate primarily on two skills-building rubrics: (1) essay writing and (2) reading comprehension and analysis. In essay writing, we learn to frame arguments as thesis statements that we defend with paragraphs of supporting evidence. In reading comprehension and analysis, we learn to pinpoint what literature is *saying*. What's this poem's perspective on life? What is this play's point of view on society? What do this novel's representations imply? What themes does this comic book contain? Do I agree with what this film is asserting, or do I want to critique it with my own thesis?

We're taught, that is, to see literature as a species of argument. We're encouraged to think that literature's main purpose is to convince us, like a charming rhetorician or a sagacious philosopher, about what is just or what is true. Which is why songs of romance, legends of magic, poems of mourning, and memoirs of perseverance are now used in literature classrooms across the globe to train us in critical thinking, persuasive writing, and the other tools of logic and disputation.

So how is it, then, that we remember the island Sophists at all? If their teaching program was plowed under with such completeness by the reason and the rhetoric of their intellectual offspring, then how have we hung on to their ancient insight that literature can be treated as a technology rich with blueprints for generating love and courage and all the other mental uplifts catalogued in this book?

The short answer, as we saw in the introduction, is that the Sophists' most crucial discovery—their method for unearthing literature's inventions—was preserved by a renegade philosopher: Aristotle. But the longer answer is that Aristotle had help. It took many other diligently curious minds to keep the Sophists' discovery alive.

And quite a bit of luck as well.

The Longer Answer

Sometime around 335 BCE, a scribe in Aristotle's school recorded the Sophists' method upon a hand-rolled scroll of delicate papyrus. And that scroll then began an itinerant ramble toward our present age.

It wended its way to the balmy shores of Hellenistic Rhodes in the days when trigonometry was first concocted and Jason's Argonauts set sail. It rested in the Great Library of Alexandria among a hundred thousand other manuscripts used by Cleopatra to mesmerize Caesar with the inkling wisdom of pharaonic Egypt. After a long spell of darkness, it resurfaced among a pile of parchment in a ninth-century Persian monastery, from whence a Nestorian churchman would convey it to Baghdad's stucco-spiraled mosques. In the eleventh century, a transcript of the scroll came into the possession of the polymathic doctor Ibn Sīnā on the banks of the Caspian Sea, and in the twelfth century, another copy rode from Morocco to al-Andalus in the baggage of an Islamic jurist by the name of Ibn Rushd. By the thirteenth century, the scroll's text had followed the wake of the Fourth Crusade to the rain-drenched winter hilltops of Arcadia. Ten decades later, it was recopied onto goatskin and carted from the gilded domes of Constantinople into the columned villas of Renaissance Italy. And there it tumbled into the famed Venetian print shop of Aldus Manutius, who in 1508 published it in a graceful paperback that would eventually make its way into book depositories from Leuven to Los Angeles.

That paperback should have spread the Sophists' invention-finding method throughout the world. But unfortunately, it did not. For on the scroll's epic journey, it had been treated so shabbily that half of it was lost asunder, while the other half was rent with scars, its words arbitrarily rubbed out and split by holes. Over the next three hundred years, diligent academics strove to repair the damage. But the task was so overwhelming that in 1786 the celebrated English antiquarian Thomas Twining could stand amid the gentle pastures of Essex and despair:

> The extreme depravation of the text, its obscurities and ambi-guities, are such that . . . a great part of my pains have been em-ployed in proving passages to be unintelligible.

The scroll, it seemed, was forever ruined—and with it, the method for discovering literature's inventions.

Yet gradually a recovery came. It began amid the mountain fortresses of nineteenth-century East Prussia, where the bow-tied academic Karl Lachmann pioneered stemmatics, a text-mending technique that em-ploys the same strategy used by paleontologists to reassemble dinosaur family trees from scattered fossil bits. This painstaking process has en-abled modern paleographers such as Leonardo Tarán and Dimitri Gutas to salvage long-lost portions of the scroll from tattered scraps of Arabic, Latin, Syriac, and Greek. And although huge chunks remain missing, enough of the Sophists' method has been reconstructed for scholars to start reusing it again.

That reuse of the method launched the next phase of the recovery, which got underway in the decades surrounding the Second World War. At the time, the textbook approach to literature was interpretation, a reading technique championed by a charismatic collection of scholars (such as Cambridge University's I. A. Richards and Yale University's Cleanth Brooks) who became known as the "New Critics." Despite the New Critics' name, interpretation was not new; it had begun its exis-tence as an old Roman synonym for "translation," until, in the fourth century, the task of translating the Bible into the Latin Vulgate was undertaken by Saint Jerome of Bethlehem. And as Jerome labored on this mighty project within a book-filled Palestinian cave, he discovered that he couldn't literally translate the Bible *verbum e verbo*—"word for word." Instead, he had to "interpret" each word of Mosaic Hebrew and Gospel Greek for its deeper "sense," extracting the unseen meaning of the sacred text before him. So, from Jerome on, interpretation became a tool for deriving hidden truths and symbolic connotations from a care-

ful study of language, a tool that would be employed by long generations of Church Fathers and Talmudic exegetes (such as Rabbi Shlomo
Yitzchaki, the eleventh-century Champagne vintner whose writing was
famed for being as effervescent as his bottled wines) to produce bountiful
commentaries on the Torah and the New Testament:

> The seven days of Genesis creation represent the seven ages of
> Man . . . The theme of Christ's parable is forgiveness . . . The
> word's deep signification is "Love."

When the New Critics transferred this hermeneutic technique onto literature, it had a similarly revelatory effect, transforming the words of
wooing sonnets, novelistic fictions, and theatrical entertainments into
instructional homilies that teemed with higher "themes" and allegorical "representations." In classrooms across early-twentieth-century Europe and America, close-reading teenagers interpreted Shakespeare's
plays—and discerned that *King Lear* was really a treatise (perhaps even
a sermon) on the themes of Nature and Mortality. Meanwhile, on college
chalkboards from Berkeley to Oxford, Macbeth was diagrammed as a
representation of Ambition, Cleopatra as a representation of Woman,
and Othello as a representation of Blackness.

But then in the mid-1930s, a patched-together copy of the ancient
scroll—now titled Aristotle's *Poetics*—fell into the hands of a fortysome-
thing professor, Ronald Salmon Crane, who sat illumined by the conic
chandeliers of the University of Chicago's Harper Library. Crane was
known to be a cautious thinker, skeptical of grand ideas. Yet as he un-
furled the scroll across a chipped oak table, his mind buzzed with the
electric realization that the Sophists' ancient method was unlike anything taught at his university—or any university in the world. Because
the method focused not on literary interpretations but on literary *inventions*, it cracked open a way of reading unimagined by the New Critics.
Instead of concentrating strictly on words, the method attended to plots,
characters, and other story nuts and bolts. Instead of seeking the veiled
meanings of literary texts, the method mapped their psychological effects: wonder, empathy, suspense. So, instead of analyzing literature in
the way that Saint Jerome had analyzed the Bible, the method explored

literature in the way that modern scientists explored the human brain, treating it as an evolved machine whose deep blueprints could be brought to light by a mixture of reverse engineering and laboratory experiment. And Crane, believing that the general public might be interested in this long-forgotten approach, set out to revive it in a six-hundred-page textbook, *Critics and Criticism*, that appeared in college bookstores in 1952.

Crane's textbook failed. Its revival of the Sophists' techno-scientific method was dismissed as strange and philistine, which is why we're still usually taught in school today that the most fruitful way to study literature is to "interpret" it for themes and representations. Yet even so, the failed textbook inspired a few rogue academics, such as James Phelan and the scholars at the Ohio State thinktank Project Narrative (where I myself work), to apply the Sophists' method to poems, plays, novels, films, television series, and comic books from across world history, building a library of literary inventions that now extends into the hundreds.

It's from those hundreds of inventions that the chapters of this book have been plucked. But as remarkable as those hundreds of inventions are, they're just the beginning of the story. For the world contains *thousands* of original literary works. And as you're reading now, there's an author somewhere on this globe who's busily engineering innovations more.

As much as we've gleaned already from the literary Sophists, there is thus still endless more left to discover. Each new poem that you read, each new page of fiction that you turn, each new stage show that draws your applause, each new pixel flashed upon your viewing screen, could contain a breakthrough. And all it takes to find that breakthrough is the method that the literary Sophists pioneered on their Mediterranean beaches twenty-five centuries ago.

The method is the one we learned in the introduction and have since practiced in every chapter of this book:

Step One. Identify the unique psychological effect of a literary work. Perhaps the effect is medicinal. Perhaps it's a well-being booster. Or perhaps it's beneficial to our gray matter in some other way. To home in on the effect, take advantage of the powerful mind-surveying gadgets housed in your local neuroscience lab.

And if you can't gain access to those gadgets, make use of your own inbuilt brain scanner—your consciousness—to characterize the literary work's unique effect as precisely as you can.

Step Two. Trace that unique effect back to an invention crafted from an original use of plot, character, storyworld, narrator, or some other element of narrative. Don't worry about themes or representations or what the author is saying. And don't get lost in the words of literature. Listen instead for the work's style, or its voice, or its story.

By practicing and practicing this two-step method through to mastery, you can carry on the search for all of literature's inventions, unlocking secret power after secret power.

Until in future years, tomorrow's generation hears about your white-sand wisdom.

And joins you on the island shores to learn.

Acknowledgments

I would like to thank Carolyn Savarese for the courage to imagine this book and Bob Bender for the courage to write it; Johanna Li, Lisa Healy, Philip Bashe, and everyone at Simon & Schuster for their enormous care with the manuscript; Lawrence Manley for Shakespeare, Madeline Puzo for the Italians, Thomas Habinek for the Greeks, Seth Lerer for Chaucer and Old English, Dimitri Gutas for Persia and the Middle East, Edward Stuenkel for Darwin, and Jim Phelan for Aristotle; the team at Project Narrative for the theory of writing, and Suzannah Showler, Alaina Belisle, Julie Garbuz, Eliza Smith, Sophie Newman, and all my Ohio State MFAs for the practice; Karen Paik, Mike Benveniste, Dan Breen, Soohyun Cho, Douglas Pfeiffer, Preeti Singh, Elizabeth Mundell Perkins, and Benjamin Card for chapter readings; and Jonathan Kramnick, John Monterosso, James Pawelski, and my other interdisciplinary collaborators for the science in art and the art in science. And I would like to thank my family for believing in me—and my daughter Marlowe for being my reason to believe.

Notes on Translations, Sources, and Further Reading

An ingenious author once observed that no book is complete *sin anotaciones en el fin*—"without annotations at its end." So here are those annotations, identifying sources antique and obscure.

Translations

All translations by the author except where credited below.

Preface: A Heaven of Invention

Enheduanna's poetry is excerpted from *The Kesh Temple Hymn* and "The Exaltation of Inana (Inana B)," available at Oxford University's *The Electronic Text Corpus of Sumerian Literature (ETCSL)*, http://etcsl.orinst.ox.ac.uk, as text numbers 4.80.1 and 4.07.2. The Mesoamerican parable is from bk. 7 of the *Florentine Codex*, originally titled *La Historia Universal de las Cosas de Nueva España*, by Bernardino de Sahagún, available from UNESCO at the World Digital Library. The pyramid text is excerpted from utterance 267 of the Unas Pyramid Texts, in Alexandre Piankoff, *The Pyramid of Unas: Texts Translated with Commentary* (Princeton, NJ: Princeton University Press, 1968). The "Love Prayer to Shu-Sin" is "A *balbale* to Inana for Šu-Suen (Šu-Suen B)" at *ETCSL*, text number 2.4.4.2. The excerpt from the *Samhita* is from mandala 2, sukta 2, line 7. The Yangtze ode is poem 82 of the *Shijing* or *Book of Poetry*, 1.7.8, available at the Chinese Text Project, https://ctext.org.

Introduction: The Lost Technology

Aristotle's discussion of plot *stretches* is *Poetics* 1452a1-4, and his discussion of the wonderful [θαυμάσιος] is *Poetics* 1452a4-7 (section 11 in most modern editions). Aristotle's mention of catharsis is *Poetics* 1449b28 (sec. 6). Aristotle's discussion of the Hurt Delay (that is, anagnorisis) and its role in Sophocles's *Oedipus Tyrannus* is *Poetics*

1452a29-33 (sec. 11). The choral chant from *Agamemnon* is lines 176–81. Ajax's rebuke to the Greeks is *Iliad* 15.508. Oedipus's cry about his posttraumatic memory [μνήμη] is *Oedipus Tyrannus* 1318, and his exchange with the chorus immediately follows in lines 1319–22. All the Greek texts above can be found at Tufts University's Perseus Digital Library, https://www.perseus.tufts.edu/hopper. William James analyzes "spiritual" experience in *The Varieties of Religious Experience: A Study in Human Nature* (New York: Longmans, Green, 1902). The recommendations on EMDR are from the American Psychiatric Association, *Practice Guideline for the Treatment of Patients with Posttraumatic Stress* (2004); the World Health Organization, *Guidelines for the Management of Conditions Specifically Related to Stress* (2013); and the Department of Veterans Affairs, *Clinical Practice Guideline for the Management of Posttraumatic Stress* (2017).

Chapter 1: Rally Your Courage

The "ancient Akan tale" is quoted from Gail E. Haley, *A Story, A Story* (New York: Aladdin, 1980). The Cherokee creation story is quoted from James Mooney, *Myths of the Cherokee: Extract from the Nineteenth Annual Report of the Bureau of American Ethnology* (Washington, DC: Government Printing Office, 1902). The lines from Aeschylus are *Persians*, 391–94, available at Tuft's Perseus Digital Library. The first use of *paean* in the *Iliad* is at line 473. The epic simile from the Bible is Genesis 49:9. This and all Bible translations are from the King James Version. The Homeric lion simile is *Iliad* 3.23–28. The poem "Achilles in the Trench," also known as "I saw a man this morning" (it was left untitled by the author, Patrick Stewart-Shaw, and dashed down on a blank leaf of A. E. Housman's *A Shropshire Lad* that he carried with him into battle), is reprinted in *The New Oxford Book of War Poetry*, ed. Jon Stallworthy (Oxford: Oxford University Press, 2014), 170–71.

Chapter 2: Rekindle the Romance

The Chinese ode is poem 73 of the *Shijing* or *Book of Poetry* 1.6.9. Sappho's first lyric (translated as "He seems to me a god") is an excerpt from Sappho's "Fragment 31," found in Longinus, *On the Sublime*, 1.10.2, available at Tuft's Perseus Digital Library. Sappho's second lyric, the trash-heap poem about Helen (translated as "Some say that horsemen") is Sappho's "Fragment Sixteen," from Papyrus Oxyrhynchus 1231, published in Bernard Pyne Grenfell and Arthur Surridge Hunt, eds., *The Oxyrhynchus Papyri* 10 (London: Egypt Exploration Fund, 1914). The Ulayya bint al-Mahdi verse (translated as "I have tucked our love inside this lyric") is خَبَّأْتُ في شِعْري اسْمَ الذي / أُردْتهُ كالحَبْ ءِ في الجَيْبِ and can be found in Abū Bakr al-Ṣūlī's tenth-century poetry anthology *Kitāb Al-Awrāq*, ed. James Heyworth Dunne (London: Luzac, 1934) and with a selection of al-Mahdi's other lyrics in *Classical Poems by Arab Women: A Bilingual Anthology*, ed. Abdullah al-Udhari (London: Saqi, 1999), 108–19.

Chapter 3: Exit Anger

Job's apology is Job 42:6. For an exploration of the connotations of *suggnômê*, see the Lewis-Short-Jones *Greek-English Lexicon* (Oxford: Oxford University Press, 1843) entry on συγγνώμη; the term is used by Herodotus, Aristotle, and others. The excerpt from *Antigone* combines lines 1266–69 (the king's lament for his son) and 1317–20 (the king's lament for his wife), available at Tuft's Perseus Digital Library. Oedipus's ἰοὺ ἰού scream is *Oedipus Tyrannus*, 1182. The excerpt from Shakespeare's *Richard III* is from the first folio, lines 3662–65 (act/scene 5.3 in most modern editions). For Aristotle's discussion of *hamartia* (ἁμαρτία) see *Poetics* 1453a10 (sec. 13).

Chapter 4: Float Above Hurt

For Socrates's definition of philosophy, "ὀρθῶς φιλοσοφοῦντες ἀποθνῄσκειν μελετῶσι," see Plato's *Phaedo* 67e4-5, available at Tuft's Perseus Digital Library. For Socrates's discussion of imitating Aesop, see *Phaedo* 60c-e. The Archilochus is "Fragment 114" and the Hipponax is "Fragment 68," both available from Loeb Classical Library, *Greek Iambic Poetry*, ed. Douglas E. Gerber (Cambridge, MA: Harvard University Press, 1999). Socrates's exchanges with Meno can be found in Plato's *Meno* 71c-d, available at Tuft's Perseus Digital Library.

Chapter 5: Excite Your Curiosity

For a selection of cuneiform riddles from ancient Sumer, see C. J. Gadd and S. N. Kramer, eds., *Ur Excavations Texts VI.2: Literary and Religious Texts* (London: British Museum Publications, 1966), 340–48. For English riddles, see Archer Taylor, *English Riddles from Oral Tradition* (Berkeley: University of California Press, 1951). For Arabic riddles, see Charles T. Scott, *Persian and Arabic Riddles: A Language-Centered Approach to Genre Definition, Publication of the Indiana University Research Center in Anthropology, Folklore, and Linguistics* 39 (Bloomington: Indiana University, 1965). Tiresias's riddling exchange with Oedipus begins at *Oedipus Tyrannus*, line 316, and culminates in lines 438–39. The riddles from *Macbeth* are from the first folio, lines 6, 12, and 1635–57 (1.1 and 4.4). The excerpt from the *Epic of Sundiata* is quoted from Djibril Tamsir Niane, *Sundiata: An Epic of Old Mali*, trans. G. D. Pickett (Essex, UK: Longman, 1965). The excerpt from *Gawain and the Green Knight* ("*Bot of alle þat here bult, of Bretaygne kynges, / Ay watz Arthur þe hendest, as I haf herde telle. / Forþi an aunter in erde I attle to schawe, / Þat a selly in ȝe summe men hit holden, / And an outtrage awenture of Arthurez wonderez. / If ȝe wyl lysten þis laye bot on littel quile, / I schal telle hit as-tit, as I in toun herde*") is from early in Passus I, eds. J. R. R. Tolkien and E. V. Gordon, rev. Norman Davis (Oxford: Clarendon Press, 1967). Regarding the prophecies of *Macbeth*, every battle is lost (by the vanquished) and won (by the victors), which means that every tomorrow is both foul (for those who suffer defeat) and fair (for those who claim victory). With that, you've solved the whole riddle of life, so let me ask you: Why are you studying these notes as if there are further answers waiting here?

Chapter 6: Free Your Mind

The phrase *mente moderna* was associated by mid-nineteenth-century Italian liberals such as Ruggiero Bonghi with Francis Bacon, an enthusiastic proponent of Machiavelli's account of innovation. (For more on Bacon, see chapter 13.) Today it's associated with a more general cluster of attitudes encouraged by Machiavelli's writings: ethical utilitarianism, technological progress, political realism, the disenchantment of nature, and a generally questioning attitude toward absolute truths and past authorities. Machiavelli's discussion of the *innovatori* is in *Il Principe*, chapter 6. The individual who accused Machiavelli of being the "enemy of the human race" and of writing "with the Devil's finger" was Cardinal Reginald Pole in his Latin polemic *Apologia ad Carolum Quintum* (1539). Dante's citation of Ovid's quote about Orpheus is from *Convivio* 2.1.3, available at Digital Dante, hosted by Columbia University Library at https://digitaldante.columbia.edu/text/library. The *oferhygd* inserted as a gloss into *Beowulf* is sec. 36, line 1743. The Bible's eye-for-an-eye injunction is Exodus 21:24. The call to Medusa, "Vegna Medusa: sì 'l farem di smalto," is *Inferno* 9.52. Dante's observation about the difference between the way that the Church and poets use allegory—"Veramenti li teologi questo senso prendono altrimenti che li poeti; ma però che mia intenzione è qui lo modo de li poeti seguitare, prendo lo senso allegorico secondo che per li poeti è usato"—is *Convivio* 2.1.4. Virgil's *parola ornata* is *Inferno* 2.67, and the invocation about "the veil of verses strange"—"O voi ch'avete li 'ntelletti sani, / mirate la dottrina che s'asconde / sotto 'l velame de li versi strain"—is *Inferno* 9.61-3. Dante's words to Cangrande—"Si vero accipiatur opus allegorice, subiectum est homo prout merendo et demerendo per arbitrii libertatem iustitie premiandi et puniendi obnoxius est"—can be found in *Dantis Alagherii Epistolae*, 13.34. Machiavelli's letter to a friend, in which he remarks that he carries with him a copy of Dante's *Comedy*—"Ho un libro sotto, o Dante"—is his letter to Francesco Vettori, December 10, 1513.

Chapter 7: Jettison Your Pessimism

On the "escaped princess" and her ultimate fate (including the role played by D'Aulnoy), see Anne Marguerite Petit du Noyer, *Lettres Historiques Et Galantes*, 5 vols. (1713), esp. vol. 1, letter 24. The phrase *Les Contes des Fées* was coined by D'Aulnoy as the title to her first fairy-tale anthology, published in Paris, 1697, and including *The Tale of Graciosa and Percinet* (*Gracieuse et Percinet*) as its third tale. The review of Cinderella as "doll-faced" is *Variety* 31 (December 1949). Perrault remarks on the importance of reason, *de raison*, in the address *A Mademoiselle*, which prefaces *Histoires ou contes du temps passé avec des moralitez* (Paris, 1697). Countess Henriette-Julie de Murat's 1699 collection is *Histoires sublimes et allégoriques*. Betty Edwards's best seller is *Drawing on the Right Side of Your Brain: A Course in Enhancing Creativity and Artistic Confidence*, which has been translated into seventeen languages, sold more than 1.7 million copies, and is now currently in its fourth edition. Robortello's definition of comedy—*"eventa quaedem fortuita, quae insperatam laetitiam afferent"*—is in the "De Comoedia" section of his *Paraphrasis in Libellum Horatii*. Straparola's fairy-tale collection is *Le Piacevoli Notti*, often translated as *The Facetious Nights* or *The Nights of Straparola*. In *Gracieuse et Percinet*, the narrator's nonexplanation for the Fairy-tale Twist is: "Hélas! quel eût été son sort, / Si de son Percinet la constance amoureuse / Ne l'avait tant de fois dérobée à la mort!" Chaplin's memory of creating the tramp is recorded in pt. 3 of his memoir, *A Comedian Sees the World*, published serially in *Women's Home Companion* from September 1933 to January 1934. The quote about "a world of chance" is from the final line of Victorian novelist Samuel Butler's *Life and Habit* (London: Jonathan Cape, 1878). Lang's quote that "Charles Perrault was a good man, a good father, a good Christian, and a good fellow" is from the introduction to *Perrault's Popular Tales* (Oxford: Clarendon Press, 1888), xvi. The story of Rhodopis can be found in Strabo, *Geographica* 17.1.33.

Chapter 8: Heal from Grief

The ghost's words to Hamlet, "Thus was I," are from the first folio *Hamlet*, lines 759–60 (1.5). Hamlet's "words" is line 1230 (2.2). Hamlet's "antic disposition" is line 868 (1.5). Hamlet's "Hold a mirror up to nature" is lines 1870–88 (3.2). The ghost's "blunted purpose" is line 2491 (3.4). Hamlet's "Alas, poor Yorick" is line 3372 (5.1). The quote from *Cardano's Comfort* is from *Cardanus Comforte*, trans. Thomas Bedingfeld (London, 1573), bk. 1, 25. Macduff's exchange with Ross and Malcolm is from the first folio *Macbeth*, lines 2047–73 (4.3). The reminiscences "so excellent . . . so loving . . . most dear life" are *Hamlet*, lines 323–24 (1.2) and line 1610 (2.2). Anthony Scoloker's quote about "Friendly Shakespeares Tragedies" is from his *Epistle to Daiphantus, or the Passions of Love* (London, 1604). The observation by the author of *Thyestes* that "In animals, grief is sharp but quick—in people, it can linger for years" is from Seneca's "Consolation to Marcia," sec. 7, "Aspice mutorum animalium quam concitata sint desideria et tamen quam breuia . . . nec ulli animali longum fetus sui desiderium est nisi homini." Hamlet's "O, God! A beast . . . would have mourn'd longer" is lines 334–35 (1.2). Hamlet's "Remember thee?" is lines 782–89 (1.5). The remark by Hamlet's mother that his grief is not "common" but "particular" is lines 252–56 (1.2). The complaint by Hamlet's uncle that Hamlet's grief is "peevish" is line 282 (1.2). Polonius's assessment that "Your noble son is mad" is line 1119 (2.2). Hamlet's "These are but the trappings and the suits of woe" is line 267 (1.2). The "O my imagination!" is *Thyestes*, lines 192–93, "age, anime, fac quod nulla posteritas probet, / sed nulla taceat," available from Loeb Classical Library, Seneca, *Tragedies, Vol. 2: Oedipus. Agamemnon. Thyestes. Hercules on Oeta. Octavia*, ed. John G. Fitch (Cambridge, MA: Harvard University Press, 2018). Keeping the memory "green" is *Hamlet*, line 180 (1.2). Hamlet's "By the image of my cause, I see the portraiture of his" is lines 3581–82 (5.2). Hamlet's "Since no man has aught of what he leaves, what is't to leave betimes?" is lines 3672–73 (5.2). "In this distracted globe" is Hamlet at line 782 (1.5). Hamlet's "Tell my story" is line 3835 (5.2).

Chapter 9: Banish Despair

John Donne's couplet on the "New Philosophy" is *An Anatomy of the World* (London, 1611), lines 205–6. Osmond's coinage of *psychedelic* can be found in his correspondence with Aldous Huxley; after Huxley proposed the term *phanerothymic* in a letter mailed from Los Angeles on March 30, 1956, Osmond replied back from Weyburn, Saskatchewan, in a letter postmarked early April 1956: "My Dear Aldous, To fathom Hell or go angelic / Just take a pinch of *PSYCHEDELIC*." The Aldous-Osmond letters are reproduced in *Psychedelic Prophets: The Letters of Aldous Huxley and Humphry Osmond*, ed. Cynthia Carson Bisbee et al. (Montreal: McGill-Queen's University Press, 2018). Russell Brain's brain-mind distinction between science and poetry is from his *Mind, Perception and Science* (Oxford: Blackwell, 1951), 88. For Kuhlenbeck's mind-brain theory, see "Further Remarks on Brain and Consciousness: The Brain-Paradox and the Meanings of Consciousness," *Confina Neurologica* 19 (1959): 462–84. For Roger Wolcott Sperry's treatment of the "Mind-Brain Problem," see "Neurology and the Mind-Brain Problem," *American Scientist* 40 (1952): 291–312. For Sperry's quote about the different consciousnesses of our right and left hemispheres, see Sperry, "Lateral Specialization in the Surgically Separated Hemispheres," in *3rd Neurosciences Study Program*, ed. F. O. Schmitt and F. G. Worden (Cambridge, MA: MIT Press, 1974).

Chapter 10: Achieve Self-Acceptance

For Master Kŏng's discussion of *chi*, or shame, see *Analects* 1.13 and 2.3, available with the *Mengzi* and *Zhuangzi* at the Chinese Text Project. Mèng Kē is usually Romanized as Mencius; his discussion of *chi* as one of the "four sprouts" or "principles" can be found in the *Mencius* or *Mengzi* 2.1.6. The twice-monthly lectures on *chi* were the public recitations and explications of the Sheng Yu; for a sample, see William Milne's *The Sacred Edict* (Shanghai: American Presbyterian Mission Press, 1870), where *shame* is mentioned explicitly in conjunction with maxims 3, 5, 6, 8, 11, and 12 but is implicit throughout. The warning against "strange teachings" is maxim 7 of the Sheng Yu. For the "Tale of Wonton," see *Zhuangzi* 7.7. *Wonton* is a rendering of *hùndùn*, which roughly means the primordial soup out of which all life comes. The story of the *Huáng dì* burying the Confucian scholars is probably apocryphal but can be found in the *Shiji* or *Records of the Grand Historian*, written by the father-son historians Sima Tan and Sima Qian between the late second century BCE and the early first century BCE. The term *Tao*, or "Way," is invoked frequently by Master Kǒng in *Analects*, including at 1.14 and 3.24. For "Dream of the Butterfly," see *Zhuangzi* 2.14. For an excellent English version of *Dream of the Red Chamber* (or *Hónglóumèng*), try the David Hawkes and John Minford translation in Penguin Classics, titled *The Story of the Stone*. There is a lively scholarly debate about how much of the novel was actually authored by Cao Xueqin, but whatever the truth of the matter, the Butterfly Immerser occurs throughout.

Chapter 11: Ward Off Heartbreak

Jane Austen's letter to her sister Cassandra is dated January 16, 1796, but contains a short addendum about Tom Lefroy dated January 17. The letter can be found in *Letters of Jane Austen, Selected from the Compilation of her Great Nephew, Edward*, ed. Sarah Chauncy Woolsey (Boston: Little, Brown, 1908). The *Don Quixote* excerpt is from bk. 1, chap. 2. Newton's quote from the *Principia*—"phaenomena naturae ad leges mathematicas revocare aggressi sint"—is from the first sentence of the "Author's Preface to the Reader." Descartes's discussion of the effects of sympathy and antipathy can be found in his *Principia Philosophiae*, pt. 4, sec. 187. Newton's alchemical writings are voluminous; although they were never prepared by their author for publication, a selection of the manuscript papers can be found at Oxford University's *The Newton Project*, http://www.newtonproject.ox.ac.uk/texts/newtons-works/alchemical. The precise quote about the "living gold" is from Keynes MS. 53, "Of the first gate," and is itself a rough translation of another alchemistical treatise, Johann de Monte Snyders's *The Metamorphosis of the Planets*, published in German in 1663; Newton's original reads "the spere of ♂." Fielding's subtitle, "*Written in Imitation of the Manner of Cervantes, Author of Don Quixote*," is from the novel *Joseph Andrews, or The History of the Adventures of Joseph Andrews and of his Friend Mr. Abraham Adams*, published in 1743, the year after *Shamela* and six years before *Tom Jones*. The *Fanny Hill* excerpt is from "Letter the First"; this author has read no further than that letter, setting down the book immediately after. The *Clarissa* excerpt is bk. 1, letter 8. Diderot's smitten response to *Clarissa* is in his 1761 "Éloge de Richardson." The *Tom Jones* excerpts are from bk. 18, chaps. 10–11. The excerpt from Horace's first satire is lines 4–8, "o fortunati mercatores gravis annis / miles ait, multo iam fractus membra labore. / contra mercator navim iactantibus Austris, / militia est potior. quid enim? concurritur: horae / momento cita mors venit aut victoria laeta," available at Tuft's Perseus Digital Library. The Chaucer excerpt is the General Prologue, lines 165–66, 184–89 ("A Monk ther was, a fair for the maistrie, / An outridere, that lovede venerie. . . . What sholde he studie and make hymselven wood, / Upon a book in cloystre alwey to poure, / Or swynken with his handes, and laboure, / As Austyn bit? How shal the world be served? / Lat Austyn have his swynk to hym reserved! / Therfore he was a prikasour aright") from *The Riverside Chaucer,* 3rd ed., ed. Larry D. Benson (Oxford: Oxford University Press, 2008). The original version of *Sense and Sensibility*, written in epistolary form like *Pamela* and *Clarissa*, no longer exists but is typically referred to now as "Elinor and Marianne" and may have been drafted as early as 1795, when Austen was still nineteen.

Chapter 12: Energize Your Life

Mary Shelley's "lover" was the poet Percy Bysshe Shelley, the "English occultist" was Lord Byron, and the "sleep-walking expert" was John William Polidori. Mary Shelley's account of the "thrilling horror" and "thrill of fear" is from her introduction to the 1831 revised edition of *Frankenstein*, pages x–xi, published by Henry Colburn and Richard Bentley. Seyle's letter in *Nature* is "A Syndrome Produced by Diverse Nocuous Agents," *Nature* 138 (July 4, 1936): 32. Walter Scott's "sort of terror" is from "Critical Introduction" in *The Castle of Otranto* (Edinburgh: John Ballantyne, 1811), xxix.

Chapter 13: Solve Every Mystery

The origins of the mystery play lie in clerical enactments of biblical passages that were meant to instruct but also engage the congregation. The precise history of these enactments is obscure, but the Church's "Four Fathers" were alive to the power of dramatic performance, and the line between holy theatrics and sin was blurry from the beginning: as early as the mid-390s, Jerome is inveighing against Ambrose for being *fautor histrionum* (a patron of actors). The mystery plays most likely seen by young Shakespeare were the ten or so from Coventry, of which two survive: the Weavers' pageant and the Tailors' pageant. They were staged about twenty miles from Shakespeare's home until they were suppressed by the Church of England in 1579, when Shakespeare was roughly fifteen. For more details, see Thomas Sharp, *Dissertation on the Pageants or Dramatic Mysteries Anciently Performed at Coventry* (Coventry, UK: Merridew, 1825). The Latin phrase *terram mobilem, Solem vero in medio universi immobilem constituit* is from the opening sentence of the "Ad lectorem" prefixed to the 1543 edition of Nicolaus Copernicus's *De Revolutionibus Orbium Coelestium. De Revolutionibus* never claims to prove that the earth goes round the sun; it merely asserts that a heliocentric solar system is simpler to model with geometry and that the final truth of the matter lies beyond mathematics. For more on Bacon's *New Atlantis* and how it incorporates a Vigilance Trigger, see Angus Fletcher, "Francis Bacon's Literary-Scientific Utopia," in *The Palgrave Handbook of Early Modern Literature, Science, and Culture*, eds. Howard Marchitello and Lyn Tribble (New York: Palgrave, 2017), 73–92. Charles Darwin's quote on the *Preliminary Discourse* is that it "stirred up in me a burning zeal to add even the most humble contribution to the noble structure of Natural Science," from *Charles Darwin: His Life Told in an Autobiographical Chapter, and in a Selected Series of his Published Letters*, ed. Francis Darwin (London: John Murray, 1892), 23. Maria Edgeworth refers to *Preliminary Discourse* in her novel *Helen* (1834), where the title character's heroic fiancée, Granville Beauclerc, effuses: "in my opinion it is the finest view of the progress of natural philosophy, the most enlarged, the most just in its judgments of the past, and in its prescience of the future; in the richness of experimental knowledge, in its theoretic invention, the greatest work by any one individual since the time of Bacon." Herschel's *"predict facts before trial"* is italicized in the original and is from *Preliminary Discourse*, pt. 2, chap. 7, sec. 215. Herschel's anecdote about the horns of Venus is from *Preliminary Discourse*, pt. 3, chap. 3, sec. 299. Brewster's discussion of the Mechanical Turk is *Letters on Natural Magic*, letter 11.

Chapter 14: Become Your Better Self

Garrison's July 4 speech is reproduced in the *Liberator*, July 7, 1854, p. 2, columns 2–4. The newspaper's full account reads: "Then holding up the U.S. Constitution, [Garrison] branded it as the source and parent of all the other atrocities,—'a covenant with death, and an agreement with hell,'—and consumed it to ashes on the spot, exclaiming, 'So perish all compromises with tyranny!' 'And let all the people say, Amen!' A tremendous shout of 'Amen!' went up to heaven in ratification of the deed." Douglass's oration was originally published as *Oration, Delivered in Corinthian Hall, Rochester, by Frederick Douglass, July 5th, 1852* (Rochester, NY: Lee, Mann, 1852). Slave narrative quotes excerpted from the works cited in the text, immediately prior. "Moral suasion" was repeatedly championed by Garrison; in the *Liberator* 15:36 (September 5, 1854), the same issue in which he advertised a "cheap edition" of Douglass's *Narrative* "sold at 25 cents single, or $2.75 per dozen," Garrison printed a letter declaring that "it is impossible . . . to abolish slavery by war . . . moral suasion alone can remove the wrongs of this world" (p. 3, column 5). The "moral suasion is moral balderdash" quote is from the first paragraph of "The Maine Law Vs. Moral Suasion," in *American Temperance* (New York: R. Van Dien, 1852), 137–42. Augustine's account of his conversion occurs in *Confessions* 8.12. The passage Augustine reads in the Bible is Romans 13:13. Augustine's "certain books of the Platonists" is *quosdam Platonicorum libros*, from *Confessions* 7.9. Augustine's ironic references to his "flesh" begin in *Confessions* 1.6, with *parentibus carnis*, "flesh parents," build in 1.13 with an allusion to Psalm 78:39, *caro eram et spiritus ambulans et non revertens*—"I was but flesh, a wind that passeth away, and cometh not again"—and continue through bk. 13. Rousseau details his childhood indiscretions—"J'avois les défauts de mon âge; j'étois babillard, gourmand, quelquefois menteur. J'aurois volé des fruits, des bonbons, de la mangeaille"—and his youthful enthusiasm for romances—"Ma mere avoit laissé des Romans. Nous mîmes à les lire après soupé, mon pere & moi"—in the *Confessions*, chap. 1. The Juan Luis Vives quote is from *De Tradendis Disciplinis* 4.4, in *De Disciplinis Libri XX* (Antwerp, Bel.: 1531). "The author has preferred variety to system" is from the preface to *The Columbian Orator* (Boston: Caleb Bingham, 1817). George Ruffin's observation that "Douglass is brim full of humor" is from the introduction to *Life and Times of Frederick Douglass, Written by Himself* (Hartford, CT: Park, 1881), vii. Mary Church Terrell's recollection about Frederick Douglass is in "Women's Debt to Frederick Douglass," part of the Mary Church Terrell Papers at the Library of Congress, MSS425490639.

Chapter 15: Bounce Back from Failure

Proudhon's "We have been defeated" is "nous sommes vaincus et humilés . . . nous voilà tous disperses, emprisonnés, désarmés, muets," from the fifth paragraph of *Les Confessions d'un Révolutionnaire* (Paris, 1849), 1. "The turning-point at which modern history failed to turn" is G. M. Trevelyan, *British History in the Nineteenth Century, 1782–1901* (London: Longmans, Green, 1922), chap. 19, p. 292. George Eliot's "millions of unfed souls and bodies" and "a sort of zoological garden" are from her letter to John Sibree in February 1848, reprinted in *George Eliot's Life, as Related in Her Letters and Journals*, ed. John Walter Cross (New York: Thomas Y. Crowell, 1884), 91–92. "Pray without ceasing. In every thing give thanks" is 1 Thessalonians 5:17–18. The *Kesh Temple Hymn* is at *ETCSL* as text number 4.80.2. "O give thanks unto the Lord" is Psalm 136. Feuerbach's *The Essence of Christianity* quoted from Eliot's translation (London: John Chapman, 1854), where Eliot is credited by her name, Mary Evans. Eliot's 1856 *Westminster Review* essay is "Silly Novels by Lady Novelists," *Westminster Review* 130 (October 1856): 243–54. Honoré de Balzac's "Behold! This Tragedy is no fiction, no Romance" is "Ah! sachez-le: ce drame n'est ni une fiction un roman," from the opening paragraph of *Le Père Goriot*. Eliot's October 25, 1859, journal entry is: "We have just finished reading aloud *Père Goriot*—a hateful book," in *George Eliot's Life*, 319. The first-person-plural *we* of *Le Père Goriot* is: "N'aimons-nous pas touts à prouver notre force au dépens de quelqu'un ou de quelque chose?" The Bible's "I long to see you . . . that I may be comforted together with you by the mutual faith both of you and me" is Romans 1:12. Guthrie's "God Is Love" is excerpted from "My Secret" in Woody Guthrie, *Born to Win*, ed. Robert Shelton (New York: Collier Books, 1967), 163 ff.

Chapter 16: Clear Your Head

On the new emperor, Hara Takeshi has written: "various stories about his bizarre behavior circulated. The most famous of these was the so-called 'telescope incident,' according to which the emperor, at the opening of the Imperial Diet [Government], rolled up the sheet of paper on which his speech was written, and instead of reading it, simply stared at the assembly through the roll." Hara Takeshi, "Taishō: An Enigmatic Emperor and His Influential Wife," in *The Modern Emperors of Japan* (Leiden, Neth.: Brill, 2008), 227–40. After taking a long relook at the telescope story, Takeshi concludes: "There is no evidence that the incident ever took place." More recently, Alison Miller has herself reevaluated the evidence and proposed that efforts to dismiss the telescope incident as "rumormongering by politicians who opposed the emperor, or . . . the product of public gossip" are themselves perhaps guilty of "overreach[ing] the available evidence. . . . This notorious incident is one of the most oft-repeated narratives from Emperor Taishō's biography, and, conspiracy theories notwithstanding, it is known that Emperor Taishō's health was deteriorating in the late 1910s." Alison Miller, "Imperial Images: The Japanese Empress Teimei in Early Twentieth-Century Newspaper Photography," *Self and Nation* 7 (2016). Mark Antony's speech is from *Julius Caesar*, first folio, lines 1614–35 (2.3). Basil Hall Chamberlain's assessment of bushido is from *The Invention of a New Religion* (London: Watts, 1912). Chiyota Shimizu's exchange with Kurosawa is recorded in Tadao Sato, *Kurosawa Akira no Sekai* (Tokyo: Sanichi Shobo, 1968), translated and reproduced in *Roshomon*, ed. Donald Richie, trans. Goro Sato (New Brunswick, NJ: Rutgers University Press, 1987), 167–72.

Chapter 17: Find Peace of Mind

"These fine December nights" is from *The Diary of Virginia Woolf*, ed. Anne Olivier Bell and Andrew McNeillie, 7 vols. (London: Hogarth Press, 1977–1984), 2.217. "A certain melancholy" is January 28, 1923, 2.227. Woolf's "tyrannical" and "Really, a doctor is worse than a husband" is October 30, 1904, *The Letters of Virginia Woolf*, ed. Nigel Nicolson and Joanne Trautmann, 6 vols. (London: Hogarth Press, 1975–80), 1.147–8. Savage's "If a . . . girl is allowed to educate herself" is *Insanity and Allied Neuroses: Practical and Clinical* (London: Cassell, 1884), chap. 3, p. 22. "You shant read this" is from Woolf's letter to Ethel Smyth on June 22, 1930, remembering Savage's instructions. The full excerpt reads: "the six months—not three—that I lay in bed taught me a good deal about what is called oneself. Indeed, I was almost crippled when I came back to the world, unable to move a foot in terror, after that discipline. Think—not one moment's freedom from a doctor's discipline—perfectly strange—conventional men; 'you shant read this' and 'you shant write a word' and 'you shall lie still and drink milk'—for six months,'" *Letters* 4.180. Woolf's lecture to the Heretics on "character in fiction" was originally published as "Character in Fiction" in *Criterion*, July 1924, then revised as *Mrs. Bennett and Mrs. Brown* and published on October 30, 1924, by Hogarth Press. Woolf's "spirit of the age" is from a draft of "Character of Fiction," which runs: "No generation in the world has known quite so much about character as our generation. . . . The average man or woman today thinks more about character than his or her grandparents; character interests them more; they get closer, they dive deeper in to the real emotions and motives of their fellow creatures. There are scientific reasons why this should be so. . . . And then there is a . . . vaguer force at work—a force which is sometimes called the Spirit of the Age," *The Essays of Virginia Woolf*, ed. Andrew McNeillie, 3 vols. (London: Hogarth, 1986–88), 3.504. Woolf's remark about Bertrand Russell, "His luminous, vigorous mind seems attached to a flimsy little car," is *Diary* 2.295. Silas Weir Mitchell's "You cure the body and some-how find that the mind also is cured" is from S. Weir Mitchell, "The Treatment by Rest, Seclusion, Etc., in Relation to Psychotherapy," *Journal of the American Medical Association* 25 (June 20, 1908): 2033–37. Mitchell's orders to Charlotte Perkins Gilman, "Never touch pen, brush, or pencil as long as you live," are recorded in *The Living of Charlotte Perkins Gilman: An Autobiography* (New York: D. Appleton-Century, 1935), 96. Woolf's "like some gigantic sow" is December 4, 1913, *Letters* 2.35. William James's "I finished the first part of Renouvier's second 'Essais'" is from his journal, April 30, 1870, cited in *The Letters of William James*, ed. Henry James, 2 vols. (Boston: Atlantic Monthly, 1920): 1.147–8. James's remark on the "feeling of effort" continues: "The stream of our thought is like a river. On the whole, easy simple flowing predom-inates in it, the drift of things is with the pull of gravity, and effortless attention is the rule. But at intervals an obstruction, a set-back, a log-jam occurs, stops the current, creates an eddy, and makes things temporarily move the other way. If a real river could feel, it would feel these eddies and set-backs as places of effort. 'I am here flow-ing,' it would say, 'in the direction of greatest resistance, instead of flowing, as usual, in the direction of least. My effort is what enables me to perform this feat,'" *The Prin-ciples of Psychology*, 2 vols. (New York: Henry Holt, 1890), 1.451–2. Bertrand Russell's citation of James's account of free will is in *The Analysis of Mind* (London: George Allen & Unwin, 1921), 285. Savage's obituary is in the *British Medical Journal* 2 (July 16, 1921): 98–99. Woolf's "I have lost three [3] teeth in vain" is *Diary* 2.176. Woolf's "everything insipid, tasteless, colourless" is recorded in July 31, 1926, *Diary* 3.103, but is her account of July 27, four days before. Woolf's "sense of physical tiredness" is July 30, and "Read some Dante" is July 31, both *Diary* 3.103. William James's article is "On Some Omissions of Introspective Psychology," *Mind* 9:33 (January 1884): 1–26. James's "chopped [it] up in bits" and "Such words as 'chain' or 'train' do not describe it fitly" are from his later elaboration of the *Mind* article in *The Principles of Psychology* 1.239; in his original *Mind* article, he more lightly accuses the great English psychol-ogists of having "broken [it] into bits," 6. "It is nothing jointed; it flows" is *Principles of Psychology* 1.239. James's discussion of "nervous shocks" and their relationship to consciousness is *Principles of Psychology* 1.152–3. "Every definite image in the mind is steeped and dyed in the free water that flows round it" is *Mind* 16 and *Principles of Psychology* 1.255. James's discussion of how authors and speakers have developed linking words that function as "psychic transitions" is *Mind* 14 and *The Principles of Psychology* 1.252–3. The diagnosis of Miriam Richardson's *Honeycomb* as a work of "neurasthenia" is the *Saturday Review of Politics, Literature, Science, and Art* 124 (November 24, 1917): 422. May Sinclair's review of Richardson is "The Novels of Dorothy Richardson," *Egoist* 5:4 (April 1918): 57–59. Woolf's "sensations, impressions, ideas and emotions glance off" is *Essays* 3.11–12. Woolf's "Oh what a bore about Joyce!" is a letter to Gerald Brenan on June 5, 1922, *Letters* 2.533. Woolf's "at large beneath the sky" and "freedom" are from "Modern Novels," *Times Literary Supplement* 899 (April 10, 1919): 189–90, revised as "Modern Fiction" in *The Common Reader* (London: Hogarth Press, 1925), where "at large beneath the sky" is altered to "enlarged and set free." Woolf's full critique of Joyce's stream-of-consciousness method runs: "But it is possible to press a little further and wonder whether we may not refer our sense of being in a bright yet narrow room, confined and shut in, rather than enlarged and set free, to some limitation imposed by the method as well as by the mind. Is it the method that inhibits the creative power?" Silas Weir Mitchell's reminiscences of his time as a Civil War doctor can be found in "The Medical Department in the Civil War," *Journal of the American Medical Association* 62 (1914): 1445–50: "Some of the symptoms of nerve-wounds we described have never been seen since in like intensity." Mitchell then goes on to remark: "It became the custom to turn over to us the cases suspected of malingering. These were the scamps or cowards, and in some cases the victims of a strange form of psychic disorder . . . making men hysteric."

Chapter 18: Feed Your Creativity

"Innate speculative principles" is John Locke, *An Essay Concerning Human Understanding* (London, 1690), 1.1. "The simple modes of the idea of space" is 2.13. "Children, idiots, etcetera" is 1.1. "Defects" and "errors" and "madness" is 2.33. "Educating young children" and the following is 2.33. Marcus E. Raichle's discovery is reported in D. A. Gusnard and M. E. Raichle, "Searching for a Baseline: Functional Imaging and the Resting Human Brain," *Nature Reviews: Neuroscience* 2 (2001): 685–94, and Marcus E. Raichle et al., "A Default Mode of Brain Function," *Proceedings of the National Academy of Sciences* 98 (2001): 676–82. *Mother Goose's Melody* was registered for publication in London by Thomas Carnan in 1780, but the earliest surviving copy dates from 1784; in the 1791 edition, "The Cat and Fiddle" is p. 32. Edward Lear's "The Owl and the Pussy-cat" is in *Nonsense Songs, Stories, Botany, and Alphabets* (Boston: James R. Osgood, 1871). John Hersey's article about "abnormally courteous, unnaturally clean boys and girls" is "Why Do Students Bog Down After the First R?" *Life* (May 24, 1954): 147–48.

Chapter 19: Unlock Salvation

Martin Luther King Jr.'s article "Out of the Long Night" is from *The Gospel Messenger* 107:6 (February 8, 1958): 3–4, 13–15. "Blessed are the poor in spirit" is Matthew 5:3. Parker's memories of childhood are from Octavius Brooks Frothingham, *Theodore Parker: A Biography* (Boston: James R. Osgood, 1874). The description of Cambridge's "orchards, gardens, and pleasure grounds" is *The Edinburgh Gazetteer: Or, Geographical Dictionary*, 6 vols. (London: Longman, Rees, Orme, Brown, and Green, 1827), 2.47. Emerson's "the infinitude of the private man" is *Journals and Miscellaneous Notebooks of Ralph Waldo Emerson*, 16 vols. (Cambridge, MA: Harvard University Press, 1960–82), 7.342. Emerson's "Now, literature, philosophy and thought are Shakespearized" is "Shakspeare [*sic*]; or, The Poet," in *The Complete Works of Ralph Waldo Emerson*, 12 vols. (Boston: Houghton, Mifflin, 1903–4), 4.204. Hamlet's "The rest is silence" is the first folio, line 3847 (5.2). Hamlet's "To be or not to be" is lines 1710–14 (5.1). Corneille's original lines are, "Père, maîtresse, honneur, amour, / Noble et dure contrainte, aimable tyrannie, / Tous mes plaisirs sont morts, ou ma gloire ternie. / L'un me rend malheureux, l'autre indigne du jour," from *Le Cid* (Paris, 1637), 1.7. Charles Lamb's observation about watching Shakespeare is from "On the Tragedies of Shakspeare, Considered with Reference to their Fitness for Stage Representation (1811)," in *The Prose Works of Charles Lamb*, 3 vols. (London: Edward Moxon, 1836) 1.99–32, 102. Lamb's following remark about being in the character's "mind" is with reference to Shakespeare's *King Lear*. Emerson's "I see you are one of the happy mortals" is from *The Complete Works*, 4.354.

Chapter 20: Renew Your Future

Gabriel García Márquez's July 1965 "flash" is "tuve la revelación: debía contar la historia como mi abuela me contaba las suyas, partiendo de aquella tarde en que el niño es llevado por su padre para conocer el hielo," recorded in *Tras las huellas de Melquiades. Historia de Cien años de soledad* (Bogotá: Norma, 2001), 69. Márquez's *Cien Años de Soledad* is quoted from Gregory Rabassa, trans., *One Hundred Years of Solitude* (New York: Harper and Row, 1970), with occasional minor adjustments. When Márquez earned the Nobel Prize in 1982, the official press release began: "With this year's Nobel Prize in Literature to the Colombian writer, Gabriel García Márquez, the Swedish Academy cannot be said to bring forward an unknown writer. García Márquez achieved unusual international success as a writer with his novel in 1967 (*One Hundred Years of Solitude*). The novel has been translated into a large number of languages and has sold millions of copies. It is still being reprinted and read with undiminished interest by new readers." Copernicus's original words are "Itaque cum mecum ipse cogitarem, quam absurdum ἀκρόαμα existimaturi essent illi, qui multorum seculorum iudiciis hanc opinionem confirmatam norunt, quod terra immobilis in medio coeli, tanquam centrum illius posita sit, si ego contra assererem terram moueri," from his preface to *De Revolutionibus Orbium Coelestium* (1543). Coleridge's extended quote runs, "The secondary Imagination . . . dissolves, diffuses, dissipates, in order to re-create. . . . It is essentially vital, even as all objects (as objects) are essentially fixed and dead," *Biographia Literaria; or Biographical Sketches of My Literary Life and Opinions*, 2 vols. (London: Rest Fenner, 1817), 1.295–6, chap. 13.

Chapter 21: Decide Wiser

The list of simultaneous inventions is from Alfred L. Kroeber, *Anthropology: Race, Language, Culture, Psychology, Prehistory*, rev. ed. (New York: Harcourt, Brace, 1948), sec. 140, p. 342. Kroeber's draft papers of the textbook are Library of Congress MSS28977. Kroeber's discussion of the "great man theory of history" is *Anthropology*, 340. Pyrrho's original words have been lost to time, but the rough outlines of his thought are preserved in *Outlines of Pyrrhonism*, composed four centuries later by the Greek physician Sextus Empiricus, who discusses both *ataraxia* and the suspension of judgment (or *epoché*) in bk. 1, chap. 12, available from Loeb Classical Library, *Outlines of Pyrrhonism*, ed. R. G. Bury (Cambridge, MA: Harvard University Press, 1933), 18–21. Herodotus's "ants bigger than foxes" is recorded in *Histories* 3.102–5. Fan Chengda's description of the Qutang gorge is from *Wuchuan lu (Diary of a Boat Trip to Wu*, composed 1177), the third of his three main travel diaries, the other two being *Lanpei lu* (1170) and *Canluan lu* (1172-3). Ibn Battuta's covetous response to the Shaykh's cloak of goat fur is from *Tuḥfat an-Nuẓẓār fī Gharā'b al-Amṣār wa 'Ajā'ib al-Asfār [A Treasury for Traveling Souls]* (c. 1354). Thomas More's original title is *Libellus vere aureus, nec minus salutaris quam festivus, de optimo rei publicae statu deque nova insula Utopia* (Leuven, 1516). Kroeber's assessment of Ishi is recorded in Theodore Kroeber, *Ishi in Two Worlds* (Berkeley: University of California Press, 1961), 229.

Chapter 22: Believe in Yourself

"You don't have to think about doing the right thing. If you're for the right thing, then you do it without thinking" is from Maya Angelou, *I Know Why the Caged Bird Sings* (New York: Random House, 1970), 290. "The strength of my words is their truth" is from the Papyrus Prisse version of *The Wisdom of Ptahhotep*, sec. 41, available at the University College London's Digital Egypt for Universities, https://www.ucl.ac.uk/museums-static/digitalegypt. Ptahhotep's "Follow your heart" is Papyrus Prisse, sec. 14. Marcus Aurelius's "Every dawn, tell yourself" is *Meditations* 2.1, available in Loeb Classical Library, *Marcus Aurelius*, ed. C. R. Haines (Cambridge, MA: Harvard University Press, 1916). "We live through work" is from sec. 9 of the *Loyalist Teaching*, as edited by Georges Posener (Geneva, 1976), available at UCL's Digital Egypt. "If a woman revels in the moment, don't cast her away" is Papyrus Prisse, sec. 40. Angelou's "I had a visitation of my mortality . . . existential in a very strange and serious way" is from Lynn Darling's interview of

Angelou in "Maya Angelou, a Woman's Heart: Inside the Raging Storm, Looking Out," *Washington Post*, October 13, 1981, D1. Sartre's "We are all born for no reason and die through collision" is "Tout existant naît sans raison, se prolonge par faiblesse et meurt par rencontre," from *La Nausée* (Paris: Éditions Gallimard, 1938). Sartre's "In despair is the start of true optimism" is from "A propos de l'existentialisme: Mise au point," *Action* (December 29, 1944), reprinted in *Les Écrits de Sartre*, ed. Michel Contat and Michel Rybalka (Paris: Gallimard, 1970), 653–58. Sartre "I seize each second, sucking it dry" is "Je me penche sur chaque seconde, j'essaie de l'épuiser," from *La Nausée*. The translation of *Les Nègres* performed by Angelou at St. Mark's Playhouse was by Bernard Frechtman, and it runs: "What a ruin! And I haven't finished sculpting myself, haven't finished carving and jagging and fashioning myself in the form of a ruin. An eternal ruin. It's not time that corrodes me, it's not fatigue that makes me forget myself, it's death that's shaping me and . . . Isn't my sublime corpse—which still moves—enough for you?"

Chapter 23: Unfreeze Your Heart

Shakespeare's *King Lear* was rewritten as *The History of King Lear* by Nahum Tate in 1681 and supplanted Shakespeare's original from the stage for the next century and a half. All Alison Bechdel quotes are from *Fun Home: A Family Tragicomic* (New York: Houghton Mifflin, 2006). For Wolpe's methods, see his *Psychotheraphy by Reciprocal Inhibition* (Stanford, CA: Stanford University Press, 1958). Death's scoff at Apollo is: "πόλλ᾽ ἂν σὺ λέξας οὐδὲν ἂν πλέον λάβοις," *Alcestis*, line 72, available at Tuft's Perseus Digital Library. The servant's "Alcestis is alive and dead" is "καὶ ζῶσαν εἰπεῖν καὶ θανοῦσαν ἔστι σοι," line 141. Eliot's nod to *Alcestis* is *On Poetry and Poets* (London: Faber and Faber, 1957), 91. "One daren't even laugh anymore" and the other lines from *Waiting for Godot* are quoted from Samuel Beckett's English translation, published in 1954 by Grove Press.

Chapter 24: Live Your Dream

The title of the false part 2 is *Segundo Tomo del Ingenioso Hidalgo Don Quixote de la Mancha,* translated into English by naval commander Captain John Stevens as *Continuation of the comical history of the most ingenious knight, Don Quixote de la Mancha, by the licentiate Alonzo Fernandez de Avellaneda. Being a third volume; never before printed in English* (London, 1705). Pseudolus's "I know, I know" is "suspicio est mihi nunc vos suspicarier, / me idcirco haec tanta facinora promittere, / quo vos oblectem, hanc fabulam dum transigam, / neque sim facturus quod facturum dixeram. / non demutabo. atque etiam certum, quod sciam, / quo id sim facturus pacto nil etiam scio, / nisi quia futurumst. nam qui in scaenam provenit, / novo módo novom aliquid inventum adferre addecet; / si id facere nequeat, det locum illi qui queat," Plautus, *Pseudolus*, 1.5.150–8, available at Tuft's Perseus Digital Library. Don Quixote's "Books are better, the truer they are" is "las historias fingidas tanto tienen de buenas y de deleitables cuanto se llegan a la verdad o la semejanza della, y las verdaderas tanto son mejores cuanto son más verdaderas," *Don Quixote*, pt. 2, chap. 62. The terms Comic Wink and Reality Shifter are translations of *indicium comicum* and *veritatis mobile*, from the anonymous thirteenth-century Andalusian compendium *Kitab al-Aikhtiraeat* (*The Book of Inventions*).

Chapter 25: Lessen Your Lonely

"O myth-made Orpheus, father of song, son of the harp of Apollo" is "ἐξ Ἀπόλλωνος δὲ φορμικτὰς ἀοιδᾶν πατὴρ ἔμολεν, εὐαίνητος, Ὀρφεύς" from Pindar's "Pythian Ode 4," line 177, available at Tuft's Perseus Digital Library. "Love feels sweeter when it follows sadness" is "Vissi già mesto e dolente; / Or gioisco, e quegli affanni / Che sofferti hò per tant'anni / Fan più caro il ben presente," *L'Orfeo*, act 2. Elena Ferrante's *L'amica Geniale* is quoted from Ann Goldstein, trans., *My Brilliant Friend* (New York: Europa, 2012).

Conclusion: Inventing Tomorrow

Quintilian's *Institutiones* is available at Tuft's Perseus Digital Library. Quintilian discusses happy accidents at 10.6.5: "non superstitiose cogitatis demum est inhaerendum. neque enim tantum habent curae, ut non sit dandus et fortunae locus, cum saepe etiam scriptis ea quae subito nata sunt inserantur," which translates as: "Don't cling superstitiously to your preconceived design; happy accidents can work better. That's why we often have unplanned epiphanies when we're writing." Quintilian's exhortation to copy multiple authors is *Institutiones* 10.2.26: "plurium bona ponamus ante oculos, ut aliud ex alio haereat, et quod cuique loco conveniat aptemus," which translates as: "Immerse yourself in lots of good authors, so you can borrow from one then another, drawing on their diversity to adapt your writing to the specific situation at hand." Quintilian observes that writing doesn't need to be true at *Institutiones* 2.17.20–1: "orator, cum falso utitur pro vero, scit esse falsum eoque se pro vero uti; non ergo falsam habet ipse opinionem, sed fallit alium . . . et pictor, cum vi artis suae efficit, ut quaedam eminere in opere, quaedam recessisse credamus, ipse ea plana esse non nescit," which translates as: "When a writer uses a fiction in place of the truth, he knows that it's a fiction and he doesn't believe it himself; he only uses it to beguile others . . . in the same way that a painter, through the power of his art, tricks our eyes into seeing things that he knows aren't really there."

Coda: The Secret History of This Book

"The tomb of time is also its womb" is "ἐξ ὧν δὲ ἡ γένεσίς ἐστι τοῖς οὖσι, καὶ τὴν φθορὰν εἰς ταῦτα γίνεσθαι κατὰ τὸ χρεών· διδόναι γὰρ αὐτὰ δίκην καὶ τίσιν ἀλλήλοις τῆς ἀδικίας κατὰ τὴν τοῦ χρόνου τάξιν," ascribed to Thales's student Anaximander by the sixth-century pagan Neoplatonist Simplicius of Cilicia in *Comments on Aristotle's Physics*, 24.18–20. Thomas Twining's despairing quote is from his October 19, 1786, letter to Charles Burney, preserved in *Recreations and Studies of a Country Clergyman of the Eighteenth Century, Being Selections from the Correspondence of the Reverend Thomas Twining*, ed. Richard Twining (London: John Murray, 1882), 139–41. Jerome's rejection of literal *verbum e verbo* translation in favor of interpretation occurs in his Epistle 57, or "Letter to Pammachius," which begins by agreeing to *de translatione respondeam* (defend Jerome's practice of translation), then pivots into a discussion of *erudito interpreti* (the educated interpreter) that includes gestures to literati such as the Roman poet Horace, and finally declares that the Apostle Paul was able to extract the true meaning of the Hebrew scriptures because *non verbum expressit e verbo, sed παραφρασικῶς, eumdem sensum aliis sermonibus indicavit*—"he did not copy them word for word, but paraphrased, uncovering their deeper sense."

The "ingenious author" who observed the need for annotations is Miguel de Cervantes in the *Prólogo* to *El ingenioso hidalgo don Quijote de la Mancha* (Madrid, 1605).

Further Reading

If you're curious to learn more about this book's scholarly method, known either as rhetorical narrative theory or story science (not cognitive narratology or cognitive approaches to literature, which, unlike this book, focus on literary *interpretations*, not literary *inventions*), the classic textbook is Aristotle's *Poetics*, as discussed in the introduction. After Aristotle, the method remained mostly forgotten until it was revived in the twentieth century by R. S. Crane and the scholars of the Chicago School, as recounted in the coda. Major works in that revival include Crane's essay "The Plot of *Tom Jones*" in *Critics and Criticism: Ancient and Modern* (Chicago: University of Chicago Press, 1952), Wayne Booth's *The Rhetoric of Fiction* (Chicago: University of Chicago Press, 1961), and James Phelan's *Narrative as Rhetoric* (Columbus: Ohio State University Press, 1996).

   If you're interested in my story science research into the psychological effects of literary inventions, one good place to start is my coauthored article with John Monterosso, "The Science of Free-Indirect Discourse: An Alternate Cognitive Effect," *Narrative* 24 (2016): 82–103, doi:10.1353/nar.2016.0004, which explores how Jane Austen's style can help our brain become more generous in love, as described in chapter 11. You can also explore the broader social benefits of literary inventions in my book *Comic Democracies* (Baltimore: Johns Hopkins University Press, 2016), which identifies a half dozen inventions—drawn from ancient comedy, through Shakespeare, to the US Declaration of Independence—that nurture curiosity, open-mindedness, flexibility, and other neural sources of democracy.

Index